Certificate Paper C1

FUNDAMENTALS OF MANAGEMENT ACCOUNTING

For assessments under the 2006 new syllabus
in 2006 and 2007

Study Text

In this July 2006 new edition

- A **user-friendly format** for easy navigation

- Regular **fast forward** summaries emphasising the key points in each chapter

- **Assessment focus points** showing you what the assessor will want you to do

- **Questions** and **quick quizzes** to test your understanding

- **Question bank** containing objective test questions with answers

- A full index

BPP's **i-Pass** product also supports this paper.

FOR ASSESSMENTS UNDER THE 2006 NEW SYLLABUS IN 2006 AND 2007

PROFESSIONAL EDUCATION

First edition July 2006

ISBN 0 7517 2647 8

British Library Cataloguing-in-Publication Data
A catalogue record for this book
is available from the British Library

Published by

BPP Professional Education
Aldine House, Aldine Place
London W12 8AW

www.bpp.com

Printed in Great Britain by
WM Print
45-47 Frederick Street
Walsall
WS2 9NE

We are grateful to the Chartered Institute of
Management Accountants for permission to reproduce
past examination questions. The suggested solutions
in the Answer bank have been prepared by BPP
Professional Education.

Contents

		Page

Introduction

The BPP Study Text – The BPP Effective Study Package – Help yourself study for your CIMA assessment – Learning outcomes and syllabus content – The assessment – Tackling multiple choice questions – Tackling objective test questions

Part A Cost determination

1	Cost accounting and cost classification	3
2	Accounting for the value of materials	29
3	Overhead costs	43
4	Marginal costing and pricing decisions	77

Part B Cost behaviour and breakeven analysis

5	Cost behaviour	99
6	Breakeven analysis and limiting factor analysis	113

Part C Standard costing

7	Standard costing	143
8	Variance analysis I	163
9	Variance analysis II	177

Part D Financial planning and control

10	Budget preparation	195
11	Flexible budgeting	217

Part E Costing and accounting systems

12	Process costing	231
13	Job, batch and contract costing	267
14	Cost bookkeeping	297
15	Service costing	325

Question bank	345
Answer bank	373
Index	399

Review form and free prize draw

Computer-based learning products from BPP

If you want to reinforce your studies by **interactive** learning, try BPP's **i-Learn** product, covering major syllabus areas in an interactive format. For **self-testing**, try **i-Pass,** which offers a large number of **objective test questions**, particularly useful where objective test questions form part of the exam.

See the order form at the back of this text for details of these innovative learning tools.

Learn Online

Learn Online uses BPP's wealth of teaching experience to produce a fully **interactive** e-learning resource **delivered via the Internet**. The site offers comprehensive **tutor support** and features areas such as **study**, **practice**, **email service**, **revision** and **useful resources**.

Visit our website www.bpp.com/cima/learnonline to sample aspects of Learn Online free of charge.

Learning to Learn Accountancy

BPP's ground-breaking **Learning to Learn Accountancy** book is designed to be used both at the outset of your CIMA studies and throughout the process of learning accountancy. It challenges you to consider how you study and gives you helpful hints about how to approach the various types of paper which you will encounter. It can help you **focus your studies on the subject and exam**, enabling you to **acquire knowledge, practise and revise efficiently and effectively**.

The BPP Study Text

Aims of this Study Text

> To provide you with the knowledge and understanding, skills and application techniques that you need if you are to be successful in your exams

This Study Text has been written around the **Fundamentals of Management Accounting** syllabus.

- It is **comprehensive**. It covers the syllabus content. No more, no less.

- It is written at the **right level**. Each chapter is written with CIMA's precise learning outcomes in mind.

- It is targeted to the **exam**. We have taken account of the pilot paper, guidance the examiner has given and the assessment methodology.

> To allow you to study in the way that best suits your learning style and the time you have available, by following your personal Study Plan (see page (viii))

You may be studying at home on your own until the date of the exam, or you may be attending a full-time course. You may like to (and have time to) read every word, or you may prefer to (or only have time to) skim-read and devote the remainder of your time to question practice. Wherever you fall in the spectrum, you will find the BPP Study Text meets your needs in designing and following your personal Study Plan.

> To tie in with the other components of the BPP Effective Study Package to ensure you have the best possible chance of passing the exam (see page (vi))

The BPP Effective Study Package

Recommended period of use	The BPP Effective Study Package
From the outset and throughout	**Learning to Learn Accountancy** Read this invaluable book as you begin your studies and refer to it as you work through the various elements of the BPP Effective Study Package. It will help you to acquire knowledge, practise and revise, efficiently and effectively.
Three to twelve months before the exam	**Study Text and i-Learn** Use the Study Text to acquire knowledge, understanding, skills and the ability to apply techniques. Use BPP's **i-Learn** product to reinforce your learning.
Throughout	**Learn Online** Study, practise, revise and take advantage of other useful resources with BPP's fully interactive e-learning site with comprehensive tutor support.
Throughout	**i-Pass** **i-Pass**, our computer-based testing package, provides objective test questions in a variety of formats and is ideal for self-assessment.
One to six months before the exam	**Practice & Revision Kit** Try the numerous examination-format questions, for which there are realistic suggested solutions prepared by BPP's own authors. Then attempt the two mock exams.
From three months before the exam until the last minute	**Passcards** Work through these short, memorable notes which are focused on what is most likely to come up in the exam you will be sitting.
One to six months before the exam	**Success CDs** The CDs cover the vital elements of your syllabus in less than 90 minutes per subject. They also contain exam hints to help you fine tune your strategy.

Help yourself study for your CIMA assessment

Exams for professional bodies such as CIMA are very different from those you have taken at college or university. You will be under **greater time pressure before** the exam – as you may be combining your study with work. There are many different ways of learning and so the BPP Study Text offers you a number of different tools to help you through. Here are some hints and tips: they are not plucked out of the air, but **based on research and experience**. (You don't need to know that long-term memory is in the same part of the brain as emotions and feelings - but it's a fact anyway.)

The right approach

1 The right attitude

Believe in yourself	Yes, there is a lot to learn. Yes, it is a challenge. But thousands have succeeded before and you can too.
Remember why you're doing it	Studying might seem a grind at times, but you are doing it for a reason: to advance your career.

2 The right focus

Read through the Syllabus and learning outcomes	These tell you what you are expected to know and are supplemented by Assessment focus points in the text.
Study the Assessment section	This will give you an indication of the style of questions you could encounter in the assessment.

3 The right method

The whole picture	You need to grasp the detail - but keeping in mind how everything fits into the whole picture will help you understand better. • The **Introduction** of each chapter puts the material in context. • The **Syllabus content, Learning outcomes** and **Exam focus points** show you what you need to **grasp**.
In your own words	To absorb the information (and to practise your written communication skills), it helps to **put it into your own words**. • **Take notes.** • Answer the **questions** in each chapter. You will practise your written communication skills, which become increasingly important as you progress through your CIMA exams. • Draw **mindmaps**. • Try **'teaching' a subject** to a colleague or friend.
Give yourself cues to jog your memory	The BPP Study Text uses **bold** to **highlight key points**. • Try **colour coding** with a highlighter pen. • Write **key points** on cards.

4   **The right review**

Review, review, review	It is a **fact** that regularly reviewing a topic in summary form can **fix it in your memory**. Because **review** is so important, the BPP Study Text helps you to do so in many ways.
	• **Chapter roundups** summarise the 'fast forward' key points in each chapter. Use them to recap each study session.
	• The **Quick quiz** is another review technique you can use to ensure that you have grasped the essentials.
	• Go through the **Examples** in each chapter a second or third time.

Developing your personal Study Plan

BPP's **Learning to Learn Accountancy** book emphasises the need to prepare (and use) a study plan. Planning and sticking to the plan are key elements of learning success.

There are four steps you should work through.

Step 1   **How do you learn?**

First you need to be aware of your style of learning. The BPP **Learning to Learn Accountancy** book commits a chapter to this **self-discovery**. What types of intelligence do you display when learning? You might be advised to brush up on certain study skills before launching into this Study Text.

BPP's **Learning to Learn Accountancy** book helps you to identify what intelligences you show more strongly and then details how you can tailor your study process to your preferences. It also includes handy hints on how to develop intelligences you exhibit less strongly, but which might be needed as you study accountancy.

Are you a **theorist** or are you more **practical**? If you would rather get to grips with a theory before trying to apply it in practice, you should follow the study sequence on page (ix). If the reverse is true (you like to know why you are learning theory before you do so), you might be advised to flick through Study Text chapters and look at examples, case studies and questions (Steps 8, 9 and 10 in the **suggested study sequence**) before reading through the detailed theory.

Step 2   **How much time do you have?**

Work out the time you have available per week, given the following.

- The standard you have set yourself
- The time you need to set aside later for work on the Practice & Revision Kit and Passcards
- The other exam(s) you are sitting
- Very importantly, practical matters such as work, travel, exercise, sleep and social life

Hours

Note your time available in box A.   A [   ]

Step 3 Allocate your time

- Take the time you have available per week for this Study Text shown in box A, multiply it by the number of weeks available and insert the result in box B. B [   ]

- Divide the figure in box B by the number of chapters in this text and insert the result in box C. C [   ]

Remember that this is only a rough guide. Some of the chapters in this book are longer and more complicated than others, and you will find some subjects easier to understand than others.

Step 4 Implement

Set about studying each chapter in the time shown in box C, following the key study steps in the order suggested by your particular learning style.

This is your personal **Study Plan**. You should try and combine it with the study sequence outlined below. You may want to modify the sequence a little (as has been suggested above) to adapt it to your **personal style**.

BPP's **Learning to Learn Accountancy** gives further guidance on developing a study plan, and deciding where and when to study.

Suggested study sequence

It is likely that the best way to approach this Study Text is to tackle the chapters in the order in which you find them. Taking into account your individual learning style, you could follow this sequence.

Key study steps	Activity
Step 1 **Topic list**	Each numbered topic is a numbered section in the chapter.
Step 2 **Introduction**	This gives you the big picture in terms of the context of the chapter, the learning outcomes the chapter covers, and the content you will read. In other words, it sets your objectives for study.
Step 3 **Knowledge brought forward boxes**	In these we highlight information and techniques that it is assumed you have 'brought forward' with you from your earlier studies. If there are topics which have changed recently due to legislation for example, these topics are explained in more detail.
Step 4 **Fast forward**	Fast forward boxes give you a quick summary of the content of each of the main chapter sections. They are listed together in the roundup at the end of each chapter to provide you with an overview of the contents of the whole chapter.
Step 5 **Explanations**	Proceed methodically through the chapter, reading each section thoroughly and making sure you understand.
Step 6 **Key terms and Exam focus points**	• Key terms can often earn you *easy marks* if you state them clearly and correctly in an appropriate exam answer (and they are highlighted in the index at the back of the text). • Exam focus points state how we think the examiner intends to examine certain topics.
Step 7 **Note taking**	Take brief notes, if you wish. Avoid the temptation to copy out too much. Remember that being able to put something into your own words is a sign of being able to understand it. If you find you cannot explain something you have read, read it again before you make the notes.

Key study steps	Activity
Step 8 **Examples**	Follow each through to its solution very carefully.
Step 9 **Case studies**	Study each one, and try to add flesh to them from your own experience. They are designed to show how the topics you are studying come alive (and often come unstuck) in the real world.
Step 10 **Questions**	Make a very good attempt at each one.
Step 11 **Answers**	Check yours against ours, and make sure you understand any discrepancies.
Step 12 **Chapter roundup**	Work through it carefully, to make sure you have grasped the significance of all the fast forward points.
Step 13 **Quick quiz**	When you are happy that you have covered the chapter, use the Quick quiz to check how much you have remembered of the topics covered and to practise questions in a variety of formats.
Step 14 **Question(s) in the Question bank**	Either at this point, or later when you are thinking about revising, make a full attempt at the Question(s) suggested at the very end of the chapter. You can find these at the end of the Study Text, along with the Answers so you can see how you did.

Short of time: Skim study technique?

You may find you simply do not have the time available to follow all the key study steps for each chapter, however you adapt them for your particular learning style. If this is the case, follow the **skim study** technique below.

- Study the chapters in the order you find them in the Study Text.

- For each chapter:

  - Follow the key study steps 1-3

  - Skim-read through step 5, looking out for the points highlighted in the fast forward boxes (step 4)

  - Jump to step 12

  - Go back to step 6

  - Follow through steps 8 and 9

  - Prepare outline answers to questions (steps 10/11)

  - Try the Quick quiz (step 13), following up any items you can't answer

  - Do a plan for the Question (step 14), comparing it against our answers

  - You should probably still follow step 7 (note-taking), although you may decide simply to rely on the BPP Passcards for this.

Moving on...

However you study, when you are ready to embark on the practice and revision phase of the BPP Effective Study Package, you should still refer back to this Study Text, both as a source of **reference** (you should find the index particularly helpful for this) and as a way to **review** (the Fast forwards, Exam focus points, Chapter roundups and Quick quizzes help you here).

And remember to keep careful hold of this Study Text – you will find it invaluable in your work.

> More advice on Study Skills can be found in BPP's **Learning to Learn Accountancy** book.

Learning outcomes and Syllabus content

Syllabus overview

Fundamentals of Management Accounting is an introduction to management accounting for students with limited knowledge or no knowledge of this subject. While this paper focuses on the application of fundamental methods and techniques, students are also expected to have an understanding of when and when not to use them. Students must also appreciate the contribution made by information technology to management accounting.

Aims

This syllabus aims to test the student's ability to:

- Explain and use concepts and processes to determine product and service costs
- Explain direct, marginal and absorption costs and their use in pricing
- Apply CVP analysis and interpret the results
- Apply a range of costing and accounting systems
- Explain the role of budgets and standard costing within organisations
- Prepare and interpret budgets, standard costs and variance statements

Assessment

The assessment is computer based and 2 hours and comprises 50 compulsory questions with one or more parts. A varied range of objective test questions will be used.

Learning outcomes and syllabus content

Learning outcomes and syllabus content

CO1A Cost determination – 25%

Learning outcomes

On completion of their studies students should be able to:

(i)   Explain why organisations need to know how much products, processes and services cost and why they need costing systems

(ii)   Explain the idea of a 'cost object'

(iii)   Explain the concept of a direct cost and an indirect cost

(iv)   Explain why the concept of "cost" needs to be qualified as direct, full, marginal etc, in order to be meaningful

(v)   Distinguish between the historical cost of an asset and the economic value of an asset to an organisation

(vi)   Apply first-in-first out (FIFO), last-in-first-out (LIFO) and average cost (AVCO) methods of accounting for stock, calculating stock values and related gross profit

(vii)   Explain why FIFO is essentially a historical cost method, while LIFO approximates economic cost

(viii) Prepare cost statements for allocation and apportionment of overheads, including reciprocal service departments

(ix)   Calculate direct, variable and full costs of products, services and activities using overhead absorption rates to trace indirect costs to cost units

(x)   Explain the use of cost information in pricing decisions, including marginal cost pricing and the calculation of "full cost" based prices to generate a specified return on sales or investment

Syllabus content

		Covered in chapter
(1)	Classification of costs and the treatment of direct costs (specifically attributed to a cost object) and indirect costs (not specifically attributable) in ascertaining the cost of a 'cost object' eg a product, service, activity, customer.	1, 3, 4
(2)	Cost measurement: historical versus economic costs.	1
(3)	Accounting for the value of materials on FIFO, LIFO and AVCO bases.	2
(4)	Overhead costs: allocation, apportionment, re-apportionment and absorption of overhead costs. *Note*. The repeated distribution method only will be used for reciprocal service department costs.	3
(5)	Marginal cost pricing and full-cost pricing to achieve specified return on sales or return on investment.	4

Note: Students are not expected to have a detailed knowledge of activity based costing (ABC).

CO1B Cost behaviour and breakeven analysis – 10%

Learning outcomes

On completion of their studies students should be able to:

(i)   Explain how costs behave as product, service or activity levels increase or decrease

(ii)   Distinguish between fixed, variable and semi-variable costs

(iii)   Explain step costs and the importance of time-scales in their treatment as either variable or fixed

(iv)   Compute the fixed and variable elements of a semi-variable cost using the high-low method and "line of best fit" method

(v)   Explain the contribution concept and its use in cost-volume-profit (CVP) analysis

(vi)   Calculate and interpret the breakeven point, profit target, margin of safety and profit/volume ratio for a single product or service

(vii)   Prepare breakeven charts and profit/volume graphs for a single product or service

(viii) Calculate the profit maximising sales mix for a multi-product company that has limited demand for each product and one other constraint or limiting factor.

Syllabus content

		Covered in chapter
(1)	Fixed, variable and semi-variable costs	5
(2)	Step costs and the importance of time-scale in analysing cost behaviour	5
(3)	High-low and graphical methods to establish fixed and variable elements of a semi-variable cost. Note. Regression analysis is not examined	5
(4)	Contribution concept and CVP analysis	6
(5)	Breakeven charts. Profit volume graphs, breakeven point, profit target, margin of safety, contribution/sales ratio	6
(6)	Limiting factor analysis	6

CO1C Standard costing – 15%

Learning outcomes

On completion of their studies students should be able to:

(i)   Explain the difference between ascertaining costs after the event and planning by establishing standard costs in advance

(ii)   Explain why planned standard costs, prices and volumes are useful in setting a benchmark for comparison and so allowing managers' attention to be directed to areas of the business that are performing below or above expectation.

(iii)   Calculate standard costs for the material, labour and variable overhead elements of a cost of a product or service

(iv)   Calculate variances for materials, labour, variable overhead, sales prices and sales volumes

(v)   Prepare a statement that reconciles budgeted contribution with actual contribution

(vi)   Interpret statements of variances for variable costs, sales prices and sales volumes including possible inter-relations between cost variances, sales price and volume variances, and cost and sales variances

(vii) Describe the possible use of standard labour costs in designing incentive schemes for factory and office workers

Syllabus content

		Covered in chapter
(1)	Principles of standard costing	7
(2)	Preparation of standards for the variable elements of cost: material, labour, variable overhead	7
(3)	Variances: materials – total, price and usage; labour – total, rate and efficiency; variable overhead – total, expenditure and efficiency; sales – sales price and sales volume contribution. *Note.* Students will be expected to calculate the sales volume contribution variance.	8, 9
(4)	Reconciliation of budgeted and actual contribution	9
(5)	Piecework and the principles of incentive schemes based on standard hours versus actual hours taken. *Note.* The details of a specific incentive scheme will be provided in the examination.	7

C01D Costing and accounting systems– 30%

Learning outcomes

On completion of their studies students should be able to:

(i)   Explain the principles of manufacturing accounts and the integration of the cost accounts with the financial accounting system

(ii)   Prepare a set of integrated accounts, given opening balances and appropriate transactional information, and show standard cost variances

(iii) Compare and contrast job, batch, contract and process costing

(iv)   Prepare ledger accounts for job, batch and process costing system

(v)   Prepare ledger accounts for contract costs

(vi)   Explain the difference between subjective and objective classifications of expenditure and the importance of tracing costs both to products/services and to responsibility centres

(vii) Construct coding systems that facilitate both subjective and objective classification of costs

(viii) Prepare financial statements that inform management

(ix)   Explain why gross revenue, value-added, contribution, gross margin, marketing expense, general and administration expenses, etc might be highlighted in management reporting

(x)   Compare and contrast managerial reports in a range of organisations including commercial enterprises, charities and public sector undertakings

Syllabus content

		Covered in chapter
(1)	Manufacturing accounts including raw material, work-in-progress, finished goods and manufacturing overhead control accounts	14
(2)	Integrated ledgers including accounting for over and under absorption of production overhead	14
(3)	The treatment of variances as period entries in integrated ledger systems	14
(4)	Job, batch, process and contract costing. *Note*. Only the average cost method will be examined for process costing but students must be able to deal with differing degrees of completion of opening and closing stocks, normal gains and abnormal gains and losses, and the treatment of scrap value	12, 13
(5)	Subjective, objective and responsibility classifications and design and coding systems to facilitate these analyses	1
(6)	Cost accounting statements for management information in production and service companies and not-for-profit organisations	15

C01E Financial planning and control – 20%

Learning outcomes

On completion of their studies students should be able to:

(i) Explain why organisations set out financial plans in the form of budgets, typically for a financial year

(ii) Prepare functional budgets for material usage and purchase, labour and overheads, including budgets for capital expenditure and depreciation

(iii) Prepare a master budget: income statement, balance sheet and cash flow statement, based on the functional budgets

(iv) Interpret budget statements and advise managers on financing projected cash shortfalls and/or investing projected cash surpluses

(v) Prepare a flexible budget based on the actual levels of sales and production and calculate appropriate variances

(vi) Compare and contrast fixed and flexible budgets

(vii) Explain the use of budgets in designing reward strategies for managers

Syllabus content

		Covered in chapter
(1)	Budgeting for planning and control	10
(2)	Budget preparation; interpretation and use of the master budget	10
(3)	Reporting of actual against budget	11
(4)	Fixed and flexible budgeting	11
(5)	Budget variances	11
(6)	Interpretation and use of budget statements and budget variances	10, 11

The assessment

Format of computer-based assessment (CBA)

The CBA will not be divided into sections. There will be a total of fifty objective test questions and you will need to answer **ALL** of them in the time allowed, 2 hours.

Frequently asked questions about CBA

Q   What are the main advantages of CBA?

A
- Assessments can be offered on a continuing basis rather than at six-monthly intervals
- Instant feedback is provided for candidates by displaying their results on the computer screen

Q   Where can I take CBA?

A
- CBA must be taken at a 'CIMA Accredited CBA Centre'. For further information on CBA, you can email CIMA at cba@cimaglobal.com.

Q   How does CBA work?

A
- Questions are displayed on a monitor

- Candidates enter their answers directly onto a computer

- Candidates have 2 hours to complete the *Fundamentals of Management Accounting* examination

- The computer automatically marks the candidate's answers when the candidate has completed the examination

- Candidates are provided with some indicative feedback on areas of weakness if the candidate is unsuccessful

Q   What sort of questions can I expect to find in CBA?

Your assessment will consist entirely of a number of different types of **objective test question**. Here are some possible examples.

- **MCQs.** Read through the information on page (xix) about MCQs and how to tackle them.

- **Data entry.** This type of OT requires you to provide figures such as the correct figure for creditors in a balance sheet.

- **Hot spots.** This question format might ask you to identify which cell on a spreadsheet contains a particular formula or where on a graph marginal revenue equals marginal cost.

- **Multiple response.** These questions provide you with a number of options and you have to identify those which fulfil certain criteria.

- **Matching.** This OT question format could ask you to classify particular costs into one of a range of cost classifications provided, to match descriptions of variances with one of a number of variances listed, and so on.

This text provides you with **plenty of opportunities to practise** these various question types. You will find OTs **within each chapter** in the text and the **Quick quizzes** at the end of each chapter are full of them. The Question Bank contains more than ninety objective test questions similar to the ones that you are likely to meet in your CBA.

Further information relating to OTs is given on page (xx).

The **Practice and Revision Kit** for this paper was published in **June 2006** and is **full of OTs**, providing you with vital revision opportunities for the fundamental techniques and skills you will require in the assessment.

Tackling multiple choice questions

In a multiple choice question on your paper, you are given how many **incorrect** options?

A   Two
B   Three
C   Four
D   Five

The correct answer is B.

The MCQs in your exam contain four possible answers. You have to **choose the option that best answers the question**. The three incorrect options are called distracters. There is a skill in answering MCQs quickly and correctly. By practising MCQs you can develop this skill, giving you a better chance of passing the exam.

You may wish to follow the approach outlined below, or you may prefer to adapt it.

Step 1   **Skim read** all the MCQs and **identify** what appear to be the easier questions.

Step 2   Attempt each question – **starting with the easier questions** identified in Step 1. Read the question thoroughly. You may prefer to work out the answer before looking at the options, or you may prefer to look at the options at the beginning. Adopt the method that works best for you.

Step 3   Read the four options and see if one matches your own answer. **Be careful with numerical questions**, as the distracters are designed to match answers that incorporate common errors. Check that your calculation is correct. Have you followed the requirement exactly? Have you included every stage of the calculation?

Step 4   You may **find that none of the options matches your answer**.

•   Re-read the question to ensure that you understand it and are answering the requirement.
•   Eliminate any obviously wrong answers.
•   Consider which of the remaining answers is the most likely to be correct and select the option.

Step 5   If you are still **unsure** make a note **and continue to the next question**.

Step 6   **Revisit unanswered** questions. When you come back to a question after a break you often find you are able to answer it correctly straight away. If you are still unsure have a guess. You are not penalised for incorrect answers, so **never leave a question unanswered!**

Exam focus. After extensive practice and revision of MCQs, you may find that you recognise a question when you sit the exam. Be aware that the detail and/or requirement may be different. If the question seems familiar read the requirement and options carefully – do not assume that it is identical.

BPP's i-Pass for this paper provides you with plenty of opportunity for further practice of MCQs.

Tackling objective test questions

Of the total marks available for the paper, objective test questions (OTs) comprise 20/50 per cent. Questions will be worth between 2 to 4 marks.

What is an objective test question?

An **OT** is made up of some form of **stimulus**, usually a question, and a **requirement** to do something.

(a)   Multiple choice questions
(b)   Filling in blanks or completing a sentence
(c)   Listing items, in any order or a specified order such as rank order
(d)   Stating a definition
(e)   Identifying a key issue, term, figure or item
(f)   Calculating a specific figure
(g)   Completing gaps in a set of data where the relevant numbers can be calculated from the information given
(h)   Identifying points/zones/ranges/areas on graphs or diagrams, labelling graphs or filling in lines on a graph
(i)   Matching items or statements
(j)   Stating whether statements are true or false
(k)   Writing brief (in a specified number of words) explanations
(l)   Deleting incorrect items
(m)   Choosing right words from a number of options
(n)   Complete an equation, or define what the symbols used in an equation mean

OT questions in CIMA exams

CIMA has offered the following **guidance** about OT questions in the exam.

•   Credit may be given for **workings** where you are asked to calculate a specific figure.

•   If you **exceed a specified limit on the number of words** you can use in an answer, you will **not be awarded any marks**.

•   If you make **more than one attempt** at a question, clearly **cross through** any answers that you do not want to submit. If you don't do this, only your first answer will be marked.

Examples of OTs are included within each chapter, in the **quick quizzes** at the end of each chapter and in the **objective test question bank**.

BPP's i-Pass for this paper provides you with plenty of opportunity for further practice of OTs.

Part A
Cost determination

1

Cost accounting and cost classification

Introduction

Welcome to BPP's Study Text for CIMA's Certificate Paper C1 **Fundamentals of Management Accounting**. This chapter will introduce the **subject of cost accounting** and explain what cost accounting is and what a **cost accountant** does.

We will then turn our attention to **costs** and consider what cost actually is! We'll then look at some of the ways in which costs can be **classified** to assist the work of the cost accountant. Terms and concepts you encounter in these sections of the chapter are vitally important and will appear throughout this text and indeed all stages of your studies.

The chapter will end with a section on **cost codes**. Once costs are classified (see Sections 4 to 7), they are coded so that they are identifiable. They can then be manipulated and used by cost accountants.

In the next chapter we will look at a specific type of cost – material costs.

Topic list	Learning outcomes	Syllabus references	Ability required
1 What is cost accounting?	A(i)	A(1)	Comprehension
2 Some cost accounting concepts	A(ii)	A(1)	Comprehension
3 The concept of cost	A(iv), (v)	A(2)	Comprehension
4 Cost classification	A(i), D(vi)	A(1), D(6)	Comprehension
5 Cost classification for inventory valuation and profit measurement	A(iii)	A(1)	Comprehension
6 Cost classification for decision making	A(i)	A(1)	Comprehension
7 Cost classification for control	A(i)	A(1)	Comprehension
8 Cost codes	D(vi), (vii)	D(5)	Comprehension, Analysis

1 What is cost accounting?

Cost accounting is a management information system which analyses past, present and future data to provide the basis for managerial action.

1.1 The cost accountant

Who can provide the answers to the following questions?

- What was the cost of goods produced or services provided last period?
- What was the cost of operating a department last month?
- What revenues were earned last week?

Yes, you've guessed it, the cost accountant.

Knowing about costs incurred or revenues earned enables management to do the following.

(a)   **Assess the profitability of a product**, a service, a department, or the whole organisation.

(b)   Perhaps, **set selling prices** with some regard for the costs of sale.

(c)   **Put a value on inventory** (raw materials, work in progress, finished goods) that are still held in store at the end of a period, for preparing a balance sheet of the company's assets and liabilities.

That was quite easy. But who could answer the following questions?

(a)   What are the future costs of goods and services likely to be?

(b)   How do actual costs compare with planned costs?

(c)   What information does management need in order to make sensible decisions about profits and costs?

Well, you may be surprised, but again it is the cost accountant.

1.2 Cost accounting and management accounting

Management accounting, and nowadays **cost accounting**, provide management information for **planning**, **control** and **decision-making** purposes.

Originally cost accounting did deal with ways of accumulating historical costs and of charging these costs to units of output, or to departments, in order to establish inventory valuations, profits and balance sheet items. It has since been extended into **planning**, **control** and **decision making**, so that the cost accountant is now able to answer the second set of questions. In today's modern industrial environment, the role of cost accounting in the provision of management information is therefore almost indistinguishable from that of management accounting, which is basically concerned with the **provision of information to assist management** with **planning**, **control** and **decision making**.

Key term

> **Cost accounting** is the 'gathering of cost information and its attachment to cost objects, the establishment of budgets, standard costs and actual costs of operations, processes, activities or products; and the analysis of variances, profitability or the social use of funds'.
>
> CIMA *Official Terminology*

So, as you can see, the cost accountant has his or her hands full! Don't worry about the terms mentioned in CIMA's definition – all will become clearer as you work through this Study Text.

1.3 Cost accounting systems

The managers of a business have the responsibility of planning and controlling the resources used. To carry out this task effectively they must be provided with **sufficiently accurate** and **detailed information**, and the cost accounting system should provide this. Indeed a costing system is the **basis of an organisation's internal financial information system for managers**.

Cost accounting systems are **not restricted to manufacturing operations**.

(a) Cost accounting information is also used in service industries, government departments and welfare organisations.

(b) Within a manufacturing organisation, the cost accounting system should be applied not only to manufacturing operations but also to administration, selling and distribution, research and development and so on.

Cost accounting is concerned with **providing information to assist** the following.

- **Establishing inventory valuations, profits and balance sheet** items
- **Planning** (for example the provision of forecast costs at different activity levels)
- **Control** (such as the provision of actual and standard costs for comparison purposes)
- **Decision making** (for example, the provision of information about actual unit costs for the period just ended for pricing decisions).

1.4 Financial accounting versus cost accounting

AST FORWARD

In general terms, **financial accounting** is for **external** reporting whereas cost accounting is for **internal** reporting.

The financial accounting and cost accounting systems in a business both record the same basic data for income and expenditure, but each set of records may analyse the data in a different way. This is because each system has a **different purpose**.

(a) **Financial accounts** are prepared for individuals **external** to an organisation eg shareholders, customers, suppliers, the Inland Revenue and employees.

(b) **Management accounts** are prepared for **internal** managers of an organisation.

The data used to prepare financial accounts and management accounts are the same. The differences between the financial accounts and the management accounts arise because the data is analysed differently.

Financial accounts	Management accounts
Financial accounts detail the performance of an organisation over a defined period and the state of affairs at the end of that period.	Management accounts are used to aid management record, plan and control the organisation's activities and to help the decision-making process.
In the UK, limited companies must, by law, prepare financial accounts.	There is no legal requirement to prepare management accounts.

Financial accounts	Management accounts
The format of published financial accounts is determined by law (mainly the Companies Acts), by Statements of Standard Accounting Practice and by Financial Reporting Standards. In principle the accounts of different organisations can therefore be easily compared.	The format of management accounts is entirely at management discretion: no strict rules govern the way they are prepared or presented. Each organisation can devise its own management accounting system and format of reports.
Financial accounts concentrate on the business as a whole, aggregating revenues and costs from different operations, and are an end in themselves.	Management accounts can focus on specific areas of an organisation's activities. Information may be produced to aid a decision rather than to be an end product of a decision.
Most financial accounting information is of a monetary nature.	Management accounts incorporate non-monetary measures. Management may need to know, for example, tonnes of aluminium produced, monthly machine hours, or miles travelled by sales representatives.
Financial accounts present an essentially historical picture of past operations.	Management accounts are both a historical record and a future planning tool.

2 Some cost accounting concepts

2.1 Functions and departments

An organisation, whether it is a manufacturing company, a provider of services (such as a bank or a hotel) or a public sector organisation (such as a hospital), may be divided into a number of different **functions** within which there are a number of **departments**. A manufacturing organisation might be structured as follows.

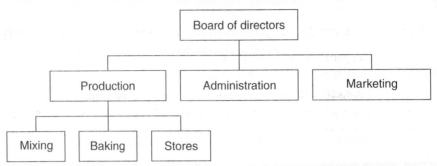

Suppose the organisation above produces chocolate cakes for a number of supermarket chains. The production function is involved with the making of the cakes, the administration department with the preparation of accounts and the employment of staff and the marketing department with the selling and distribution of the cakes.

Within the production function there are three departments, two of which are production departments (the mixing department and the baking department) which are actively involved in the production of the cakes and one of which is a service department (stores department) which provides a service or back-up to the production departments.

2.2 Cost objects

ST FORWARD

If the users of accounting information want to know the cost of something, that something is called a **cost object**.

Examples of cost objects include:

- A product
- A service to a hotel guest
- A sales territory

Key term

> A **cost object** is 'for example a product, service, centre, activity, customer or distribution channel in relation to which costs are ascertained'.   CIMA *Official Terminology*

In our example, cost objects include:

- Chocolate cakes
- The provision of supply to one of the supermarkets
- The administration department

2.3 Cost centres

ST FORWARD

Cost centres are **collecting places** for costs before they are further analysed.

In general, for cost accounting purposes, departments are termed **cost centres** and the product produced by an organisation is termed the **cost unit**. In our example, the cost centres of the production function could be the mixing department, the baking department and the stores department and the organisation's cost unit could be one chocolate cake.

When costs are incurred, they are generally allocated to a **cost centre**. Cost centres may include the following.

- A **department** (as in our example above)
- A **machine** or group of machines
- A **project** (eg the installation of a new computer system)
- A **new product** (to enable the costs of development and production to be identified)

ssessment ocus point

> A typical objective testing (OT) question on the contents of this chapter might be to ask you to select appropriate cost centres from a number of suggestions for a particular organisation.

2.4 Cost units

AST FORWARD

Cost units are the **basic control units** for costing purposes.

Key term

> A **cost unit** is a 'unit of product or service in relation to which costs are ascertained'.   CIMA *Official Terminology*

Once costs have been traced to cost centres, they can be further analysed in order to establish a **cost per cost unit**. Alternatively, some items of costs may be charged directly to a cost unit, for example direct materials and direct labour costs, which you will meet later in this text.

Different organisations use different cost units. Here are some suggestions.

Organisation	Possible cost unit
Steelworks	Tonne of steel produced Tonne of coke used
Hospital	Patient/day Operation Out-patient visit
Freight organisation	Tonne/kilometre
Passenger transport organisation	Passenger/kilometre
Accounting firm	Audit performed Chargeable hour
Restaurant	Meal served

2.5 Composite cost units

Notice that some of the cost units in this table are made up of **two parts**. For example the patient/day cost unit for the hospital. These two-part cost units are known as **composite cost units** and they are used most often in service organisations.

Composite cost units help to improve cost control. For example the measure of 'cost per patient' **might not be particularly useful for control purposes**. The cost per patient will vary depending on the length of the patient's stay, therefore monitoring costs using this basis would be difficult.

The cost per patient/day is not affected by the length of the individual patient's stay. Therefore it would be more useful for **monitoring and controlling costs**. Similarly, in a freight organisation the **cost per tonne/kilometre** (the cost of carrying one tonne for one kilometre) would be more meaningful for control than the cost per tonne carried, which would vary with the distance travelled.

Question   **Cost centres and cost units**

Identify the following as suitable cost centres or cost units for a hospital.

Ward
Operating theatre
Bed/night
Patient/day
Outpatient visit
Operating theatre hour

Cost unit	Cost Centre

Answer

Cost unit	Cost Centre
Bed/night	Ward
Patient/day	Operating theatre
Operating theatre hour	
Outpatient visit	

3 The concept of cost

3.1 Cost measurement

ST FORWARD In practice most cost accounting transactions are recorded at **historic cost**, but costs can be measured in terms of **economic cost.**

Cost accounting transactions, indeed all accounting transactions, can be measured (or valued) on numerous bases. For example:

(a)   Cost accounts kept on a historical cost basis use original/past values.
(b)   Cost accounts kept on a current cost basis use up-to-date market values.

Transactions can also be recorded at **economic cost**.

3.1.1 Economic cost

Economic cost, also referred to as **opportunity cost**, is the value of the best alternative course of action that was not chosen. In other words, it is **what could have been accomplished with the resources used in the course of action not chosen.** It represents opportunities forgone.

If a person has a job offer that pays $25 for an hour's work, and instead chooses to take a nap for an hour, the historical cost of the nap is zero; the person did not hand over any money in order to nap. The economic cost of the nap is the $25 that could have been earned working.

In practice **most cost accounting systems use historical cost as a measurement basis**.

3.2 Economic value

AST FORWARD **Economic value** is the amount someone is willing to pay.

The economic value of a particular item, for example a kilogram of rice, is measured by the maximum amount of other things that a person is willing to give up to have that kilogram of rice. If we simplify our example 'economy' so that the person only has two goods to choose from, rice and pasta, the value of a kilogram of rice would be measured by the amount of pasta that the person is willing to give up to have one more kilogram of rice.

Economic value is therefore measured by **the most someone is willing to give up in other products and services in order to obtain a product or service**. Dollars (or some other currency) are a universally accepted measure of economic value in many markets, because the number of **dollars** that a person is willing to pay for something tells how much of all other goods and services they are willing to give up to get that item. This is often referred to as 'willingness to pay'.

3.3 Qualifying the concept of cost

Key term

> As a noun, **cost** is 'The amount of cash or cash equivalent paid ….'
>
> As a verb, cost is 'To ascertain the cost of a specified thing or activity.
>
> The word *cost* can rarely stand alone and should be qualified as to its nature and limitations.'
>
> CIMA *Official Terminology*

Costs need to be **qualified or classified in some way** so that they can be **arranged into logical groups** in order to **facilitate** an efficient **system for collecting and analysing costs**.

As you work through this text you will encounter many different types of cost, each of which has its usefulness and limitations in various circumstances.

4 Cost classification

Before the cost accountant can plan, control or make decisions, all costs (whether labour, material or overheads) must be accurately **classified** and their destination in the costing system (cost units because they are direct costs or cost centres because they are indirect costs) identified via a **coding** system.

We'll look at coding later in the chapter. First we consider classification.

Key term

> **Cost classification** is the 'arrangement of elements of cost into logical groups with respect to their nature (fixed, variable, value adding), function (production, selling) or use in the business of the entity'.   CIMA *Official Terminology*

Classification can be by **nature (subjective)**, by **purpose (objective)** or by **responsibility**.

4.1 Classification by nature

Subjective classification of expenditure indicates the **nature** of the expenditure.

- Material
- Labour
- Expense

Each grouping may be subdivided. For example the materials classification may be subdivided into:

- Raw materials
- Components
- Consumables

4.2 Classification by purpose

Objective classification of expenditure indicates the **purpose** of the expenditure, the reason why the expenditure has taken place, which might be for:

- Stock valuation and profit measurement
- Decision making
- Control

We'll be looking at objective classification in the next few sections.

4.3 Classification by responsibility

Responsibility classification indicates who is responsible for the expenditure, and so is linked with objective classification for control. We'll look at this in detail in Section 7.

5 Cost classification for inventory valuation and profit measurement

5.1 Cost elements

For the purposes of inventory valuation and profit measurement, the cost accountant must calculate the cost of one unit. The total cost of a cost unit is made up of the following three **elements of cost**.

- Materials
- Labour
- Other expenses (such as rent and rates, interest charges and so on)

Key term

> **Cost elements** are 'constituent parts of costs according to the factors upon which expenditure is incurred, namely material, labour and expenses'.
> CIMA *Official Terminology*

Cost elements can be classified as **direct** costs or **indirect** costs.

5.2 Direct cost and prime cost

AST FORWARD

> A **direct cost** is a cost that can be traced in full to the product, service, or department that is being costed.

Key term

> A **direct cost** is 'expenditure that can be attributed to a specific cost unit, for example material that forms part of a product'.
> CIMA *Official Terminology*

Direct costs are therefore **directly attributable to cost objects**.

(a) **Direct material costs** are the costs of materials that are known to have been used in making and selling a product (or providing a service).

(b) **Direct labour costs** are the specific costs of the workforce used to make a product or provide a service. Direct labour costs are established by measuring the time taken for a job, or the time taken in 'direct production work'.

(c)   **Other direct expenses** are those expenses that have been incurred in full as a direct consequence of making a product, or providing a service, or running a department.

We look at these types of direct cost in more detail below.

FAST FORWARD

Prime cost = direct material cost + direct labour cost + direct expenses

Key term

Prime cost is the 'total of direct material, direct labour and direct expenses'.   CIMA *Official Terminology*

5.2.1 Direct material

Direct material is **all material becoming part of the product** (unless used in negligible amounts and/or having negligible cost).

Direct material costs are charged to the product as part of the **prime cost**. Examples of direct material are as follows.

(a)   **Component parts** or other materials specially purchased for a particular job, order or process.

(b)   **Part-finished work** which is transferred from department 1 to department 2 becomes finished work of department 1 and a direct material cost in department 2.

(c)   **Primary packing materials** like cartons and boxes.

Materials used in negligible amounts and/or having negligible cost can be grouped under indirect materials as part of overhead (see Section 5.3).

5.2.2 Direct wages or direct labour costs

Direct wages are all **wages paid for labour** (either as basic hours or as overtime expended on work on the product itself).

Direct wages costs are charged to the product as part of the **prime cost**.

Examples of groups of labour receiving payment as direct wages are as follows.

(a)   Workers engaged in **altering** the condition, conformation or composition of the product.

(b)   Inspectors, analysts and testers **specifically required** for such production.

5.2.3 Direct expenses

Direct expenses are any expenses which are incurred on a specific product **other than direct material cost and direct wages**.

Direct expenses are charged to the product as part of the **prime** cost. Examples of direct expenses are as follows.

- The cost of special designs, drawings or layouts
- The hire of tools or equipment for a particular job

Direct expenses are also referred to as **chargeable expenses.**

5.3 Indirect cost/overhead

> An **indirect cost** (or **overhead**) is a cost that is incurred in the course of making a product, providing a service or running a department, but which cannot be traced directly and in full to the product, service or department.

> An **indirect cost** or **overhead** is 'expenditure on labour, materials or services that cannot be economically identified with a specific saleable cost unit'.
> CIMA *Official Terminology*

Indirect costs are therefore **not directly attributable to cost objects**.

Examples of indirect costs might be the cost of supervisors' wages on a production line, cleaning materials and buildings insurance for a factory.

Total expenditure may therefore be **analysed** as follows.

Materials cost	=	Direct materials cost	+	Indirect materials cost
+		+		+
Labour cost	=	Direct labour cost	+	Indirect labour cost
+		+		+
Expenses	=	Direct expenses	+	Indirect expenses
Total cost	=	Direct cost/prime cost	+	Overhead cost

5.3.1 Production overhead

Production (or factory) overhead includes all indirect material cost, indirect wages and indirect expenses **incurred in the factory from receipt of the order until its completion**, including:

(a) **Indirect materials** which cannot be traced in the finished product.

- Consumable stores, eg material used in negligible amounts

(b) **Indirect wages**, meaning all wages not charged directly to a product.

- Salaries of non-productive personnel in the production department, eg supervisor

(c) **Indirect expenses** (other than material and labour) not charged directly to production

- Rent, rates and insurance of a factory
- Depreciation, fuel, power and maintenance of plant and buildings

5.3.2 Administration overhead

Administration overhead is all indirect material costs, wages and expenses **incurred in the direction, control and administration of an undertaking**, including:

- **Depreciation** of office equipment
- **Office salaries**, including the salaries of secretaries and accountants
- Rent, rates, insurance, telephone, heat and light cost of general offices

5.3.3 Selling overhead

Selling overhead is all indirect materials costs, wages and expenses **incurred in promoting sales and retaining customers**, including:

- **Printing** and **stationery**, such as catalogues and price lists
- **Salaries** and **commission** of sales representatives
- **Advertising** and **sales promotion**, market research
- Rent, rates and insurance for sales offices and showrooms

5.3.4 Distribution overhead

Distribution overhead is all indirect material costs, wages and expenses **incurred in making the packed product ready for despatch and delivering it to the customer**, including:

- Cost of packing cases
- Wages of packers, drivers and despatch clerks
- Depreciation and running expenses of delivery vehicles

Question   Direct and indirect labour costs

Classify the following labour costs as either direct or indirect.

(a)   The basic pay of direct workers (cash paid, tax and other deductions) is a ⬚ cost.

(b)   The basic pay of indirect workers is a ⬚ cost.

(c)   Overtime premium, ie the premium above basic pay, for working overtime is a ⬚ cost.

(d)   Bonus payments under a group bonus scheme is a ⬚ cost.

(e)   Employer's National Insurance contributions is a ⬚ cost.

(f)   Idle time of direct workers, paid while waiting for work is a ⬚ cost.

Answer

(a)   The basic pay of direct workers is a ⬚ direct ⬚ cost to the unit, job or process.

(b)   The basic pay of indirect workers is an ⬚ indirect ⬚ cost, unless a customer asks for an order to be carried out which involves the dedicated use of indirect workers' time, when the cost of this time would be a direct labour cost of the order.

(c)   Overtime premium paid to both direct and indirect workers is usually an ⬚ indirect ⬚ cost because it is 'unfair' to charge the items produced in overtime hours with the premium. Why should an item made in overtime be more costly just because, by chance, it was made after the employee normally clocks off for the day?

There are two particular circumstances in which the overtime premium might be a direct cost.

(i)   If overtime is worked at the specific request of a customer to get his order completed, the overtime premium paid is a direct cost of the order.

(ii) If overtime is worked regularly by a production department in the normal course of operations, the overtime premium paid to direct workers could be incorporated into the (average) direct labour hourly rate.

(d) Bonus payments are generally an [indirect] cost.

(e) Employer's National Insurance contributions (which are added to employees' total pay as a wages cost) are normally treated as an [indirect] labour cost.

(f) Idle time is an overhead cost, that is an [indirect] labour cost.

Question   **Direct labour costs**

A production worker is paid the following in week 5.

		$
(a)	Basic pay for normal hours worked, 36 hours at $4 per hour =	144
(b)	Pay at the basic rate for overtime, 6 hours at $4 per hour =	24
(c)	Overtime shift premium, with overtime paid at time-and-a-quarter $\frac{1}{4} \times 6$ hours $\times$ $4 per hour =	6
(d)	A bonus payment under a group bonus (or 'incentive') scheme (bonus for the month)	30
(e)	Employer National Insurance	18
(f)	Idle time	14
	Total gross wages in week 5 for 42 hours of work	236

What is the direct labour cost for this employee in week 5?

A $144   B $168   C $230   D $236

Answer

The correct answer is B.

Let's start by considering a general approach to answering multiple choice questions (MCQs). In a numerical question like this, the best way to begin is to ignore the options and work out your own answer from the available data. If your solution corresponds to one of the four options then mark this as your chosen answer and move on. Don't waste time working out whether any of the other options might be correct. If your answer does not appear among the available options then check your workings. If it still does not correspond to any of the options then you need to take a calculated guess. **Never leave a question out because CIMA does not penalise an incorrect answer.**

Do not make the common error of simply selecting the answer which is closest to yours. The best thing to do is to first eliminate any answers which you know or suspect are incorrect. For example you could eliminate C and D because you should now know that costs such as group bonus schemes are usually indirect costs. You are then left with a choice between A and B, and at least you have now improved your chances if you really are guessing.

The correct answer is B because the basic rate for overtime is a part of direct wages cost. It is only the overtime premium that is usually regarded as an overhead or indirect cost.

5.4 Product costs and period costs

For the preparation of financial statements, costs are often classified as either **product costs** or **period costs**. Product costs are costs identified with goods produced or purchased for resale. Period costs are costs deducted as expenses during the current period.

Key terms

A **product cost** is a 'cost of a finished product built up from its cost elements'.

A **period cost** is a 'cost relating to a time period rather than to the output of products or services'.

CIMA *Official Terminology*

Consider a retailer who acquires goods for resale without changing their basic form. The only product cost is therefore the purchase cost of the goods. Any unsold goods are held as inventory, valued at the lower of purchase cost and net realisable value and included as an asset in the balance sheet. As the goods are sold, their cost becomes an expense in the form of 'cost of goods sold'. A retailer will also incur a variety of selling and administration expenses. Such costs are **period costs** because they are **deducted from revenue** without ever being regarded as part of the **value of inventory**.

Now consider a manufacturing firm in which direct materials are transformed into saleable goods with the help of direct labour and factory overheads. All these costs are **product costs** because they are allocated to the value of inventory until the goods are sold. As with the retailer, selling and administration expenses are regarded as **period costs.**

5.5 Functional costs

Classification by function involves classifying costs as production/manufacturing costs, administration costs or marketing/selling and distribution costs.

This way of classifying costs involves relating the costs to the activity causing the cost. In a 'traditional' costing system for a manufacturing organisation, costs are classified by function as follows.

- **Production or manufacturing** costs
- **Administration** costs
- **Marketing, or selling and distribution costs**

Many expenses fall comfortably into one or other of these three broad classifications. Other expenses that do not fall fully into one of these classifications might be categorised as **general overheads** or even classified on their own (for example **research and development costs**).

Question

Classification of costs

Within the costing system of a manufacturing company the following types of expense are incurred.

Reference number

1   Cost of oils used to lubricate production machinery
2   Motor vehicle licences for lorries
3   Depreciation of factory plant and equipment
4   Cost of chemicals used in the laboratory
5   Commission paid to sales representatives
6   Salary of the secretary to the finance director

7   Trade discount given to customers
8   Holiday pay of machine operatives
9   Salary of security guard in raw materials warehouse
10   Fees to advertising agency
11   Rent of finished goods warehouse
12   Salary of scientist in laboratory
13   Insurance of the company's premises
14   Salary of supervisor working in the factory
15   Cost of typewriter ribbons in the general office
16   Protective clothing for machine operatives

Required

Place each expense within the following classifications using the reference numbers above. Each type of expense should appear only once in your answer.

Classifications		Reference numbers of expenses
(a)	Production costs	
(b)	Selling and distribution costs	
(c)	Administration costs	
(d)	Research and development costs	

Answer

The reference number for each expense can be classified as follows.

Classifications		Reference numbers of expenses
(a)	Production costs	1, 3, 8, 9, 14, 16
(b)	Selling and distribution costs	2, 5, 7, 10,11
(c)	Administration costs	6, 13, 15
(d)	Research and development costs	4, 12

6 Cost classification for decision making

ST FORWARD

A different way of classifying costs is into **fixed costs** and **variable costs**. Many costs are part fixed and part variable and so are called **semi-fixed**, **semi-variable** or **mixed costs**. A knowledge of how costs vary at different levels of activity (or volume) is essential to decision making.

Decision making is concerned with **future events** and so managers require information on **expected future costs and revenues**. Although cost accounting systems are designed to accumulate **past costs and revenues** this historical information may provide a starting point for **forecasting future events**.

6.1 Fixed costs and variable costs

Key terms

- A **fixed cost** is a 'cost incurred for an accounting period, that, within certain output or turnover limits, tends to be unaffected by fluctuations in the levels of activity (output or turnover)'.

- A **variable cost** is a 'cost that varies with a measure of activity'.

- A **semi-variable cost** is a 'cost containing both fixed and variable components and thus partly affected by a change in the level of activity'.

CIMA *Official Terminology*

(a) Direct material costs are **variable costs** because they rise as more units of a product are manufactured.

(b) Sales commission is often a fixed percentage of sales revenue, and so is a **variable cost** that varies with the level of sales.

(c) Telephone call charges are likely to increase if the volume of business expands, and so they are a **variable overhead cost.**

(d) The rental cost of business premises is a constant amount, at least within a stated time period, and so it is a **fixed cost.**

Note that costs can be classified as direct costs or indirect costs/overheads, or as fixed costs or variable costs. These alternative classifications are not, however, mutually exclusive, but are complementary to each other, so that we can find **some direct costs that are fixed costs (although they are commonly variable costs)** and **some overhead costs that are fixed** and **some overhead costs that are variable**.

7 Cost classification for control

FAST FORWARD

Classification by responsibility requires costs to be divided into those that are **controllable** and those that are **uncontrollable**. A system of **responsibility accounting** is therefore required.

There is little point allocating costs to products for the purposes of control as the production of a product, say, may consist of a number of operations, each of which is the responsibility of a different person. A product cost does not therefore provide a link between costs incurred and areas of responsibility. So costs (and revenues) must be traced in another way to the individuals responsible for their incurrence. This 'other way' is known as **responsibility accounting.**

7.1 Responsibility accounting and responsibility centres

Key terms

Responsibility accounting is a system of accounting that segregates revenue and costs into areas of personal responsibility in order to monitor and assess the performance of each part of an organisation.

A **responsibility centre** is a department or function whose performance is the direct responsibility of a specific manager.

Managers of responsibility centres should only be held accountable for costs over which they have some influence. From a motivation point of view this is important because it can be very demoralising for managers who feel that their performance is being judged on the basis of something over which they have no influence. It is also important from a control point of view in that control reports should ensure that information on costs is reported to the manager who is able to take action to control them.

Responsibility accounting attempts to associate costs, revenues, assets and liabilities with the managers most capable of controlling them. As a system of accounting, it therefore distinguishes between controllable and uncontrollable costs.

7.2 Controllable and uncontrollable costs

A **controllable cost** is a cost which can be influenced by management decisions and actions.

An **uncontrollable cost** is a cost which cannot be affected by management within a given time span.

Most **variable costs** within a department are thought to be **controllable in the short term** because managers can influence the efficiency with which resources are used, even if they cannot do anything to raise or lower price levels.

A cost which is not controllable by a junior manager might be controllable by a senior manager. For example, there may be high direct labour costs in a department caused by excessive overtime working. The junior manager may feel obliged to continue with the overtime to meet production schedules, but his senior may be able to reduce costs by hiring extra full-time staff, thereby reducing the requirements for overtime.

A cost which is not controllable by a manager in one department may be controllable by a manager in another department. For example, an increase in material costs may be caused by buying at higher prices than expected (controllable by the purchasing department) or by excessive wastage (controllable by the production department) or by a faulty machine producing rejects (controllable by the maintenance department).

Some costs are **non-controllable**, such as increases in expenditure items due to inflation. Other costs are **controllable, but in the long term rather than the short term**. For example, production costs might be reduced by the introduction of new machinery and technology, but in the short term, management must attempt to do the best they can with the resources and machinery at their disposal.

7.2.1 The controllability of fixed costs

It is often assumed that all fixed costs are non-controllable in the short run. This is not so.

(a) **Committed fixed costs** are those costs arising from the possession of plant, equipment, buildings and an administration department to **support the long-term needs of the business**. These costs (depreciation, rent, administration salaries) are largely **non-controllable in the short term** because they have been committed by longer-term decisions affecting longer-term needs. When a company decides to cut production drastically, the long-term committed fixed costs will be reduced, but only after redundancy terms have been settled and assets sold.

(b) **Discretionary fixed costs**, such as advertising and research and development costs, are incurred as a result of a top management decision, but could be **raised or lowered at fairly short notice** (irrespective of the actual volume of production and sales).

7.2.2 Controllability and dual responsibility

Quite often a particular cost might be the **responsibility of two or more managers**. For example, raw materials costs might be the responsibility of the purchasing manager (prices) and the production manager (usage). A **reporting system must allocate responsibility appropriately**. The purchasing manager must be responsible for any increase in raw materials prices whereas the production manager should be responsible for any increase in raw materials usage.

Attention!

You can see that there are **no clear cut rules** as to which costs are controllable and which are not. Each situation and cost must be reviewed separately and a decision taken according to the control value of the information and its behavioural impact.

8 Cost codes

Once costs have been classified, a **coding system** can be applied to make it easier to manage the cost data, both in manual systems and in computerised systems.

Key term

A **code** is a 'brief, accurate reference designed to assist classification of items by facilitating entry, collation and analysis'.

CIMA *Official Terminology*

Coding is the way in which the classification system that we have been looking at is applied.

Step 1 Costs are classified.

Step 2 Costs are coded.

Each individual cost should be identifiable by its code. This is possible by building up the individual characteristics of the cost into the code.

The characteristics which are normally identified are as follows.

- The **nature** of the cost (materials, labour, overhead), which is known as a **subjective classification**

- The **type** of cost (direct, indirect and so on)

- The **cost centre** to which the cost should be allocated or **cost unit** which should be charged, which is known as an **objective classification**

- The **department** which the particular cost centre is in

8.1 Features of a good coding system

An efficient and effective coding system, whether manual or computerised, should incorporate the following features.

(a) The code must be **easy to use and communicate**.

(b) Each item should have a **unique code**.

(c) The coding system must **allow for expansion**.

(d) If there is conflict between the ease of using the code by the people involved and its manipulation on a computer, the **human interest should dominate**.

(e) The code should be **flexible** so that small changes in a cost's classification can be incorporated without major changes to the coding system itself.

(f) The coding system should provide a **comprehensive** system, whereby every recorded item can be suitably coded.

(g) The coding system should be **brief**, to save clerical time in writing out codes and to save storage space in computer memory and on computer files. At the same time codes must be **long enough** to allow for the suitable coding of all items.

(h) The likelihood of **errors** going undetected should be minimised.

(i) There should be a readily available **index or reference book** of codes.

(j) Existing codes should be **reviewed** regularly and out-of-date codes removed.

(k) Code numbers should be **issued from a single central point**. Different people should not be allowed to add new codes to the existing list independently.

(l) The code should be either **entirely numeric or entirely alphabetic**. In a computerised system, numeric characters are preferable. The use of dots, dashes, colons and so on should be avoided.

(m) Codes should be **uniform** (that is, have the same length and the same structure) to assist in the detection of missing characters and to facilitate processing.

(n) The coding system should avoid problems such as confusion between I and 1, O and 0 (zero), S and 5 and so on.

(o) The coding system should, if possible, be **significant** (in other words, the actual code should signify something about the item being coded).

(p) If the code consists of alphabetic characters, it should be derived from the item's description or name (that is, **mnemonics** should be used).

8.2 Types of code

8.2.1 Composite codes

The CIMA *Official Terminology* definition of a code describes a composite code.

'For example, in costing, the first three digits in the **composite code** 211.392 might indicate the **nature** of the expenditure (**subjective classification**) and the last three digits might indicate the **cost centre or cost unit to be charged (objective classification).**

So the digits 211 might refer to:

2   Materials
1   Raw materials
1   Timber

This would indicate to anyone familiar with the coding system that the expenditure was incurred on timber.

The digits 392 might refer to:

3   Direct cost
9   Factory alpha
2   Assembly department

This would indicate the expenditure was to be charged as a direct material cost to the assembly department in factory alpha.

8.2.2 Other types of code

Here are some other examples of codes.

(a)   **Sequence (or progressive) codes**

Numbers are given to items in ordinary numerical sequence, so that there is no obvious connection between an item and its code. For example:

000042	4cm nails
000043	Office stapler
000044	Hand wrench

(b)   **Group classification codes**

These are an improvement on simple sequences codes, in that a digit (often the first one) indicates the classification of an item. For example:

4NNNNN	Nails
5NNNNN	Screws
6NNNNN	Bolts

(Note. 'N' stands for another digit; 'NNNNN' indicates there are five further digits in the code.)

(c)   **Faceted codes**

These are a refinement of group classification codes, in that each digit of the code gives information about an item. For example:

(i)	The first digit:	1	Nails
		2	Screws
		3	Bolts
			etc…

(ii)	The second digit:	1	Steel
		2	Brass
		3	Copper
			etc…

(iii)	The third digit:	1	50mm
		2	60mm
		3	75mm
			etc…

A 60mm steel screw would have a code of 212.

(d)   **Significant digit codes**

These incorporate some digit(s) which is (are) part of the description of the item being coded. For example:

5000	Screws
5050	50mm screws
5060	60mm screws
5075	75mm screws

(e)   **Hierarchical codes**

This is a type of faceted code where each digit represents a classification, and each digit further to the right represents a smaller subset than those to the left. For example:

3	=	Screws
31	=	Flat headed screws
32	=	Round headed screws
322	=	Steel (round headed) screws
		and so on

A coding system does not have to be structured entirely on any one of the above systems. It can mix the various features according to the items which need to be coded.

8.3 Example: coding systems

Formulate a coding system suitable for computer application for the cost accounts of a small manufacturing company.

Solution

A suggested computer-based four-digit numerical coding system is set out below.

Basic structure	Code number	Allocation
First division	1000-4999	This range provides for cost accounts and is divided into four main departmental sections with ten cost centre subsections in each department, allowing for a maximum of 99 accounts of each cost centre.
Second division	1000-1999	Department 1
	2000-2999	Department 2
	3000-3999	Department 3
	4000-4999	Department 4
Third division	100-999	Facility for ten cost centres in each department
Fourth division		Breakdown of costs in each cost centre
	01-39	Direct costs
	40-59	Variable costs
	60-79	Fixed costs
	80-99	Spare capacity

Codes 5000-9999 could be used for the organisation's financial accounts.

An illustration of the coding of steel screws might be as follows.

Department 2

Cost centre	1	2	3	4
Consumable stores	2109	2209	2309	2409

The four-digit codes above indicate the following.

- The first digit, 2, refers to the department.
- The second digit, 1, 2, 3 or 4, refers to the cost centre which incurred the cost.
- The last two digits, 09, refer to 'materials costs, steel screws'.

8.4 The advantages of a coding system

(a)   A code is usually **briefer** than a description, thereby saving clerical time in a manual system and storage space in a computerised system.

(b)   A code is **more precise** than a description and therefore **reduces ambiguity**.

(c)   Coding **facilitates data processing**.

Chapter Roundup

- **Cost accounting** is a management information system which analyses past, present and future data to provide the basis for managerial action.

- **Management accounting**, and nowadays **cost accounting**, provide management information for **planning**, **control** and **decision-making** purposes.

- In general terms, **financial accounting** is for **external** reporting whereas **cost accounting** is for **internal** reporting.

- If the users of accounting information want to know the cost of something, that something is called a **cost object**.

- **Cost centres** are **collecting places** for costs before they are further analysed.

- **Cost units** are the **basic control units** for costing purposes.

- In practice most cost accounting transactions are recorded at **historic cost**, but costs can be measured in terms of **economic cost.**

- **Economic value** is the amount someone is willing to pay.

- Before the cost accountant can plan, control or make decisions, all costs (whether labour, material or overheads) must be accurately **classified** and their destination in the costing system (cost units because they are direct costs or cost centres because they are indirect costs) identified via a **coding** system.

- **Classification** can be by **nature** (**subjective**), by **purpose** (**objective**) or by **responsibility**.

- A **direct cost** is a cost that can be traced in full to the product, service or department that is being costed.

- **Prime cost** = direct material cost + direct labour cost + direct expenses

- An **indirect cost** (or **overhead**) is a cost that is incurred in the course of making a product, providing a service or running a department, but which cannot be traced directly and in full to the product, service or department.

- For the preparation of financial statements, costs are often classified as either **product costs** or **period costs**. Product costs are costs identified with goods produced or purchased for resale. Period costs are costs deducted as expenses during the current period.

- **Classification by function** involves classifying costs as production/manufacturing costs, administration costs or marketing/selling and distribution costs.

- A different way of classifying costs is into **fixed costs** and **variable costs**. Many costs are part fixed and part variable and so are called **semi-fixed**, **semi-variable** or **mixed costs**. A knowledge of how costs vary at different levels of activity (or volume) is essential to decision making.

- **Classification by responsibility** requires costs to be divided into those that are **controllable** and those that are **uncontrollable**. A system of **responsibility accounting** is therefore required.

- Once costs have been classified, a **coding system** can be applied to make it easier to manage the cost data, both in manual systems and in computerised systems.

Quick Quiz

1   In general terms, financial accounting is for internal reporting whereas cost accounting is for external reporting.

   True [ ]

   False [ ]

2   (a)   A .... is a unit of product or service to which costs can be related. It is the basic control unit for costing purposes.

   (b)   A .... acts as a collecting place for certain costs before they are analysed further.

   (c)   A .... is anything that users of accounting information want to know the cost of.

3   *Choose the correct words from those highlighted.*

   In practice, most cost accounting systems use **historical cost/economic cost/economic value/cost value** as a measurement basis.

4   Classification of expenditure into material, labour and expenses, say, is an example of:

   A   subjective classification
   B   objective classification
   C   classification by responsibility
   D   classification by behaviour

5   There are a number of different ways in which costs can be classified.

   (a)   .... and .... (or overhead) costs

   (b)   .... costs (production costs, distribution and selling costs, administration costs and financing costs)

   (c)   Fixed costs and ....costs

6   A fixed cost is a cost which tends to vary with the level of activity.

   True [ ]

   False [ ]

7   Categorise these costs:

   Sales commission   Functional cost

   Rent   ?   Fixed cost

   Research and development costs   Variable cost

8   Which of the following would be classified as indirect labour?

   A   Assembly workers in a company manufacturing televisions
   B   A stores assistant in a factory store
   C   Plasterers in a construction company
   D   An audit clerk in a firm of auditors

9   In the composite code 374.152, the last three digits indicate the cost centre to be charged. This is:

A   classification by responsibility
B   cost classification
C   objective classification
D   subjective classification

Answers to Quick Quiz

1 False. Cost accounting is mainly concerned with the preparation of management accounts for **internal** managers of an organisation. Financial accounts are prepared for individuals **external** to an organisation eg shareholders, customers and so on.

2 (a) Cost unit
  (b) Cost centre
  (c) Cost object

3 Historical cost

4 A

5 (a) Direct, indirect (overhead) costs
  (b) Functional
  (c) Variable

6 False. Fixed costs are unaffected by changes in the level of activity.

7

8 B

9 C

Now try the questions below from the Question Bank

Question numbers	Page
1–5	345

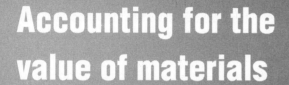

Accounting for the value of materials

Introduction

The investment in inventory is a very important one for most businesses, both in terms of monetary value and relationships with customers (no inventory, no sale, loss of customer goodwill). It is therefore vital that management are aware of the major costing problem relating to materials, that of pricing materials issues and valuing inventory at the end of each period.

In this chapter we will therefore consider the methods for **pricing materials issues/valuing inventory**. We will look at the various methods, their advantages and disadvantages and their impact on profitability.

Topic list	Learning outcomes	Syllabus references	Ability required
1 Inventory valuation	A(vi)	A(3)	Application
2 FIFO (first in, first out)	A(vi), (vii)	A(3)	Application, Comprehension
3 LIFO (last in, first out)	A(vi), (vii)	A(3)	Application, Comprehension
4 AVCO (cumulative weighted average pricing)	A(vi)	A(3)	Application
5 Inventory valuation and profitability	A(vi)	A(3)	Application

1 Inventory valuation

The correct **pricing of issues and valuation of inventory** are of the utmost importance because they have a direct effect on the calculation of profit. Several different methods can be used in practice.

1.1 Valuing inventory in financial accounts

You may be aware from your studies for the Fundamentals of Financial Accounting paper that, for financial accounting purposes, inventories are valued at the **lower of cost and net realisable value**. In practice, inventories will probably be valued at cost in the stores records throughout the course of an accounting period. Only when the period ends will the value of the inventory in hand be reconsidered so that items with a net realisable value below their original cost will be revalued downwards, and the inventory records altered accordingly.

1.2 Charging units of inventory to cost of production or cost of sales

It is important to be able to distinguish between the way in which the physical items in inventory are actually issued. In practice a storekeeper may issue goods in the following way.

- The oldest goods first
- The latest goods received first
- Randomly
- Those which are easiest to reach

By comparison the cost of the goods issued must be determined on a **consistently applied basis**, and must ignore the likelihood that the materials issued will be costed at a price different to the amount paid for them.

This may seem a little confusing at first, and it may be helpful to explain the point further by looking at an example.

1.3 Example: inventory valuation

Suppose that there are three units of a particular material in inventory.

Units	Date received	Purchase cost
A	June 20X1	$100
B	July 20X1	$106
C	August 20X1	$109

In September, one unit is issued to production. As it happened, the physical unit actually issued was B. The accounting department must put a value or cost on the material issued, but the value would not be the cost of B, $106. The principles used to value the materials issued are not concerned with the actual unit issued, A, B, or C. Nevertheless, the accountant may choose to make one of the following assumptions.

(a) The unit issued is valued as though it were the earliest unit in inventory, ie at the purchase cost of A, $100. This valuation principle is called **FIFO**, or **first in, first out**.

(b) The unit issued is valued as though it were the most recent unit received into inventory, ie at the purchase cost of C, $109. This method of valuation is **LIFO**, or **last in, first out**.

(c) The unit issued is valued at an **average** price of A, B and C, ie $105.

1.4 A chapter example

In the following sections we will consider each of the pricing methods detailed above (and a few more), using the following transactions to illustrate the principles in each case.

TRANSACTIONS DURING MAY 20X6

	Quantity	Unit cost	Total cost	Market value per unit on date of transaction
	Units	$	$	$
Opening balance, 1 May	100	2.00	200	
Receipts, 3 May	400	2.10	840	2.11
Issues, 4 May	200			2.11
Receipts, 9 May	300	2.12	636	2.15
Issues, 11 May	400			2.20
Receipts, 18 May	100	2.40	240	2.35
Issues, 20 May	100			2.35
Closing balance, 31 May	200			2.38
			1,916	

2 FIFO (first in, first out)

ST FORWARD

FIFO assumes that materials are issued out of inventory in the order in which they were delivered into inventory: issues are priced at the cost of the earliest delivery remaining in inventory.

Key term

FIFO (first in, first out) is 'used to price issues of goods or materials based on the cost of the oldest units held, irrespective of the sequence in which the actual issue of units held takes place. Closing stock is, therefore, valued at the cost of the oldest purchases.'   CIMA *Official Terminology*

2.1 Example: FIFO

Using **FIFO**, the cost of issues and the closing inventory value in the transactions in section 1.4 would be as follows.

Date of issue	Quantity issued	Value		
	Units		$	$
4 May	200	100 o/s at $2	200	
		100 at $2.10	210	
				410
11 May	400	300 at $2.10	630	
		100 at $2.12	212	
				842
20 May	100	100 at $2.12		212
Cost of issues				1,464
Closing inventory value	200	100 at $2.12	212	
		100 at $2.40	240	
				452
				1,916

Notes

(a) The cost of materials issued plus the value of closing inventory equals the cost of purchases plus the value of opening inventory ($1,916).

(b) The market price of purchased materials is rising dramatically. In a period of inflation, there is a tendency with FIFO for materials to be issued at a cost lower than the current market value, although closing inventories tend to be valued at a cost approximating to current market value. FIFO is therefore essentially a **historical cost method**, materials included in cost of production being valued at historical cost.

2.2 Advantages and disadvantages of the FIFO method

Advantages	Disadvantages
It is a logical pricing method which probably represents what is physically happening: in practice the oldest inventory is likely to be used first.	FIFO can be cumbersome to operate because of the need to identify each batch of material separately.
It is easy to understand and explain to managers.	Managers may find it difficult to compare costs and make decisions when they are charged with varying prices for the same materials.
The inventory valuation can be near to a valuation based on replacement cost.	In a period of high inflation, inventory issue prices will lag behind current market value.

Question

FIFO

Complete the table below in as much detail as possible using the information in Sections 1.4 and 2.1.

Date	Receipts			Issues			Inventory		
	Quantity	Unit price $	Amount $	Quantity	Unit price $	Amount $	Quantity	Unit price $	Amount $

Answer

Date	Receipts			Issues			Inventory		
	Quantity	Unit price $	Amount $	Quantity	Unit price $	Amount $	Quantity	Unit price $	Amount $
1.5.X3							100	2.00	200.00
3.5.X3	400	2.10	840.00				100	2.00	200.00
							400	2.10	840.00
							500		1,040.00
4.5.X3				100	2.00	200.00			
				100	2.10	210.00	300	2.10	630.00
9.5.X3	300	2.12	636.00				300	2.10	630.00
							300	2.12	636.00
							600		1,266.00
11.5.X				300	2.10	630.00			
				100	2.12	212.00	200	2.12	424.00
18.5.X	100	2.40	240.00				200	2.12	424.00
							100	2.40	240.00
							300		664.00
20.5.X				100	2.12	212.00	100	2.12	212.00
							100	2.40	240.00
31.5.X							200		452.00

3 LIFO (last in, first out)

FAST FORWARD

LIFO assumes that materials are issued out of inventory in the reverse order to which they were delivered: the most recent deliveries are issued before earlier ones, and issues are priced accordingly.

Key term

LIFO (last in, first out) is 'used to price issues of goods or materials based on the cost of the most recently received units. Cost of sales in the income statement is, therefore, valued at the cost of the most recent purchases.'

CIMA *Official Terminology*

3.1 Example: LIFO

Using LIFO, the cost of issues and the closing inventory value in the example above would be as follows.

Date of issue	Quantity issued	Valuation		
	Units		$	$
4 May	200	200 at $2.10		420
11 May	400	300 at $2.12	636	
		100 at $2.10	210	
				846
20 May	100	100 at $2.40		240
Cost of issues				1,506
Closing inventory value	200	100 at $2.10	210	
		100 at $2.00	200	
				410
				1,916

Notes

(a)   The cost of materials issued plus the value of closing inventory equals the cost of purchases plus the value of opening inventory ($1,916).

(b)   In a period of inflation there is a tendency with **LIFO** for the following to occur.

(i)   Materials are issued at a price which approximates to current market value (or **economic cost**).

(ii)   Closing inventories become undervalued when compared to market value.

3.2 Advantages and disadvantages of the LIFO method

Advantages	Disadvantages
Inventories are issued at a price which is close to current market value.	The method can be cumbersome to operate because it sometimes results in several batches being only part-used in the inventory records before another batch is received.
Managers are continually aware of recent costs when making decisions, because the costs being charged to their department or products will be current costs.	LIFO is often the opposite to what is physically happening and can therefore be difficult to explain to managers.
	As with FIFO, decision making can be difficult because of the variations in prices.

4 AVCO (cumulative weighted average pricing)

The cumulative weighted average pricing method (or AVCO) calculates a **weighted average price** for all units in inventory. Issues are priced at this average cost, and the balance of inventory remaining would have the same unit valuation. The average price is determined by dividing the total cost by the total number of units.

A new weighted average price is calculated whenever a new delivery of materials is received into store. This is the key feature of cumulative weighted average pricing.

Average cost is 'used to price issues of goods or materials at the weighted average cost of all units held'.

CIMA *Official Terminology*

4.1 Example: AVCO

In our example, issue costs and closing inventory values would be as follows.

Date	Received Units	Issued Units	Balance Units	Total inventory value $	Unit cost $	$
Opening inventory			100	200	2.00	
3 May	400			840	2.10	
			* 500	1,040	2.08	
4 May		200		(416)	2.08	416
			300	624	2.08	
9 May	300			636	2.12	
			* 600	1,260	2.10	
11 May		400		(840)	2.10	840
			200	420	2.10	
18 May	100			240	2.40	
			* 300	660	2.20	
20 May		100		(220)	2.20	220
						1,476
Closing inventory value			200	440	2.20	440
						1,916

* A new inventory value per unit is calculated whenever a new receipt of materials occurs.

Notes

(a) The cost of materials issued plus the value of closing inventory equals the cost of purchases plus the value of opening inventory ($1,916).

(b) In a period of inflation, using the cumulative weighted average pricing system, the value of material issues will rise gradually, but will tend to lag a little behind the current market value at the date of issue. Closing inventory values will also be a little below current market value.

4.2 Advantages and disadvantages of AVCO

Advantages	Disadvantages
Fluctuations in prices are smoothed out, making it easier to use the data for decision making.	The resulting issue price is rarely an actual price that has been paid, and can run to several decimal places.
It is easier to administer than FIFO and LIFO, because there is no need to identify each batch separately.	Prices tend to lag a little behind current market values when there is gradual inflation.

Question

Inventory valuation methods

Shown below is an extract from records for inventory code no 988988.

Date	Qty	Receipts Value $	Total $	Qty	Issues Value $	Total $	Qty	Balance Value $	Total $
5 June							30	2.50	75
8 June	20	3.00	60						
10 June				10		A			
14 June				20		B			
18 June	40	2.40	96						
20 June				6		C			D

(a) The values that would be entered on the stores ledger card for A, B, C and D in a cumulative weighted average pricing system would be:

A $ [   ]

B $ [   ]

C $ [   ]

D $ [   ]

(b) The values that would be entered on the stores ledger card for A, B, C and D in a LIFO system would be:

A $ [   ]

B $ [   ]

C $ [   ]

D $ [   ]

Answer

(a)   A $ 27

    B $ 54

    C $ 15

    D $ 135

Workings

				$
8 June	Inventory balance =	30	units @ $2.50	75
		20	units @ $3.00	60
		50		135
			Weighted average price	= $135/50
				= $2.70
10 June	Issues =	10	units × $2.70 =	$27
14 June	Issues =	20	units × $2.70 =	$54
18 June	Inventory balance =	20	units @ $2.70	54
	remaining receipts	40	units @ $2.40	96
		60		150
			Weighted average price	= $150/60
				= $2.50
20 June	Issues =	6	units × $2.50 =	$15
	Inventory balance =	54	units × $2.50 =	$135

(b)   A $ 30

    B $ 55

    C $ 14.40

    D $ 131.60

Workings

10 June		10	units × $3.00	$30
14 June	Remaining	10	units × $3.00 =	$30
		10	units × $2.50 =	$25
				$55
20 June	Issues:	6	units × $2.40 =	$14.40
	Balance:	34	units × $2.40	81.60
		20	units × $2.50	50.00
		54		131.60

5 Inventory valuation and profitability

Each method of inventory valuation (usually) produces different figures for both the value of closing inventories and also the cost of material issues. Since materials costs affect the cost of production, and the cost of production works through eventually into the cost of sales (which is also affected by the value of closing inventories), it follows that **different methods of inventory valuation will provide different profit figures**.

The following example will help to illustrate the point.

5.1 Example: inventory valuation and profitability

On 1 November 20X2, Delilah's Dresses Ltd held 3 pink satin dresses with orange sashes, designed by Freda Swoggs. These were valued at $120 each. During November 20X2, 12 more of the dresses were delivered as follows.

Date	Units received	Purchase cost per dress
10 November	4	$125
20 November	4	$140
25 November	4	$150

A number of the pink satin dresses with orange sashes were sold during November as follows.

Date	Dresses sold	Sales price per dress
14 November	5	$200
21 November	5	$200
28 November	1	$200

Required

Calculate the gross profit (sales – (opening inventory + purchases – closing inventory)) from selling the pink satin dresses with orange sashes in November 20X2, applying the following principles of inventory valuation.

(a)   FIFO
(b)   LIFO
(c)   AVCO

Solution

(a)   **FIFO**

Date	Cost of sales	Total $	Closing inventory $
14 November	3 units × $120 + 2 units × $125		
		610	
21 November	2 units × $125 + 3 units × $140		
		670	
28 November	1 unit × $140	140	
Closing inventory	4 units × $150		600
		1,420	600

(b) LIFO

Date	Cost of sales	Total $	Closing inventory $
14 November	4 units × $125 + 1 unit × $120		
		620	
21 November	4 units × $140 + 1 unit × $120		
		680	
28 November	1 unit × $150	150	
Closing inventory	3 units × $150 + 1 unit × $120		
			570
		1,450	570

(c) AVCO

	Units	Unit cost $	Balance in inventory $	Cost of sales $	Closing inventory $
1 November	3	120.00	360		
10 November	4	125.00	500		
	7	122.86	860		
14 November	5	122.86	614	614	
	2		246		
20 November	4	140.00	560		
	6	134.33	806		
21 November	5	134.33	672	672	
	1		134		
25 November	4	150.00	600		
	5	146.80	734		
28 November	1	146.80	147	147	
30 November	4	146.80	587	1,433	587

Profitability

	FIFO $	LIFO $	Weighted average $
Opening inventory	360	360	360
Purchases	1,660	1,660	1,660
	2,020	2,020	2,020
Closing inventory	600	570	587
Cost of sales	1,420	1,450	1,433
Sales (11 × $200)	2,200	2,200	2,200
Gross profit	780	750	767

5.2 Profit differences

In the example above, **different inventory valuation methods produced different costs of sale and hence different gross profits. As opening inventory values and purchase costs are the same for each method, the different costs of sale are due to different closing inventory valuations. The differences in gross profits therefore equal the differences in closing inventory valuations.**

The profit differences are only **temporary**. In the example, the opening inventory in December 20X2 will be $600, $570 or $587, depending on the inventory valuation method used. Different opening inventory values will affect the cost of sales and profits in December, so that in the long run, inequalities in costs of sales each month will even themselves out.

Assessment focus point

It is highly likely that your assessment will include a question on inventory valuation and the pricing of materials issues and/or the affect on profit as it is relatively easy to set questions on this topic.

Chapter Roundup

- The correct **pricing of issues and valuation of inventory** are of the utmost importance because they have a direct effect on the calculation of profit. Several different methods can be used in practice.

- **FIFO** assumes that materials are issued out of inventory in the order in which they were delivered into inventory: issues are priced at the cost of the earliest delivery remaining in inventory.

- **LIFO** assumes that materials are issued out of inventory in the reverse order to which they were delivered: the most recent deliveries are issued before earlier ones, and issues are priced accordingly.

- The cumulative weighted average pricing method (or AVCO) calculates a **weighted average price** for all units in inventory. Issues are priced at this average cost, and the balance of inventory remaining would have the same unit valuation. The average price is determined by dividing the total cost by the total number of units.

  A new weighted average price is calculated whenever a new delivery of materials is received into store. This is the key feature of cumulative weighted average pricing.

- Each method of inventory valuation (usually) produces different figures for both the value of closing inventories and also the cost of material issues. Since materials costs affect the cost of production, and the cost of production works through eventually into the cost of sales (which is also affected by the value of closing inventories), it follows that **different methods of inventory valuation will provide different profit figures**.

Quick Quiz

1   Which of the following are true?

I   With FIFO, the inventory valuation will be very close to replacement cost.

II   With LIFO, inventories are issued at a price which is close to the current market value.

III   Decision making can be difficult with both FIFO and LIFO because of the variations in prices.

IV   A disadvantage of the weighted average method of inventory valuation is that the resulting issue price is rarely an actual price that has been paid and it may be calculated to several decimal places.

A   I and II only
B   I, II and III only
C   I and III only
D   I, II, III and IV

2   LIFO is essentially an historical cost method.

True   ☐

False ☐

3   *Fill in the blanks.*

When using .... method of inventory valuation, issues are at a price which approximates to economic cost.

4   *Choose the correct words from those highlighted.*

AVCO requires that a new weighted average price is calculated whenever **materials are issued/a new delivery of materials is received/at the end of each accounting period**.

Answers to Quick Quiz

1   D

2   False. FIFO is an historical cost method

3   LIFO

4   When a new delivery of materials is received

Now try the questions below from the Question Bank

Question numbers	Page
6–10	346

Overhead costs

Introduction

In Chapter 2 we looked at how to account for material costs. Here we study one method of dealing with overheads, **absorption costing**, which is defined in CIMA *Official Terminology* as a cost accounting method that 'assigns direct costs *and* all or part of overhead to cost units using one or more overhead absorption rates'. (It is sometimes referred to as **full costing**.)

Absorption costing is a method for sharing overheads between a number of different products on a fair basis. The chapter begins by looking at the three stages of absorption costing: **allocation, apportionment and absorption**. We then move on to the important issue of **over/under absorption**. Over/under absorption is very likely to be included in your assessment, so ensure you know how to deal with it.

In the next chapter we'll see an alternative approach to accounting for overheads – **marginal costing**.

Topic list	Learning outcomes	Syllabus references	Ability required
1 Overhead allocation	A(viii)	A(4)	Application
2 Overhead apportionment	A(viii)	A(4)	Application
3 Overhead absorption	A(ix)	A(4)	Application
4 Blanket absorption rates and departmental absorption rates	A(ix)	A(4)	Application
5 Over and under absorption of overheads	A(ix)	A(4)	Application
6 Activity based costing	A(viii), (ix)	A(4)	Application

1 Overhead allocation

The first step in absorption costing is **allocation**. Allocation is the process by which whole cost items are charged direct to a cost unit or cost centre.

Key term

Allocation is 'to assign a whole item of cost, or of revenue, to a single cost unit, centre, account or time period'.

CIMA *Official Terminology*

Cost centres may be one of the following types.

(a) A **production department**, to which production overheads are charged.

(b) A **production area service department**, to which production overheads are charged.

(c) An **administrative department**, to which administration overheads are charged.

(d) A **selling** or a **distribution department**, to which sales and distribution overheads are charged.

(e) An **overhead cost centre**, to which items of expense which are shared by a number of departments, such as rent and rates, heat and light and the canteen, are charged.

The following are examples of costs which would be charged direct to cost centres via the process of allocation.

(a) The cost of a warehouse security guard will be charged to the warehouse cost centre.

(b) Paper on which computer output is recorded will be charged to the computer department.

1.1 Example: overhead allocation

Consider the following costs of a company.

Wages of the supervisor of department A	$200
Wages of the supervisor of department B	$150
Indirect materials consumed in department A	$50
Rent of the premises shared by departments A and B	$300

The cost accounting system might include three cost centres.

Cost centre: 101 Department A
102 Department B
201 Rent

Overhead costs would be allocated directly to each cost centre, ie $200 + $50 to cost centre 101, $150 to cost centre 102 and $300 to cost centre 201. The rent of the factory will be subsequently shared between the two production departments, but for the purpose of day to day cost recording in this particular system, the rent will first of all be charged in full to a separate cost centre.

2 Overhead apportionment

The second step in absorption costing is overhead **apportionment**. This involves apportioning general overheads to cost centres and then reapportioning the costs of service cost centres to production departments.

Key term

Apportion is 'to spread indirect revenues or costs over two or more cost units, centres, accounts or time periods'.

CIMA *Official Terminology*

2.1 First stage: apportioning general overheads

Overhead apportionment follows on from overhead allocation. The first stage of overhead apportionment is to identify all overhead costs as production department, production service department, administration or selling and distribution overhead. This means that the costs for heat and light, rent and rates, the canteen and so on (that is, costs which have been allocated to general overhead cost centres) must be shared out between the other cost centres.

2.1.1 Bases of apportionment

Overhead costs should be shared out on a fair basis. You will appreciate that because of the complexity of items of cost it is rarely possible to use only one method of apportioning costs to the various departments of an organisation. The bases of apportionment for the most usual cases are given below.

Overhead to which the basis applies	Basis
Rent, rates, heating and light, repairs and depreciation of buildings	Floor area occupied by each cost centre
Depreciation, insurance of equipment	Cost or book value of equipment
Personnel office, canteen, welfare, wages and cost offices, first aid	Number of employees, or labour hours worked in each cost centre
Heating, lighting (see above)	Volume of space occupied by each cost centre

Question
Bases of apportionment

The following **bases of apportionment** are used by a factory.

A   Volume of cost centre
B   Value of machinery in cost centre
C   Number of employees in cost centre
D   Floor area of cost centre

Complete the table below using one of A to D to show the bases on which the **production overheads listed in the table** should be **apportioned**.

Production overheads	Basis
Rent	
Heating costs	
Insurance of machinery	
Cleaning costs	
Canteen costs	

Answer

Production overheads	Basis
Rent	D
Heating costs	A
Insurance of machinery	B
Cleaning costs	D
Canteen costs	C

2.1.2 Example: overhead apportionment

McQueen Co has incurred the following overhead costs.

	$'000
Depreciation of factory	100
Factory repairs and maintenance	60
Factory office costs (treat as production overhead)	150
Depreciation of equipment	80
Insurance of equipment	20
Heating	39
Lighting	10
Canteen	90
	549

Information relating to the production and service departments in the factory is as follows.

	Department			
	Production 1	Production 2	Service 100	Service 101
Floor space (square metres)	1,200	1,600	800	400
Volume (cubic metres)	3,000	6,000	2,400	1,600
Number of employees	30	30	15	15
Book value of equipment	$30,000	$20,000	$10,000	$20,000

Required

Determine how the overhead costs should be apportioned between the four departments.

Solution

Costs are apportioned using the following general formula.

$$\frac{\text{Total overhead cost}}{\text{Total value of apportionment base}} \times \text{value of apportionment base of cost centre}$$

For example, heating for department 1 = $\dfrac{\$39,000}{13,000} \times 3,000 = \$9,000$

Item of cost	Basis of apportionment	Total cost	To Department 1	2	100	101
		$	$	$	$	$
Factory depreciation	(floor area)	100	30.0	40	20.0	10.0
Factory repairs	(floor area)	60	18.0	24	12.0	6.0
Factory office costs	(number of employees)	150	50.0	50	25.0	25.0
Equipment depreciation	(book value)	80	30.0	20	10.0	20.0
Equipment insurance	(book value)	20	7.5	5	2.5	5.0
Heating	(volume)	39	9.0	18	7.2	4.8
Lighting	(floor area)	10	3.0	4	2.0	1.0
Canteen	(number of employees)	90	30.0	30	15.0	15.0
Total		549	177.5	191	93.7	86.8

Question

Pippin Co has three production departments (forming, machines and assembly) and two service departments (maintenance and general).

The following is an analysis of budgeted overhead costs for a twelve-month period.

	$	$
Rent and rates		8,000
Power		750
Light, heat		5,000
Repairs, maintenance:		
Forming	800	
Machines	1,800	
Assembly	300	
Maintenance	200	
General	100	
		3,200
Departmental expenses:		
Forming	1,500	
Machines	2,300	
Assembly	1,100	
Maintenance	900	
General	1,500	
		7,300
Depreciation:		
Plant		10,000
Fixtures and fittings		250
Insurance:		
Plant		2,000
Buildings		500
Indirect labour:		
Forming	3,000	
Machines	5,000	
Assembly	1,500	
Maintenance	4,000	
General	2,000	
		15,500
		52,500

Other available data are as follows

	Floor area sq.ft	Plant value $	Fixtures & fittings $	Effective horse-power	Direct cost for year $	Labour hours worked	Machine hours worked
Forming	2,000	25,000	1,000	40	20,500	14,400	12,000
Machines	4,000	60,000	500	90	30,300	20,500	21,600
Assembly	3,000	7,500	2,000	15	24,200	20,200	2,000
Maintenance	500	7,500	1,000	5	-	-	-
General	500	-	500	-	-	-	-
	10,000	100,000	5,000	150	75,000	55,100	35,600

The overheads apportioned to:

(a)   Forming is $ [   ]

(b)   Machines is $ [   ]

(c)   Assembly is $ [   ]

(d)   Maintenance is $ [   ]

(e)   General is $ [   ]

Answer

(a)   **Forming $** [11,250]

(b)   **Machines $** [22,175]

(c)   **Assembly $** [81,025]

(d)   **Maintenance $** [6,750]

(e)   **General $** [4,300]

Workings

	Basis	Forming $	Machines $	Assembly $	Maint'nce $	General $	Total $
Directly allocated overheads:							
Repairs, maintenance		800	1,800	300	200	100	3,200
Departmental expenses		1,500	2,300	1,100	900	1,500	7,300
Indirect labour		3,000	5,000	1,500	4,000	2,000	15,500
Apportionment of other overheads:							
Rent, rates	1	1,600	3,200	2,400	400	400	8,000
Power	2	200	450	75	25	0	750
Light, heat	1	1,000	2,000	1,500	250	250	5,000
Dep'n of plant	3	2,500	6,000	750	750	0	10,000
Dep'n of F & F	4	50	25	100	50	25	250
Insurance of plant	3	500	1,200	150	150	0	2,000
Insurance of buildings	1	100	200	150	25	25	500
		11,250	22,175	8,025	6,750	4,300	52,500

Basis of apportionment:

1 floor area
2 effective horsepower
3 plant value
4 fixtures and fittings value

2.2 Second stage: service cost centre cost apportionment

The second stage of overhead apportionment concerns the treatment of **service cost centres**. A factory is divided into several production departments and also a number of service departments, but only the production departments are directly involved in the manufacture of the units. In order to be able to add production overheads to unit costs, it is necessary to have all the overheads charged to (or located in) the production departments. The next stage in absorption costing is, therefore, to apportion the costs of service cost centres to the production cost centres. Examples of possible apportionment bases are as follows.

Service cost centre	Possible basis of apportionment
Stores	Number of materials requisitions
Maintenance	Hours of maintenance work done for each cost centre
Production planning	Direct labour hours worked in each production cost centre

ST FORWARD

There are two main methods of reapportioning the service department overheads to production departments.

- **Direct method** (ignores inter-service department work)
- **Repeated distribution method** (recognises inter-service department work)

Key term

Re-apportion is 'the re-spread of costs apportioned to service departments to production departments'.

CIMA *Official Terminology*

2.2.1 Example: service centre cost apportionment

A company has two production and two service departments (stores and maintenance). The following information about activity in the recent costing period is available.

	Production departments		Stores	Maintenance
	A	B	department	department
Overhead costs	$10,030	$8,970	$10,000	$8,000
Cost of material requisitions	$30,000	$50,000	–	$20,000
Maintenance hours needed	8,000	1,000	1,000	–

(a)   Direct method

If service department overheads were apportioned **directly** to production departments, the apportionment would be as follows.

Service department	Basis of apportionment	Total cost $		A $		B $
Stores	Material requisitions	10,000	(3/8)	3,750	(5/8)	6,250
Maintenance	Maintenance hours	8,000	(8/9)	7,111	(1/9)	889
		18,000		10,861		7,139
Overheads of departments A and B		19,000		10,030		8,970
		37,000		20,891		16,109

(b)   Repeated distribution method

If, however, recognition is made of the fact that the stores and maintenance department do work for each other, and the basis of apportionment remains the same, we ought to apportion service department costs as follows.

	Dept A	Dept B	Stores	Maintenance
Stores (100%)	30%	50%	-	20%
Maintenance (100%)	80%	10%	10%	-

This situation where the service departments do work for each other is known as **reciprocal servicing**. The re-apportionment of service department costs in this situation can be done using the **repeated distribution method of apportionment**.

	Production dept A $	Production dept B $	Stores $	Maintenance $
Overhead costs	10,030	8,970	10,000	8,000
First stores apportionment (see note (a))	3,000	5,000	(10,000)	2,000
			0	10,000
First maintenance apportionment	8,000	1,000	1,000	(10,000)
			1,000	0
Second stores apportionment	300	500	(1,000)	200
Second maintenance apportionment	160	20	20	(200)
Third stores apportionment	6	10	(20)	4
Third maintenance apportionment	4	-	-	(4)
	21,500	15,500	0	0

Notes

(a)   The first apportionment could have been the costs of maintenance, rather than stores; there is no difference to the final results.

(b)   When the repeated distributions bring service department costs down to small numbers (here $4) the final apportionment to production departments is an approximate rounding.

Important!   You should note the difference in the final overhead apportionment to each production department using the different service department apportionment methods. Unless the difference is substantial, the **direct apportionment method** might be preferred because it is clerically simpler to use.

Question

Using your answer to the previous question (apportioning overheads) and the following information, apportion the overheads of the two service departments using the repeated distribution method.

Service department costs are apportioned as follows

	Maintenance	General
	%	%
Forming	20	20
Machines	50	60
Assembly	20	10
General	10	-
Maintenance	-	10
	100	100

(a) The forming department overheads after service department apportionment are $ [   ]

(b) The machines department overheads after service department apportionment are $ [   ]

(c) The assembly department overheads after service department apportionment are $ [   ]

Answer

(a) The forming department overheads after service department apportionment are $ 13,705

(b) The machines department overheads after service department apportionment are $ 28,817

(c) The assembly department overheads after service department apportionment are $ 9,978

Workings

Apportionment of service department overheads to production departments, using the repeated distribution method.

	Forming	Machines	Assembly	Maintenance	General	Total
	$	$	$	$	$	$
Overheads	11,250	22,175	8,025	6,750	4,300	52,500
Apportion maintenance (2:5:2:1)	1,350	3,375	1,350	(6,750)	675	
					4,975	
Apportion general (2:6:1:1)	995	2,985	498	497	(4,975)	
Apportion maintenance (2:5:2:1)	99	249	99	(497)	50	
Apportion general (2:6:1:1)	10	30	5	5	(50)	
Apportion maintenance (2:5:2:1)	1	3	1	(5)		
	13,705	28,817	9,978	0	0	52,500

Remember!

Apportioning service department overheads is only useful if the resulting product costs reflect accurately the amounts expended by service departments. If, however, the apportionment is arbitrary or ill-considered, the absorption of service department costs into product costs may be misleading.

3 Overhead absorption

3.1 Introduction

Having allocated and/or apportioned all overheads, the next stage in absorption costing is to add them to, or **absorb them into**, the cost of production or sales.

(a) **Production overheads** are added to the prime cost (direct materials, labour and expenses), the total of the two being the factory cost, or full cost of production. Production overheads are therefore included in the value of inventories of finished goods.

(b) **Administration and selling and distribution overheads** are then added, the sum of the factory cost and these overheads being the total cost of sales. These overheads are therefore not included in the value of closing inventory.

3.2 Predetermined absorption rates

FAST FORWARD

In absorption costing, it is usual to add overheads into product costs by applying a **predetermined overhead absorption rate**. The predetermined rate is set annually, in the budget.

Key term

> **Overhead absorption rate** is 'a means of attributing overhead to a product or service, based for example on direct labour hours, direct labour cost or machine hours'.
> CIMA *Official Terminology*

Overheads are not absorbed on the basis of the actual overheads incurred but on the basis of estimated or budgeted figures (calculated prior to the beginning of the period). The rate at which overheads are included in cost of sales (**absorption rate**) is predetermined before the accounting period actually begins for a number of reasons.

(a) Goods are produced and sold throughout the year, but many actual overheads are not known until the end of the year. It would be inconvenient to wait until the year end in order to decide what overhead costs should be.

(b) An attempt to calculate overhead costs more regularly (such as each month) is possible, although estimated costs must be added for occasional expenditures such as rent and rates (incurred once or twice a year). The difficulty with this approach would be that actual overheads from month to month would fluctuate randomly; therefore, overhead costs charged to production would depend on a certain extent on random events and changes. A unit made in one week might be charged with $4 of overhead, in a subsequent week with $5, and in a third week with $4.50. Only units made in winter would be charged with the heating overhead. Such charges are considered misleading for costing purposes and administratively and clerically inconvenient to deal with.

(c) Similarly, production output might vary each month. For example actual overhead costs might be $20,000 per month and output might vary from, say, 1,000 units to 20,000 units per month. The unit rate for overhead would be $20 and $1 per unit respectively, which would again lead to administration and control problems.

3.3 Calculating predetermined overhead absorption rates

The **absorption ratxe** is calculated by dividing the budgeted overhead by the budgeted level of activity. For production overheads the level of activity is often budgeted direct labour hours or budgeted machine hours.

Overhead absorption rates are therefore predetermined as follows.

(a) The overhead **likely to be incurred** during the coming period is estimated.

(b) The total hours, units, or direct costs on which the overhead absorption rates are to be based (activity level) are estimated.

(c) The estimated overhead is divided by the budgeted activity level to arrive at an absorption rate for the forthcoming period.

3.4 Selecting the appropriate absorption base

Management should try to establish an absorption rate that provides a **reasonably 'accurate' estimate** of overhead costs for jobs, products or services.

There are a number of different **bases of absorption** (or 'overhead **recovery** rates') which can be used. Examples are as follows.

- A percentage of direct materials cost
- A percentage of direct labour cost
- A percentage of prime cost
- A rate per machine hour
- A rate per direct labour hour
- A rate per unit

The choice of an absorption basis is a matter of judgement and common sense. There are no strict rules or formulae involved, although factors which should be taken into account are set out below. What is required is an absorption basis which realistically reflects the characteristics of a given cost centre and which avoids undue anomalies.

Many factories use a **direct labour hour rate** or **machine hour rate** in preference to a rate based on a percentage of direct materials cost, wages or prime cost.

(a) A **direct labour** hour basis is most appropriate in a **labour intensive** environment.

(b) A **machine hour** rate would be used in departments where production is controlled or dictated by **machines**. This basis is becoming more appropriate as factories become more heavily automated.

(c) In a standard costing environment, both of these time-based methods would use **standard hours** as the absorption basis. We will return to study **standard labour hour** and **standard machine hour** absorption rates when we learn about standard costing.

A **rate per unit** would be effective only if all units were identical.

3.5 Example: overhead absorption bases

The budgeted production overheads and other budget data of Calculator Co are as follows.

Budget	Production dept 1	Production dept 2
Overhead cost	$36,000	$5,000
Direct materials cost	$32,000	
Direct labour cost	$40,000	
Machine hours	10,000	
Direct labour hours	18,000	
Units of production		1,000

Required

Calculate the production overhead absorption rate using the various bases of apportionment.

Solution

(a)   Department 1

  (i)   Percentage of direct materials cost = $\dfrac{\$36,000}{\$32,000} \times 100\% = 112.5\%$

  (ii)   Percentage of direct labour cost = $\dfrac{\$36,000}{\$40,000} \times 100\% = 90\%$

  (iii)   Percentage of prime cost = $\dfrac{\$36,000}{\$72,000} \times 100\% = 50\%$

  (iv)   Rate per machine hour = $\dfrac{\$36,000}{10,000 \text{ hrs}} = \$3.60$ per machine hour

  (v)   Rate per direct labour hour = $\dfrac{\$36,000}{18,000 \text{ hrs}} = \$2$ per direct labour hour

(b)   The department 2 absorption rate will be based on units of output.

  $\dfrac{\$5,000}{1,000 \text{ units}} = \$5$ per unit produced

3.6 The impact of different absorption bases

The choice of the basis of absorption is significant in determining the cost of individual units, or jobs, produced. Using the previous example, suppose that an individual product has a material cost of $80, a labour cost of $85, and requires 36 labour hours and 23 machine hours to complete. The overhead cost of the product would vary, depending on the basis of absorption used by the company for overhead recovery.

(a)   As a percentage of direct materials cost, the overhead cost would be 112.5% × $80   = $90.00

(b)   As a percentage of direct labour cost, the overhead cost would be 90% × $85   = $76.50

(c)   As a percentage of prime cost, the overhead cost would be 50% × $165   = $82.50

(d)   Using a machine hour basis of absorption, the overhead cost would be 23 hrs × $3.60 = $82.80

(e)   Using a labour hour basis, the overhead cost would be 36 hrs × $2   = $72.00

In theory, each basis of absorption would be possible, but the company should choose a basis for its own costs which seems to be 'fairest'. In our example, this choice will be significant in determining the cost of individual products, as the following summary shows, but the **total cost** of production overheads is the budgeted overhead expenditure, no matter what basis of absorption is selected. It is the relative share of overhead costs borne by individual products and jobs which is affected by the choice of overhead absorption basis.

A summary of the product costs in the previous example is shown below.

	Basis of overhead recovery				
	Percentage of materials cost	Percentage of labour cost	Percentage of prime cost	Machine hours	Direct labour hours
	$	$	$	$	$
Direct material	80	80.00	80.00	80.00	80
Direct labour	85	85.00	85.00	85.00	85
Production overhead	90	76.50	82.50	82.80	72
Total production cost	255	241.50	247.50	247.80	237

Question

Overhead absorption rates

Using your answer to the previous question (repeated distribution method) and the following information, determine suitable overhead absorption rates for Pippin Co's three production departments.

	Forming	Machines	Assembly
Budgeted direct labour hours per annum	5,482	790	4,989
Budgeted machine hours per annum	1,350	5,240	147

(a)   The forming department rate is $ _____ per direct labour hour/direct machine hour (delete as appropriate)

(b)   The machines department rate is $ _____ per direct labour hour/direct machine hour (delete as appropriate)

(c)   The assembly department rate is $ _____ per direct labour hour/direct machine hour (delete as appropriate)

Answer

(a)   **Forming (labour intensive)** $\dfrac{\$13,705}{5,482}$ = $ **2.50** per direct labour hour

(b)   **Machines (machine intensive)** $\dfrac{\$28,817}{5,240}$ = $ **5.50** per machine hour

(c)   **Assembly (labour intensive)** $\dfrac{\$9,978}{4,989}$ = $ **2** per direct labour hour

B Co has five cost centres.

(a)   Machining department
(b)   Assembly department
(c)   Finishing department
(d)   Stores department
(e)   Building occupancy - this cost centre is charged with all costs relating to the use of the building

In the cost accounting treatment of the costs of these cost centres, the total costs of building occupancy are apportioned before the stores department costs are apportioned.

Costs incurred and data available for Period 7 of the current year were as follows.

Allocated costs	Total	Machining	Assembly	Finishing	Stores
	$	$	$	$	$
Indirect materials	2,800	500	1,700	600	-
Indirect wages	46,600	11,000	21,900	6,700	7,000
Other expenses	5,500	3,700	1,100	400	300
	54,900	15,200	24,700	7,700	7,300

Other costs	$
Rent	3,000
Rates	800
Lighting and heating	200
Plant and equipment depreciation	19,800
Insurance on plant and equipment	1,980
Insurance on building	200
Company pension scheme	28,000
Factory administration	12,500
Contract costs of cleaning factory buildings	1,400
Building repairs	400
	68,280

General information	Department			
	Machining	Assembly	Finishing	Stores
Area occupied (square metres)	3,000	4,000	2,000	1,000
Plant and equipment at cost ($'000)	1,400	380	150	50
Number of employees	100	350	150	25
Direct labour hours	24,000	80,000	35,000	–
Machine hours	52,725	20,500	10,200	–
Direct wages ($)	24,000	89,400	36,000	–
Number of stores requisitions	556	1,164	270	–

Required

(a)   The total of building occupancy costs for Period 7 is $ ⎡‾‾‾‾‾‾‾‾⎤

(b)   The cost accountant has begun work on the first stage of the analysis of overheads for Period 7. An extract from the working paper is shown below.

Overhead analysis sheet – first stage

	Basis	Total $	Machining $	Assembly $	Finishing $	Stores $
Allocated costs						
Indirect materials		2,800	500	1,700	600	0
Indirect wages		46,600	11,000	21,900	6,700	7,000
Other expenses		5,500	3,700	1,100	400	300
		54,900	15,200	24,700	7,700	7,300
Apportioned costs	*Basis*					
Plant depreciation	*	19,800	A			
Plant insurance	B					
Pension scheme	**	28,000		C		
Factory admin			2,000	7,000	D	500
Building occupancy	E					
		123,180	39,400	54,180	19,650	9,950

* Cost of plant and equipment
** Total labour cost

The entries to be shown as A to E in the boxes on the overhead analysis sheet are:

A $ [   ]

B   [   ]

C $ [   ]

D $ [   ]

E   [   ]

(c)   After the re-apportionment of the stores cost to the production cost centres, the total cost centre overheads will be:

Machining $ [   ]

Assembly $ [   ]

Finishing $ [   ]

(d)   Appropriate overhead absorption rates (to the nearest penny) for the three production cost centres are:

Machining $ [   ]   for each [   ]

Assembly $ [   ]   for each [   ]

Finishing $ [   ]   for each [   ]

Answer

(a)   The total of building occupancy costs for Period 7 is $ | 6,000 |

Workings

	$
Rent	3,000
Rates	800
Lighting and heating	200
Insurance on building	200
Contract costs of cleaning	1,400
Building repairs	400
	6,000

(b)   **A**   **$14,000**
      B   **Cost of plant and equipment**
      C   **$15,900**
      D   **$3,000**
      E   **Area occupied**

Workings

A: Total cost of plant and equipment ($'000) = 1,400 + 380 + 150 + 50 = 1,980

Apportioned cost of plant depreciation in Machinery $= \dfrac{1,400}{1,980} \times \$19,800$

$= \$14,000$

C: Total direct and indirect labour costs in the four departments:

	$
Direct wages (24,000 + 89,400 + 36,000)	149,400
Indirect wages	46,600
Total wages	196,000

Pension scheme costs (1/7 of wages cost) = $28,000

Apportioned pension cost to Assembly department:

	$
Direct wages	89,400
Indirect wages	21,900
	111,300

Apportioned cost = 1/7 × $111,300 = $15,900

D: Apportionment basis for factory administration costs = number of employees

$12,500 ÷ 625 employees = $20 per employee

Apportioned factory administration cost to finishing department = $20 × 150 = $3,000

(c)   **Machining** $ | 42,180 |

    Assembly $ | 60,000 |

    Finishing $ | 21,000 |

Workings: Overhead analysis sheet – second stage

	Total $	Machining $	Assembly $	Finishing $	Stores $
Allocated and apportioned overhead	123,180	39,400	54,180	19,650	9,950
Apportionment of stores costs (see note)		2,780	5,820	1,350	(9,950)
	123,180	42,180	60,000	21,000	0

Note. Stores costs are apportioned on the basis of the number of stores requisitions.

$$\text{Stores cost} \quad \frac{£9,950}{(556 + 1,164 + 270)} = \$5 \text{ per requisition}$$

(d)   Machining: \$ 0.75   for each **machine hour**

Assembly: \$ 0.60   for each **direct labour hour**

Finishing: \$ 0.80   for each **direct labour hour**

Workings

	Machining	Assembly	Finishing
Overhead cost	$42,180	$60,000	$21,000
Machine hours/direct labour hours	52,725	80,000	35,000
Absorption rate per machine hour/direct labour hour	$0.80	$0.75	$0.60

4 Blanket absorption rates and departmental absorption rates

ST FORWARD

The use of **separate departmental absorption rates** instead of **blanket (or single factory) absorption rates** will produce more realistic product costs.

4.1 Blanket absorption rates

A **blanket or single factory overhead absorption rate** is an absorption rate **used throughout a factory** and for all jobs and units of output irrespective of the department in which they were produced.

For example, if total overheads were $500,000 and there were 250,000 direct machine hours during the period, the **blanket overhead rate** would be $2 per direct machine hour and all units of output passing through the factory would be charged at that rate.

Such a rate is not appropriate, however, if there are a number of departments and units of output do not spend an equal amount of time in each department.

4.2 Are blanket overhead absorption rates 'fair'?

It is argued that if a single factory overhead absorption rate is used, some products will receive a higher overhead charge than they ought 'fairly' to bear, whereas other products will be under-charged. By using a separate absorption rate for each department, charging of overheads will be equitable and the full cost of production of items will be more representative of the cost of the efforts and resources put into making them. An example may help to illustrate this point.

4.3 Example: separate absorption rates

AB Co has two production departments, for which the following budgeted information is available.

	Department 1	Department 2	Total
Budgeted overheads	$360,000	$200,000	$560,000
Budgeted direct labour hours	200,000 hrs	40,000 hrs	240,000 hrs

If a single factory overhead absorption rate is applied, the rate of overhead recovery would be:

$$\frac{\$560,000}{240,000 \text{ hours}} = \$2.33 \text{ per direct labour hour}$$

If separate departmental rates are applied, these would be:

Department 1

$$\frac{\$360,000}{200,000 \text{ hours}} = \$1.80 \text{ per direct labour hour}$$

Department 2

$$\frac{\$200,000}{40,000 \text{ hours}} = \$5 \text{ per direct labour hour}$$

Department 2 has a higher overhead cost per hour worked than department 1.

Now let us consider two separate products.

(a) Product A has a prime cost of $100, takes 30 hours in department 2 and does not involve any work in department 1.
(b) Product B has a prime cost of $100, takes 28 hours in department 1 and 2 hours in department 2.

What would be the factory cost of each product, using the following rates of overhead recovery.

(a) A single factory rate of overhead recovery
(b) Separate departmental rates of overhead recovery

Solution

				Product A		Product B
				$		$
(a)	**Single factory rate**					
	Prime cost			100		100
	Factory overhead (30 × $2.33)			70		70
	Factory cost			170		170
(b)	**Separate departmental rates**			$		$
	Prime cost			100		100.00
	Factory overhead:	department 1		0	(28 × $1.80)	50.40
		department 2	(30 × $5)	150	(2 × $5)	10.00
	Factory cost			250		160.40

Using a single factory overhead absorption rate, both products would cost the same. However, since product A is done entirely within department 2 where overhead costs are relatively higher, whereas product B is done mostly within department 1, where overhead costs are relatively lower, it is arguable that product A should cost more than product B.

This will occur if separate departmental overhead recovery rates are used to reflect the work done on each job in each department separately.

Question
Machine hour absorption rate

The following data relate to one year in department A.

Budgeted machine hours	25,000
Actual machine hours	21,875
Budgeted overheads	$350,000
Actual overheads	$350,000

Based on the data above, what is the machine hour absorption rate as conventionally calculated?

A $12 B $14 C $16 D $18

Answer

The correct answer is B.

Don't forget, if your calculations produce a solution which does not correspond with any of the options available, then eliminate the unlikely options and make a guess from the remainder. Never leave out an assessment question.

A common pitfall is to think 'we haven't had answer A for a while, so I'll guess that'. The computerised assessment does *not* produce an even spread of A, B, C and D answers. There is no reason why the answer to *every* question cannot be D!

The correct answer in this case is B.

$$\text{Overhead absorption rate} = \frac{\text{Budgeted overheads}}{\text{Budgeted machine hours}} = \frac{\$350,000}{25,000} = \$14 \text{ per machine hour}$$

5 Over and under absorption of overheads

ST FORWARD

The rate of overhead absorption is based on **estimates** (of both numerator and denominator) and it is quite likely that either one or both of the estimates will not agree with what *actually* occurs. Actual overheads incurred will probably be either greater than or less than overheads absorbed into the cost of production.

(a) **Over absorption** means that the overheads charged to the cost of production are greater than the overheads actually incurred.

(b) **Under absorption** means that insufficient overheads have been included in the cost of production.

Key terms

Absorbed overhead is 'overhead attached to products or services by means of an absorption rate, or rates'.

Under or over absorbed overhead is 'the difference between overhead incurred and overhead absorbed, using an estimated rate, in a given period. If overhead absorbed is less than that incurred there is under-absorption, if overhead absorbed is more than that incurred there is over-absorption. Over- and under-absorptions are treated as period cost adjustments'.

CIMA *Official Terminology*

5.1 Example: over and under absorption of overheads

Suppose that the budgeted overhead in a production department is $80,000 and the budgeted activity is 40,000 direct labour hours. The overhead recovery rate (using a direct labour hour basis) would be $2 per direct labour hour.

Actual overheads in the period are, say $84,000 and 45,000 direct labour hours are worked.

	$
Overhead incurred (actual)	84,000
Overhead absorbed (45,000 × $2)	90,000
Over absorption of overhead	6,000

In this example, the cost of produced units or jobs has been charged with $6,000 more than was actually spent. An adjustment to reconcile the overheads charged to the actual overhead is necessary and the over-absorbed overhead will be written as a credit to the **income statement** at the end of the accounting period.

Assessment focus point

You can always work out whether overheads are under- or over-absorbed by using the following rule.

- If **Actual** overhead incurred – **Absorbed** overhead = **NEGATIVE** (N), then overheads are **over-absorbed** (O) (NO)
- If **Actual** overhead incurred – **Absorbed** overhead = **POSITIVE** (P), then overheads are **under-absorbed** (U) (PU)

So, remember the **NOPU** rule when you go into your assessment and you won't have any trouble in deciding whether overheads are under- or over-absorbed!

5.2 The reasons for under-/over-absorbed overhead

The overhead absorption rate is **predetermined from budget estimates** of overhead cost and the expected volume of activity. Under or over recovery of overhead will occur in the following circumstances.

- Actual overhead costs are different from budgeted overheads.
- The actual activity level is different from the budgeted activity level.
- Both actual overhead costs and actual activity level are different from budget.

5.3 Example: under and over absorption of overheads

Rex Co is a small company which manufactures two products, A and B, in two production departments, machining and assembly. A canteen is operated as a separate production service department.

The budgeted production and sales in the year to 31 March 20X3 are as follows.

	Product A	Product B
Sales price per unit	$50	$70
Sales (units)	2,200	1,400
Production (units)	2,000	1,500
Material cost per unit	$14	$12

	Product A Hours per unit	Product B Hours per unit
Direct labour:		
Machining department ($8 per hour)	2	3
Assembly department ($6 per hour)	1	2
Machine hours per unit:		
Machining department	3	4
Assembly department	1/2	

Budgeted production overheads are as follows.

	Machining department $	Assembly department $	Canteen $	Total $
Allocated costs	10,000	25,000	12,000	47,000
Apportionment of other general production overheads	26,000	12,000	8,000	46,000
	36,000	37,000	20,000	93,000
Number of employees	30	20	1	51
Floor area (square metres)	5,000	2,000	500	7,500

Required

(a) Calculate an absorption rate for overheads in each production department for the year to 31 March 20X3 and the budgeted cost per unit of products A and B.

(b) Suppose that in the year to 31 March 20X3, 2,200 units of Product A are produced and 1,500 units of Product B. Direct labour hours per unit and machine hours per unit in both departments were as budgeted.

Actual production overheads are as follows.

	Machining department $	Assembly department $	Canteen $	Total $
Allocated costs	30,700	27,600	10,000	68,300
Apportioned share of general production overheads	17,000	8,000	5,000	30,000
	47,700	35,600	15,000	98,300

Calculate the under- or over-absorbed overhead in each production department and in total.

Solution

(a) **Choose absorption rates**

Since machine time appears to be more significant than labour time in the machining department, a machine hour rate of absorption will be used for overhead recovery in this department. On the other hand, machining is insignificant in the assembly department, and a direct labour hour rate of absorption would seem to be the basis which will give the fairest method of overhead recovery.

Apportion budgeted overheads

Next we need to apportion budgeted overheads to the two production departments. Canteen costs will be apportioned on the basis of the number of employees in each department. (Direct labour hours in each department are an alternative basis of apportionment, but the number of employees seems to be more directly relevant to canteen costs.)

	Machining department $	Assembly department $	Total $
Budgeted allocated costs	10,000	25,000	35,000
Share of general overheads	26,000	12,000	38,000
Apportioned canteen costs (30:20)	12,000	8,000	20,000
	48,000	45,000	93,000

Calculate overhead absorption rates

The overhead absorption rates are predetermined, using budgeted estimates. Since the overheads are production overheads, the budgeted activity relates to the volume of production, in units (the production hours required for volume of sales being irrelevant).

	Product A	Product B	Total
Budgeted production (units)	2,000	1,500	
Machining department: machine hours	6,000 hrs	6,000 hrs	12,000 hrs
Assembly department: direct labour hours	2,000 hrs	3,000 hrs	5,000 hrs

The overhead absorption rates will be as follows.

	Machining department	Assembly department
Budgeted overheads	$48,000	$45,000
Budgeted activity	12,000 hrs	5,000 hrs
Absorption rate	$4 per machine hour	$9 per direct labour hour

Determine a budgeted cost per unit

The budgeted cost per unit would be as follows.

	Product A		Product B	
	$	$	$	$
Direct materials		14		12
Direct labour:				
Machining department	16		24	
Assembly department	6		12	
		22		36
Prime cost		36		48
Production overhead:				
Machining department	12		16	
Assembly department	9		18	
		21		34
Full production cost		57		82

(b) **Apportion actual service department overhead to production departments**

When the actual costs are analysed, the 'actual' overhead of the canteen department ($15,000) would be split between the machining and assembly departments.

	Machining department	Assembly department	Total
	$	$	$
Allocated cost	30,700	27,600	58,300
Apportioned general overhead	17,000	8,000	25,000
Canteen (30:20)	9,000	6,000	15,000
	56,700	41,600	98,300

Establish the over- or under-absorption of overheads

There would be an over- or under-absorption of overheads as follows.

		Machining department $		Assembly department $	Total $
Overheads absorbed					
Product A (2,200 units)	(× $4 × 3hrs)	26,400	(× $9 × 1hr)	19,800	46,200
Product B (1,500 units)	(× $4 × 4hrs)	24,000	(× $9 × 2hrs)	27,000	51,000
		50,400		46,800	97,200
Overheads incurred		56,700		41,600	98,300
Over-/(under)-absorbed overhead		(6,300)		5,200	(1,100)

The total under-absorbed overhead of $1,100 will be written off to the income statement at the end of the year, to compensate for the fact that overheads charged to production ($97,200) were less than the overheads actually incurred ($98,300).

Question   Under and over absorption of overheads

Using your answer to an earlier question (entitled 'Overhead absorption rates') and the following information, determine whether the overhead in each of the three production departments of Pippin Co is under or over absorbed and by how much for the twelve-month period.

	Forming	Machines	Assembly
Actual direct labour hours	5,370	950	5,400
Actual machine hours	1,300	6,370	100
Actual overhead	$13,900	$30,300	$8,500

(a)   The overhead in the forming department is [   ] absorbed by $ [   ]

(b)   The overhead in the machines department is [   ] absorbed by $ [   ]

(c)   The overhead in the assembly department is [   ] absorbed by $ [   ]

Answer

(a)   [Under] absorbed by $ [475]

(b)   [Over] absorbed by $ [4,735]

(c)   [Over] absorbed by $ [2,300]

Working

	$
Forming	
Overhead absorbed ($2.50 × 5,370)	13,425
Overhead incurred	13,900
Under-absorbed overhead	475

Machines

	$
Overhead absorbed ($5.50 × 6,370)	35,035
Overhead incurred	30,300
Over-absorbed overhead	4,735

Assembly

	$
Overhead absorbed ($2 × 5,400)	10,800
Overhead incurred	8,500
Over-absorbed overhead	2,300

Important!

It is important that you should be completely confident in handling under and over absorption of overheads. This question will demonstrate that the techniques which you have just learned can also be applied in a service organisation.

Question   Budget overhead absorption rate

A management consultancy recovers overheads on chargeable consulting hours. Budgeted overheads were $615,000 and actual consulting hours were 32,150. Overheads were under-recovered by $35,000.

If actual overheads were $694,075 what was the budgeted overhead absorption rate per hour?

A $19.13   B $20.50   C $21.59   D $22.68

Answer

The correct answer is B.

	$
Actual overheads	694,075
Under-recovered overheads	35,000
Overheads recovered for 32,150 hours at budgeted overhead absorption rate (x)	659,075

$$32,150x = 659,075$$

$$x = \frac{659,075}{32,150} = \$20.50$$

6 Activity based costing

Activity based costing (ABC) is an alternative approach to absorption costing. It involves the identification of the factors (**cost drivers**) which cause the costs of an organisation's major activities.

6.1 The reasons for the development of ABC

6.1.1 In the past

Most organisations used to produce **only a few products**. **Direct labour costs** and **direct material costs** accounted for the **largest proportion** of total costs and so it was these variable costs that needed to be **controlled**.

Overhead costs were only a **very small fraction** of total costs and so it did not particularly matter what absorption costing bases were used to apportion overheads to products.

6.1.2 Nowadays

Costs tend to be **fixed** and **overheads huge**.

Manufacturing is **capital and machine intensive** rather than labour intensive and so direct labour might account for as little as 5% of a product's cost. For example, furniture is no longer made by skilled workers. Instead complicated expensive machines are programmed with the necessary skills and workers become machine minders.

Advanced manufacturing technology (such as robotics) has had a significant impact on the level of overheads. For example, the marginal cost of producing a piece of computer software might be just a few pounds but the fixed (initial) cost of the software development might run into millions of pounds.

Many resources are used in **support activities** such as setting-up, production scheduling, first item inspection and data processing. These support activities help with the manufacture of a wide range of products and are **not**, in general, **affected by changes in production volume**. They tend to **vary** instead in the **long term** according to the **range** and **complexity** of the products manufactured.

The wider the range and the more complex the products, the more support services will be required. Suppose factory X produces 10,000 units of one product, the Alpha. Factory Y also produces 10,000 units, made up of 1,000 units each of ten slightly different versions of the Alpha. Consider the setting-up activity.

- Factory X will only need to set-up once.

- Factory Y will have to set-up the production run at least ten times for the ten different products and so will incur more set-up costs.

6.1.3 Problems of using absorption costing in today's environment

Overhead absorption rates might be 200% or 300% of unit labour costs. Unit **costs** are **distorted** and so cost information is **misleading**.

Overheads are **not controlled** because they are hidden within unit production costs rather than being shown as individual totals.

Products bear an arbitrary share of overheads which **do not reflect the benefits** they receive.

Absorption costing **assumes** all products **consume all resources** in **proportion** to their **production volumes**.

- It tends to **allocate too great a proportion** of overheads to **high volume products** (which cause relatively little diversity and hence use fewer support services).

- It tends to **allocate too small a proportion** of overheads to **low volume products** (which cause greater diversity and therefore use more support services).

Activity based costing (ABC) attempts to overcome these problems.

Key term

> **Activity based costing (ABC)** is an 'approach to the costing and monitoring of activities which involves tracing resource consumption and costing final outputs. Resources are assigned to activities, and activities to cost objects based on consumption estimates. The latter utilise cost drivers to attach activity costs to outputs.' CIMA *Official Terminology*

6.2 ABC and using it to calculate product costs

6.2.1 Major ideas behind ABC

Activities cause costs.	Activities include ordering and despatching.
The costs of an activity are caused or driven by factors known as **cost drivers**.	The cost of the ordering activity might be driven by the number of orders placed, the cost of the despatching activity by the number of despatches made.
The costs of an activity are assigned to products on the basis of the number of the activity's cost driver products generate.	If product A requires 5 orders to be placed, and product B 15 orders, ¼ (ie 5/(5 + 15)) of the ordering cost will be assigned to product A and ¾ (ie 15/(5 + 15)) to product B.

6.2.2 Cost drivers

Key term

A **cost driver** is 'a factor influencing the level of cost'.   CIMA *Official Terminology*

For those costs that **vary with production levels in the short term**, ABC uses **volume-related cost drivers** such as labour hours or machine hours. The cost of oil used as a lubricant on machines would therefore be added to products on the basis of the number of machine hours, since oil would have to be used for each hour the machine ran.

For costs that **vary with some other activity and not volume of production**, ABC uses **transaction-related cost drivers** such as the number of production runs for the production scheduling activity.

6.2.3 Calculating product costs using ABC

Step 1
Identify an organisation's major activities.

Step 2
Identify the factors (cost drivers) which cause the costs of the activities.

Step 3
Collect the costs associated with each activity into **cost pools**.

Cost pools are equivalent to cost centres used with traditional absorption costing.

Step 4
Charge the costs of activities to products on the basis of their usage of the activities. A product's usage of an activity is measured by the number of the activity's cost driver it generates.

Suppose the cost pool for the ordering activity totalled $100,000 and that there were 10,000 orders (orders being the cost driver). Each product would therefore be charged with $10 for each order it required. A batch requiring five orders would therefore be charged with $50.

6.2.4 Example: ABC

Suppose that Cooplan Co manufactures four products, W, X, Y and Z. Output and cost data for the period just ended are as follows.

	Output Units	No of production runs in the period	Material cost per unit $	Direct labour hours per unit	Machine hours per unit
W	10	2	20	1	1
X	10	2	80	3	3
Y	100	5	20	1	1
Z	100	5	80	3	3
		14			

Direct labour cost per hour is $5. Overhead costs are as follows.

	$
Short-run variable costs	3,080
Set-up costs	10,920
Production and scheduling costs	9,100
Materials handling costs	7,700
	30,800

Required:

Calculate product costs using absorption costing and ABC.

Solution

Using absorption costing and an absorption rate based on either direct labour hours or machine hours, the product costs would be as follows.

	W $	X $	Y $	Z $	Total $
Direct material	200	800	2,000	8,000	11,000
Direct labour	50	150	500	1,500	2,200
Overheads *	700	2,100	7,000	21,000	30,800
	950	3,050	9,500	30,500	44,000
Units produced	10	10	100	100	
Cost per unit	$95	$305	$95	$305	

* $30,800 ÷ 440 hours = $70 per direct labour or machine hour

Using activity based costing and assuming that the number of production runs is the cost driver for set-up costs, production and scheduling costs and materials handling costs and that machine hours are the cost driver for short-run variable costs, unit costs would be as follows.

	W	X	Y	Z	Total
	$	$	$	$	$
Direct material	200	800	2,000	8,000	11,000
Direct labour	50	150	500	1,500	2,200
Short-run variable overheads (W1)	70	210	700	2,100	3,080
Set-up costs (W2)	1,560	1,560	3,900	3,900	10,920
Production and scheduling costs (W3)	1,300	1,300	3,250	3,250	9,100
Materials handling costs (W4)	1,100	1,100	2,750	2,750	7,700
	4,280	5,120	13,100	21,500	44,000
Units produced	10	10	100	100	
Cost per unit	$428	$512	$131	$215	

Workings

1    $3,080 ÷ 440 machine hours   = $7 per machine hour
2    $10,920 ÷ 14 production runs   = $780 per run
3    $9,100 ÷ 14 production runs   = $650 per run
4    $7,700 ÷ 14 production runs   = $550 per run

Summary

Product	Absorption costing Unit cost	ABC Unit cost	Difference
	$	$	$
W	95	428	+ 333
X	305	512	+ 207
Y	95	131	+ 36
Z	305	215	− 90

The figures suggest that the traditional volume-based absorption costing system is flawed.

- It under allocates overhead costs to low-volume products (here, W and X) and over allocates overheads to higher-volume products (here Z in particular).

- It under allocates overhead costs to less complex products (here W and Y with just one hour of work needed per unit) and over allocates overheads to more complex products (here X and particularly Z).

Question

Having attended a AAT course on activity based costing (ABC) you decide to experiment by applying the principles of ABC to the four products currently made and sold by your company. Details of the four products and relevant information are given below for one period.

Product	P1	P2	P3	P4
Output in units	120	100	80	120
Costs per unit:	$	$	$	$
Direct material	40	50	30	60
Direct labour	28	21	14	21

The four products are similar and are usually produced in production runs of 20 units.

The total of the production overhead for the period has been analysed as follows.

	$
Set up costs	5,250
Stores receiving	3,600
Inspection/quality control	2,100
Materials handling and despatch	4,620

You have ascertained that the following 'cost drivers' are to be used for the costs shown.

Cost	Cost driver
Set up costs	Number of production runs
Stores receiving	Requisitions raised
Inspection/quality control	Number of production runs
Materials handling and despatch	Orders executed

The number of requisitions raised on the stores was 20 for each product and the number of orders executed was 42, each order being for a batch of 10 of a product.

Required:

(a)   The total costs for each product using activity based costing are:

(i) $ ⬚ for P1

(ii) $ ⬚ for P2

(iii) $ ⬚ for P3

(iv) $ ⬚ for P4

(b)   The unit costs are:

(i) $ ⬚ for P1

(ii) $ ⬚ for P2

(iii) $ ⬚ for P3

(iv) $ ⬚ for P4

Answer

(a)   (i) $ ☐ 12,480

    (ii) $ ☐ 10,850

    (iii) $ ☐ 6,700

    (iv) $ ☐ 14,040

(b)   (i) $ ☐ 104

    (ii) $ ☐ 108.50

    (iii) $ ☐ 83.75

    (iv) $ ☐ 117

Workings

		P1	P2	P3	P4
		$	$	$	$
Direct material		4,800	5,000	2,400	7,200
Direct labour		3,360	2,100	1,120	2,520
Production overhead *					
Set up costs		1,500	1,250	1,000	1,500
Stores receiving		900	900	900	900
Inspection/quality control		600	500	400	600
Material handling and despatch		1,320	1,100	880	1,320
(a)	Total cost	12,480	10,850	6,700	14,040
(b)	Unit costs	(÷120) $104	(÷ 100) $108.50	(÷ 80) $83.75	(÷ 120) $117

* Overhead costs will be divided in the following ratios, depending upon the number of production runs, requisitions or orders per product.

	P1	P2	P3	P4
Production runs	6	5	4	6
Requisitions raised	20	20	20	20
Orders executed	12	10	8	12

Chapter Roundup

- The first step in absorption costing is **allocation**. Allocation is the process by which whole cost items are charged direct to a cost unit or cost centre.

- The second step in absorption costing is overhead **apportionment**. This involves apportioning general overheads to cost centres and then reapportioning the costs of service cost centres to production departments.

- There are two main methods of reapportioning service department overheads to production departments.

    - **Direct method** (ignores inter-service department work)
    - **Repeated distribution method** (recognises inter-service department work)

- In absorption costing, it is usual to add overheads into product costs by applying a **predetermined overhead absorption rate**. The predetermined rate is set annually, in the budget.

- The **absorption rate** is calculated by dividing the budgeted overhead by the budgeted level of activity. For production overheads, the level of activity is often budgeted direct labour hours or budgeted machine hours.

- Management should try to establish an absorption rate that provides a **reasonably 'accurate' estimate** of overhead costs for jobs, products or services.

- The use of **separate departmental absorption rates** instead of **blanket (or single factory) absorption rates** will produce more realistic product costs.

- The rate of overhead absorption is based on **estimates** (of both numerator and denominator) and it is quite likely that either one or both of the estimates will not agree with what *actually* occurs. Actual overheads incurred will probably be either greater than or less than overheads absorbed into the cost of production.

    (a) **Over absorption** means that the overheads charged to the cost of production are greater than the overheads actually incurred.

    (b) **Under absorption** means that insufficient overheads have been included in the cost of production.

- **Activity based costing (ABC)** is an alternative approach to absorption costing. It involves the identification of the factors (**cost drivers**) which cause the costs of an organisation's major activities.

Quick Quiz

1   Allocation involves spreading overhead costs across cost centres.

True ☐

False ☐

2   Match the following overheads with the most appropriate basis of apportionment.

Overhead		**Basis of apportionment**	
(a)	Depreciation of equipment	(1)	Direct machine hours
(b)	Heat and light costs	(2)	Number of employees
(c)	Canteen	(3)	Book value of equipment
(d)	Insurance of equipment	(4)	Floor area

3   Which of the following departments are directly involved in production?

Department	Involved in production (✓)
Finished goods warehouse	
Canteen	
Machining department	
Offices	
Assembly department	

4   In relation to calculating total absorption cost, label the following descriptions in the correct order as Steps 1 – 5.

Description		**Step**
A	Apportion fixed costs over departments	
B	Establish the overhead absorption rate	
C	Choose fair methods of apportionment	
D	Apply the overhead absorption rate to products	
E	Reapportion service departments costs	

5   In order to recognise the work service departments do for each other, the .... method of reapportioning service department overheads should be used.

6   A direct labour hour basis is most appropriate in which of the following environments?

A   Machine-intensive
B   Labour-intensive
C   When all units produced are identical
D   None of the above

7   Over absorption occurs when absorbed overheads are greater than actual overheads.

True ☐

False ☐

8   *Choose the correct words from those highlighted.*

Traditional costing systems tend to allocate **too great/too small** a proportion of overheads to high volume products and **too great/too small** a proportion of overheads to low volume products.

Answers to Quick Quiz

1   False. It is the process whereby whole cost items are charged direct to a cost unit or cost centre.

2   (a)   (3)
      (b)   (4)
      (c)   (2)
      (d)   (3)

3

Department Involved in production (✓)	
Finished goods warehouse	
Canteen	
Machining department	✓
Offices	
Assembly department	✓

4   A = 2
      B = 4
      C = 1
      D = 5
      E = 3

5   Repeated distribution method

6   B

7   True

8   Traditional costing systems tend to allocate **too great** a proportion of overheads to high volume products and **too small** a proportion of overheads to low volume products.

Now try the questions below from the Question Bank

Question numbers	Page
11–15	347

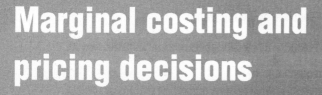

Marginal costing and pricing decisions

Introduction

In Chapter 3 we saw how product costs are absorbed into the cost of units of output using absorption costing.

This chapter describes **marginal costing**, an alternative method of dealing with overheads. Whereas absorption costing recognises fixed costs (usually fixed production costs) as part of the cost of a unit of output and hence classifies them as product costs, marginal costing treats all fixed costs as period costs. (Remember we covered product costs and period costs in Chapter 1.)

This chapter then goes on to cover how unit costs (whether full product costs derived using absorption costing, or marginal costs) can be used as the basis for setting **prices**.

Topic list	Learning outcomes	Syllabus references	Ability required
1 Marginal cost	A(ix)	A(5)	Application
2 Marginal costing	A(ix)	A(5)	Application
3 Pricing decisions	A(x)	A(5)	Comprehension

PART A   COST DETERMINATION

1 Marginal cost

Whereas fully absorbed product costs include fixed overhead, the **marginal cost** of a product usually consists of variable costs only.

1.1 Marginal cost

Key term

Marginal cost is 'part of the cost of one unit of product or service that would be avoided if the unit were not produced, or that would increase if one extra unit were produced'.
CIMA *Official Terminology*

The marginal production cost per unit of an item usually consists of the following.

- Direct materials
- Direct labour
- Variable production overheads

1.2 Contribution

Contribution is an important measure in marginal costing, and it is calculated as the difference between sales value and marginal or variable cost.

Key term

Contribution is '(sales value – variable cost of sales)'.
CIMA *Official Terminology*

The term 'contribution' is really short for 'contribution towards covering fixed overheads and making a profit'.

Question
Contribution

A particular electrical good is sold for $1,009.99. The direct material cost per unit is $320, the direct labour cost per unit is $192 and the variable production overhead cost per unit is $132. Fixed overheads per annum are $100,000 and the budgeted production level is 1,000 units.

The contribution per unit of the electrical good is $ [   ].

Answer

The contribution per unit is $ | 365.99 |

Workings

	$	$
Selling price per unit		1009.99
Marginal cost per unit		
Direct material	320	
Direct labour	192	
Variable production overhead	132	
		644.00
Contribution per unit		365.99

We do *not* include absorbed fixed overheads in the calculation of marginal cost per unit and contribution per unit.

BPP
PROFESSIONAL EDUCATION

2 Marginal costing

FORWARD

Marginal costing is an alternative method of costing to absorption costing. In marginal costing, only variable costs are charged as a cost of sale and a contribution is calculated. Closing inventories of work in progress or finished goods are valued at marginal (variable) production cost. Fixed costs are treated as a period cost, and are charged in full against profit in the accounting period in which they are incurred.

Key term

Marginal (or **variable**) **costing** 'assigns only variable costs to cost units while fixed costs are written off as period costs'.

CIMA *Official Terminology*

Fixed costs are a period charge and are the **same for any volume of sales and production** (within the relevant range). So if an extra unit is sold the following happens.

- Revenue will increase by the sales value of the item sold.

- Costs will increase by the variable cost per unit.

- Profit will increase by the **difference between sales value per unit and variable cost per unit (contribution)**.

Therefore **only variable costs** are **charged** to the **cost of sales**.

Fixed costs are **deducted** from **total contribution** (the difference between sales revenue and the cost of sales) **to derive profit** for the period.

When a unit of product is made, the extra costs incurred in its manufacture are the variable production costs. Fixed costs are unaffected – no extra fixed costs are incurred when output is increased. The **valuation of units of output** and hence **closing stocks** is therefore at **variable production cost** because these are the only costs properly attributable to the product.

Before explaining marginal costing principles any further, it will be helpful to look at a numerical example.

2.1 Example: marginal costing

Water Co makes a product, the Splash, which has a variable production cost of $6 per unit and a sales price of $10 per unit. At the beginning of September 20X0, there were no opening inventories and production during the month was 20,000 units. Fixed costs for the month were $45,000 (production, administration, sales and distribution). There were no variable marketing costs.

Required

Calculate at each of the following sales levels, the total contribution and total profit for September 20X0 and the contribution per unit and the profit/loss per unit, using marginal costing principles.

(a)   10,000 Splashes
(b)   15,000 Splashes
(c)   20,000 Splashes

Solution

The first stage in the profit calculation must be to identify the variable costs, and then the contribution. Fixed costs are deducted from the total contribution to derive the profit. All closing inventories are valued at marginal production cost ($6 per unit).

	10,000 Splashes		15,000 Splashes		20,000 Splashes	
	$	$	$	$	$	$
Sales (at $10)		100,000		150,000		200,000
Opening inventory	0		0		0	
Variable production cost	120,000		120,000		120,000	
	120,000		120,000		120,000	
Less value of closing inventory (at marginal cost)	60,000		30,000		-	
Variable cost of sales		60,000		90,000		120,000
Contribution		40,000		60,000		80,000
Less fixed costs		45,000		45,000		45,000
Profit/(loss)		(5,000)		15,000		35,000
Profit/(loss) per unit		$(0.50)		$1		$1.75
Contribution per unit		$4		$4		$4

The conclusions which may be drawn from this example are as follows.

(a)   The **profit per unit varies** at differing levels of sales, because the average fixed overhead cost per unit changes with the volume of output and sales.

(b)   The **contribution per unit is constant** at all levels of output and sales. Total contribution, which is the contribution per unit multiplied by the number of units sold, increases in direct proportion to the volume of sales.

(c)   Since the **contribution per unit does not change**, the most effective way of calculating the expected profit at any level of output and sales would be as follows.

(i)   First calculate the total contribution.

(ii)   Then deduct fixed costs as a period charge in order to find the profit.

(d)   In our example the expected profit from the sale of 17,000 Splashes would be as follows.

	$
Total contribution (17,000 × $4)	68,000
Less fixed costs	45,000
Profit	23,000

2.2 Profits, losses and breakeven point

(a)   If total contribution exceeds fixed costs, a profit is made.

(b)   If total contribution exactly equals fixed costs, no profit and no loss is made and breakeven point is reached.

(c)   If total contribution is less than fixed costs, there will be a loss.

Question

Marginal costing principles

PC company makes two products, the Loo and the Wash. Information relating to each of these products for April 20X1 is as follows.

	Loo	Wash
Opening inventory	nil	nil
Production (units)	15,000	6,000
Sales (units)	10,000	5,000
	$	$
Sales price per unit	20	30
Unit costs		
Direct materials	8	14
Direct labour	4	2
Variable production overhead	2	1
Variable sales overhead	2	3

Fixed costs for the month	$
Production costs	40,000
Administration costs	15,000
Sales and distribution costs	25,000

Using the approach set out in the answer to the example in Section 2.1 above, the marginal costing profit for April 20X1 is $ ☐ .

Answer

The profit is $ 10,000

Workings

	$
Contribution from Loos (unit contribution = $20 – $16 = $4 × 10,000)	40,000
Contribution from Washes (unit contribution = $30 – $20 = $10 × 5,000)	50,000
Total contribution	90,000
Fixed costs for the period	80,000
Profit	10,000

2.3 Inventory valuation using absorption costing and marginal costing

Marginal costing is significantly different from absorption costing. It is an **alternative method** of accounting for costs and profit, which rejects the principles of absorbing fixed overheads into unit costs.

(a) **In marginal costing**

    (i)   Closing inventories are valued at **marginal production cost**.

    (ii)   Fixed costs are charged in full against the profit of the period in which they are incurred.

(b) **In absorption costing**

    (i)   Closing inventories are valued at full production cost, and include a share of fixed production costs.

(ii)   This means that the cost of sales in a period will include some fixed overhead incurred in a previous period (in opening inventory values) and will exclude some fixed overhead incurred in the current period but carried forward in closing inventory values as a charge to a subsequent accounting period.

With this in mind work through the following example.

2.4 Example: marginal and absorption costing

TLF Company manufactures a single product, the Claud. The following figures relate to the Claud for a one-year period.

Activity level	50%	100%
Sales and productions (units)	400	800

	$	$
Sales	8,000	16,000
Production costs: variable	3,200	6,400
fixed	1,600	1,600
Sales and distribution costs:		
variable	1,600	3,200
fixed	2,400	2,400

The normal level of activity for the year is 800 units. Fixed costs are incurred evenly throughout the year, and actual fixed costs are the same as budgeted.

There were no inventories of Claud at the beginning of the year.

In the first quarter, 220 units were produced and 160 units sold.

Required

(a)   Calculate the fixed production costs absorbed by Clauds in the first quarter if absorption costing is used.
(b)   Calculate the under/over recovery of overheads during the quarter.
(c)   Calculate the profit using absorption costing.
(d)   Calculate the profit using marginal costing.

Solution

(a) $$\frac{\text{Budgeted fixed production costs}}{\text{Budgeted output (normal level of activity)}} = \frac{\$1,600}{800 \text{ units}}$$

Absorption rate = $2 per unit produced.

During the quarter, the fixed production overhead absorbed was 220 units × $2 = $440.

(b)

	$
Actual fixed production overhead	400 (1/4 of $1,600)
Absorbed fixed production overhead	440
Over absorption of overhead	40

(c)   Profit for the quarter, absorption costing

	$	$
Sales (160 × $20)		3,200
Production costs		
Variable (220 × $8)	1,760	
Fixed (absorbed overhead (220 × $2))	440	
Total (220 × $10)	2,200	
Less closing inventories (60 × $10)	600	
Production cost of sales	1,600	
Adjustment for over-absorbed overhead	40	
Total production costs		1,560
Gross profit		1,640
Less: sales and distribution costs		
variable (160 × $4)	640	
fixed (1/4 of $2,400)	600	
		1,240
Net profit		400

(d)   Profit for the quarter, marginal costing

	$	$
Sales		3,200
Variable production costs	1,760	
Less closing inventories (60 × $8)	480	
Variable production cost of sales	1,280	
Variable sales and distribution costs	640	
Total variable costs of sales		1,920
Total contribution		1,280
Less:		
Fixed production costs incurred	400	
Fixed sales and distribution costs	600	
		1,000
Net profit		280

Now have a go at the following questions to assess whether or not you can use both absorption costing and marginal costing.

Question	Calculating profits

Suppose that a company makes and sells a single product. At the beginning of period 1, there are no opening inventories of the product, for which the variable production cost is $4 and the sales price $6 per unit. Fixed costs are $2,000 per period, of which $1,500 are fixed production costs.

	Period 1	Period 2
Sales	1,200 units	1,800 units
Production	1,500 units	1,500 units

(a)   Assuming normal output is 1,500 units per period, the absorption costing profit in each period and in total would be:

(i)   Period 1 $☐

(ii)   Period 2 $☐

(iii)   Total $☐

(b)   The marginal costing profit in each period and in total would be:

(i)   Period 1 $ _____

(ii)   Period 2 $ _____

(iii)   Total $ _____

Answer

(a)   (i)   **Period 1** $ | 700 |

(ii)   **Period 2** $ | 1,300 |

(iii)   **Total** $ | 2,000 |

Workings

The absorption rate for fixed production overhead is

$$\frac{\$1,500}{1,500 \text{ units}} = \$1 \text{ per unit}$$

	Period 1		Period 2		Total	
	$	$	$	$	$	$
Sales		7,200		10,800		18,000
Production costs						
Variable	6,000		6,000		12,000	
Fixed	1,500		1,500		3,000	
	7,500		7,500		15,000	
Add opening inventory b/f	-		1,500			
	7,500		9,000		15,000	
Less closing inventory c/f	(1,500)		(-)		(-)	
Production cost of sales	6,000		9,000		15,000	
(Under-)/over-absorbed overhead	-		-		-	
Total production costs		6,000		9,000		15,000
Gross profit		1,200		1,800		3,000
Other costs		500		500		1,000
Net profit		700		1,300		2,000

(b)   (i)   **Period 1** $ | 400 |

(ii)   **Period 2** $ | 1,600 |

(iii)   **Total** $ | 2,000 |

Workings

	Period 1		Period 2		Total	
	$	$	$	$	$	$
Sales		7,200		10,800		18,000
Variable production cost	6,000		6,000		12,000	
Add opening inventory b/f	-		1,200		-	
	6,000		7,200		12,000	
Less closing inventory c/f	(1,200)		(-)		(-)	
Variable production cost of sales		4,800		7,200		12,000
Contribution		2,400		3,600		6,000
Fixed costs		2,000		2,000		4,000
Profit		400		1,600		2,000

Question

Two approaches to dealing with overheads

X Co commenced business on 1 March making one product only. The standard cost of one unit is as follows.

	$
Direct labour	5
Direct material	8
Variable production overhead	2
Fixed production overhead	5
Standard production cost	20

The fixed production overhead figure has been calculated on the basis of a budgeted normal output of 36,000 units per annum.

You are to assume that all the budgeted fixed expenses are incurred evenly over the year. March and April are to be taken as equal period months.

Selling, distribution and administration expenses are as follows.

Fixed $120,000 per annum
Variable   15% of the sales value

The selling price per unit is $35 and the number of units produced and sold was as follows.

	March Units	April Units
Production	2,000	3,200
Sales	1,500	3,000

(a)   If a marginal costing system is in operation:

    (i)   The value of the closing inventory for each month will be:

        March $ ☐

        April $ ☐

    (ii) The loss reported for March will be $ ☐

    (iii) The profit reported for April will be $ ☐

(b)   If an absorption costing system is in operation:

(i)   The value of the closing inventory for each month will be:

March $ [   ]

April $ [   ]

(ii)   The production overhead for March will be [   ] absorbed by $ [   ]

(iii)   The production overhead for April will be [   ] absorbed by $ [   ]

(iv)   The loss reported for March will be $ [   ]

(v)   The profit reported for April will be $ [   ]

Answer

(a)   (i)   **March $**   7,500   (500 units × $15)

             April $ 10,500   (700 units × $15)

     (ii)   **The loss reported for March will be $**   2,875

             Workings

             Contribution per unit:

	$ per unit
Selling price	35.00
Variable production cost	(15.00)
Variable selling expenses ($35 × 15%)	(5.25)
Contribution per unit	14.75

             Loss for March:

	$
Contribution (1,500 × $14.75)	22,125
Fixed production overhead ($5 × 36,000 × 1/12)	(15,000)
Fixed selling expenses	(10,000)
Loss	(2,875)

     (iii)   **The profit reported for April will be $**   19,250

             Workings

	$
Contribution (3,000 × $14.75)	44,250
Fixed production overhead	(15,000)
Fixed selling expenses	(10,000)
	19,250

(b)   (i)   **March $**   10,000   (500 units × $20)

             April $ 14,000   (700 units × $20)

     (ii)   **The production overhead for March will be**   under   **absorbed by $**   5,000

     (iii)   **The production overhead for April will be**   over   **absorbed by $**   1,000

Workings

		March $		April $
Overhead absorbed	(2,000 × $5)	10,000	(3,200 × $5)	16,000
Overhead incurred	($5 × 36,000 × 1/12)	15,000		15,000
Under/(over) absorbed		5,000		(1,000)

(iv) **The loss reported for March will be $** | 375 |

(v) **The profit reported for April will be $** | 20,250 |

Workings

	March $	April $
Marginal costing (loss)/profit	(2,875)	19,250
Plus increase in inventory @ $5 fixed overhead per unit:		
500 units × $5	2,500	
200 units × $5		1,000
Absorption costing (loss)/profit	(375)	20,250

3 Pricing decisions

3.1 Full cost plus pricing

A price determined using **full cost plus pricing** is based on full cost plus a percentage mark-up for profit.

A traditional approach to pricing products is full cost plus pricing, whereby the sales price is determined by **calculating the full cost of the product and adding a percentage mark-up for profit.**

In full cost plus pricing, the full cost may be a fully absorbed *production* cost only, or it may include some absorbed administration, selling and distribution overhead.

A business might have an idea of the percentage profit margin it would like to earn and so might decide on an average profit mark-up as a general guideline for pricing decisions. This would be particularly **useful for** businesses that carry out a large amount of **contract work** or **jobbing work**, for which individual job or contract prices must be quoted regularly to prospective customers.

However, the **percentage profit mark-up** does not have to be fixed, but can be **varied to suit the circumstances**. In particular, the percentage mark-up can be varied to suit demand conditions in the market.

3.1.1 Problems with full cost plus pricing

(a) Prices must be adjusted to market and demand conditions, the decision cannot simply be made on a cost basis only. A company may need to match the prices of rival firms when these take a price-cutting initiative.

(b) A full cost plus basis for a pricing decision is a means of ensuring that, in the long run, a company succeeds in covering all its fixed costs and making a profit out of revenue earned. However, in the short term it is **inflexible**.

(1)   A firm tendering for a contract may quote a cost plus price that results in the contract going elsewhere, although a lower price would have been sufficient to cover all incremental costs and opportunity costs.

(2)   In the short term, rapidly-changing environmental factors might dictate the need for lower (or higher) prices than long-term considerations would indicate.

(c)   Where more than one product is sold by a company, the price decided by a cost plus formula depends on the method of apportioning fixed costs between the products.

3.1.2 Example: full cost plus pricing with more than one product

GL Company is attempting to decide sales prices for two products, Lyons and Tygers. The products are both made by the same workforce and in the same department. 30,000 direct labour hours are budgeted for the year. The budgeted fixed costs are $30,000 and it is expected that the department will operate at full capacity. Variable costs per unit are as follows.

		Lyons		Tygers
		$		$
Materials		4		4
Labour	(2 hours)	6	(3 hours)	9
Expenses	(1 machine hour)	2	(1 machine hour)	2
		12		15

Expected demand is 7,500 Lyons and 5,000 Tygers.

Required

Calculate the unit prices which give a profit of 20% on full cost if overheads are absorbed on the following bases.

(a)   On a direct labour hour basis
(b)   On a machine hour basis

Solution

(a)   **A direct labour hour basis**

$$\frac{\text{Budgeted fixed costs}}{\text{Budgeted labour costs}} = \frac{\$30,000}{(15,000+15,000)} = \$1$$

Absorption rate $1 per direct labour hour

	Lyons	Tygers
	$	$
Variable costs	12.00	15.00
Overhead absorbed	2.00	3.00
	14.00	18.00
Profit (20%)	2.80	3.60
Price	16.80	21.60

The total budgeted profit would be $(2.80 × 7,500) + ($3.60 × 5,000) = $39,000

(b)   **A machine hour basis**

$$\frac{\text{Budgeted fixed costs}}{\text{Budgeted machine hours}} = \frac{\$30,000}{(7,500+5,000)} = \frac{\$30,000}{12,500} = \$2.40$$

Absorption rate $2.40 per machine hour

	Lyons	Tygers
	$	$
Variable costs	12.00	15.00
Overhead absorbed	2.40	2.40
Full cost	14.40	17.40
Profit (20%)	2.88	3.48
Price	17.28	20.88

The total budgeted profit would be $(2.88 × 7,500) + ($3.48 × 5,000) = $39,000

(c) The different bases for charging overheads result in different prices for both Lyons (difference of 48c per unit) and Tygers (difference of 72c per unit).

It is unlikely that the expected sales demand for the products would be the same at both sales prices. It is questionable whether one (or either) product might achieve expected sales demand at the higher price. In other words, although the budgeted profit is $39,000 whichever overhead absorption method is used, this assumes that budgeted sales would be achieved regardless of the unit price of each product. This is an unrealistic basis on which to make a decision.

3.1.3 Advantages of full cost plus pricing

(a) Since the size of the profit margin can be varied at management's discretion, a decision based on a price in excess of full cost should ensure that a company working at normal capacity will cover all its fixed costs and make a profit. Companies may benefit from cost plus pricing in the following circumstances.

   (i) When they carry out large contracts which must make a sufficient profit margin to cover a fair share of fixed costs

   (ii) If they must justify their prices to potential customers (for example for government contracts)

   (iii) If they find it difficult to estimate expected demand at different sales prices

(b) It is a **simple, quick and cheap** method of pricing which can be delegated to junior managers. This may be particularly important with jobbing work where many prices must be decided and quoted each day.

Question	Mark up

A company's product's full cost is $4.75 and it is sold at full cost plus 70%. A competitor has just launched a similar product selling for $7.99. The company needs to change the price of its product to match that of the competitor.

The margin of the first product should change to [   ] %.

Answer

The margin should change to [68.2] %

Workings

Margin in $ = $(7.99 − 4.75) = $3.24.
Margin as % of full cost = (3.24/4.75) × 100% = 68.2%.

3.1.4 Generating a return on sales or investment

Full cost plus pricing is a form of **target pricing**, which means setting a price so as to achieve a target return on sales or investment.

Let's start with looking at a **target return on sales**.

Suppose LM Company wishes to make a 20% **return on sales**. The full cost of product K is $100. The price that LM Company needs to set is therefore calculated as follows.

Let the selling price = P
P– full cost = 20% of P= 0.2P
Therefore P – 0.2P = full cost
Therefore 0.8P = full cost = $100
Therefore P = $100/0.8 = $125

Now let's look at a **target return on investment**.

Suppose sales of product Z for the coming year are expected to be 500 units. A return of 15% in the coming year is required on the annual investment of $250,000 in product Z. The full cost of product Z is $175. The required selling price is calculated as follows.

Required return = 15% × $250,000 = $37,500
Expected cost = 500 × $175 = $87,500
Required revenue – expected cost = required return
Therefore expected revenue = $(37,500 + 87,500) = $125,000
Therefore selling price = $125,000/500 = $250

Question	Pricing to generate a return on investment

MM Company requires a 30% return on investment from its products. It will invest $800,000 in product B in the coming year, when it expects to sell 50,000 units.

If the full cost of product B is $100, the required selling price is $ ☐ .

Answer

The required selling price is $ 104.80

Workings

Required return = 30% × $800,000 = $240,000

Expected cost = 50,000 × $100 = $5,000,000

Required revenue = $(5,000,000 + 240,000) = $5,240,000

Selling price = $5,240,000/50,000 = $104.80

Assessment focus point   Watch out for OT questions in the assessment on this area in particular.

3.2 Marginal cost plus pricing

Marginal cost plus prices are based on the marginal cost of production or the marginal cost of sales, plus a profit margin.

Instead of pricing products or services by adding a profit margin on to full cost, a business might **add a profit margin on to marginal cost (either the marginal cost of production or else the marginal cost of sales)**.

For example, if a company budgets to make 10,000 units of a product for which the variable cost of production is $3 a unit and the fixed production cost $60,000 a year, it might decide to fix a price by adding, say, $33\frac{1}{3}$% to full production cost to give a price of $9 × 1$\frac{1}{3}$ = $12 a unit. Alternatively, it might decide to add a profit margin of, say, 250% on to the variable production cost, to give a price of $3 × 350% = $10.50.

3.2.1 Advantages of a marginal cost plus approach

(a) It is a **simple and easy** method to use.

(b) The **mark-up can be varied**, and so provided that a rigid mark-up is not used, mark-up pricing can be adjusted to reflect demand conditions.

(c) It draws management attention to contribution and the effects of higher or lower sales volumes on profit. This helps to **create a better awareness of** the concepts and implications of **marginal costing and breakeven analysis (**a topic we cover in Chapter 4). For example, if a product costs $10 a unit and a mark-up of 150% is added to reach a price of $25 a unit, management should be clearly aware that every additional $1 of sales revenue would add 60c to contribution and profit.

(d) Mark-up pricing is **convenient where there is a readily identifiable basic variable cost. Retail industries** are the most obvious example, and it is quite common for the prices of goods in shops to be fixed by adding a mark-up (20% or $33\frac{1}{3}$%, say) to the purchase cost. For example, a department store might buy in items of pottery at $3 each, add a mark-up of one third and resell the items at $4.

3.2.2 Drawbacks to marginal cost plus pricing

(a) Although the size of the mark-up can be varied in accordance with demand conditions, it does not ensure that sufficient attention is paid to demand conditions and competitors' prices.

(b) It ignores fixed overheads in the pricing decision, but the price must be high enough to ensure that a profit is made after covering fixed costs. Pricing decisions cannot ignore fixed costs altogether.

Question		Profit margin

A product has the following costs.

	$
Direct materials	5
Direct labour	3
Variable overhead	7

Fixed overheads are $10,000 per month. Budgeted sales for the month are 400 units.

The profit margin that needs to be added to marginal cost to break even is [   ] %

Answer

The profit margin is | 167 | **%**

Workings

Total costs for the month = variable costs + fixed costs

= ($15 × 400) + $10,000 = $16,000

∴ Sales revenue must equal $16,000

∴ Selling price per unit = $16,000/400 = $40

∴ Mark-up = $(40 − 15) = $25

Mark-up % = (25/15) × 100% = 167%

3.2.3 Margins and mark-ups

Consider the following **cost/profit/sales structure.**

	%
Cost	80
Profit	20
Sales	100

The **profit added** to the full cost or marginal cost of a product may be expressed in one of two ways.

- Percentage of **cost of sales**, such as **25%** ($^{20}/_{80}$) **mark-up**
- Percentage of **sales**, such as **20%** ($^{20}/_{100}$) **margin**

Alternatively, the **cost/profit/sales structure** could be:

	%
Cost	100
Profit	20
Sales	120

- Mark-up = $^{20}/_{100}$ = 20%
- Margin = $^{20}/_{120}$ = 16.7%

Question

Selling price and unit cost

(a) Product B's unit cost is $50. A selling price is set based on a margin of 15%. The selling price is $ [   ]

(b) Product L sells for $750. The mark-up is 10%. The unit cost of product L is $ [   ]

Answer

(a)   **The selling price is $ 58.82**

Workings

	$	%
Cost	50	85
Profit	?	15
Selling price	?	100

∴ Selling price = $50/0.85 = $58.82

(b)   **The unit cost is $ 681.82**

Workings

	$	%
Cost	?	100
Profit	?	10
Selling price	750	110

Cost = $750/1.1 = $681.82

Chapter Roundup

- Whereas fully absorbed product costs include fixed overhead, the **marginal cost** of a product usually consists of variable costs only.

- **Contribution** is an important measure in marginal costing, and it is calculated as the difference between sales value and marginal or variable cost.

- **Marginal costing** is an alternative method of costing to absorption costing. In marginal costing, only variable costs are charged as a cost of sale and a contribution is calculated. Closing inventories of work in progress or finished goods are valued at marginal (variable) production cost. Fixed costs are treated as a period cost, and are charged in full against profit in the accounting period in which they are incurred.

- A price determined using **full cost plus pricing** is based on full cost plus a percentage mark-up for profit.

- **Marginal cost plus prices** are based on the marginal cost of production or the marginal cost of sales, plus a profit margin.

Quick Quiz

1   Sales value – marginal cost of sales = ...

2   Identify which of the following relate to either

A = Absorption costing
M = Marginal costing

		A or M
(a)	Closing inventories valued at marginal production cost	
(b)	Closing inventories valued at full production cost	
(c)	Cost of sales include some fixed overhead incurred in previous period in opening inventory values	
(d)	Fixed costs are charged in full against profit for the period	

3   Which of the following are arguments in favour of marginal costing?

(a)   Closing inventory is valued in accordance with SSAP 9.
(b)   It is simple to operate.
(c)   There is no under or over absorption of overheads.
(d)   Fixed costs are the same regardless of activity levels.
(e)   The information from this costing method may be used for decision making.

4   ABC Co plans to sell 1,200 units of product B. A 12% return is required on the $1,000,000 annual investment in product B. A selling price of $550 per unit has been set.

The full cost of product B is $ [   ] .

BPP
PROFESSIONAL EDUCATION

Answers to quick quiz

1   Contribution

2

		A or M
(a)	Closing inventory valued at marginal production cost	M
(b)	Closing inventory valued at full production cost	A
(c)	Cost of sales include some fixed overhead incurred in previous period in opening inventory values	A
(d)	Fixed costs are charged in full against profit for the period	M

3   (b), (c), (d), (e)

4   Required return = 12% × $1,000,000 = $120,000

Expected revenue = 1,200 × $500 = $600,000

Expected cost = expected revenue − required return

∴ Expected cost = $(600,000 − 120,000) = $480,000

∴ Full cost per unit = $480,000/1,200 = $400

Now try the questions below from the Question Bank

Question numbers	Page
16–20	348

Part B

Cost behaviour and breakeven analysis

Cost behaviour

Introduction

In Chapter 1 we introduced the concept of the division of costs into those that vary directly with changes in activity level (**variable costs**) and those that do not (**fixed costs**). This chapter examines further this particular two-way split of **cost behaviour** and explains two methods of splitting total costs into these two elements, the **line of best fit** (or **scattergraph**) method and the **high-low** method.

You will need to rely on concepts covered in this chapter in the other chapters in this Study Text (but particularly the next chapter) and in the remainder of your management accounting studies both at the Certificate stage and at future examination levels.

Topic list	Learning outcomes	Syllabus references	Ability required
1 Cost behaviour and levels of activity	B(i)	B(1)	Comprehension
2 Cost behaviour patterns	B(ii), B(iii)	B(1), B(2)	Comprehension
3 Determining the fixed and variable elements of semi-variable costs	B(iv)	B(3)	Application

1 Cost behaviour and levels of activity

Cost behaviour is the way in which a cost changes as activity level changes.

Key term

Cost behaviour is the 'Variability of input costs with activity undertaken. Cost may increase proportionately with increasing activity (the usual assumption for variable cost), or it may not change with increased activity (a fixed cost). Some costs (semi-variable) may have both variable and fixed elements. Other behaviour is possible; costs may increase more or less than in direct proportion, and there may be step changes in cost, for example. To a large extent, cost behaviour will be dependent on the timescale assumed.' CIMA *Official Terminology*

1.1 Levels of activity

The level of activity refers to the amount of work done, or the number of events that have occurred. Depending on circumstances, the level of activity may refer to measures such as the following.

- The volume of production in a period
- The number of items sold
- The number of invoices issued
- The number of units of electricity consumed

1.2 Basic principle of cost behaviour

The basic principle of cost behaviour is that as the level of activity rises, costs will usually rise. It will probably cost more to produce 2,000 units of output than it will cost to produce 1,000 units; it will usually cost more to make five telephone calls than to make one call and so on. The problem for the accountant is to determine, for each item of cost, the way in which costs rise and by how much as the level of activity increases.

For our purposes in this chapter, the level of activity will generally be taken to be the volume of production/output.

2 Cost behaviour patterns

2.1 Fixed costs

Costs which are not affected by the level of activity are **fixed costs** or **period costs**.

Key term

A **fixed cost** is a 'cost incurred for an accounting period, that, within certain output or turnover limits, tends to be unaffected by fluctuations in the levels of activity (output or turnover)'. CIMA *Official Terminology*

We discussed fixed costs briefly in Chapter 1. A **fixed cost** is a cost which tends to be unaffected by increases or decreases in the volume of output. Fixed costs are a **period charge**, in that they relate to a span of time; as the time span increases, so too will the fixed costs. A sketch graph of a fixed cost would look like this.

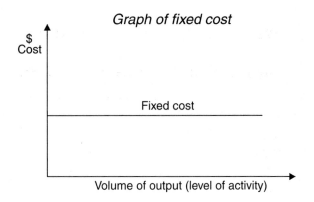

Graph of fixed cost

2.1.1 Examples of fixed costs

- The salary of the managing director (per month or per annum)
- The rent of a single factory building (per month or per annum)
- Straight line depreciation of a single machine (per month or per annum)

2.2 Variable costs

Variable costs increase or decrease with the level of activity.

A **variable cost** is a 'cost that varies with a measure of activity'.   CIMA *Official Terminology*

We discussed variable costs briefly in Chapter 1. A **variable cost** is a cost which tends to vary directly with the volume of output. The variable cost **per unit** is the same amount for each unit produced whereas **total** variable cost increases as volume of output increases. A sketch graph of a variable cost would look like this.

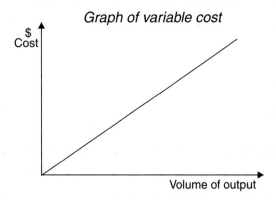

Graph of variable cost

2.2.1 Examples of variable costs

(a) The cost of raw materials (where there is no discount for bulk purchasing since bulk purchase discounts reduce the unit cost of purchases).

(b) Direct labour costs are, for very important reasons which you will study in Chapter 7, usually classed as a variable cost even though basic wages are often fixed.

(c) Sales commission is variable in relation to the volume or value of sales.

2.3 Step costs

FAST FORWARD

A **step cost** is a cost which is fixed in nature but only within certain levels of activity. Depending on the time frame being considered, it may appear as fixed or variable.

Consider the depreciation of a machine which may be fixed if production remains below 1,000 units per month. If production exceeds 1,000 units, a second machine may be required, and the cost of depreciation (on two machines) would go up a step. A sketch graph of a step cost could look like this.

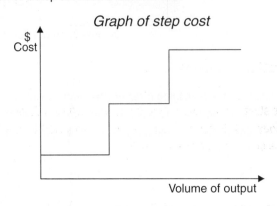

Graph of step cost

2.3.1 Examples of step costs

(a)   Rent is a step cost in situations where accommodation requirements increase as output levels get higher.

(b)   Basic pay of employees is nowadays usually fixed, but as output rises, more employees (direct workers, supervisors, managers and so on) are required.

2.3.2 The importance of time scale

The time scale over which we consider the behaviour of what appears to be a step cost can actually result in its classification as a fixed cost or a variable cost.

Over the short to medium term, a cost such as rent will appear as fixed, steps in the cost only occurring after a certain length of time.

Many **variable costs** also appear **fixed over a short period of time**. For example, spending on direct labour (traditionally classified as a variable cost) will be fixed in relation to changes in activity level as it takes time to respond to changes in activity and alter spending levels.

Over longer periods of time, however, say a number of years, **all costs will tend to vary in response to large changes in activity level.** For this reason **fixed costs** are sometimes called **long-term variable costs**. Costs traditionally classified as fixed will become step costs as no cost can remain unchanged forever. And so as the **time span increases, step costs become variable costs, varying with the passing of time**. For example, when considered over many years, rent will appear as a variable cost, varying in the long term with large changes in the level of activity.

2.4 Non-linear variable costs

Although variable costs are usually assumed to be linear, there are situations where variable costs are **curvilinear**. Have a look at the following graphs.

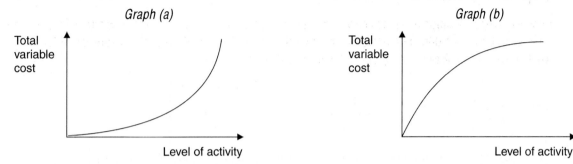

Graph (a) becomes steeper as levels of activity increase. Each additional unit of activity is adding more to total variable cost than the previous unit. Graph (b) becomes less steep as levels of activity increase. Each additional unit is adding less to total variable cost than the previous unit.

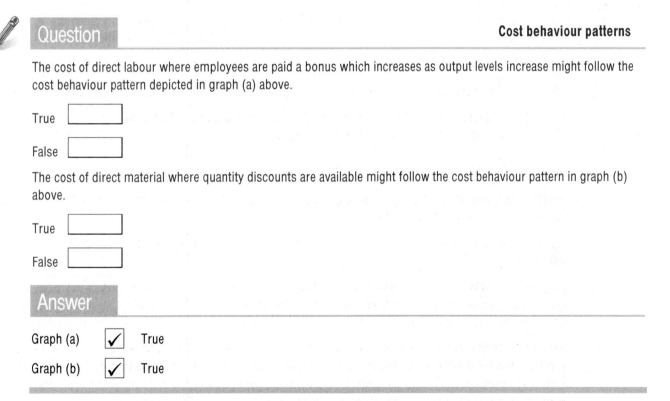

Question   **Cost behaviour patterns**

The cost of direct labour where employees are paid a bonus which increases as output levels increase might follow the cost behaviour pattern depicted in graph (a) above.

True ☐

False ☐

The cost of direct material where quantity discounts are available might follow the cost behaviour pattern in graph (b) above.

True ☐

False ☐

Answer

Graph (a) ☑ True

Graph (b) ☑ True

2.5 Semi-variable costs (or semi-fixed costs or mixed costs)

Semi-variable, semi-fixed or **mixed costs** are costs which are part-fixed and part-variable and are therefore partly affected by a change in the level of activity.

Key term

A **semi-variable cost** is a 'cost containing both fixed and variable components and thus partly affected by a change in the level of activity'.

CIMA *Official Terminology*

2.5.1 Examples of semi-variable costs

(a)   **Electricity and gas bills**. There is a basic charge plus a charge per unit of consumption.

(b)   **Sales representative's salary**. The sales representative may earn a basic monthly amount of, say, $1,000 and then commission of 10% of the value of sales made.

The behaviour of a semi-variable cost can be presented graphically as follows.

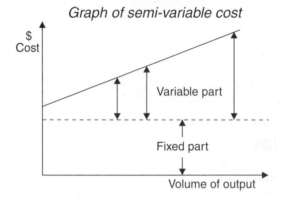

Graph of semi-variable cost

2.6 Cost behaviour and total and unit costs

If the variable cost of producing a unit is $5 per unit then it will remain at that cost per unit no matter how many units are produced. However if the business's fixed costs are $5,000 then the fixed cost **per unit** will decrease the more units are produced: one unit will have fixed costs of $5,000 per unit; if 2,500 are produced the fixed cost per unit will be $2; if 5,000 are produced the fixed cost per unit will be only $1. Thus as the level of activity increases the total costs **per unit** (fixed cost plus variable cost) will decrease.

In sketch graph form this may be illustrated as follows.

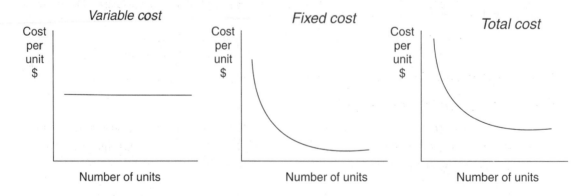

Question

Fixed, variable and mixed costs

Tick the appropriate box for each cost.

		Fixed	Variable	Mixed
(a)	Telephone bill	☐	☐	☐
(b)	Annual salary of the chief accountant	☐	☐	☐
(c)	The management accountant's annual membership fee to CIMA (paid by the company)	☐	☐	☐
(d)	Cost of materials used to pack 20 units of product X into a box	☐	☐	☐

Answer

(a)	Mixed	☑
(b)	Fixed	☑
(c)	Fixed	☑
(d)	Variable	☑

2.7 Assumption about cost behaviour

2.7.1 The relevant range

Key term

> The **relevant range** is 'activity levels within which assumptions about cost behaviour in breakeven analysis remain valid'.
> CIMA *Official Terminology*

The relevant range also broadly represents the **activity levels at which an organisation has had experience of operating at in the past** and for which **cost information is available**. It can therefore be dangerous to attempt to predict costs at activity levels which are outside the relevant range.

2.7.2 Assumptions

It is often possible to assume that, within the normal or relevant range of output, costs are either fixed, variable or semi-variable.

Question

Activity levels

Select the correct words in the following sentence.

The basic principle of cost behaviour is that as the level of activity rises, costs will usually (a) **rise/fall/stay the same**. In general, as activity levels rise, the variable cost per unit will (b) **rise/fall/stay the same**, the fixed cost per unit will (c) **rise/fall/stay the same** and the total cost per unit will (d) **rise/fall/stay the same**.

Answer

(a)   Rise
(b)   Stay the same
(c)   Fall
(d)   Fall

Question   **Cost behaviour graphs**

Match the sketches (1) to (5) below to the listed items of expense. In each case the vertical axis relates to total cost, the horizontal axis to activity level.

(a)   Electricity bill: a standing charge for each period plus a charge for each unit of electricity consumed.

(b)   Supervisory labour.

(c)   Production bonus, which is payable when output in a period exceeds 10,000 units. The bonus amounts in total to $20,000 plus $50 per unit for additional output above 10,000 units.

(d)   Sales commission, which amounts to 2% of sales revenue.

(e)   Machine rental costs of a single item of equipment. The rental agreement is that $10 should be paid for every machine hour worked each month, subject to a maximum monthly charge of $480.

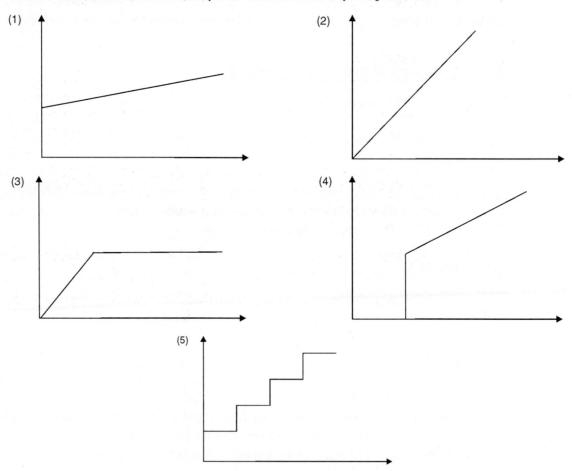

Answer

(a)   Graph (1)
(b)   Graph (5)
(c)   Graph (4)
(d)   Graph (2)
(e)   Graph (3)

3 Determining the fixed and variable elements of semi-variable costs

T FORWARD

The fixed and variable elements of semi-variable costs can be determined by the **high/low method** or the **'line of best fit' (scattergraph) method**.

There are several ways in which fixed cost elements and variable cost elements within semi-variable costs may be ascertained. Each method only gives an estimate, and can therefore give differing results from the other methods. The main methods that you need to know about for your assessment are the **high/low method** and the **line of best bit (scattergraph)** method.

3.1 High/low method

Key term

The **high/low method** is a 'method of estimating cost behaviour by comparing the total costs associated with two different levels of output. The difference in costs is assumed to be caused by variable costs increasing, allowing unit variable cost to be calculated. Following from this, since total cost is known, the fixed cost can be derived.'

CIMA *Official Terminology*

(a)   Records of costs in previous periods are reviewed and the costs of the following two periods are selected.

- The period with the **highest** volume of activity
- The period with the **lowest** volume of activity

(b)   The difference between the total cost of these two periods will be the **variable cost** of the difference in activity levels (since the same fixed cost is included in each total cost).

(c)   The variable cost per unit may be calculated from this (difference in total costs ÷ difference in activity levels), and the **fixed cost** may then be determined by substitution.

3.1.1 Example: the high/low method

The costs of operating the maintenance department of a computer manufacturer, Bread and Butter company, for the last four months have been as follows.

Month	Cost	Production volume
	$	Units
1	110,000	7,000
2	115,000	8,000
3	111,000	7,700
4	97,000	6,000

Required

Calculate the costs that should be expected in month five when output is expected to be 7,500 units. Ignore inflation.

Solution

(a)

	Units		$
High output	8,000	total cost	115,000
Low output	6,000	total cost	97,000
Variable cost of	2,000		18,000

Variable cost per unit $18,000/2,000 = $9

(b)   Substituting in either the high or low volume cost:

		High		Low
		$		$
Total cost		115,000		97,000
Variable costs	(8,000 × $9)	72,000	(6,000 × $9)	54,000
Fixed costs		43,000		43,000

(c)   Estimated maintenance costs when output is 7,500 units:

	$
Fixed costs	43,000
Variable costs (7,500 × $9)	67,500
Total costs	110,500

Question

High/low method

The Valuation Department of a large firm of surveyors wishes to develop a method of predicting its total costs in a period. The following past costs have been recorded at two activity levels.

	Number of valuations (V)	Total cost (TC)
Period 1	420	82,200
Period 2	515	90,275

The total cost model for a period could be represented as follows.

A   TC = $46,500 + 85V
B   TC = $42,000 + 95V
C   TC = $46,500 − 85V
D   TC = $51,500 − 95V

BPP
PROFESSIONAL EDUCATION

Answer

The correct answer is A.

Although we only have two activity levels in this question we can still apply the high/low method.

	Valuations	Total cost
	V	$
Period 2	515	90,275
Period 1	420	82,200
Change due to variable cost	95	8,075

∴ Variable cost per valuation = $8,075/95 = $85.

Period 2: fixed cost = $90,275 – (515 × $85)
= $46,500

Using good MCQ technique, you should have managed to eliminate C and D as incorrect options straightaway. The variable cost must be added to the fixed cost, rather than subtracted from it. Once you had calculated the variable cost as $85 per valuation (as shown above), you should have been able to select option A without going on to calculate the fixed cost (we have shown this calculation above for completeness).

Assessment focus point

The high-low method was frequently tested in the form of multiple choice questions under the previous syllabus of this paper. The information in questions often relates to **two** activity levels only. The high-low method is still an appropriate method for identifying the fixed and variable elements of costs where two levels of activity are concerned – you still have a **high** and a **low** activity level.

3.2 'Line of best fit' or scattergraph method

A scattergraph of costs in previous periods can be prepared (with cost on the vertical axis and volume of output on the horizontal axis). A **line of best fit**, which is a line drawn **by judgement** to pass through the middle of the points, thereby having as many points above the line as below it, can then be drawn and the fixed and variable costs determined.

A scattergraph of the cost and volume data in Section 3.1.1 is shown below.

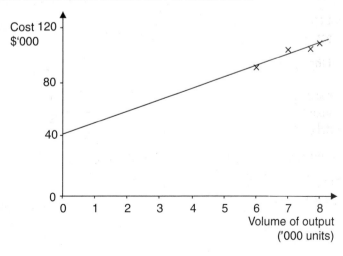

The point where the line cuts the vertical axis (approximately $40,000) is the fixed cost (the cost if there is no output). If we take the value of one of the plotted points which lies close to the line and deduct the fixed cost from the total cost, we can calculate the variable cost per unit.

Total cost for 8,000 units   = $115,000
Variable cost for 8,000 units   = $(115,000 – 40,000) = $75,000
Variable cost per unit   = $75,000/8,000 = $9.375

Assessment focus point

Although you would not actually be required to draw a scattergraph, you could perhaps be required to answer a multiple choice question about how the technique works, or its advantages and limitations.

Chapter Roundup

- **Cost behaviour** is the way in which a cost changes as activity level changes.

- Costs which are not affected by the level of activity are **fixed costs** or **period costs**.

- **Variable costs** increase or decrease with the level of activity.

- A **step cost** is a cost which is fixed in nature but only within certain levels of activity. Depending on the time frame being considered, it may appear as fixed or variable.

- **Semi-variable, semi-fixed** or **mixed costs** are costs which are part-fixed and part-variable and are therefore partly affected by a change in the level of activity.

- The fixed and variable elements of semi-variable costs can be determined by the **high-low method** or the **'line of best fit' (scattergraph) method**.

BPP
PROFESSIONAL EDUCATION

Quick Quiz

1   The basic principle of cost behaviour is that as the level of activity rises, costs will usually fall.

True ☐

False ☐

2   Fill in the gaps for each of the graph titles below.

(a)

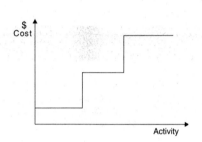

Graph of a ………………… cost

Example:

(b)

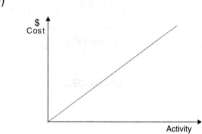

Graph of a ………………… cost

Example:

(c)

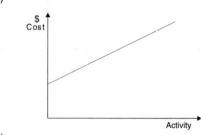

Graph of a ………………… cost

Example:

(d)

Graph of a ……………….. cost

Example:

3   Costs are assumed to be either fixed, variable or semi-variable within the normal or relevant range of output.

True ☐

False ☐

4   The costs of operating the canteen at 'Eat a lot Company' for the past three months is as follows.

Month	Cost $	Employees
1	72,500	1,250
2	75,000	1,300
3	68,750	1,175

Variable cost (per employee per month) =

Fixed cost per month =

Answers to Quick Quiz

1   False. They will rise.

2   (a)   Step cost. Example: rent, supervisors' salaries
      (b)   Variable cost. Example: raw materials, direct labour
      (c)   Semi-variable cost. Example: electricity and telephone
      (d)   Fixed. Example: rent, depreciation (straight-line)

3   True

4   Variable cost = $50 per employee per month
     Fixed costs = $10,000 per month

	Activity	Cost $
High	1,300	75,000
Low	1,175	68,750
	125	6,250

Variable cost per employee = $6,250/125 = $50

For 1,175 employees, total cost = $68,750

Total cost   = variable cost + fixed cost
$68,750   = (1,175 × $50) + fixed cost
∴ Fixed cost = $68,750 − $58,750
               = $10,000

Now try the questions below from the Question Bank

Question numbers	Page
21–25	349

Breakeven analysis and limiting factor analysis

Introduction

You should by now realise that the cost accountant needs estimates of **fixed** and **variable costs**, and **revenues**, at various output levels. Cost accountants must also be fully aware of **cost behaviour** because, to be able to estimate costs, they must know what a particular cost will do given particular conditions.

An understanding of cost behaviour is not all that you may need to know, however. The application of **breakeven analysis**, which is based on cost behaviour principles and marginal costing ideas, is sometimes necessary so that the appropriate decision-making information can be provided. As you may have guessed, this chapter is going to look at that very topic.

We're also going to take a look at **limiting factor analysis**, another technique using marginal costing ideas. This one helps us to determine the profit-maximising production or sales mix.

Topic list	Learning outcomes	Syllabus references	Ability required
1 Breakeven analysis and contribution	B(v)	B(4)	Comprehension
2 Breakeven point	B(vi)	B(5)	Application/Analysis
3 The contribution/sales (C/S) ratio	B(vi)	B(5)	Application/Analysis
4 The margin of safety	B(vi)	B(5)	Application/Analysis
5 Breakeven arithmetic and profit targets	B(vi)	B(5)	Application/Analysis
6 Breakeven charts and profit/volume graphs	B(vii)	B(5)	Application
7 Limitations of breakeven analysis	B(v)	B(5)	Comprehension
8 Limiting factor analysis	B(viii)	B(6)	Application

1 Breakeven analysis and contribution

Breakeven analysis or **cost-volume-profit (CVP) analysis** is the study of the interrelationships between costs, volume and profit at various levels of activity.

Key term

Cost-volume-profit analysis (CVP) is the 'study of the effects on future profit of changes in fixed cost, variable cost, sales price, quantity and mix'.   CIMA *Official Terminology*

1.1 Contribution

Contribution, a concept we encountered in Chapter 4, is fundamental to CVP analysis. As you know, contribution per unit is the difference between selling price per unit and variable costs per unit. The **total contribution** from the sales volume for a period can be **compared with the fixed costs** for the period. Any **excess of contribution** is **profit**, any **deficit** of contribution is a **loss**.

2 Breakeven point

The **breakeven point** occurs when there is neither a profit nor a loss and so fixed costs equal contribution.

Key term

The **breakeven point** is the 'level of activity at which there is neither profit nor loss'.   CIMA *Official Terminology*

The management of an organisation usually wishes to know the profit likely to be made if the aimed-for production and sales for the year are achieved. Management may also be interested to know the activity level at which there is neither profit nor loss. This is known as the **breakeven point**.

The breakeven point (BEP) can be calculated arithmetically.

Formula to learn

$$\text{Breakeven point} = \text{Number of units of sale required to break even}$$

$$= \frac{\text{Total fixed costs}}{\text{Contribution per unit}}$$

$$= \frac{\text{Contribution required to break even}}{\text{Contribution per unit}}$$

2.1 Example: breakeven point

Expected sales	10,000 units at $8 = $80,000
Variable cost	$5 per unit
Fixed costs	$21,000

Required

Compute the breakeven point.

Solution

The contribution per unit is $(8-5)   = $3

Contribution required to break even   =   fixed costs = $21,000

Breakeven point (BEP)   =   21,000 ÷ 3

   =   7,000 units

In revenue, BEP   =   (7,000 × $8) = $56,000

Sales above $56,000 will result in profit of $3 per unit of additional sales and sales below $56,000 will mean a loss of $3 per unit for each unit by which sales fall short of 7,000 units. In other words, profit will improve or worsen by the amount of contribution per unit.

	7,000 units	7,001 units
	$	$
Revenue	56,000	56,008
Less variable costs	35,000	35,005
Contribution	21,000	21,003
Less fixed costs	21,000	21,000
Profit	0 (= breakeven)	3

3 The contribution/sales (C/S) ratio

ST FORWARD

The **C/S ratio** (or **P/V ratio**) is a measure of how much contribution is earned from each $1 of sales.

3.1 C/S ratio and breakeven point

An alternative way of calculating the breakeven point to give an answer in terms of sales revenue and using the C/S ratio is as follows.

Formula to learn

Breakeven point = **Sales revenue** required to break even

$$= \frac{\text{Contribution required to break even}}{\text{C/S ratio}}$$

$$= \frac{\text{Fixed costs}}{\text{C/S ratio}}$$

3.2 Example: C/S ratio

In the example in Section 2.1 the C/S ratio is $\frac{\$3}{\$8}$ = 37.5%

Breakeven is where sales revenue equals $\frac{\$21,000}{37.5\%}$ = $56,000. At a price of $8 per unit, this represents 7,000 units of sales.

The C/S ratio is a measure of how much contribution is earned from each $1 of sales. The C/S ratio of 37.5% in the above example means that for every $1 of sales, a contribution of 37.5c is earned. Thus, in order to earn a total contribution of $21,000 and if contribution increases by 37.5c per $1 of sales, sales must be:

$$\frac{\$1}{37.5c} \times \$21,000 = \$56,000$$

Important! | The C/S (contribution/sales) ratio is sometimes called the **profit/volume or P/V ratio**.

Question C/S ratio

The C/S ratio of product W is 20%. IB, the manufacturer of product W, wishes to make a contribution of $50,000 towards fixed costs.

If the selling price is $10 per unit, the number of units of W that must be sold is ⬚ .

Answer

The number of units that must be sold is ⬚ 25,000 ⬚ .

Workings

$$\frac{\text{Required contribution}}{\text{C/S ratio}} = \frac{\$50,000}{20\%} = \$250,000$$

∴ Number of units = $250,000 ÷ $10 = 25,000.

4 The margin of safety

FAST FORWARD

The **margin of safety** is the difference in units between the budgeted sales volume and the breakeven sales volume. It is sometimes expressed as a percentage of the budgeted sales volume. Alternatively the margin of safety can be expressed as the difference between the budgeted sales revenue and breakeven sales revenue, expressed as a percentage of the budgeted sales revenue.

As well as being interested in the breakeven point, management may also be interested in the amount by which actual sales can fall below anticipated sales without a loss being incurred. This is the **margin of safety**.

Key term

The **margin of safety** 'indicates the percentage by which forecast revenue exceeds or falls short of that required to break even'.

CIMA Official Terminology

4.1 Example: margin of safety

Mal de Mer Co makes and sells a product which has a variable cost of $30 and which sells for $40. Budgeted fixed costs are $70,000 and budgeted sales are 8,000 units.

Required

Calculate the breakeven point and the margin of safety.

BPP
PROFESSIONAL EDUCATION

Solution

(a)   Breakeven point $= \dfrac{\text{Total fixed costs}}{\text{Contribution per unit}} = \dfrac{\$70,000}{\$(40-30)}$

                     $=$ 7,000 units

(b)   Margin of safety $=$ 8,000 – 7,000 units = 1,000 units

      which may be expressed as $\dfrac{1{,}000 \text{ units}}{8{,}000 \text{ units}} \times 100\%$ = 12½% of budget

(c)   The margin of safety indicates to management that actual sales can fall short of budget by 1,000 units or 12½% before the breakeven point is reached and no profit at all is made.

5 Breakeven arithmetic and profit targets

5.1 Breakeven arithmetic

At the **breakeven point**, there is no profit or loss and so **sales revenue = total costs** or **total contribution = fixed costs**.

At the **breakeven point**, sales revenue equals total costs and there is no profit.

     S $= V + F$

where S   = Sales revenue

         V   = Total variable costs

         F   = Total fixed costs

Subtracting V from each side of the equation, we get:

     $S - V = F$, that is, **total contribution = fixed costs**

5.2 Example: breakeven arithmetic

Butterfingers Company makes a product which has a variable cost of $7 per unit.

Required

If fixed costs are $63,000 per annum, calculate the selling price per unit if the company wishes to break even with a sales volume of 12,000 units.

Solution

			$
Contribution required to break even (= Fixed costs)	=	$63,000	
Volume of sales	=	12,000 units	
Required contribution per unit (S – V)	=	$63,000 ÷ 12,000 =	5.25
Variable cost per unit (V)	=		7.00
Required sales price per unit (S)	=		12.25

5.3 Target profits

The **target profit** is achieved when sales revenue equals variable costs plus fixed costs plus profit. Therefore the **total contribution required** for a target profit = **fixed costs + required profit.**

A similar formula may be applied where a company wishes to achieve a certain profit during a period. To achieve this profit, sales must cover all costs and leave the required profit.

Formula to learn

The **target profit** is achieved when: S = V + F + P,

Where S = Sales revenue
       V = Variable costs
       F = Fixed costs
       P = required profit

Subtracting V from each side of the equation, we get:

$$S - V = F + P, \text{ so}$$

Total contribution required   = F + P

5.4 Example: target profits

RB Co makes and sells a single product, for which variable costs are as follows.

	$
Direct materials	10
Direct labour	8
Variable production overhead	6
	24

The sales price is $30 per unit, and fixed costs per annum are $68,000. The company wishes to make a profit of $16,000 per annum.

Required

Determine the sales required to achieve this profit.

Solution

Required contribution = fixed costs + profit = $68,000 + $16,000 = $84,000

Required sales can be calculated in one of two ways.

(a) $\dfrac{\text{Required contribution}}{\text{Contribution perunit}} = \dfrac{\$84,000}{\$(30 - 24)} = 14,000$ units, or $420,000 in revenue

(b) $\dfrac{\text{Required contribution}}{\text{C/S ratio}} = \dfrac{\$84,000}{20\% *} = \$420,000$ of revenue, or 14,000 units.

$* \text{ C/S ratio} = \dfrac{\$30 - \$24}{\$30} = \dfrac{\$6}{\$30} = 0.2 = 20\%.$

Question

SLB Co wishes to sell 14,000 units of its product, which has a variable cost of $15 to make and sell. Fixed costs are $47,000 and the required profit is $23,000.

The required sales price per unit is $ ☐ .

Answer

The required sales price per unit is $ ☐ 20 ☐ .

Workings

Required contribution	=	fixed costs plus profit
	=	$47,000 + $23,000
	=	$70,000
Required sales		14,000 units

	$
Required contribution per unit sold	5
Variable cost per unit	15
Required sales price per unit	20

5.5 Variations on breakeven and profit target calculations

You may come across variations on breakeven and profit target calculations in which you will be expected to consider the effect of altering the selling price, variable cost per unit or fixed cost.

5.5.1 Example: change in selling price

Stomer Cakes Co bake and sell a single type of cake. The variable cost of production is 15c and the current sales price is 25c. Fixed costs are $2,600 per month, and the annual profit for the company at current sales volume is $36,000. The volume of sales demand is constant throughout the year.

The sales manager, Ian Digestion, wishes to raise the sales price to 29c per cake, but considers that a price rise will result in some loss of sales.

Required

Ascertain the minimum volume of sales required each month to raise the price to 29c.

Solution

The minimum volume of demand which would justify a price of 29c is one which would leave total profit at least the same as before, ie $3,000 per month. Required profit should be converted into required contribution, as follows.

	$
Monthly fixed costs	2,600
Monthly profit, minimum required	3,000
Current monthly contribution	5,600

Contribution per unit (25c – 15c)   10c
Current monthly sales   56,000 cakes

The minimum volume of sales required after the price rise will be an amount which earns a contribution of $5,600 per month, no worse than at the moment. The contribution per cake at a sales price of 29c would be 14c.

$$\text{Required sales} = \frac{\text{required contribution}}{\text{contribution per unit}} = \frac{\$5,600}{14c} = 40,000 \text{ cakes per month.}$$

5.5.2 Example: change in production costs

Close Brickett Co makes a product which has a variable production cost of $8 and a variable sales cost of $2 per unit. Fixed costs are $40,000 per annum, the sales price per unit is $18, and the current volume of output and sales is 6,000 units.

The company is considering whether to have an improved machine for production. Annual hire costs would be $10,000 and it is expected that the variable cost of production would fall to $6 per unit.

Required

(a)   Determine the number of units that must be produced and sold to achieve the same profit as is currently earned, if the machine is hired.

(b)   Calculate the annual profit with the machine if output and sales remain at 6,000 units per annum.

Solution

The current unit contribution is $(18 – (8+2)) = $8

(a) $
       Current contribution (6,000 × $8)   48,000
       Less current fixed costs   40,000
       Current profit   8,000

With the new machine fixed costs will go up by $10,000 to $50,000 per annum. The variable cost per unit will fall to $(6 + 2) = $8, and the contribution per unit will be $10.

                                                                           $
       Required profit (as currently earned)   8,000
       Fixed costs   50,000
       Required contribution   58,000

       Contribution per unit $10
       Sales required to earn $8,000 profit   5,800 units

(b)   **If sales are 6,000 units**

                                                            $ $
       Sales (6,000 × $18)   108,000
       Variable costs: production (6,000 × $6)   36,000
                        sales (6,000 × $2)   12,000
                                                                         48,000
       Contribution (6,000 × $10)   60,000
       Less fixed costs   50,000
       Profit   10,000

	$
Alternative calculation	
Profit at 5,800 units of sale (see (a))	8,000
Contribution from sale of extra 200 units (× $10)	2,000
Profit at 6,000 units of sale	10,000

5.6 More applications of breakeven arithmetic

It may be clear by now that, given no change in fixed costs, **total profit is maximised when the total contribution is at its maximum**. Total contribution in turn depends on the unit contribution and on the sales volume.

An increase in the sales price will increase unit contribution, but sales volume is likely to fall because fewer customers will be prepared to pay the higher price. A decrease in sales price will reduce the unit contribution, but sales volume may increase because the goods on offer are now cheaper. The **optimum combination** of sales price and sales volume is arguably the one which **maximises total contribution**.

5.6.1 Example: profit maximisation

C Co has developed a new product which is about to be launched on to the market. The variable cost of selling the product is $12 per unit. The marketing department has estimated that at a sales price of $20, annual demand would be 10,000 units.

However, if the sales price is set above $20, sales demand would fall by 500 units for each 50c increase above $20. Similarly, if the price is set below $20, demand would increase by 500 units for each 50c stepped reduction in price below $20.

Required

Determine the price which would maximise C Co's profit in the next year.

Solution

At a price of $20 per unit, the unit contribution would be $(20 − 12) = $8. Each 50c increase (or decrease) in price would raise (or lower) the unit contribution by 50p. The total contribution is calculated at each sales price by multiplying the unit contribution by the expected sales volume.

	Unit price $	Unit contribution $	Sales volume Units	Total contribution $
	20.00	8.00	10,000	80,000
(a)	**Reduce price**			
	19.50	7.50	10,500	78,750
	19.00	7.00	11,000	77,000
(b)	**Increase price**			
	20.50	8.50	9,500	80,750
	21.00	9.00	9,000	81,000
	21.50	9.50	8,500	80,750
	22.00	10.00	8,000	80,000
	22.50	10.50	7,500	78,750

The total contribution would be maximised, and therefore profit maximised, at a sales price of $21 per unit, and sales demand of 9,000 units.

Question

Betty Battle Co manufactures a product which has a selling price of $20 and a variable cost of $10 per unit. The compan incurs annual fixed costs of $29,000. Annual sales demand is 9,000 units.

New production methods are under consideration, which would cause a $1,000 increase in fixed costs and a reduction i variable cost to $9 per unit. The new production methods would result in a superior product and would enable sales to be increased to 9,750 units per annum at a price of $21 each.

If the change in production methods were to take place, the breakeven output level would be:

A   400 units higher
B   400 units lower
C   100 units higher
D   100 units lower

Answer

The correct answer is B.

	Current $	Revised $	Difference
Selling price	20	21	
Variable costs	10	9	
Contribution per unit	10	12	
Fixed costs	$29,000	$30,000	
Breakeven point (units)	2,900	2,500	400 lower

$$\text{Breakeven point (BEP)} = \frac{\text{Total fixed costs}}{\text{Contribution per unit}}$$

$$\text{Current BEP} = \frac{\$29,000}{\$10} = 2,900 \text{ units}$$

$$\text{Revised BEP} = \frac{\$30,000}{\$12} = 2,500 \text{ units}$$

6 Breakeven charts and profit/volume graphs

6.1 Breakeven charts

FAST FORWARD

The breakeven point can also be determined graphically using a **breakeven chart**.

Key term

A **breakeven chart** is a chart that indicates approximate profit or loss at different levels of sales volume within a limited range.

A breakeven chart has the following axes.

- A **horizontal** axis showing the **sales/output** (in value or units)
- A **vertical axis** showing $ for **sales revenues** and **costs**

> Although you will not be required to draw a breakeven chart in the assessment, a question may require you to identify certain points on a chart provided. Furthermore, you may need to draw a chart for a task at work, or in examinations for other subjects in the future. If you follow the description below carefully, it will provide a firm basis for your current and future understanding and interpretation of breakeven charts.

6.1.1 Lines on a breakeven chart

The following lines are drawn on the breakeven chart.

(a) The **sales line**
- Starts at the origin
- Ends at the point signifying expected sales

(b) The **fixed costs line**
- Runs parallel to the horizontal axis
- Meets the vertical axis at a point which represents total fixed costs

(c) The **total costs line**
- Starts where the fixed costs line meets the vertical axis
- Ends at the point which represents anticipated sales on the horizontal axis and total costs of anticipated sales on the vertical axis

The **breakeven point** is the **intersection** of the **sales line** and the **total costs line**.

The distance between the **breakeven point** and the **expected (or budgeted) sales**, in units, indicates the **margin of safety**.

6.1.2 Example: a breakeven chart

The budgeted annual output of a factory is 120,000 units. The fixed overheads amount to $40,000 and the variable costs are 50p per unit. The sales price is $1 per unit.

Required

Construct a breakeven chart showing the current breakeven point and profit earned up to the present maximum capacity.

Solution

We begin by calculating the profit at the budgeted annual output.

	$
Sales (120,000 units)	120,000
Variable costs	60,000
Contribution	60,000
Fixed costs	40,000
Profit	20,000

The breakeven chart is shown on the following page.

The chart is drawn as follows.

(a)   The **vertical axis** represents **money** (costs and revenue) and the **horizontal axis** represents the **level of activity** (production and sales).

(b)   The fixed costs are represented by a **straight line parallel to the horizontal axis** (in our example, at $40,000).

(c)   The **variable costs** are added 'on top of' fixed costs, to give **total costs**. It is assumed that fixed costs are the same in total and variable costs are the same per unit at all levels of output.

The line of costs is therefore a straight line and only two points need to be plotted and joined up. Perhaps the two most convenient points to plot are total costs at zero output, and total costs at the budgeted output and sales.

- At zero output, costs are equal to the amount of fixed costs only, $40,000, since there are no variable costs.

- At the budgeted output of 120,000 units, costs are $100,000.

	$
Fixed costs	40,000
Variable costs 120,000 × 50c	60,000
Total costs	100,000

(d)   The sales line is also drawn by plotting two points and joining them up.

- At zero sales, revenue is nil.
- At the budgeted output and sales of 120,000 units, revenue is $120,000.

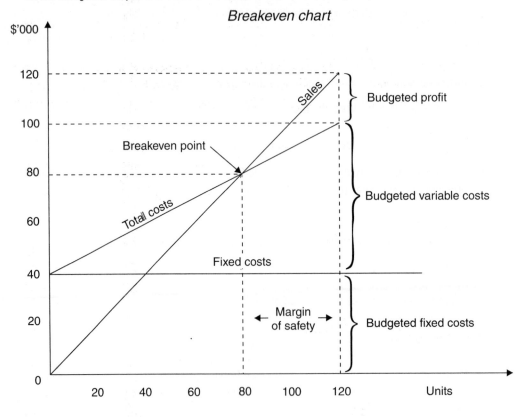

Breakeven chart

6.1.3 Interpreting the breakeven chart

The breakeven point is where total costs are matched exactly by total revenue. From the chart, this can be seen to occur at output and sales of 80,000 units, when revenue and costs are both $80,000. This breakeven point can be proved mathematically as:

$$\frac{\text{Required contribution } (= \text{fixed costs})}{\text{Contribution per unit}} = \frac{\$40,000}{50c \text{ per unit}} = 80,000 \text{ units}$$

The margin of safety can be seen on the chart as the difference between the budgeted level of activity and the breakeven level.

6.1.4 The value of breakeven charts

Breakeven charts are used as follows.

- To **plan** the production of a company's products
- To **market** a company's products
- To give a **visual display** of breakeven arithmetic

6.2 The contribution breakeven chart

T FORWARD

A **contribution breakeven chart** depicts variable costs, so that contribution can be read directly from the chart.

The main problem with the traditional breakeven chart is that it is not possible to read contribution directly from the chart.

The contribution breakeven chart remedies this by **drawing the variable cost line instead of the fixed cost line**. A contribution breakeven chart for the example in Section 6.1.2 would include the variable cost line passing through the origin and the total variable cost of $60,000 for 120,000 units. The contribution breakeven chart is shown below.

Contribution breakeven chart

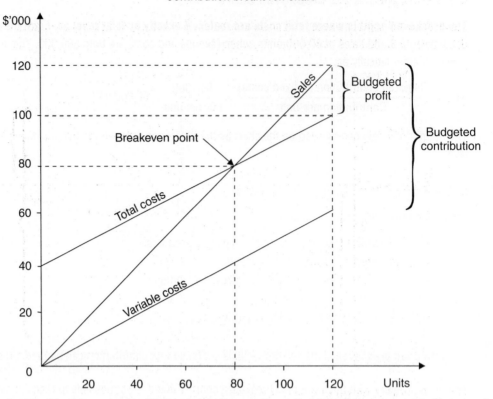

If you look back at the breakeven chart in Section 6.1.2(d) you will see that the breakeven point is the same, but that the budgeted contribution can now be read more easily from the chart.

6.3 The profit/volume (P/V) graph

The **profit/volume (P/V) graph** is a variation of the breakeven chart and illustrates the relationship of profit to sales volume.

6.3.1 Construction of a profit/volume graph

A P/V graph is constructed as follows (look at the chart in the example that follows as you read the explanation).

(a) 'P' is on the y axis and actually comprises not only 'profit' but contribution to profit (in monetary value), extending above and below the x axis with a zero point at the intersection of the two axes, and the negative section below the x axis representing fixed costs. This means that at zero production, the firm is incurring a loss equal to the fixed costs.

(b) 'V' is on the x axis and comprises either volume of sales or value of sales (revenue).

(c) The profit-volume line is a straight line drawn with its starting point (at zero production) at the intercept on the y axis representing the level of fixed costs, and with a gradient of contribution/unit (or the C/S ratio if sales value is used rather than units). The P/V line will cut the x axis at the breakeven point of sales volume. Any point on the P/V line above the x axis represents the profit to the firm (as measured on the vertical axis) for that particular level of sales.

6.3.2 Example: P/V graph

Let us draw a P/V graph for our example in Section 6.1.2. At sales of 120,000 units, total contribution will be 120,000 × $(1 − 0.5) = $60,000 and total profit will be $20,000.

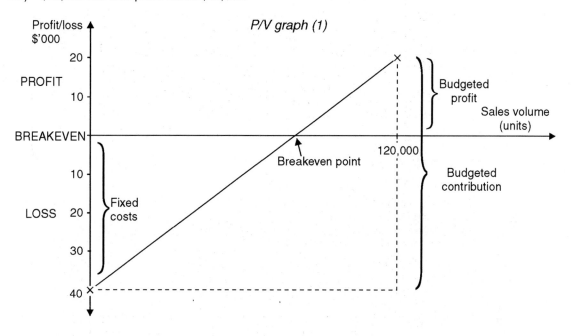

6.3.3 The advantage of the P/V graph

(a)   If the budgeted selling price of the product in our example is increased to $1.20, with the result that demand drops to 105,000 units despite additional fixed costs of $10,000 being spent on advertising, we could add a line representing this situation to our P/V chart.

(b)   At sales of 105,000 units, contribution will be 105,000 × $(1.20 − 0.50) = $73,500 and total profit will be $23,500 (fixed costs being $50,000).

(c)   The diagram shows that if the selling price is increased, the breakeven point occurs at a lower level of sales revenue (71,429 units instead of 80,000 units), although this is not a particularly large decrease when viewed in the context of the projected sales volume. It is also possible to see that for sales above 50,000 units, the profit achieved will be higher (and the loss achieved lower) if the price is $1.20. For sales volumes below 50,000 units the first option will yield lower losses.

(d)   The P/V graph is the clearest way of presenting such information; two conventional breakeven charts on one set of axes would be very confusing.

(e)   Changes in the variable cost per unit or in fixed costs at certain activity levels can also be incorporated easily into a P/V graph. The profit or loss at each point where the cost structure changes should be calculated and plotted on the graph so that the profit/volume line becomes a series of straight lines.

(f)   For example, suppose that in our example, at sales levels in excess of 120,000 units the variable cost per unit increases to $0.60 (perhaps because of overtime premiums that are incurred when production exceeds a certain level). At sales of 130,000 units, contribution would therefore be 130,000 × $(1 - 0.60) = $52,000 and total profit would be $12,000.

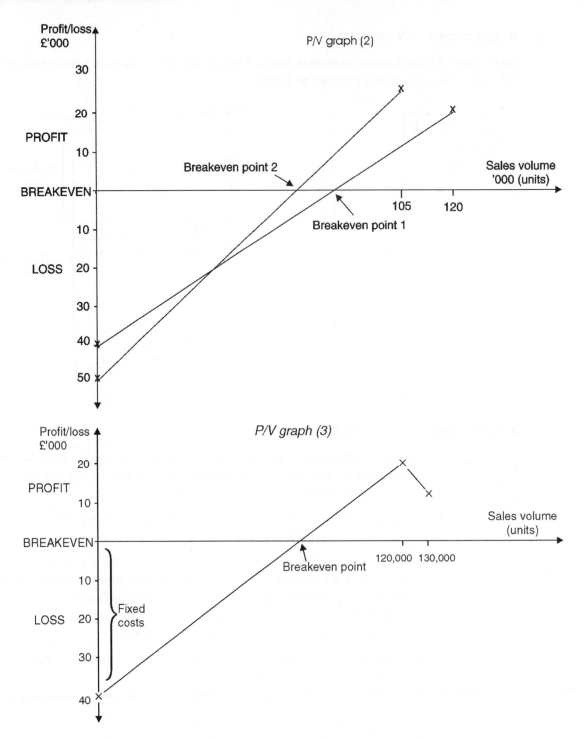

Question

Match the following labels to (a), (b), (c) and (d) marked on the breakeven chart below.

| Fixed costs | Margin of safety | Budgeted profit | Budgeted variable costs |

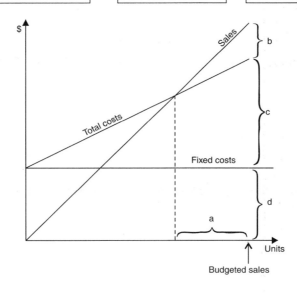

Answer

Fixed costs (d)
Margin of safety (a)
Budgeted profit (b)
Budgeted variable costs (c)

Question

G Limited

G Co manufactures and sells a single product. The profit statement for May is as follows.

	$
Sales value	80,000
Variable cost of sales	48,000
Contribution	32,000
Fixed costs	15,000
Profit	17,000

The management accountant has used the data for May to draw the following profit/volume graph.

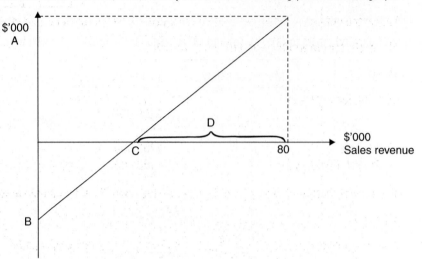

(a)   The monetary values indicated on the graph as A, B and C are:

A $ _____

B $ _____

C $ _____

(b)   The term used to describe the distance D on the graph is the _____

(c)   For the whole of the current year, G Co budgets to achieve a sales value of $900,000. Assuming that the unit variable costs and selling price achieved will be the same as that achieved during May, and that fixed costs for the year will be $180,000, the profit for the whole year will be

$ _____

(d)   The annual margin of safety for G Co's product is _____ % of budgeted sales.

Answer

(a)   **A $17,000**
B   (–$15,000)
C $37,500

Workings

A: profit achieved from $80,000 sales revenue = $17,000
B: loss at zero sales revenue = fixed costs = (–$15,000)
C: breakeven point = $37,500 sales revenue (see below)

C/S ratio = 32/80 = 40%

$$\text{Breakeven point} = \frac{\text{fixed costs}}{\text{C/S ratio}} = \frac{\$15,000}{0.4} = \$37,500 \text{ sales revenue}$$

(b)   **The term used to describe the distance D on the graph is the** | margin of safety |.

This is the difference between the sales revenue budgeted or achieved, and the revenue required to break even.

(c)   **The profit for the whole year will be $** | **180,000** |.

Workings

Contribution achieved	=	sales revenue × C/S ratio
	=	$900,000 × 0.4
	=	$360,000
Fixed costs		$180,000
∴ Profit for whole year		$180,000

(d)   **The annual margin of safety for G Co's product is** | **50** | **% of budgeted sales.**

Workings

$$\text{Annual breakeven point} = \frac{\text{fixed costs}}{\text{C/S ratio}} = \frac{\$18,000}{0.4} = \$450,000 \text{ sales revenue}$$

Margin of safety = $900,000 − $450,000   = $450,000 sales revenue
= 50% of budgeted sales

7 Limitations of breakeven analysis

ST FORWARD

Despite the **advantages** of breakeven analysis, the technique has some serious **limitations**.

CVP analysis is a useful technique for managers. It can provide **simple** and **quick** estimates, and **breakeven charts** provide a **graphical representation** of breakeven arithmetic. It does, however, have a number of limitations.

- It **can only apply to a single product** or a single mix of a group of products.
- A breakeven chart may be **time-consuming** to prepare.
- It **assumes** fixed costs are constant at all levels of output.
- It **assumes** that **variable costs** are the **same** per unit at all levels of output.
- It **assumes** that **sales prices** are **constant** at all levels of output.
- It assumes **production** and **sales** are the **same** (inventory levels are ignored).
- It **ignores** the **uncertainty** in the estimates of fixed costs and variable cost per unit.

8 Limiting factor analysis

In a **limiting factor situation**, contribution will be maximised by earning the biggest possible contribution per unit of limiting factor.

8.1 Limiting factors

One of the more common problems faced by management is a situation where there are not enough resources to meet the potential sales demand, and so a decision has to be made about what mix of products to produce, using what resources there are as effectively as possible. The resource that limits the organisation's ability to meet sales demand is called a **limiting factor** or **key factor**.

Key term

A **limiting factor** or **key factor** is 'anything which limits the activity of an entity. An entity seeks to optimise the benefit it obtains from the limiting factor. Examples are a shortage of supply of a resource or a restriction on sales demand at a particular price'.

CIMA *Official Terminology*

A **limiting factor** could be sales if there is a limit to sales demand but any one of the organisation's resources (labour, materials and so on) may be insufficient to meet the level of production demanded.

It is assumed in limiting factor analysis that management wishes to maximise profit and that **profit will be maximised when contribution is maximised** (given no change in fixed cost expenditure incurred). In other words, **marginal costing ideas are applied**.

8.2 Limiting factor situations

For example if grade A labour is the limiting factor, contribution will be maximised by earning the biggest contribution from each hour of grade A labour worked.

The limiting factor decision therefore involves the determination of **the contribution earned by each different product from each unit of the limiting factor**.

8.2.1 Example: limiting factor

AB Co makes two products, the Ay and the Be. Unit variable costs are as follows.

	Ay	Be
	$	$
Direct materials	1	3
Direct labour ($3 per hour)	6	3
Variable overhead	1	1
	8	7

The sales price per unit is $14 per Ay and $11 per Be. During July 20X2 the available direct labour is limited to 8,000 hours. Sales demand in July is expected to be 3,000 units for Ays and 5,000 units for Bes.

Required

Determine the profit-maximising production mix, assuming that monthly fixed costs are $20,000, and that opening inventories of finished goods and work in progress are nil.

Solution

Step 1 Confirm that the limiting factor is something other than sales demand.

	Ays	Bes	Total
Labour hours per unit	2 hrs	1 hr	
Sales demand	3,000 units	5,000 units	
Labour hours needed	6,000 hrs	5,000 hrs	11,000 hrs
Labour hours available			8,000 hrs
Shortfall			3,000 hrs

Labour is the limiting factor on production.

Step 2 Identify the contribution earned by each product per unit of limiting factor, that is per labour hour worked.

	Ays	Bes
	$	$
Sales price	14	11
Variable cost	8	7
Unit contribution	6	4
Labour hours per unit	2 hrs	1 hr
Contribution per labour hour (= unit of limiting factor)	$3	$4

Although Ays have a higher unit contribution than Bes, two Bes can be made in the time it takes to make one Ay. Because labour is in short supply it is more profitable to make Bes than Ays.

Step 3 Determine the **optimum production plan**. Sufficient Bes will be made to meet the full sales demand, and the remaining labour hours available will then be used to make Ays.

(a)

Product	Demand	Hours required	Hours available	Priority of manufacture
Bes	5,000	5,000	5,000	1st
Ays	3,000	6,000	3,000 (bal)	2nd
		11,000	8,000	

(b)

Product	Units	Hours needed	Contribution per unit	Total
			$	$
Bes	5,000	5,000	4	20,000
Ays	1,500	3,000	3	9,000
		8,000		29,000
Less fixed costs				20,000
Profit				9,000

Conclusion

(a) Unit contribution is *not* the correct way to decide priorities.

(b) Labour hours are the scarce resource, and therefore contribution **per labour hour** is the correct way to decide priorities.

(c) The Be earns $4 contribution per labour hour, and the Ay earns $3 contribution per labour hour. Bes therefore make more profitable use of the scarce resource, and should be manufactured first.

Assessment focus point

If an assessment question asks you to determine the optimum production plan, you might find it useful to follow the five-step approach used in the example above and shown below.

Step 1   Identify the limiting factor

Step 2   Calculate contribution per unit for each product

Step 3   Calculate contribution per unit of limiting factor

Step 4   Rank products (make product with highest contribution per unit of limiting factor first)

Step 5   Make products in rank order until scarce resource is used up **(optimal production plan)**

Question

Limiting factors

LF Co makes a single product for which the standard cost details are as follows.

	$
Direct material ($3 per kg)	12
Direct labour ($8 per hour)	72
Production overhead	18
Total production cost	102

Demand for next period will be 20,000 units. No inventories are held and only 75,000 kg of material and 190,000 hours of labour will be available. What will be the limiting factor next period?

A   Material only

B   Labour only

C   Material and labour

D   There will be no limiting factor next period

Answer

The correct answer is A.

Material required = 20,000 units × ($12/$3) = 80,000 kg

Material is therefore a limiting factor, since only 75,000 kg are available. This eliminates options B and D.

Labour required = 20,000 units × ($72/$8) = 180,000 hours.

Labour is not a limiting factor, since 190,000 labour hours are available. This eliminates option C.

Question

POV Ltd

POV Co manufactures three products - X, Y and Z - that use the same machines. The budgeted income statements for the three products are as follows:

	X	Y	Z
	$'000	$'000	$'000
Sales	1,000	1,125	625
Prime costs	(500)	(562.5)	(437.5)
Variable overheads	(250)	(187.5)	(62.5)
Fixed overheads	(200)	(315)	(130)
Profit/(loss)	50	60	(5)
Annual sales demand (units)	5,000	7,500	2,500
Machine hours per unit	20	21	26

However, after the budget had been formulated, an unforeseen condition has meant that during the next period the available machine capacity has been limited to 296,500 hours.

(a)   The shortfall in available machine hours for next period is [   ] hours

(b)   The contribution earned per machine hour used on product X is $ [   ]

(c)   The management accountant has ranked the products in order of preference for production as follows:

1st   product X
2nd   product Y
3rd   product Z

The number of units of each product that should be manufactured next period is:

(i)   Product X   [   ] units

(ii)   Product Y   [   ] units

(iii)   Product Z   [   ] units

Answer

(a)   **The shortfall in available machine hours for next period is** [**26,000**] **hours.**

Workings

Machine hours required to satisfy annual sales demand:

		Hours
Product X	5,000 units × 20 hrs	100,000
Product Y	7,500 units × 21 hrs	157,500
Product Z	2,500 units × 26 hrs	65,000
Total machine hours required		322,500
Machine hours available		296,500
Shortfall in available machine hours		26,000

(b)   **The contribution earned per machine hour used on product X is $ 2.50 .**

Workings

		$'000
Sales revenue		1,000
Prime costs		(500)
Variable overheads		(250)
Contribution		250
Contribution per unit	(÷ 5,000)	$50
Contribution per machine hour	(÷ 20)	$2.50

(c)   (i)   **Product X   5,000   units**

(ii)   **Product Y   7,500   units**

(iii)   **Product Z   1,500   units**

Workings

Ranking	Product	Demand units	Hours required	Hours available	Production units
1st	X	5,000 (× 20)	100,000	100,000	5,000
2nd	Y	7,500 (× 21)	157,500	157,500	7,500
3rd	Z	2,500 (× 26)	65,000	39,000*	1,500
				296,500	

* Balance (296,500 – 100,000 – 157,500)

Chapter Roundup

- **Breakeven analysis** or **cost-volume-profit analysis (CVP) analysis** is the study of the interrelationships between costs, volume and profits at various levels of activity.

- The **breakeven point** occurs when there is neither a profit nor a loss and so fixed costs equal contribution.

- The **C/S ratio** (or **P/V ratio**) is a measure of how much contribution is earned from each $1 of sales.

- The **margin of safety** is the difference in units between the budgeted sales volume and the breakeven sales volume. It is sometimes expressed as a percentage of the budgeted sales volume.

- The **margin of safety** is the difference in units between the budgeted sales volume and the breakeven sales volume. It is sometimes expressed as a percentage of the budgeted sales volume. Alternatively the margin of safety can be expressed as the difference between the budgeted sales revenue and breakeven sales revenue, expressed as a percentage of the budgeted sales revenue.

- At the **breakeven point,** there is no profit or loss and so **sales revenue = total costs** or **total contribution = fixed costs.**

- The **target profit** is achieved when sales revenue equals variable costs plus fixed costs plus profit. Therefore the **total contribution required** for a target profit = **fixed costs + required profit.**

- The breakeven point can also be determined graphically using a **breakeven chart**.

- A **contribution breakeven chart** depicts variable costs, so that contribution can be read directly from the chart.

- The **profit/volume (P/V) graph** is a variation of the breakeven chart and illustrates the relationship of profit to sales volume.

- Despite the **advantages** of breakeven analysis, the technique has some serious **limitations**.

- In a **limiting factor situation**, contribution will be maximised by earning the biggest possible contribution per unit of limiting factor.

Quick Quiz

1   Use the following to make up four formulae which can be used to calculate the breakeven point.

Contribution per unit
Contribution per unit
Fixed costs
Fixed costs
Contribution required to break even
Contribution required to break even
C/S ratio
C/S ratio

(a)   Breakeven point (sales units)   =   _____

or   _____

(b)   Breakeven point (sales revenue) =   _____

or   _____

2   The P/V ratio is a measure of how much profit is earned from each $1 of sales.

True   ☐

False   ☐

3   Profits are maximised at the breakeven point.

True   ☐

False   ☐

4   At the breakeven point, total contribution = ...

5   The total contribution required for a target profit = ...

6   Breakeven charts show approximate levels of profit or loss at different sales volume levels within a limited range. Which of the following are true?

I   The sales line starts at the origin
II   The fixed costs line runs parallel to the vertical axis
III   Breakeven charts have a horizontal axis showing the sales/output (in value or units)
IV   Breakeven charts have a vertical axis showing $ for revenues and costs
V   The breakeven point is the intersection of the sales line and the fixed cost line

A   I and II

B   I and III

C   I, III and IV

D   I, III, IV, and V

7   On a breakeven chart, the distance between the breakeven point and the expected (or budgeted) sales, in units, indicates the ....

8   Give seven limitations of CVP analysis.

- ....
- ....
- ....
- ....
- ....
- ....
- ....

9   When determining the optimum production plan using limiting factor analysis, what five steps are involved?

Step 1..

Step 2..

Step 3..

Step 4..

Step 5..

Answers to Quick Quiz

1   (a)   Breakeven point (sales units)   = $\dfrac{\text{Fixed costs}}{\text{Contribution per unit}}$

or $\dfrac{\text{Contribution required to break even}}{\text{Contribution per unit}}$

(b)   Breakeven point (sales revenue)   = $\dfrac{\text{Fixed costs}}{\text{C/S ratio}}$

or $\dfrac{\text{Contribution required to break even}}{\text{C/S ratio}}$

2   False. The P/V ratio is a measure of how much **contribution** is earned from each $1 of sales.

3   False. At the breakeven point there is no profit.

4   At the breakeven point, total contribution = fixed costs

5   The total contribution required for a target profit = fixed costs + required profit

6   C

7   Margin of safety

8   • It **can only apply to a single product** or a single mix of a group of products.
   • A breakeven chart may be **time-consuming** to prepare.
   • It **assumes** fixed costs are constant at all levels of output.
   • It **assumes** that **variable costs** are the **same** per unit at all levels of output.
   • It **assumes** that **sales prices** are **constant** at all levels of output.
   • It assumes **production** and **sales** are the **same** (inventory levels are ignored).
   • It **ignores** the **uncertainty** in the estimates of fixed costs and variable cost per unit.

9   **Step 1**   Identify the limiting factor

   Step 2   Calculate contribution per unit for each product

   Step 3   Calculate contribution per unit of limiting factor

   Step 4   Rank products (make product with highest contribution per unit of limiting factor first)

   Step 5   Make products in rank order until scarce resource is used up **(optimal production plan)**

Now try the questions below from the Question Bank

Question numbers	Page
26–31	351

Part C
Standard costing

Standard costing

Introduction

Just as there are **standards** for most things in our daily lives (cleanliness in hamburger restaurants, educational achievement of nine year olds, number of trains running on time), there are standards for the costs of products and services. Moreover, just as the standards in our daily lives are not always met, the standards for the costs of products and services are not always met. We will not, however, be considering the standards of cleanliness of hamburger restaurants in this chapter but we will be looking at standards for **costs**, what they are used for and how they are set.

In the next chapter we will see how **standard costing** forms the basis of a process called **variance analysis**, a vital management control tool.

Topic list	Learning outcomes	Syllabus references	Ability required
1 Standard costing	C(i), C(ii)	C(1)	Comprehension
2 Preparation of standards	C(iii)	C(2)	Application
3 Other aspects of standard costing	C(i), (ii)	C(1)	Comprehension
4 The standard hour	C(vii)	C(5)	Analysis
5 Standard labour costs and incentive schemes	C(vii)	C(5)	Analysis

1 Standard costing

Standard costing is the preparation of standard costs to value inventories/cost products and/or to use in variance analysis, a key management control tool.

1.1 Standard cost

Key term

A **standard cost** is a 'planned unit cost of a product, component or service'.

CIMA *Official Terminology*

A **standard cost card** shows full details of the standard cost of each product.

The standard variable cost of product 1234 is set out below.

STANDARD COST CARD - PRODUCT 1234

	$	$
Direct materials		
Material X – 3 kg at $4 per kg	12	
Material Y – 9 litres at $2 per litre	18	
		30
Direct labour		
Grade A – 6 hours at $7 per hour	42	
Grade B – 8 hours at $8 per hour	64	
		106
Standard direct cost		136
Variable production overhead – 14 hours at $0.50 per hour		7
Standard variable cost of production		143
Fixed production overhead – 14 hours at $4.50 per hour		63
Standard full production cost		206
Administration and marketing overhead		15
Standard cost of sale		221
Standard profit		20
Standard sales price		241

Notice how the total standard cost is built up from standards for each cost element: standard quantities of materials at standard prices, standard quantities of labour time at standard rates and so on. It is therefore determined by management's estimates of the following.

- The expected prices of materials, labour and expenses
- Efficiency levels in the use of materials and labour
- Budgeted overhead costs and budgeted volumes of activity

1.2 The uses of standard costing

Standard costing has a variety of uses but its two principal ones are as follows.

(a) To **value inventories** and **cost production** for cost accounting purposes. It is an alternative method of valuation to methods like FIFO and LIFO which we looked at in Chapter 2.

(b) To act as a **control device** by establishing standards (planned costs), highlighting (via **variance analysis** which we will cover in the next chapter) activities that are not conforming to plan and thus **alerting management** to areas which may be out of control and in need of corrective action.

Question

B Company makes one product, the J. Two types of labour are involved in the preparation of a J, skilled and semi-skilled. Skilled labour is paid $10 per hour and semi-skilled $5 per hour. Twice as many skilled labour hours as semi-skilled labour hours are needed to produce a J, four semi-skilled labour hours being needed.

A J is made up of three different direct materials. Seven kilograms of direct material A, four litres of direct material B and three metres of direct material C are needed. Direct material A costs $1 per kilogram, direct material B $2 per litre and direct material C $3 per metre.

Variable production overheads are incurred at B Company at the rate of $2.50 per direct labour (skilled) hour.

A system of absorption costing is in operation at B Company. The basis of absorption is direct labour (skilled) hours. For the forthcoming accounting period, budgeted fixed production overheads are $250,000 and budgeted production of the J is 5,000 units.

Administration, selling and distribution overheads are added to products at the rate of $10 per unit.

A mark-up of 25% is made on the J.

Required

Using the above information complete the standard cost card below for the J.

STANDARD COST CARD – PRODUCT J

	$	$
Direct materials		
Direct labour		
Standard direct cost		
Variable production overhead		
Standard variable cost of production		
Fixed production overhead		
Standard full production cost		
Administration, selling and distribution overhead		
Standard cost of sale		
Standard profit		
Standard sales price		

Answer

STANDARD COST CARD - PRODUCT J

Direct materials	$	$
A 7 kgs × $1	7	
B 4 litres × $2	8	
C 3m × $3	9	
		24

Direct labour		
Skilled – 8 × $10	80	
Semi-skilled – 4 × $5	20	
		100

Standard direct cost		124
Variable production overhead 8 × $2.50		20
Standard variable cost of production		144
Fixed production overhead 8 × $6.25 (W)		50
Standard full production cost		194
Administration, selling and distribution overhead		10
Standard cost of sale		204
Standard profit 25% × 204		51
Standard sales price		255

Working

Overhead absorption rate = $\dfrac{\$250,000}{5,000 \times 8}$ = $6.25 per skilled labour hour

1.3 Standard costing as a control technique

Key term

Standard costing is a 'control technique that reports variances by comparing actual costs to pre-set standards so facilitating action through management by exception'.
CIMA *Official Terminology*

Standard costing (for control) therefore involves the following.

- The establishment of predetermined estimates of the costs of products or services
- The collection of actual costs
- The comparison of the actual costs with the predetermined estimates.

The predetermined costs are known as **standard costs** and the difference between standard and actual cost is known as a **variance**. The process by which the total difference between standard and actual results is analysed is known as **variance analysis**.

1.4 Historical costs versus standard costs

A **focus on the future** is one of the principal **differences** between the **work of the cost and management accountant and the work of the financial accountant**.

(a) Financial accountants are concerned with ensuring that the accounting records show a true and fair view of the organisation's operations over the accounting period (say 12 months).

(b) **Cost and management accountants**, on the other hand, are not so worried about the absolute validity, accuracy and verifiability of past events and transactions. Given their focus on planning, control and decision making they are more concerned with **what is likely to happen in the future**.

That's not to say that cost and management accounting is not concerned with the past. In the **final part of this text** we will look in depth at the **basic role of costing in accumulating, classifying, recording and ascertaining both historical unit costs and historical total costs of operations**. And it is only after basic cost accounting methods and processes have provided information about the historical costs of running an organisation that, in essence, the cost and management accounting role of providing information for planning, control and decision making can begin.

Standard costing is an integral part of an organisation's system of planning and control and is based on **standard costs** that are **established in advance**, before events and transactions occur. They represent what should happen rather than what has happened.

1.5 Standard costing and management by exception

Standard costs, when established, are **average expected unit costs**. Because they are only averages and **not a rigid specification, actual results will vary to some extent above or below the average**. Standard costs can therefore be viewed as **benchmarks** for comparison purposes, and **variances** (the differences between standard costs and actual costs) should only be **reported** and investigated if there is a **significant difference** between actual and standard. The problem is in deciding whether a variation from standard should be considered significant and worthy of investigation. **Tolerance limits** can be set and only variances that exceed such limits would require investigation.

Standard costing therefore enables the principle of **management by exception** to be practised.

Key term

> **Management by exception** is the 'Practice of concentrating on activities that require attention and ignoring those which appear to be conforming to expectations. Typically standard cost variances or variances from budget are used to identify those activities that require attention.'
>
> CIMA *Official Terminology*

2 Preparation of standards

> **Standards** for each cost element are made up of a monetary component and a resources requirement component.

Standard costs may be used in both absorption costing and in marginal costing systems. We shall, however, confine our description to standard costs in marginal costing systems.

As we noted earlier, the standard cost of a product (or service) is made up of a number of different standards, one for each cost element, each of which has to be set by management.

2.1 Monetary parts of standards

2.1.1 Standard direct material prices

Direct material prices will be estimated by the purchasing department from their knowledge of the following.

- Purchase contracts already agreed
- Pricing discussions with regular suppliers
- The forecast movement of prices in the market
- The availability of bulk purchase discounts

Price inflation can cause difficulties in setting realistic standard prices. Suppose that a material costs $10 per kilogram at the moment and during the course of the next twelve months it is expected to go up in price by 20% to $12 per kilogram. What standard price should be selected?

- The current price of $10 per kilogram
- The average expected price for the year, say $11 per kilogram

Either would be possible, but neither would be entirely satisfactory.

(a)   If the **current price** were used in the standard, the reported price variance will become adverse as soon as prices go up, which might be very early in the year. If prices go up gradually rather than in one big jump, it would be difficult to select an appropriate time for revising the standard.

(b)   If an **estimated mid-year price** were used, price variances should be favourable in the first half of the year and adverse in the second half of the year, again assuming that prices go up gradually throughout the year. Management could only really check that in any month, the price variance did not become excessively adverse (or favourable) and that the price variance switched from being favourable to adverse around month six or seven and not sooner.

2.1.2 Standard direct labour rates

Direct labour rates per hour will be set by discussion with the personnel department and by reference to the payroll and to any agreements on pay rises with trade union representatives of the employees.

(a)   A separate hourly rate or weekly wage will be set for each different labour grade/type of employee.

(b)   An average hourly rate will be applied for each grade (even though individual rates of pay may vary according to age and experience).

Similar problems when dealing with inflation to those described for material prices can be met when setting labour standards.

2.2 Standard resource requirements

To estimate the materials required to make each product (**material usage**) and also the labour hours required (**labour efficiency**), **technical specifications** must be prepared for each product by production experts (either in the production department or the work study department).

(a) The **'standard product specification'** for materials must list the quantities required per unit of each material in the product. These standard input quantities must be made known to the operators in the production department so that control action by management to deal with **excess material wastage** will be understood by them.

(b) The **'standard operation sheet'** for labour will specify the expected hours required by each grade of labour in each department to make one unit of product. These standard times must be carefully set (for example by work study) and must be understood by the labour force. Where necessary, **standard procedures** or **operating methods** should be stated.

2.3 Standard variable overhead rates

Establishing the input of labour and material required for each unit of output is usually a fairly straightforward task. For example, if a unit of output requires five labour hours and each hours costs $10, the standard labour cost is $50.

It is not so easy to determine the cost of variable overhead resources per unit of output as there is no observable direct relationship between resources required and units of output. The relationship therefore has to be established using data from the past.

Variable overhead rates can be estimated by looking at **past relationships** between changes in costs and changes in activity level. The problem is in establishing which type of activity exerts the greatest influence on the cost (direct labour hours, machine hours, quantity of material used, units of output and so on).

Using one or more of a range of **statistical techniques** (including, at the basic level, the scattergraph and the hi/low method which we looked at earlier in this text), the activity measure that best explains the variations in the level of costs should be selected.

In practice, direct labour hours and machine hours are the activity measures most frequently used.

The variable overhead rate per direct labour hour (or machine hour or whatever measure is selected) is then applied to the standard labour (or machine) usage per unit to derive a standard variable overhead cost per unit of output.

2.4 Performance standards

ST FORWARD

Performance standards are used to set efficiency targets. There are four types: **ideal**, **attainable**, **current** and **basic**.

The setting of standards raises the problem of **how demanding** the standard should be. Should the standard represent perfect performance or easily attainable performance?

There are four different types of **performance standard** that an organisation could aim for.

Key terms

Ideal standards are based on the most favourable operating conditions, with no wastage, no inefficiencies, no idle time and no breakdowns. These standards are likely to have an unfavourable motivational impact, because employees will often feel that the goals are unattainable and not work so hard.

Key terms (cont'd)

Attainable standards are based on efficient (but not perfect) operating conditions. Some allowance is made for wastage, inefficiencies, machine breakdowns and fatigue. If well-set they provide a useful psychological incentive, and for this reason they should be introduced whenever possible. The consent and co-operation of employees involved in improving the standard are required.

Current standards are standards based on current working conditions (current wastage, current inefficiencies). The disadvantage of current standards is that they do not attempt to improve on current levels of efficiency, which may be poor and capable of significant improvement.

Basic standards are standards which are kept unaltered over a long period of time, and may be out-of-date. They are used to show changes in efficiency or performance over an extended time period. Basic standards are perhaps the least useful and least common type of standard in use.

2.5 Taking account of wastage, losses etc

If, during processing, the quantity of material input to the process is likely to reduce (due to wastage, evaporation and so on), the quantity input must be greater than the quantity in the finished product and a material standard must take account of this.

Suppose that the fresh raspberry juice content of a litre of Purple Pop is 100ml and that there is a 10% loss of raspberry juice during process due to evaporation. The standard material usage of raspberry juice per litre of Purple Pop will be:

$$100ml \times \frac{100\%}{(100-10)\%} = 100ml \times \frac{100\%}{90\%} = 111.11ml$$

Assessment focus point

Make sure that you understand how to account for wastage and losses etc when calculating standard costs. Assessment questions could well ask you to calculate the standard cost of a product given that there is loss due to evaporation or idle time and so on.

Question   **Standard labour costs**

A unit of product X requires 24 active labour hours for completion. It is anticipated that there will be 20% idle time which is to be incorporated into the standard times for all products. If the wage rate is $10 per hour, what is the standard labour cost of one unit of product X?

A $192   B $240   C $288   D $300

Answer

The correct answer is D.

The basic labour cost for 24 hours is $240. However with idle time it will be necessary to pay for more than 24 hours in order to achieve 24 hours of actual work Therefore options A and B are incorrect.

Standard labour cost = active hours for completion $\times \dfrac{125}{100} \times$ $10 = 24 \times 1.25 \times$ $10 = $300

Option C is incorrect because it results from simply adding an extra 20 per cent to the labour hours. However the idle hours are 20 per cent of the *total* hours worked, therefore we need to add 25 per cent to the required active hours, as shown in the working.

BPP
PROFESSIONAL EDUCATION

3 Other aspects of standard costing

FORWARD

There are a number of **advantages** and **disadvantages** of standard costing.

3.1 Problems in setting standards

(a) Deciding how to incorporate **inflation** into planned unit costs

(b) Agreeing on a **performance standard** (attainable or ideal)

(c) Deciding on the **quality** of materials to be used (a better quality of material will cost more, but perhaps reduce material wastage)

(d) Estimating materials **prices** where seasonal price variations or bulk purchase discounts may be significant

(e) Finding sufficient **time** to construct accurate standards as standard setting can be a **time-consuming process**

(f) Incurring the **cost of setting up and maintaining a system** for establishing standards

(g) Dealing with possible **behavioural problems**, managers responsible for the achievement of standards possibly resisting the use of a standard costing control system for fear of being blamed for any adverse variances

3.1.1 Standard costing and inflation

Note that standard costing is most difficult in times of inflation but it is still worthwhile.

(a) **Usage** and **efficiency** variances will still be meaningful.

(b) **Inflation is measurable**: there is no reason why its effects cannot be removed from the variances reported.

(c) Standard costs can be **revised** so long as this is **not done too frequently**.

3.2 The advantages of standard costing

(a) Carefully planned standards are an **aid to more accurate budgeting**.

(b) Standard costs provide a **yardstick** against which actual costs can be measured.

(c) The **setting of standards** involves determining the best materials and methods which may lead to **economies**.

(d) A **target of efficiency** is set for employees to reach and **cost consciousness** is stimulated.

(e) Variances can be calculated which enable the principle of '**management by exception**' to be operated. Only the variances which exceed acceptable tolerance limits need to be investigated by management with a view to control action.

(f) Standard costs **simplify the process of bookkeeping** in cost accounting, because they are easier to use than LIFO, FIFO and weighted average costs.

(g) Standard times **simplify the process of production scheduling**.

(h) Standard performance levels might provide an **incentive for individuals** to achieve targets for themselves at work.

3.3 The applicability of standard costing

Standard costing systems can be **adapted** to remain useful in the modern business environment.

3.3.1 Criticisms of standard costing

Critics of standard costing have argued that standard costing is not appropriate in the modern business environment.

(a)   The use of standard costing relies on the existence of **repetitive operations** and relatively **homogeneous** output. Nowadays many organisations are forced continually to respond to customers' changing requirements, with the result that output and operations are not so repetitive.

(b)   Standard costing systems were developed when the business environment was more stable and less prone to **change**. The current business environment is more dynamic and it is not possible to assume stable conditions.

(c)   Standard costing systems assume that performance to standard is acceptable. Today's business environment is more focused on **continuous improvement**.

(d)   Standard costing was developed in an environment of predominantly **mass production** and **repetitive assembly work**. It is not particularly useful in today's growing **service sector** of the economy.

3.3.2 Using standard costing today

This long list of criticisms of standard costing may lead you to believe that such systems have little use in today's business environment. However standard costing systems can be adapted to remain useful.

(a)   Even when output is not standardised, it may be possible to identify a number of **standard components and activities** whose costs may be controlled effectively by the setting of standard costs and identification of variances.

(b)   The use of computer power enables standards to be **updated rapidly** and more frequently, so that they remain useful for the purposes of control by comparison.

(c)   The use of **ideal standards** and more demanding performance levels can combine the benefits of **continuous improvement** and standard costing control.

(d)   Standard costing can be applied in **service industries**, where a **measurable cost unit** can be established. For example it is possible to set a standard cost for the following.

- Transport cost per tonne-mile
- Laundry cost per hotel room night
- Cost per chargeable consultant hour
- Cost per equivalent full time student
- Cost per medical examination

4 The standard hour

FORWARD

The **standard hour** can be used to overcome the problem of how to measure output when a number of dissimilar products are manufactured.

4.1 Example: standard hour

S Co manufactures plates, mugs and eggcups. Production during the first two quarters of 20X5 was as follows.

	Quarter 1	Quarter 2
Plates	1,000	800
Mugs	1,200	1,500
Eggcups	800	900

The fact that 3,000 products were produced in quarter 1 and 3,200 in quarter 2 does not tell us anything about S Co's performance over the two periods because plates, mugs and eggcups are so different. The fact that the production mix has changed is not revealed by considering the total number of units produced. This is where the concept of the standard hour is useful.

The standard hour (or standard minute) is the **amount of work achievable, at standard efficiency levels, in an hour or minute.**

(a) The standard time allowed to produce one unit of each of S Co's products is as follows.

	Standard time
Plate	½ hour
Mug	$1/_3$ hour
Eggcup	¼ hour

(b) By measuring the standard hours of output in each quarter, a more useful output measure is obtained.

		Quarter 1		Quarter 2	
Product	Standard hours per unit	Production	Standard hours	Production	Standard hours
Plate	½	1,000	500	800	400
Mug	$1/_3$	1,200	400	1,500	500
Eggcup	¼	800	200	900	225
			1,100		1,125

The output level in the two quarters was therefore very similar.

5 Standard labour costs and incentive schemes

ST FORWARD

Bonus/incentive schemes often incorporate labour standards as targets.

5.1 Remuneration methods

(a) **Time-based systems**. These are based on the principle of paying an employee for the hours attended, regardless of the amount of work achieved (wages = hours worked × rate of pay per hour).

- Overtime premium = **extra** rate per hour for hours over and above the basic hours.
- Quality of output is more important than quantity of output.
- There is no incentive for improvements in employee performance.

(b)   **Piecework systems**. Here the employee is paid according to the output achieved (wages = units produced × rate of pay per unit).

(c)   **Incentive/bonus schemes**. There are a variety of these schemes, all of which are designed to encourage workers to be more productive.

We're going to be looking at piecework systems and incentive/bonus schemes and how standard labour costs can be used in them.

5.2 Piecework schemes

5.2.1 Straight piece rate schemes

A type of scheme where the employee is paid a constant rate per unit of output is called a straight piece rate scheme.

Suppose for example, an employee is paid $1 for each unit produced and works a 40 hour week. Production overhead is added at the rate of $2 per direct labour hour.

Weekly production	Pay (40 hours)	Overhead	Conversion cost	Conversion cost per unit
Units	$	$	$	$
40	40	80	120	3.00
50	50	80	130	2.60
60	60	80	140	2.33
70	70	80	150	2.14

As his output increases, his wage increases and at the same time unit costs of output are reduced.

These schemes can be unfair to employees if there are production problems, therefore many piecework schemes offer a **guaranteed minimum wage**, so that employees do not suffer loss of earnings when production is low through no fault of their own.

5.2.2 Schemes with standard time allowances

If an employee makes several different types of product, it may not be possible to add up the units for payment purposes. Instead, a **standard time allowance** is given for each unit to arrive at a total of piecework hours for payment.

For example, suppose an employee is paid $8 per piecework hour produced. In a 40 hour week he produces the following output.

		Piecework time allowed per unit
15 units of product X		0.5 hours
20 units of product Y		2.0 hours

Piecework hours produced are as follows.

Product X	15 × 0.5 hours	7.5 hours
Product Y	20 × 2.0 hours	40.0 hours
Total piecework hours		47.5 hours

Therefore employee's pay = 47.5 × $8 = $380 for the week.

5.2.3 Differential piecework schemes

Differential piecework schemes offer an incentive to employees to increase their output by paying higher rates for increased levels of production. For example:

up to and including 80 units, rate of pay per unit in this band	= $1.00
81 to 90 units, rate of pay per unit in this band	= $1.20
above 90 units, rate of pay per unit in this band	= $1.30

An employee producing 97 units would therefore receive (80 × $1.00) + (10 × $1.20) + (7 × $1.30) = $101.10.

Employers should obviously be careful to make it clear whether they intend to pay the increased rate on all units produced, or on the extra output only.

5.2.4 Piecework schemes – advantages and disadvantages

- They enjoy fluctuating popularity.
- They are occasionally used by employers as a means of increasing pay levels.
- They are frequently condemned as a means of driving employees to work too hard to earn a satisfactory wage.
- Careful inspection of output is necessary to ensure that quality is maintained as production increases.

Question   **Remuneration schemes**

Match the descriptions of remuneration schemes to the graphs below.

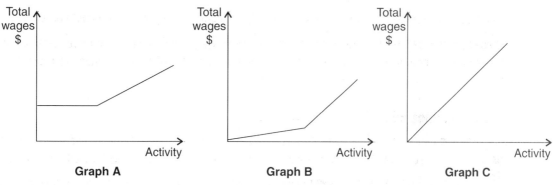

Descriptions

(a) A basic hourly rate is paid for hours worked, with an overtime premium payable for hours worked in excess of 35 per week.

(b) A straight piecework scheme is operated.

(c) A straight piecework scheme is operated, with a minimum guaranteed weekly wage.

Answer

(a) Graph B
(b) Graph C
(c) Graph A

5.3 Bonus/incentive schemes

In general, bonus schemes were introduced to compensate workers paid under a time-based system for their inability to increase earnings by working more efficiently. Various types of incentive and bonus schemes have been devised which encourage greater productivity. The characteristics of such schemes are as follows.

(a)   A target is set and actual performance is compared with target. Here is where we see the **role of standard labour costs**.

(b)   Employees are paid more for their efficiency.

(c)   In spite of the extra labour cost, the unit cost of output is reduced and the profit earned per unit of sale is increased; in other words the profits arising from productivity improvements are shared between employer and employee.

(d)   Morale of employees should be expected to improve since they are seen to receive extra reward for extra effort.

5.3.1 Conditions for successful operation of incentive schemes

Whatever scheme is used, it must satisfy certain conditions to operate successfully.

(a)   Its **objectives** should be **clearly stated** and **attainable** by the employees.

(b)   The **rules** and conditions of the scheme should be **easy to understand** and not liable to be misinterpreted.

(c)   It must win the full **acceptance** of everyone concerned including, of course, trade union negotiators and officials.

(d)   It should be seen to be **fair to employees and employers**. Other groups of employees should not feel unjustly excluded from the scheme, as their work might be affected by their dissatisfaction.

(e)   The bonus should ideally be **paid soon after the extra effort has been made** by the employees, to associate the ideas of effort and reward.

(f)   **Allowances** should be made for external factors outside the employees' control which reduce their productivity such as machine breakdowns or raw materials shortages.

(g)   Only those employees who make the extra effort should be rewarded. It would not be an incentive, for example, to institute a scheme in all factories in a country-wide organisation and to pay a productivity bonus to employees in London for work done by employees in a factory in the North of England (especially if these North of England employees fail to get an adequate bonus for their efforts as a result of this sharing).

(h)   The scheme must be **properly communicated** to employees.

5.3.2 Types of incentive schemes

There are many possible types of incentive scheme. Some organisations employ a variety of incentive schemes. A scheme for a production labour force may not necessarily be appropriate for clerical workers. An organisation's incentive schemes may be regularly reviewed, and altered as circumstances dictate.

(a)   A **high day-rate system** is an incentive scheme where employees are paid a high hourly wage rate in the expectation that they will work more efficiently than similar employees on a lower hourly rate in a different company.

(b)   Under an **individual bonus scheme**, individual employees qualify for a bonus on top of their basic wage, with each person's bonus being calculated separately.

(c)   Where individual effort cannot be measured, and employees work as a team, an individual incentive scheme is impractical but a **group bonus scheme** is feasible.

(d)   In a **profit sharing scheme**, employees receive a certain proportion of their company's year-end profits (the size of their bonus being related to their position in the company and the length of their employment to date).

(e)   Companies operating **incentive schemes involving shares** use their shares, or the right to acquire them, as a form of incentive.

5.3.3 Example: incentive schemes

EF Co manufactures a single product. Its work force consists of 10 employees, who work a 36-hour week exclusive of lunch and tea breaks. The standard time required to make one unit of the product is two hours, but the current efficiency (or productivity) ratio being achieved is 80%. No overtime is worked, and the work force is paid $8 per attendance hour.

Because of agreements with the work force about work procedures, there is some unavoidable idle time due to bottlenecks in production, and about four hours per week per person are lost in this way.

The company can sell all the output it manufactures, and makes a 'cash profit' of $40 per unit sold, after deducting currently achievable costs of production but *before* deducting labour costs.

An incentive scheme is proposed whereby the work force would be paid $10 per hour in exchange for agreeing to new work procedures that would reduce idle time per employee per week to two hours and also raise the efficiency ratio to 90%. Evaluate the incentive scheme from the point of view of profitability.

Solution

The current situation

Hours in attendance $10 \times 36 = 360$ hours

Hours spent working $10 \times 32 = 320$ hours

Units produced, at 80% efficiency $\dfrac{320}{2} \times \dfrac{80}{100} = 128$ units

	$
Cash profits before deducting labour costs (128 × $40)	5,120
Less labour costs ($8 × 360 hours)	2,880
Net profit	2,240

The incentive scheme

Hours spent working $10 \times 34 = 340$ hours

Units produced, at 90% efficiency $\dfrac{340}{2} \times \dfrac{90}{100} = 153$ units

	$
Cash profits before deducting labour costs (153 × $40)	6,120
Less labour costs ($10 × 360)	3,600
Net profit	2,520

In spite of a 25% increase in labour costs, profits would rise by $280 per week. The company and the workforce would both benefit provided, of course, that management can hold the work force to their promise of work reorganisation and improved productivity.

Question

The following data relate to work at a certain factory.

Normal working day	8 hours
Basic rate of pay per hour	$6
Standard time allowed to produce 1 unit	2 minutes
Premium bonus	75% of time saved at basic rate

What will be the labour cost in a day when 340 units are made?

   A $48   B $51   C $63   D $68

Answer

The correct answer is C.

Standard time for 340 units (× 2 minutes)	680 minutes
Actual time (8 hours per day)	480 minutes
Time saved	200 minutes

	$
Bonus = 75% × 200 minutes × $6 per hour	15
Basic pay = 8 hours × $6	48
Total labour cost	63

Using basic MCQ technique you can eliminate option A because this is simply the basic pay without consideration of any bonus. You can also eliminate option D, which is based on the standard time allowance without considering the basic pay for the eight-hour day. Hopefully you were not forced to guess, but had you been you would have had a 50% chance of selecting the correct answer (B or C) instead of a 25% chance because you were able to eliminate two of the options straightaway.

Assessment focus point

If an assessment question requires you to calculate labour costs with a bonus system, you must read the description of the system carefully and use the data supplied to calculate the required cost.

Chapter Roundup

- **Standard costing** is the preparation of standard costs to value inventories/cost products and/or to use in variance analysis, a key management control tool.

- **Standards** for each cost element are made up of a monetary component and a resources requirement component.

- **Performance standards** are used to set efficiency targets. There are four types: **ideal, attainable, current and basic**.

- There are a number of **advantages** and **disadvantages** of standard costing.

- Standard costing systems can be **adapted** to remain useful in the modern business environment.

- The **standard hour** can be used to overcome the problem of how to measure output when a number of dissimilar products are manufactured.

- **Bonus/incentive schemes** often incorporate labour standards as targets.

Quick Quiz

1   *Choose the correct words from those highlighted.*

    A standard cost is a **planned/historical unit/total** cost.

2   The only use of standard costing is to value inventory.

    True   ☐

    False   ☐

3   A control technique which compares standard costs and revenues with actual results to obtain variances which are used to stimulate improved performance is known as:

    A   Standard costing
    B   Variance analysis
    C   Budgetary control
    D   Budgeting

4   Standard costs may only be used in absorption costing.

    True   ☐

    False   ☐

5   Four types of performance standard are

    (a)   …………………………..
    (b)   …………………………..
    (c)   …………………………..
    (d)   …………………………..

6   The formula for standard material cost per unit = …………………………

7   List three problems in setting standards.

    (a)   ……………………………………………
    (b)   ……………………………………………
    (c)   ……………………………………………

8   The standard time per unit of product W is five hours. Ten employees work a 40-hour week. Idle time is two hours per employee per week. Efficiency levels are 125%.

    The weekly output is ☐ units.

Answers to Quick Quiz

1   A standard cost is a **planned unit** cost.

2   False. It has a number of uses including:

  (a)   To value inventory and cost production for cost accounting purposes.

  (b)   To act as a control device by establishing standards and highlighting activities that are not conforming to plan and bringing these to the attention of management.

3   A

4   False

5   (a)   Ideal
  (b)   Attainable
  (c)   Current
  (d)   Basic

6   Standard material cost per unit = standard material usage × standard material price

7   (a)   Deciding how to incorporate **inflation** into planned unit costs

  (b)   Agreeing on a **performance standard** (attainable or ideal)

  (c)   Deciding on the **quality** of materials to be used (a better quality of material will cost more, but perhaps reduce material wastage)

  (d)   Estimating materials **prices** where seasonal price variations or bulk purchase discounts may be significant

  (e)   Finding sufficient **time** to construct accurate standards as standard setting can be a **time-consuming process**

  (f)   Incurring the **cost of setting up and maintaining a system** for establishing standards

  (g)   Dealing with possible **behavioural problems**, managers responsible for the achievement of standards possibly resisting the use of a standard costing control system for fear of being blamed for any adverse variances

8   Active hours = (40 − 2) × 10 = 380

  Units produced = 380/5 × 125% = $\boxed{95}$ units

Now try the questions below from the Question Bank

Question numbers	Page
32-36	353

Variance analysis I

Introduction

The actual results achieved by an organisation during a reporting period (week, month, quarter, year) will, more than likely, be different from the expected results (the expected results being the standard costs and revenues which we looked at in the previous chapter). Such differences may occur between individual items, such as the cost of labour and the volume of sales, and between the total expected contribution and the total actual contribution.

Management will have spent considerable time and trouble setting standards. Actual results have differed from the standards. The wise manager will consider the differences that have occurred and use the results of these considerations to assist in attempts to attain the standards. The wise manager will use **variance analysis** as a method of **control**.

This chapter examines **variance analysis** and sets out the method of calculating the following variances.

- Direct material variances
- Direct labour variances
- Variable overhead variances

We will then go on to look at the reasons for cost variances.

Chapter 7 of this Study Text will build on the basics set down in this chapter by introducing, among other things, sales variances and operating statements.

Topic list	Learning outcomes	Syllabus references	Ability required
1 Variances	C(iv)	C(3)	Application
2 Direct material variances	C(iv)	C(3)	Application
3 Direct labour variances	C(iv)	C(3)	Application
4 Variable overhead variances	C(iv)	C(3)	Application
5 The reasons for cost variances	C(vi)	C(3)	Analysis

1 Variances

FAST FORWARD

Variances measure the difference between actual results and expected results. The process by which the total difference between standard and actual results is analysed is known as **variance analysis**.

Key terms

A **variance** is 'the difference between a planned, budgeted, or standard cost and the actual cost incurred. The same comparisons may be made for revenues.'

Variance analysis is defined as the 'evaluation of performance by means of variances, whose timely reporting should maximise the opportunity for managerial action'.

CIMA *Official Terminology*

When actual results are better than expected results, we have a **favourable variance** (F). If, on the other hand, actual results are worse than expected results, we have an **adverse variance** (A).

2 Direct material variances

Key term

The **direct labour total variance** is the 'measurement of the difference between the standard material cost of the output produced and the actual material cost incurred'. CIMA *Official Terminology*

FAST FORWARD

The **direct material total variance** (the difference between what the output actually cost and what it should have cost, in terms of material) can be divided into the **direct material price variance** and the **direct material usage variance**.

(a) **The direct material price variance**

This is the **difference between the standard cost and the actual cost for the actual quantity of material used or purchased.** In other words, it is the difference between what the material did cost and what it should have cost.

Key term

The **direct material price variance** is the 'difference between the actual price paid for the purchased materials and their standard cost'. CIMA *Official Terminology*

(b) **The direct material usage variance**

This is the **difference between the standard quantity of materials that should have been used for the number of units actually produced, and the actual quantity of materials used, valued at the standard cost per unit of material.** In other words, it is the difference between how much material should have been used and how much material was used, valued at standard cost.

Key term

The **direct material usage variance** 'measures efficiency in the use of material, by comparing standard material usage for actual production with actual material used, the difference is valued at standard cost'. CIMA *Official Terminology*

2.1 Example: direct material variances

Product X has a standard direct material cost as follows.

10 kilograms of material Y at $10 per kilogram = $100 per unit of X.

During period 4, 1,000 units of X were manufactured, using 11,700 kilograms of material Y which cost $98,600.

Required

Calculate the following variances.

(a)   The direct material total variance
(b)   The direct material price variance
(c)   The direct material usage variance

Solution

(a)   **The direct material total variance**

This is the difference between what 1,000 units should have cost and what they did cost.

	$
1,000 units should have cost (× $100)	100,000
but did cost	98,600
Direct material total variance	1,400 (F)

The variance is **favourable** because the units cost less than they should have cost.

Now we can break down the direct material total variance into its two constituent parts: the direct material **price** variance and the direct material **usage** variance.

(b)   **The direct material price variance**

This is the difference between what 11,700 kgs should have cost and what 11,700 kgs did cost.

	$
11,700 kgs of Y should have cost (× $10)	117,000
but did cost	98,600
Material Y price variance	18,400 (F)

The variance is **favourable** because the material cost less than it should have.

(c)   **The direct material usage variance**

This is the difference between how many kilograms of Y should have been used to produce 1,000 units of X and how many kilograms were used, valued at the standard cost per kilogram.

1,000 units should have used (× 10 kgs)	10,000 kgs
but did use	11,700 kgs
Usage variance in kgs	1,700 kgs (A)
× standard cost per kilogram	× $10
Usage variance in $	$17,000 (A)

The variance is **adverse** because more material was used than should have been used.

(d)   **Summary**

	$
Price variance	18,400 (F)
Usage variance	17,000 (A)
Total variance	1,400 (F)

2.2 Materials variances and opening and closing inventory

Suppose that a company uses raw material P in production, and that this raw material has a standard price of $3 per metre. During one month 6,000 metres are bought for $18,600, and 5,000 metres are used in production. At the end of the month, inventory will have been increased by 1,000 metres. In variance analysis, the problem is to decide the **material price variance**. Should it be calculated on the basis of **materials purchased** (6,000 metres) or on the basis of **materials used** (5,000 metres)? The answer to this problem depends on how **closing inventories** of the raw materials will be valued.

(a)   If closing inventories of raw materials are valued at **standard cost**, (1,000 units at $3 per unit) the price variance is calculated on material **purchases** in the period.

(b)   If closing inventories of raw materials are valued at **actual cost** (FIFO) (1,000 units at $3.10 per unit) the price variance is calculated on materials **used in production** in the period.

2.3 When to calculate the direct material price variance

Since material inventories are usually valued at **standard cost** in a standard costing system, direct material price variances are usually extracted at the time of **receipt** of the materials, rather than at the time of usage.

A **full standard costing system** is usually in operation and therefore the price variance is usually calculated on **purchases** in the period. The variance on the full 6,000 metres will be written off to the costing income statement, even though only 5,000 metres are included in the cost of production.

There are two main advantages in extracting the material price variance at the time of **receipt**.

(a)   If variances are extracted at the time of receipt they will be **brought to the attention of managers earlier** than if they are extracted as the material is used. If it is necessary to correct any variances then management action can be more timely.

(b)   Since variances are extracted at the time of receipt, **all inventories will be valued at standard price**. This is administratively easier and it means that all issues from inventories can be made at standard price. If inventories are held at actual cost it is necessary to calculate a separate price variance on each batch as it is issued. Since issues are usually made in a number of small batches this can be a time-consuming task, especially with a manual system.

2.3.1 Calculation of the direct material price variance

The price variance would be calculated as follows.

	$
6,000 metres of material P purchased should cost (× $3)	18,000
but did cost	18,600
Price variance	600 (A)

Question

Select the correct words in each of the following sentences.

(a)   If material inventories are valued at standard cost, the material price variance should be based on the materials **purchased/used** in the period.

(b)   If material inventories are valued at actual cost, the material price variance should be based on the materials **purchased/used** in the period.

Answer

(a)   purchased
(b)   used

3 Direct labour variances

The calculation of **direct labour variances** is very similar to the calculation of direct material variances.

> **FORWARD**
>
> The **direct labour total variance** (the difference between what the output should have cost and what it did cost, in terms of labour) can be divided into the **direct labour rate variance** and the **direct labour efficiency variance**.

Key term

> The **direct labour total variance** 'indicates the difference between the standard direct labour cost of the output which has been produced and the actual direct labour cost incurred'. CIMA *Official Terminology*

(a)   **The direct labour rate variance**

This is similar to the direct material price variance. It is the **difference between the standard cost and the actual cost for the actual number of hours paid for**.

In other words, it is the difference between what the labour did cost and what it should have cost.

Key term

> The **direct labour rate variance** 'indicates the actual cost of any change from the standard labour rate of remuneration'. CIMA *Official Terminology*

(b)   **The direct labour efficiency variance**

This is similar to the direct material usage variance. It is the **difference between the hours that should have been worked for the number of units actually produced, and the actual number of hours worked, valued at the standard rate per hour**.

In other words, it is the difference between how many hours should have been worked and how many hours were worked, valued at the standard rate per hour.

Key term

> The **direct labour efficiency variance** is the 'standard labour cost of any change from the standard level of labour efficiency'. CIMA *Official Terminology*

3.1 Example: direct labour variances

The standard direct labour cost of product X is as follows.

> 2 hours of grade Z labour at $5 per hour = $10 per unit of product X.

During period 4, 1,000 units of product X were made, and the direct labour cost of grade Z labour was $8,900 for 2,300 hours of work.

Required

Calculate the following variances.

(a) The direct labour total variance
(b) The direct labour rate variance
(c) The direct labour efficiency (productivity) variance

Solution

(a) **The direct labour total variance**

This is the difference between what 1,000 units should have cost and what they did cost.

	$
1,000 units should have cost (× $10)	10,000
but did cost	8,900
Direct labour total variance	1,100 (F)

The variance is **favourable** because the units cost less than they should have done.

Again we can analyse this total variance into its two constituent parts.

(b) **The direct labour rate variance**

This is the difference between what 2,300 hours should have cost and what 2,300 hours did cost.

	$
2,300 hours of work should have cost (× $5 per hr)	11,500
but did cost	8,900
Direct labour rate variance	2,600 (F)

The variance is **favourable** because the labour cost less than it should have cost.

(c) **The direct labour efficiency variance**

1,000 units of X should have taken (× 2 hrs)	2,000 hrs
but did take	2,300 hrs
Efficiency variance in hours	300 hrs (A)
× standard rate per hour	× $5
Efficiency variance in $	$1,500 (A)

The variance is **adverse** because more hours were worked than should have been worked.

(d) **Summary**

	$
Rate variance	2,600 (F)
Efficiency variance	1,500 (A)
Total variance	1,100 (F)

3.2 Idle time variance

If idle time arises, it is usual to calculate a separate **idle time variance**, and to base the calculation of the efficiency variance on **active hours** (when labour actually worked) only. It is always an **adverse** variance.

The **direct labour idle time variance** 'occurs when the hours paid exceed the hours worked and there is an extra cost caused by this idle time. Its computation increases the accuracy of the labour efficiency variance'.

CIMA *Official Terminology*

A company may operate a costing system in which any **idle time** is recorded. Idle time may be caused by machine breakdowns or not having work to give to employees, perhaps because of bottlenecks in production or a shortage of orders from customers. When idle time occurs, the labour force is still paid wages for time at work, but no actual work is done. Time paid for without any work being done is unproductive and therefore inefficient. In variance analysis, **idle time is always an adverse efficiency variance**.

When idle time is recorded separately, it is helpful to provide control information which identifies the cost of idle time separately, and in variance analysis, there will be an idle time variance **as a separate part of the total labour efficiency variance**. The remaining efficiency variance will then relate only to the productivity of the labour force during the hours spent **actively working**.

3.2.1 Example: labour variances with idle time

Refer to the standard cost data in Section 3.1. During period 5, 1,500 units of product X were made and the cost of grade Z labour was $17,500 for 3,080 hours. During the period, however, there was a shortage of customer orders and 100 hours were recorded as idle time.

Required

Calculate the following variances.

(a) The direct labour total variance
(b) The direct labour rate variance
(c) The idle time variance
(d) The direct labour efficiency variance

Solution

(a) **The direct labour total variance**

	$
1,500 units of product X should have cost (× $10)	15,000
but did cost	17,500
Direct labour total variance	2,500 (A)

Actual cost is greater than standard cost. The variance is therefore **adverse**.

(b)   **The direct labour rate variance**

The rate variance is a comparison of what the hours paid should have cost and what they did cost.

	$
3,080 hours of grade Z labour should have cost (× $5)	15,400
but did cost	17,500
Direct labour rate variance	2,100 (A)

Actual cost is greater than standard cost. The variance is therefore **adverse**.

(c)   **The idle time variance**

The idle time variance is the hours of idle time, valued at the standard rate per hour.

Idle time variance = 100 hours (A) × $5 = $500 (A)

Idle time is **always** an adverse variance.

(d)   **The direct labour efficiency variance**

The efficiency variance considers the hours actively worked (the difference between hours paid for and idle time hours). In our example, there were (3,080 – 100) = 2,980 hours when the labour force was not idle. The variance is calculated by taking the amount of output produced (1,500 units of product X) and comparing the time it should have taken to make them, with the actual time spent **actively** making them (2,980 hours). Once again, the variance in hours is valued at the **standard rate per labour hour.**

1,500 units of product X should take (× 2hrs)	3,000 hrs
but did take (3,080 – 100)	2,980 hrs
Direct labour efficiency variance in hours	20 hrs (F)
× standard rate per hour	× $5
Direct labour efficiency variance in $	$100 (F)

(e)   **Summary**

	$
Direct labour rate variance	2,100 (A)
Idle time variance	500 (A)
Direct labour efficiency variance	100 (F)
Direct labour total variance	2,500 (A)

Important!

> Remember that, if idle time is recorded, the actual hours used in the efficiency variance calculation are the **active hours worked and not the hours paid for**.

Question Variances

Growler Co is planning to make 100,000 units per period of product AA. Each unit of AA should require 2 hours to produce, with labour being paid $11 per hour. Attainable work hours are less than clock hours, so 250,000 hours have been budgeted in the period.

Actual data for the period was:

Units produced	120,000
Direct labour cost	$3,200,000
Clock hours	280,000

(a)   The labour rate variance is $ ☐

(b)   The labour efficiency variance is $ ☐

(c)   The idle time variance is $ ☐

Answer

(a)   The labour rate variance is $ 120 (A)

(b)   The labour efficiency variance is $ 176,000 (F)

(c)   The idle time variance is $ 616,000 (A)

Workings

The information means that clock hours have to be multiplied by $\dfrac{200,000}{250,000}$ (80%) in order to arrive at a realistic efficiency variance.

(a)   **Labour rate variance**

	$'000
280,000 hours should have cost (× $11)	3,080
but did cost	3,200
Labour rate variance	120 (A)

(b)   **Labour efficiency variance**

120,000 units should have taken (× 2 hours)	240,000 hrs
but did take (280,000 × 80%)	224,000 hrs
	16,000 hrs (F)
	× $11
Labour efficiency variance	$176,000 (F)

(c)   **Idle time variance**

280,000 × 20%	56,000 hrs
	× $11
	$616,000 (A)

4 Variable overhead variances

The **variable overhead total variance** can be subdivided into the variable overhead **expenditure variance** and the variable overhead **efficiency variance** (**based on active hours**).

Key terms

The **variable production overhead total variance** 'measures the difference between variable overhead that should be used for actual output and variable production overhead actually used'.

The **variable production overhead expenditure variance** 'indicates the actual cost of any change from the standard rate per hour'.

The **variable production overhead efficiency variance** is the 'standard variable overhead cost of any change from the standard level of efficiency'.

CIMA *Official Terminology*

4.1 Example: variable overhead variances

Suppose that the variable production overhead cost of product X is as follows.

2 hours at $1.50 = $3 per unit

During period 6, 400 units of product X were made. The labour force worked 820 hours, of which 60 hours were recorded as idle time. The variable overhead cost was $1,230.

Calculate the following variances.

(a)   The variable production overhead total variance
(b)   The variable production overhead expenditure variance
(c)   The variable production overhead efficiency variance

Since this example relates to variable production costs, the total variance is based on actual units of production. (If the overhead had been a variable selling cost, the variance would be based on sales volumes.)

	$
400 units of product X should cost (× $3)	1,200
but did cost	1,230
Variable production overhead total variance	30 (A)

4.2 Subdividing the variable overhead total variance

In many variance reporting systems, the variance analysis goes no further, and expenditure and efficiency variances are not calculated. However, the adverse variance of $30 may be explained as the sum of two factors.

(a)   The hourly rate of spending on variable production overheads was higher than it should have been, that is there is an **expenditure variance**.

(b)   The labour force worked inefficiently, and took longer to make the output than it should have done. This means that spending on variable production overhead was higher than it should have been, in other words there is an **efficiency (productivity) variance**. The variable production overhead efficiency variance is exactly the same, in hours, as the direct labour efficiency variance, and occurs for the same reasons.

It is usually assumed that **variable overheads are incurred during active working hours**, but are not incurred during idle time (for example the machines are not running, therefore power is not being consumed, and no direct materials are being used). This means in our example that although the labour force was paid for 820 hours, they were actively working for only 760 of those hours and so variable production overhead spending occurred during 760 hours.

4.2.1 The variable overhead expenditure variance

This is the difference between the amount of variable overhead that should have been incurred in the actual hours actively worked, and the actual amount of variable overhead incurred. Refer to the data in Section 4.1.

	$
760 hours of variable production overhead should cost (× $1.50)	1,140
but did cost	1,230
Variable production overhead expenditure variance	90 (A)

4.2.2 The variable overhead efficiency variance

If you already know the direct labour efficiency variance, the variable overhead efficiency variance is exactly the same in hours, but priced at the variable production overhead rate per hour. In the example in Section 4.1, the efficiency variance would be as follows.

400 units of product X should take (× 2hrs)	800 hrs
but did take (active hours)	760 hrs
Variable production overhead efficiency variance in hours	40 hrs (F)
× standard rate per hour	× $1.50
Variable production overhead efficiency variance in $	$60 (F)

4.2.3 Summary

	$
Variable production overhead expenditure variance	90 (A)
Variable production overhead efficiency variance	60 (F)
Variable production overhead total variance	30 (A)

5 The reasons for cost variances

ST FORWARD

There are a wide range of **reasons** for the occurrence of adverse and favourable cost **variances**.

sessment
cus point

This is not an exhaustive list and in an assessment question might suggest other possible causes. You should review the information provided and select any causes that are consistent with the reported variances.

Variance	Favourable	Adverse
(a) Material price	Unforeseen discounts received More care taken in purchasing Change in material standard	Price increase Careless purchasing Change in material standard
(b) Material usage	Material used of higher quality than standard More effective use made of material Errors in allocating material to jobs	Defective material Excessive waste Theft Stricter quality control Errors in allocating material to jobs
(c) Labour rate	Use of apprentices or other workers at a rate of pay lower than standard	Wage rate increase Use of higher grade labour
(d) Idle time	The idle time variance is always adverse	Machine breakdown Non-availability of material Illness or injury to worker
(e) Labour efficiency	Output produced more quickly than expected because of work motivation, better quality of equipment or materials, or better methods. Errors in allocating time to jobs	Lost time in excess of standard allowed Output lower than standard set because of deliberate restriction, lack of training, or sub-standard material used Errors in allocating time to jobs
(f) Variable overhead expenditure	Change in types of overhead or their cost	Change in type of overhead or their cost
(g) Variable overhead efficiency	As for labour efficiency (if based on labour hours)	As for labour efficiency (if based on labour hours)

Chapter Roundup

- **Variances** measure the difference between actual results and expected results. The process by which the total difference between standard and actual results is analysed is known as **variance analysis**.

- The **direct material total variance** (the difference between what the output actually cost and what it should have cost, in terms of material) can be divided into the **direct material price variance** and the **direct material usage variance**.

- Since material inventories are usually valued at **standard cost** in a standard costing system, direct material price variances are usually extracted at the time of **receipt** of the materials, rather than at the time of usage.

- The **direct labour total variance** (the difference between what the output should have cost and what it did cost, in terms of labour) can be divided into the **direct labour rate variance** and the **direct labour efficiency variance**.

- If idle time arises, it is usual to calculate a separate **idle time variance**, and to base the calculation of the **efficiency variance** on **active hours** (when labour actually worked) only. It is always an **adverse** variance.

- The **variable overhead total variance** can be subdivided into the variable overhead **expenditure variance** and the variable overhead **efficiency variance (based on active hours).**

- There are a wide range of **reasons** for the occurrence of adverse and favourable cost **variances**.

Quick Quiz

1 Subdivide the following variances.

    (a)   Direct materials cost variance

    (b)   Direct labour cost variance

    (c)   Variable production overhead variance

2 What are the two main advantages in calculating the material price variance at the time of receipt of materials?

3 Idle time variances are always adverse.

    True   ☐

    False   ☐

4 Adverse material usage variances might occur for the following reasons.

    I   Defective material
    II   Excessive waste
    III   Theft
    IV   Unforeseen discounts received

    A   I
    B   I and II
    C   I, II and III
    D   I, II, III and IV

Answers to Quick Quiz

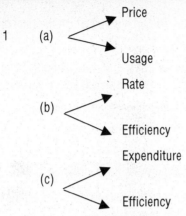

1   (a)   Price
            Usage

     (b)   Rate
            Efficiency

     (c)   Expenditure
            Efficiency

2   (a)   The earlier variances are extracted, the sooner they will be brought to the attention of managers.
     (b)   All inventories will be valued at standard price which requires less administration effort.

3   True

4   C

Now try the questions below from the Question Bank

Question numbers	Page
37–41	355

Variance analysis II

Introduction

The objective of cost variance analysis, which we looked at in the previous chapter, is to assist management in the **control of costs**. Costs are, however, only one factor which contribute to the achievement of planned contribution. **Sales** are another important factor and sales variances can be calculated to aid management's control of their business. We will therefore begin this chapter by examining **sales price** and **sales volume contribution variances**.

Having discussed the variances you need to know about, we will be looking in Section 2 at the **ways in which variances should be presented to management** to aid their control of the organisation.

Finally we will examine two further topics. We will consider **how actual data can be derived from standard cost details and variances** and we'll look at the **interrelationship** (or **interdependence**) between various variances.

Topic list	Learning outcomes	Syllabus references	Ability required
1 Sales variances	C(iv)	C(3)	Application
2 Operating statements	C(v)	C(4)	Application
3 Deriving actual data from standard cost details and variances	C(iv)	C(3)	Application
4 Inter-relationships between variances	C(vi)	C(3)	Analysis

1 Sales variances

1.1 Sales price variance

The **sales price variance** is a measure of the effect on expected contribution of a different selling price to standard selling price. It is calculated as the difference between what the sales revenue should have been for the actual quantity sold, and what it was.

Key term

The **sales price variance** is the 'change in revenue caused by the actual selling price differing from that budgeted'.

CIMA *Official Terminology*

Suppose that the standard selling price of product X is $15. Actual sales in 20X3 were 2,000 units at $15.30 per unit. The sales price variance is calculated as follows.

	$
Sales revenue from 2,000 units should have been (× $15)	30,000
but was	30,600
Sales price variance	600 (F)

The variance is favourable because the price was higher than expected.

1.2 Sales volume contribution variance

The **sales volume contribution variance** is the difference between the actual units sold and the budgeted quantity, valued at the standard contribution per unit. In other words, it measures the increase or decrease in standard contribution as a result of the sales volume being higher or lower than budgeted.

Key term

The **sales volume contribution variance** is a 'measure of the effect on contribution of not achieving the budgeted volume of sales'.

CIMA *Official Terminology*

Suppose that a company budgets to sell 8,000 units of product J for $12 per unit. The standard variable cost per unit is $7. Actual sales were 7,700 units, at $12.50 per unit.

The sales volume contribution variance is calculated as follows.

	$
Budgeted sales volume	8,000 units
Actual sales volume	7,700 units
Sales volume contribution variance in units	300 units (A)
× standard contribution per unit $(12 – 7)	× $5
Sales volume contribution variance	1,500 (A)

The variance is adverse because actual sales were less than budgeted.

Question

Jasper Co has the following budget and actual figures for 20X4.

	Budget	Actual
Sales units	600	620
Selling price per unit	$30	$29

Standard marginal cost of production = $28 per unit.

(a)   The sales price variance is $ [   ]

(b)   The sales volume contribution variance is $ [   ]

Answer

(a)   **The sales price variance is $** [**620 (A)**]

(b)   **The sales volume contribution variance is $** [**40 (F)**]

Workings

	$
Sales revenue from 620 units should have been (× $30)	18,600
but was (× $29)	17,980
Sales price variance	620 (A)
Budgeted sales volume	600 units
Actual sales volume	620 units
Sales volume contribution variance in units	20 units (F)
× standard contribution per unit ($(30 − 28))	× $2
Sales volume contribution variance	$40 (F)

2 Operating statements

ST FORWARD

Operating statements show how the combination of variances reconcile budgeted contribution and actual contribution.

So far, we have considered how variances are calculated without considering how they combine to reconcile the difference between budgeted contribution and actual contribution during a period. This reconciliation is usually presented as a report to senior management at the end of each control period. The report is called an operating statement or statement of variances.

Let's have a look at an example. This will provide you with the opportunity to revise the variance calculations already described, and will also show you how to combine them into an operating statement.

2.1 Example: variances and operating statements

Sydney Co manufactures one product, and the entire product is sold as soon as it is produced. There are no opening or inventories and work in progress is negligible. The company operates a standard costing system and analysis of variances is made every month. The standard cost card for a product is as follows.

STANDARD COST CARD

		$
Direct materials	0.5 kilos at $4 per kilo	2.00
Direct wages	2 hours at $8.00 per hour	16.00
Variable overheads	2 hours at $0.30 per hour	0.60
Standard variable cost		18.60
Standard contribution		13.40
Standing selling price		32.00

Budgeted output for the month of June 20X7 was 5,100 units. Actual results for June 20X7 were as follows.

Production of 4,850 units was sold for $150,350.
Materials consumed in production amounted to 2,300 kgs at a total cost of $9,800.
Labour hours paid for amounted to 8,500 hours at a cost of $67,800.
Actual operating hours amounted to 8,000 hours.
Variable overheads amounted to $2,600.

Required

Calculate all variances and prepare an operating statement for the month ended 30 June 20X7.

Solution

(a)		$
	2,300 kg of material should cost (× $4)	9,200
	but did cost	9,800
	Material price variance	600 (A)

(b)		
	4,850 units should use (× 0.5 kgs)	2,425 kg
	but did use	2,300 kg
	Material usage variance in kgs	125 kg (F)
	× standard price per kg	× $4
	Material usage variance in $	$500 (F)

(c)		$
	8,500 hours of labour should cost (× $8)	68,000
	but did cost	67,800
	Labour rate variance	200 (F)

(d)		
	4,850 units should take (× 2 hrs)	9,700 hrs
	but did take (active hours)	8,000 hrs
	Labour efficiency variance in hours	1,700 hrs (F)
	× standard rate per hour	× $8
	Labour efficiency variance in $	$13,600 (F)

(e)		
	Idle time variance 500 hours (A) × $8	$4,000 (A)

(f)		$
	8,000 hours incurring variable o/hd expenditure should cost (× $0.30)	2,400
	but did cost	2,600
	Variable overhead expenditure variance	200 (A)

(g)   Variable overhead efficiency variance in hours is the same as the
       labour efficiency variance:
       1,700 hours (F) × $0.30 per hour $ 510 (F)

(h) $
       Revenue from 4,850 units should be (× $32)   155,200
         but was   150,350
       Sales price variance   4,850 (A)

(i)
       Budgeted sales volume   5,100 units
       Actual sales volume   4,850 units
       Sales volume contribution variance in units   250 units (A)
       × standard contribution per unit   × $13.40
       Sales volume contribution variance $3,350 (A)

Now let's turn our attention to the operating statement.

There are several ways in which an operating statement can be presented. Perhaps the most common format is one which **reconciles budgeted contribution to actual contribution.**

- **Budgeted contribution** is adjusted by the **sales volume variance** to give the **budgeted contribution from actual sales**.

- The **sales price variance** is then included to give a figure representing the **actual sales revenue minus the standard variable cost of sales**.

- **Cost variances** are then taken into account to produce a figure for **actual contribution.**

SYDNEY CO – OPERATING STATEMENT JUNE 20X7

			$
Budgeted contribution ($13.40 × 5,100)			68,340
Sales volume variance			3,350 (A)
Budgeted contribution from actual sales			64,990
Sales price variance			4,850 (A)
Actual sales minus the standard variable cost of sales			60,140

Cost variances	(F)	(A)	
	$	$	
Material price		600	
Material usage	500		
Labour rate	200		
Labour efficiency	13,600		
Labour idle time		4,000	
Variable overhead expenditure		200	
Variable overhead efficiency	510		
	14,810	4,800	10,010 (F)
Actual contribution			70,150

Check	$	$
Sales		150,350
Materials	9,800	
Labour	67,800	
Variable overhead	2,600	
		80,200
Actual contribution		70,150

Question

NN Co manufactures a single product, the SK. The standard variable cost for this item is as follows.

	$	$
Direct materials:		
P (8 kg at $0.40 per kg)	3.20	
Q (4 kg at $0.70 per kg)	2.80	
		6.00
Direct labour (3 hours at $7.50)		22.50
Variable production overhead (3 hours at $0.50)		1.50
		30.00

The standard sales price per unit is $40. The budgeted production and sales for period 7 were 3,000 units.

Actual results for period 7 were as follows.

Sales and production	2,800 units
Sales revenue	$113,200

Direct materials purchased and used:

P	19,000 kg	Cost $7,500
Q	14,000 kg	Cost $10,250

Direct labour 8,600 hours   Cost $67,100

It is known that 300 hours of this labour was recorded as idle time.

Variable production overhead $4,100

Complete the operating statement for period 7 shown below. You should insert each cost variance into the correct box according to whether it is adverse or favourable. For the sales variances, indicate in the box whether they are adverse (A) or favourable (F).

OPERATING STATEMENT FOR PERIOD 7

		$
	Budgeted contribution	30,000
(a)	Sales volume contribution variance	
(b)	Sales price variance	
	Actual sales less standard variable cost of sales	

	Cost variances	$ Favourable	$ Adverse
(c)	Direct material price		
(d)	Direct material usage		
(e)	Direct labour rate		
(f)	Direct labour efficiency		
(g)	Idle time		
(h)	Variable production overhead expenditure		
(i)	Variable production overhead efficiency		

	Total cost variances	
	Actual contribution	24,250

Answer

OPERATING STATEMENT FOR PERIOD 7

		$
	Budgeted contribution	30,000
(a)	Sales volume contribution variance	2,000 (A)
(b)	Sales price variance	1,200 (F)
	Actual sales less standard variable cost of sales	29,200

	Cost variances	$ Favourable	$ Adverse
(c)	Direct material price		350
(d)	Direct material usage		600
(e)	Direct labour rate		2,600
(f)	Direct labour efficiency	750	
(g)	Idle time		2,250
(h)	Variable production overhead expenditure	50	
(i)	Variable production overhead efficiency	50	

	Total cost variances	4,950 (A)
	Actual contribution	24,250

Workings

(a) **Sales volume**

		$
Budgeted sales volume		3,000 units
Actual sales volume		2,800 units
Sales volume variance in units		200 units (A)
× standard contribution per unit ($(40 – 30))		× $10
Sales volume variance in $		$2,000 (A)

(b) **Sales price**

	$
Revenue from 2,800 units should have been (× $40)	112,000
but was	113,200
Sales price variance	1,200 (F)

(c) **Material price**

	$	$	
19,000 kg of P should cost (× 40c)	7,600		
did cost	7,500		
Material P price variance		100	(F)
14,000 kg of Q should cost (× 70c)	9,800		
did cost	10,250		
Material Q price variance		450	(A)
Total material price variance		350	(A)

(d) **Material usage**

Material P

2,800 units of SK should use (× 8 kgs)	22,400	kgs
did use	19,000	kgs
Material P usage variance in kgs	3,400	kgs (F)
× standard price per kg	× $0.40	
Material P usage variance in $	$1,360	(F)

Material Q

2,800 units of SK should use (× 4 kgs)	11,200	kgs
did use	14,000	kgs
Material Q usage variance in kgs	2,800	kgs (A)
× standard price per kg	× $0.70	
Material Q usage variance in $	$1,960	(A)
Total material usage variance ($1,960 – $1,360)	$600	(A)

(e) **Direct labour rate**

	$	
8,600 hours of labour should cost (× $7.50)	64,500	
did cost	67,100	
Direct labour rate variance	2,600	(A)

(f) **Direct labour efficiency**

To make 2,800 units of SK should take (× 3 hrs)	8,400	hrs
did take (active hours)	8,300	hrs
Direct labour variance in hrs	100	hrs (F)
× standard rate per hour	× $7.50	
Direct labour efficiency variance in $	$750	(F)

(g) **Idle time variance** 300 hours (A) × $7.50 = $2,250   (A)

(h) **Variable production overhead expenditure**

	$	
8,300 worked hours should cost (× $0.50)	4,150	
did cost	4,100	
Variable overhead expenditure variance	50	(F)

(i) **Variable production overhead efficiency** (same as direct labour)
100 hrs (F) × standard rate ($0.50) $50   (F)

Question   Further variance analysis

P Co, a manufacturing firm, operates a standard marginal costing system. It makes a single product, PG, using a single raw material.

Standard costs relating to PG have been calculated as follows.

Standard cost schedule – PG	Per unit
	$
Direct material, 100 kg at $5 per kg	500
Direct labour, 10 hours at $8 per hour	80
Variable production overhead, 10 hours at $2 per hour	20
	600

The standard selling price of a PG is $900 and P Co plan to produce and sell 1,020 units a month.

During December 20X0, 1,000 units of PG were produced and sold. Relevant details of this production are as follows.

Direct material

90,000 kgs costing $720,000 were bought and used.

Direct labour

8,200 hours were worked during the month and total wages were $63,000.

Variable production overhead

The actual cost for the month was $25,000.

Inventories of the direct material are valued at the standard price of $5 per kg.

Each PG was sold for $975.

(a) The variable production cost variance for December 20X0 is $ [   ]

(b) (i) The direct labour rate variance is $ [   ]

(ii) The direct labour efficiency variance is $ [   ]

(c) (i) The direct material price variance is $ [   ]

(ii) The direct material usage variance is $ [   ]

(d) (i) The variable production overhead expenditure variance is $ [   ]

(ii) The variable production overhead efficiency variance is $ [   ]

(e) (i) The sales volume contribution variance is $ [   ]

(ii) The sales price variance is $ [   ]

Answer

(a) **The variable production cost variance is $ | 208,000 (A) |**

Workings

This is simply a 'total' variance.

	$
1,000 units should have cost (× $600)	600,000
but did cost (see working)	808,000
Variable production cost variance	208,000 (A)

(b) (i) **The direct labour rate variance is $ | 2,600 (F) |**

Workings

	$
8,200 hours should cost (× $8)	65,600
but did cost	63,000
Direct labour rate variance	2,600 (F)

(ii) **The direct labour efficiency variance is $ | 14,400 (F) |**

Workings

1,000 units should take (× 10 hours)	10,000 hrs
but did take	8,200 hrs
Direct labour efficiency variance in hrs	1,800 hrs (F)
× standard rate per hour	× $8
Direct labour efficiency variance in $	$14,400 (F)

(c) (i) **The direct material price variance is $ | 270,000 (A) |**

Workings

	$
90,000 kg should cost (× $5)	450,000
but did cost	720,000
Direct material price variance	270,000 (A)

(ii) **The direct material usage variance is $ 50,000 (F)**

Workings

1,000 units should use (× 100 kg)	100,000 kg
but did use	90,000 kg
Direct material usage variance in kgs	10,000 kg (F)
× standard cost per kg	× $5
Direct material usage variance in $	$50,000 (F)

(d) (i) **The variable production overhead expenditure variance is $ 8,600 (A)**

Workings

	$
8,200 hours incurring o/hd should cost (× $2)	16,400
but did cost	25,000
Variable production overhead expenditure variance	8,600 (A)

(ii) **The variable production overhead efficiency variance is $ 3,600 (F)**

Workings

Efficiency variance in hrs (from (b)(ii))	1,800 hrs (F)
× standard rate per hour	× $2
Variable production overhead efficiency variance	$3,600 (F)

(e) (i) **The sales volume contribution variance is $ 6,000 (A)**

Workings

Budgeted sales volume	1,020 units
Actual sales volume	1,000 units
Sales volume contribution variance in units	20 units (A)
× standard contribution per unit ($(900 − 600))	× $300
	$6,000 (A)

(ii) **The sales price variance is $ 75,000 (F)**

Workings

	$
Revenue should have been (1,000 × $900)	900,000
but was (1,000 × $975)	975,000
	75,000 (F)

3 Deriving actual data from standard cost details and variances

> **Variances** can be **manipulated** so as to derive actual data from standard cost details.

3.1 Example: deriving actual data

The standard marginal cost card for the TR, one of the products made by P Co, is as follows.

	$
Direct material 16 kgs × $6 per kg	96
Direct labour 6 hours × $12 per hour	72
	168

P Co reported the following variances in control period 13 in relation to the TR.

Direct material price: $18,840 favourable
Direct material usage: $480 adverse
Direct labour rate: $10,598 adverse
Direct labour efficiency: $8,478 favourable

Actual direct wages cost $171,320. P Co paid $5.50 for each kg of direct material. There was no opening or closing inventories of the material.

Required

Calculate the following.

(a)   Actual output
(b)   Actual hours worked
(c)   Average actual wage rate per hour
(d)   Actual number of kilograms purchased and used

Solution

(a)		$
	Total direct wages cost	171,320
	Adjust for variances:	
	labour rate	(10,598)
	labour efficiency	8,478
	Standard direct wages cost	169,200

∴ Actual output   = Total standard cost ÷ unit standard cost
                          = $169,200 ÷ $72
                          = 2,350 units

(b)		$
	Total direct wages cost	171,320.0
	Less rate variance	(10,598.0)
	Standard rate for actual hours	160,722.0
	÷ standard rate per hour	÷ $12.0
	Actual hours worked	13,393.5 hrs

(c)   Average actual wage rate per hour = actual wages/actual hours = $171,320/13,393.5 = $12.79 per hour.

(d)   Number of kgs purchased and used = x

	$
x kgs should have cost (× $6)	6.0x
but did cost (× $5.50)	5.5x
Direct material price variance	0.5x

∴ $0.5x   = $18,840
∴   x   = 37,680 kgs

Question   **Actual rate of pay**

XYZ Co uses standard costing. The following data relates to labour grade II.

Actual hours worked	10,400 hours
Standard allowance for actual production	8,320 hours
Standard rate per hour	$5
Rate variance (adverse)	$416

What was the actual rate of pay per hour?

A $4.95
B $4.96
C $5.04
D $5.05

Answer

The correct answer is C.

Rate variance per hour worked = $\dfrac{\$416}{10,400}$ = $0.04 (A)

Actual rate per hour = $(5.00 + 0.04) = $5.04.

You should have been able to eliminate options A and B because they are both below the standard rate per hour. If the rate variance is adverse then the actual rate must be above standard.

Option D is incorrect because it results from basing the calculations on standard hours rather than actual hours.

Question   **Quantity of material X**

The standard material content of one unit of product A is 10kgs of material X which should cost $10 per kilogram. In June 20X4, 5,750 units of product A were produced and there was an adverse material usage variance of $1,500.

The quantity of material X used in June 20X4 is ☐ kgs.

Answer

The quantity used is $\boxed{57,650}$ kgs.

Workings

Let the quantity of material X used = Y

5,750 units should have used (× 10kgs)	57,500 kgs
but did use	Y kgs
Usage variance in kgs	(Y − 57,500) kgs
× standard price per kg	× $10
Usage variance in $	$1,500 (A)

$$\therefore \quad 10(Y - 57,500) = 1,500$$
$$Y - 57,500 \quad = 150$$
$$\therefore \quad Y \quad\quad\quad = 57,650 \text{ kgs}$$

Assessment focus point

Make sure you can deal with this sort of variance analysis question as it is an ideal way of assessing your competence in this area.

4 Inter-relationships between variances

Quite possibly, individual variances should not be looked at in isolation. One variance might be inter-related with another, and much of it might have occurred only because the other, inter-related, variance occurred too.

FAST FORWARD

When two variances are **interdependent** (**interrelated**) one will usually be adverse and the other one favourable.

Here are some examples of interdependent variables.

(a) **Materials price and usage**

It may be decided to purchase cheaper materials for a job in order to obtain a favourable price variance, possibly with the consequence that materials wastage is higher and an adverse usage variance occurs. If the cheaper materials are more difficult to handle, there might be an adverse labour efficiency variance too.

If a decision is made to purchase more expensive materials, which perhaps have a longer service life, the price variance will be adverse but the usage variance might be favourable.

(b) **Labour rate and efficiency**

If employees in a workforce are paid higher rates for experience and skill, using a highly skilled team to do some work would incur an adverse rate variance, but should also obtain a favourable efficiency variance. In contrast, a favourable rate variance might indicate a larger-than-expected proportion of inexperienced workers in the workforce, which could result in an adverse labour efficiency variance, and perhaps poor materials handling and high rates of rejects too (adverse materials usage variance).

(c) **Sales price and sales volume**

The possible interdependence between sales price and sales volume variances should (hopefully) be obvious to you. A reduction in the sales price might stimulate bigger sales demand, so that an adverse sales price variance might be offset by a favourable sales volume variance. Similarly a price rise would give a favourable price variance, but possible at the cost of a fall in demand and an adverse sales volume variance.

(d) **Cost and sales variances**

(i) If there are **favourable cost variances** (perhaps cheaper labour or material have been used, say, so that there are favourable labour rate or material price variances), the possible drop in quality of the product could lead to an **adverse sales volume variance** because customers don't wish to buy the lower quality product.

(ii) If product quality is improved this might result in an **adverse cost variance**.

- If more expensive material is used (adverse material price variance)

- If labour are more careful in production of the product and hence take longer than standard (adverse labour efficiency variance)

- If more skilled labour is used (adverse labour rate variance)

But the change in quality might result in a **favourable sales volume variance**, customers wanting to buy more of the higher-quality product.

(iii) If costs have risen (resulting in **adverse labour rate, material price and variable overhead expenditure variances**), the sales price might have to be increased to cover the extra costs. This would result in a **favourable sales price variance.**

Chapter Roundup

- The **sales price variance** is a measure of the effect on expected contribution of a different selling price to standard selling price. It is calculated as the difference between what the sales revenue should have been for the actual quantity sold, and what it was.

- The **sales volume contribution variance** is the difference between the actual units sold and the budgeted quantity, valued at the standard contribution per unit. In other words, it measures the increase or decrease in standard contribution as a result of the sales volume being higher or lower than budgeted.

- **Operating statements** show how the combination of variances reconcile budgeted contribution and actual contribution.

- **Variances** can be **manipulated** so as to derive actual data from standard cost details.

- When two variances are **interdependent (interrelated)** one will usually be adverse and the other one favourable.

Quick Quiz

1   A regular report for management of actual cost and revenue, and usually comparing actual with budget (and showing variances) is known as

    A   Bank statement
    B   Variance statement
    C   Budget statement
    D   Operating statement

2   A favourable sales price variance can result from a combination of a lower than budgeted sales volume and a higher than standard selling price.

    True   ☐

    False   ☐

3   If two variances are interdependent, both must be either favourable or adverse.

    True   ☐

    False   ☐

4   The sales volume variance considers the difference between .... sales volume and .... sales volume.

Fill in the gaps using two of the following words.

• total	• budgeted	• actual	• future
• incremental	• estimated	• past	• confirmed

Answers to Quick Quiz

1   D

2   False. The variance is favourable if the actual price is higher than standard.

3   False. Favourable material price and adverse material usage variances might be interdependent, for example.

4   The correct words are **budgeted** and **actual**.

Now try the questions below from the Question Bank

Question numbers	Page
42–46	356

Part D
Financial planning and control

Budget preparation

Introduction

This chapter is the first of two on a new topic, **budgeting**. It is a topic which you will meet at all stages of your examination studies so it is vital that you get a firm grasp of the basics now. The chapter begins by explaining the **reasons** why an organisation might prepare a budget and goes on to detail the **steps in the preparation of a budget**. The method of preparing and the relationship between the various **functional budgets** is then set out.

The chapter also considers the construction of **cash budgets** and **budgeted income statements and balance sheets**, the these three budgets making up what is known as a **master budget**.

In Chapter 11 we will build on the general awareness of budgeting gained in this chapter and look at more specific budgeting issues.

Topic list	Learning outcomes	Syllabus references	Ability required
1 Why do organisations prepare budgets?	E(i)	E(1)	Comprehension
2 A framework for budgeting	E(i), (ii)	E(1)	Comprehension/ Application
3 Steps in the preparation of a budget	E(i), (ii)	E(2)	Comprehension/ Application
4 Functional budgets	E(ii)	E(2)	Application
5 Cash budgets	E(iii), E(iv)	E(2)	Application, Analysis
6 Master budgets	E(iii)	E(2)	Application
7 Capital expenditure budgets	E(ii)	E(2)	Application

1 Why do organisations prepare budgets?

FAST FORWARD

Budgeting is a **multi-purpose activity**.

1.1 Reasons for preparing budgets

Here are some of the reasons why budgets are used.

Function	Detail
Compel planning	Budgeting forces management to look ahead, to set out detailed plans for achieving the targets for each department, operation and (ideally) each manager and to anticipate problems.
Communicate ideas and plans	A formal system is necessary to ensure that each person affected by the plans is aware of what he or she is supposed to be doing. Communication might be one-way, with managers giving orders to subordinates, or there might be a two-way communication .
Coordinate activities	The activities of different departments need to be coordinated to ensure everyone in an organisation is working towards the same goals. This means, for example, that the purchasing department should base its budget on production requirements and that the production budget should in turn be based on sales expectations.
Provide a framework for responsibility accounting	Budgets require that managers are made responsible for the achievement of budget targets for the operations under their personal control.
Establish a system of control	Control over actual performance is provided by the comparisons of actual results against the budget plan. Departures from budget can then be investigated and the reasons for the departures can be divided into controllable and uncontrollable factors.
Provide a means of performance evaluation	Budgets provide targets which can be compared with actual outcomes in order to assess employee performance.
Motivate employees to improve their performance	The interest and commitment of employees can be retained if there is a system that lets them know how well or badly they are performing. The identification of controllable reasons for departures from budget with managers responsible provides an incentive for improving future performance.

Here's what the *Official Terminology* has to say:

Key term

> **Budget purposes**: 'Budgets may help in authorising expenditure, communicating objectives and plans, controlling operations, co-ordinating activities, evaluating performance, planning and rewarding performance. Often, reward systems involve comparison of actual with budgeted performance.'
> CIMA *Official Terminology*

1.2 Different things to different people

A **budget**, since it has different purposes, **might mean different things to different people**.

ORWARD ▶▶

A budget might be a **forecast**, a **means of allocating resources,** a **yardstick** or a **target.**

What it might mean	Detail
Forecast	It helps managers to plan for the future. Given uncertainty about the future, however, it is quite likely that a budget will become outdated as events occur and so the budget will cease to be a realistic forecast. New forecasts might be prepared that differ from the budget. (A **forecast** is **what is likely to happen**; a **budget** is **what an organisation wants to happen**. These are not necessarily the same thing.)
Means of allocating resources	It can be used to decide how many resources are needed (cash, labour and so on) and how many should be given to each area of the organisation's activities. As we saw when we looked at limiting factor analysis, resource allocation is particularly important when some resources are in short supply. Budgets often set ceilings or limits on how much administrative departments and other service departments are allowed to spend in the period. Public expenditure budgets, for example, set spending limits for each government department.
Yardstick	By comparing it with actual performance, the budget provides a means of indicating where and when control action may be necessary (and possibly where some managers or employees are open to censure for achieving poor results).
Target	A budget might be a means of motivating the workforce to greater personal accomplishment, another aspect of control.

Key term

A **budget** is a 'quantitative expression of a plan for a defined period of time. It may include planned sales volumes and revenues; resource quantities, costs and expenses; assets, liabilities and cash flows.'   CIMA *Official Terminology*

2 A framework for budgeting

2.1 Budget committee

ST FORWARD ▶▶

The **budget committee** is the coordinating body in the preparation and administration of budgets.

The budget committee is usually headed up by the managing director (as chairman) and is assisted by a **budget officer** who is usually an accountant. Every part of the organisation should be represented on the committee, so there should be a representative from sales, production, marketing and so on. Functions of the budget committee include the following.

- Coordination and allocation of responsibility for the preparation of budgets
- Issuing of the budget manual
- Timetabling
- Provision of information to assist in the preparation of budgets
- Communication of final budgets to the appropriate managers
- Monitoring the budgeting process by comparing actual and budgeted results

2.2 The budget period

Key term

> A **budget period** is a 'period for which a budget is prepared, and used, which may then be sub-divided into control periods'.
>
> *CIMA Official Terminology*

Except for capital expenditure budgets, the budget period is usually the accounting year (sub-divided into 12 or 13 control periods).

2.3 Responsibility for budgets

FAST FORWARD

> The manager responsible for preparing each budget should ideally be the manager responsible for carrying out the budget.

For example, the preparation of particular budgets might be allocated as follows.

(a) The **sales manager** should draft the **sales budget** and the selling overhead cost centre budgets.

(b) The **purchasing manager** should draft the **material purchases budget**.

(c) The **production manager** should draft the **direct production cost budgets.**

Question

Budget committee

Which of the following is the budget committee *not* responsible for?

A   Preparing functional budgets
B   Timetabling the budgeting operation
C   Allocating responsibility for the budget preparation
D   Monitoring the budgeting process

Answer

The correct answer is A.

The manager responsible for implementing the budget that must prepare it, not the budget committee.

If you don't know the answer, remember not to fall for the common pitfall of thinking, 'Well, we haven't had a D for a while, so I'll guess that'. It is good practice to guess if you don't know the answer (never leave out an assessment question) but first eliminate some of the options if you can.

Since the committee is a co-ordinating body we can definitely say that they are responsible for B and D. Similarly, a co-ordinating body is more likely to allocate responsibility than to actually undertake the budget preparation, so eliminate C and select A as the correct answer.

2.4 The budget manual

The **budget manual** is a collection of instructions governing the responsibilities of persons and the procedures, forms and records relating to the preparation and use of budgetary data.

The **budget manual** is a 'detailed set of guidelines and information about the budget process typically including a calendar of budgetary events, specimen budget forms, a statement of budgetary objectives and desired results, listing of budgetary activities and budget assumptions, regarding, for example, inflation and interest rates'.

CIMA *Official Terminology*

A budget manual may contain the following.

(a) An explanation of the **objectives** of the budgetary process

- The purpose of budgetary planning and control
- The objectives of the various stages of the budgetary process
- The importance of budgets in the long-term planning of the business

(b) **Organisational structures**

- An organisation chart
- A list of individuals holding budget responsibilities

(c) An **outline of the principal budgets** and the **relationship between them**

(d) **Administrative details of budget preparation**

- Membership and terms of reference of the budget committee
- The sequence in which budgets are to be prepared
- A timetable

(e) **Procedural matters**

- Specimen forms and instructions for their completion
- Specimen reports
- Account codes (or a chart of accounts)
- The name of the budget officer to whom enquiries must be sent

3 Steps in the preparation of a budget

The first task in the budgetary process is to identify the **principal budget factor**. This is also known as the **key budget factor** or **limiting budget factor**. The principal budget factor is the factor which limits the activities of an organisation.

The procedures for preparing a budget will differ from organisation to organisation but the steps described below will be indicative of the steps followed by many organisations. The preparation of a budget may take weeks or months and the **budget committee** may meet several times before the **master budget** (budgeted income statement, budgeted balance sheet and budgeted cash flow) is finally agreed. **Functional budgets** (sales budgets, production budgets, direct labour budgets and so on), which are amalgamated into the master budget, may need to be amended many times over as a consequence of discussions between departments, changes in market conditions and so on during the course of budget preparation.

3.1 Identifying the principal budget factor

The **principal budget factor** 'limits the activities of an undertaking. Identification of the principal budget factor is often the starting point in the budget setting process. Often the principal budget factor will be sales demand but it could be production capacity or material supply.'

CIMA *Official Terminology*

The **principal budget factor** is usually **sales demand**. A company is usually restricted from making and selling more of its products because there would be no sales demand for the increased output at a price which would be acceptable/profitable to the company. The principal budget factor may also be machine capacity, distribution and selling resources, the availability of key raw materials or the availability of cash. Once this factor is defined then the remainder of the budgets can be prepared. For example, if sales are the principal budget factor then the production manager can only prepare his budget after the sales budget is complete.

3.2 The order of budget preparation

Assuming that the principal budget factor has been identified as being sales, the stages involved in the preparation of a budget can be summarised as follows.

(a)   The **sales budget** is prepared in units of product and sales value. The **finished goods inventory budget** can be prepared at the same time. This budget decides the planned increase or decrease in finished goods inventory levels.

(b)   With the information from the sales and inventory budgets, the **production budget** can be prepared. This is, in effect, the sales budget in units plus (or minus) the increase (or decrease) in finished goods inventory. The production budget will be stated in terms of units.

(c)   This leads on logically to budgeting the **resources for production**. This involves preparing a **materials usage budget, machine usage budget and a labour budget**.

(d)   In addition to the materials usage budget, a **materials inventory budget** will be prepared, to decide the planned increase or decrease in the level of inventory held. Once the raw materials usage requirements and the raw materials inventory budget are known, the purchasing department can prepare a **raw materials purchases budget** in quantities and value for each type of material purchased.

(e)   During the preparation of the sales and production budgets, the managers of the cost centres of the organisation will prepare their draft budgets for the department **overhead costs**. Such overheads will include maintenance, stores, administration, selling and research and development.

(f)   From the above information a **budgeted income statement** can be produced.

(g)   In addition several other budgets must be prepared in order to arrive at the **budgeted balance sheet**. These are the **capital expenditure budget** (for non-current assets), the **working capital budget** (for budgeted increases or decreases in the level of receivables and accounts payable as well as inventories), and a **cash budget**.

4 Functional budgets

Functional/departmental budgets include budgets for sales, production, purchases and labour.

A **departmental/functional budget** is a 'budget of income and/or expenditure applicable to a particular function frequently including sales budget, production cost budget (based on budgeted production, efficiency and utilisation), purchasing budget, human resources budget, marketing budget and research and development budget'.

CIMA *Official Terminology*

Having seen the theory of budget preparation, let us look at **functional** (or **departmental**) budget preparation, which are best explained by means of an example.

4.1 Example: preparing a materials purchases budget

ECO Co manufactures two products, S and T, which use the same raw materials, D and E. One unit of S uses 3 litres of D and 4 kilograms of E. One unit of T uses 5 litres of D and 2 kilograms of E. A litre of D is expected to cost $3 and a kilogram of E $7.

Budgeted sales for 20X2 are 8,000 units of S and 6,000 units of T; finished goods in inventory at 1 January 20X2 are 1,500 units of S and 300 units of T, and the company plans to hold inventories of 600 units of each product at 31 December 20X2.

Inventories of raw material are 6,000 litres of D and 2,800 kilograms of E at 1 January and the company plans to hold 5,000 litres and 3,500 kilograms respectively at 31 December 20X2.

The warehouse and stores managers have suggested that a provision should be made for damages and deterioration of items held in store, as follows.

Product S :   loss of 50 units
Product T :   loss of 100 units
Material D :   loss of 500 litres
Material E :   loss of 200 kilograms

Required

Prepare a material purchases budget for the year 20X2.

Solution

To calculate material purchases requirements it is first necessary to calculate the material usage requirements. That in turn depends on calculating the budgeted production volumes.

	Product S Units	Product T Units
Production required		
To meet sales demand	8,000	6,000
To provide for inventory loss	50	100
For closing inventory	600	600
	8,650	6,700
Less inventory already in hand	1,500	300
Budgeted production volume	7,150	6,400

	Material D Litres	Material E Kgs
Usage requirements		
To produce 7,150 units of S	21,450	28,600
To produce 6,400 units of T	32,000	12,800
To provide for inventory loss	500	200
For closing inventory	5,000	3,500
	58,950	45,100
Less inventory already in hand	6,000	2,800
Budgeted material purchases	52,950	42,300
Unit cost	$3	$7
Cost of material purchases	$158,850	$296,100
Total cost of material purchases	$454,950	

Important! | The basics of the preparation of each functional budget are similar to those above. Work carefully through the following question which covers the preparation of a number of different types of functional budget.

Question   **Functional budgets**

XYZ company produces three products X, Y and Z. For the coming accounting period budgets are to be prepared based on the following information.

Budgeted sales

Product X	2,000 at $100 each
Product Y	4,000 at $130 each
Product Z	3,000 at $150 each

Budgeted usage of raw material

	RM11	RM22	RM33
Product X	5	2	-
Product Y	3	2	2
Product Z	2	1	3
Cost per unit of material	$5	$3	$4

Finished inventories budget

	Product X	Product Y	Product Z
Opening	500	800	700
Closing	600	1,000	800

Raw materials inventory budget

	RM11	RM22	RM33
Opening	21,000	10,000	16,000
Closing	18,000	9,000	12,000

	Product X	Product Y	Product Z
Expected hours per unit	4	6	8
Expected hourly rate (labour)	$9	$9	$9

Fill in the blanks.

(a) **Sales budget**

	Product X	Product Y	Product Z	Total
Sales quantity	☐	☐	☐	
Sales value	$ ☐	$ ☐	$ ☐	$ ☐

(b) **Production budget**

	Product X Units	Product Y Units	Product Z Units
Budgeted production	☐	☐	☐

(c) **Material usage budget**

	RM11 Units	RM22 Units	RM33 Units
Budgeted material usage	☐	☐	☐

(d) **Material purchases budget**

	RM11	RM22	RM33
Budgeted material purchases	$ ☐	$ ☐	$ ☐

(e) **Labour budget**

Budgeted total wages	$ ☐

Answer

(a)

Sales budget			
	Product X	Product Y	Product Z	Total
---	---	---	---	---
Sales quantity	2,000	4,000	3,000	
Sales price	$100	$130	$150	
Sales value	$ 200,000	$ 520,000	$ 450,000	$ 1,170,000

(b)

	Production budget		
	Product X	Product Y	Product Z
	Units	Units	Units
Sales quantity	2,000	4,000	3,000
Closing inventories	600	1,000	800
	2,600	5,000	3,800
Less opening inventories	500	800	700
Budgeted production	2,100	4,200	3,100

(c)

	Material usage budget			
	Production	RM11	RM22	RM33
	Units	Units	Units	Units
Product X	2,100	10,500	4,200	-
Product Y	4,200	12,600	8,400	8,400
Product Z	3,100	6,200	3,100	9,300
Budgeted material usage		29,300	15,700	17,700

(d)

	Material purchases budget		
	RM11	RM22	RM33
	Units	Units	Units
Budgeted material usage	29,300	15,700	17,700
Closing inventories	18,000	9,000	12,000
	47,300	24,700	29,700
Less opening inventories	21,000	10,000	16,000
Budgeted material purchases	26,300	14,700	13,700
Standard cost per unit	$5	$3	$4
Budgeted material purchases	$ 131,500	$ 44,100	$ 54,800

(e)

		Labour budget			
Product	Production	Hours required per unit	Total hours	Rate per hour	Cost
	Units			$	$
X	2,100	4	8,400	9	75,600
Y	4,200	6	25,200	9	226,800
Z	3,100	8	24,800	9	223,200
Budgeted total wages					525,600

5 Cash budgets

> A **cash budget** is a statement in which estimated future cash receipts and payments are tabulated in such a way as to show the forecast cash balance of a business at defined intervals.

> A **cash budget** is a 'detailed budget of estimated cash inflows and outflows incorporating both revenue and capital items'.
>
> CIMA *Official Terminology*

5.1 Preparing cash budgets

For example, in December 20X2 an accounts department might wish to estimate the cash position of the business during the three following months, January to March 20X3. A cash budget might be drawn up in the following format.

	Jan $	Feb $	Mar $
Estimated cash receipts			
From accounts payable	14,000	16,500	17,000
From cash sales	3,000	4,000	4,500
Proceeds on disposal of non-current assets		2,200	
Total cash receipts	17,000	22,700	21,500
Estimated cash payments			
To suppliers of goods	8,000	7,800	10,500
To employees (wages)	3,000	3,500	3,500
Purchase of non-current assets		16,000	
Rent and rates			1,000
Other overheads	1,200	1,200	1,200
Repayment of loan	2,500		
	14,700	28,500	16,200
Net surplus/(deficit) for month	2,300	(5,800)	5,300
Opening cash balance	1,200	3,500	(2,300)
Closing cash balance	3,500	(2,300)	3,000

In this example (where the figures are purely for illustration) the accounts department has calculated that the cash balance at the beginning of the budget period, 1 January, will be $1,200. Estimates have been made of the cash which is likely to be received by the business (from cash and credit sales, and from a planned disposal of non-current assets in February). Similar estimates have been made of cash due to be paid out by the business (payments to suppliers and employees, payments for rent, rates and other overheads, payment for a planned purchase of non-current assets in February and a loan repayment due in January).

From these estimates it is a simple step to calculate the excess of cash receipts over cash payments in each month. In some months cash payments may exceed cash receipts and there will be a **deficit** for the month; this occurs during February in the above example because of the large investment in non-current assets in that month.

The last part of the cash budget above shows how the business's estimated cash balance can then be rolled along from month to month. Starting with the opening balance of $1,200 at 1 January a cash surplus of $2,300 is generated in January. This leads to a closing January balance of $3,500 which becomes the opening balance for February. The deficit of $5,800 in February throws the business's cash position into **overdraft** and the overdrawn balance of $2,300 becomes the opening balance for March. Finally, the healthy cash surplus of $5,300 in March leaves the business with a favourable cash position of $3,000 at the end of the budget period.

5.2 The usefulness of cash budgets

FAST FORWARD

The **usefulness of cash budgets** is that they enable management to make any **forward planning decisions** that may be needed, such as advising their bank of estimated overdraft requirements or strengthening their credit control procedures to ensure that customers pay more quickly.

The cash budget is one of the most important planning tools that an organisation can use. It shows the **cash effect of all plans made within the budgetary process** and hence its preparation can lead to a **modification of budgets** if it shows that there are insufficient cash resources to finance the planned operations.

It can also give management an indication of **potential problems** that could arise and allows them the opportunity to take action to avoid such problems. A cash budget can show **four positions**. Management will need to take appropriate action depending on the potential position.

5.3 Potential cash positions

Cash position	Appropriate management action
Short-term surplus	• Pay suppliers early to obtain discount • Attempt to increase sales by increasing receivables and inventories • Make short-term investments
Short-term shortfall	• Increase accounts payable • Reduce receivables • Arrange an overdraft
Long-term surplus	• Make long-term investments • Expand • Diversify • Replace/update non-current assets
Long-term shortfall	• Raise long-term finance (such as via issue of share capital) • Consider shutdown/disinvestment opportunities

Question
Cash budget

Tick the boxes to show which of the following should be included in a **cash** budget.

	Include	Do not include
Funds from the receipt of a bank loan		
Revaluation of a non-current asset		
Receipt of dividends from outside the business		
Depreciation of distribution vehicles		
Bad debts written off		
Share dividend paid		

Answer

Any item that is a **cash** flow will be included. Non-cash items are excluded from a cash budget.

	Include	Do not include
Funds from the receipt of a bank loan	✓	
Revaluation of a non-current asset		✓
Receipt of dividends from outside the business	✓	
Depreciation of distribution vehicles		✓
Bad debts written off		✓
Share dividend paid	✓	

5.4 Example: cash budgets again

Peter Blair has worked for some years as a sales representative, but has recently been made redundant. He intends to start up in business on his own account, using $15,000 which he currently has invested with a building society. Peter maintains a bank account showing a small credit balance, and he plans to approach his bank for the necessary additional finance. Peter asks you for advice and provides the following additional information.

(a) Arrangements have been made to purchase non-current assets costing $8,000. These will be paid for at the end of September and are expected to have a five-year life, at the end of which they will possess a nil residual value.

(b) Inventories costing $5,000 will be acquired on 28 September and subsequent monthly purchases will be at a level sufficient to replace forecast sales for the month.

(c) Forecast monthly sales are $3,000 for October, $6,000 for November and December, and $10,500 from January 20X4 onwards.

(d) Selling price is fixed at the cost of inventory plus 50%.

(e) Two months' credit will be allowed to customers but only one month's credit will be received from suppliers of inventory.

(f) Running expenses, including rent but excluding depreciation of non-current assets, are estimated at $1,600 per month.

(g) Blair intends to make monthly cash drawings of $1,000.

Required

Prepare a cash budget for the six months to 31 March 20X4.

Solution

The opening cash balance at 1 October will consist of Peter's initial $15,000 less the $8,000 expended on non-current assets purchased in September. In other words, the opening balance is $7,000. Cash receipts from credit customers arise two months after the relevant sales.

Payments to suppliers are a little more tricky. We are told that cost of sales is 100/150 × sales. Thus for October cost of sales is 100/150 × $3,000 = $2,000. These goods will be purchased in October but not paid for until November. Similar calculations can be made for later months. The initial inventory of $5,000 is purchased in September and consequently paid for in October. **Depreciation is not a cash flow and so is *not* included in a cash budget.**

The cash budget can now be constructed.

CASH BUDGET FOR THE SIX MONTHS ENDING 31 MARCH 20X4

	Oct $	*Nov* $	*Dec* $	*Jan* $	*Feb* $	*Mar* $
Payments						
Suppliers	5,000	2,000	4,000	4,000	7,000	7,000
Running expenses	1,600	1,600	1,600	1,600	1,600	1,600
Drawings	1,000	1,000	1,000	1,000	1,000	1,000
	7,600	4,600	6,600	6,600	9,600	9,600
Receipts						
Receivables	-	-	3,000	6,000	6,000	10,500
Surplus/(shortfall)	(7,600)	(4,600)	(3,600)	(600)	(3,600)	900
Opening balance	7,000	(600)	(5,200)	(8,800)	(9,400)	(13,000)
Closing balance	(600)	(5,200)	(8,800)	(9,400)	(13,000)	(12,100)

 Question

Cash budget

You are presented with the budgeted data shown in Annex A for the period November 20X1 to June 20X2 by your firm. It has been extracted from the other functional budgets that have been prepared.

You are also told the following.

(a) Sales are 40% cash, 60% credit. Credit sales are paid two months after the month of sale.
(b) Purchases are paid the month following purchase.
(c) 75% of wages are paid in the current month and 25% the following month.
(d) Overheads are paid the month after they are incurred.
(e) Dividends are paid three months after they are declared.
(f) Capital expenditure is paid two months after it is incurred.
(g) The opening cash balance is $15,000.

Annex A

	Nov X1	Dec X1	Jan X2	Feb X2	Mar X2	Apr X2	May X2	June X2
	$	$	$	$	$	$	$	$
Sales	80,000	100,000	110,000	130,000	140,000	150,000	160,000	180,000
Purchases	40,000	60,000	80,000	90,000	110,000	130,000	140,000	150,000
Wages	10,000	12,000	16,000	20,000	24,000	28,000	32,000	36,000
Overheads	10,000	10,000	15,000	15,000	15,000	20,000	20,000	20,000
Dividends		20,000						40,000
Capital expenditure			30,000			40,000		

The net cash balance carried forward at the end of June 20X2 is $ [   ].

Answer

The net cash balance carried forward at the end of June 20X2 is $ (156,000) .

Workings

	January $'000	February $'000	March $'000	April $'000	May $'000	June $'000
Receipts						
Sales revenue						
Cash	44	52	56	60	64	72
Credit	48	60	66	78	84	90
	92	112	122	138	148	162
Payments						
Purchases	60	80	90	110	130	140
Wages						
75%	12	15	18	21	24	27
25%	3	4	5	6	7	8
Overheads	10	15	15	15	20	20
Dividends			20			
Capital expenditure			30			40
	85	114	178	152	181	235
Net cash flow	7	(2)	(56)	(14)	(33)	(73)
b/f	15	22	20	(36)	(50)	(83)
c/f	22	20	(36)	(50)	(83)	(156)

5.5 Example: using cash budgets

Suppose that a bank overdraft with a ceiling of $50,000 has been arranged to accommodate the increased inventory levels and wage bill for overtime required to support the rising sales shown in Annex A in the question above.

What advice might be offered, given the cash budget prepared in answering the question?

Solution

The overdraft arrangements are quite inadequate to service the cash needs of the business over the six month period. If the figures are realistic then action should be taken now to avoid difficulties in the near future. The following are possible courses of action.

(a) Activities could be curtailed.

(b) Other sources of cash could be explored, for example a long-term loan to finance the capital expenditure and a factoring arrangement to provide cash due from customers more quickly.

(c) Efforts to increase the speed of debt collection could be made.

(d) Payments to suppliers could be delayed.

(e) The dividend payments could be postponed (the figures indicate that this is a small company, possibly owner-managed).

(f) Staff might be persuaded to work at a lower rate in return for, say, an annual bonus or a profit-sharing agreement.

(g) Extra staff might be taken on to reduce the amount of overtime paid.

(h) The stockholding policy should be reviewed: it may be possible to meet demand from current production and minimise cash tied up in inventories.

Assessment focus point	Questions on functional and cash budget preparation are likely to appear in your assessment.

6 Master budgets

> **FAST FORWARD**
>
> The **master budget** provides a consolidation of all the subsidiary budgets and normally consists of a budgeted income statement, budgeted balance sheet, and a cash budget.

As well as wishing to forecast its cash position, a business might want to estimate its profitability and its financial position for a coming period. This would involve the preparation of a budgeted income statement and balance sheet, both of which form a part of the **master budget**.

6.1 Example: preparing a budgeted income statement and balance sheet

Using the information in Section 5.4, you are required to prepare Peter Blair's budgeted income statement for the six months ending on 31 March 20X4 and a budgeted balance sheet as at that date.

Solution

The income statement is straightforward. The first figure is sales, which can be computed very easily from the information in Section 5.4(c). It is sufficient to add up the monthly sales figures given there; for the income statement there is no need to worry about any closing receivables. Similarly, cost of sales is calculated directly from the information on gross margin contained in Section 5.4(d).

FORECAST TRADING AND INCOME STATEMENT
FOR THE SIX MONTHS ENDING 31 MARCH 20X4

	$	$
Sales (3,000 + (2 × 6,000) + (3 × 10,500))		46,500
Cost of sales (2/3 × $46,500)		31,000
Gross profit		15,500
Expenses		
Running expenses (6 × $1,600)	9,600	
Depreciation ($8,000 × 20% × 6/12)	800	
		10,400
Net profit		5,100

Items will be shown in the balance sheet as follows.

(a)   Inventory will comprise the initial purchases of $5,000.
(b)   Receivables will comprise sales made in February and March (not paid until April and May respectively).
(c)   Accounts payable will comprise purchases made in March (not paid for until April).
(d)   The bank overdraft is the closing cash figure computed in the cash budget.

FORECAST BALANCE SHEET AT 31 MARCH 20X4

	$	$
Non-current assets $(8,000 – 800)		7,200
Current assets		
Inventories	5,000	
Receivables (2 × $10,500)	21,000	
	26,000	
Current liabilities		
Bank overdraft	12,100	
Trade suppliers (March purchases)	7,000	
	19,100	
Net current assets		6,900
		14,100
Proprietor's interest		
Capital introduced		15,000
Profit for the period	5,100	
Less drawings	(6,000)	
Deficit retained		(900)
		14,100

We have now prepared all of the elements of Peter Blair's **master budget**: the budgeted income statement and balance sheet, and the budgeted cash flow from Section 5.4

6.2 A few hints

Budget questions are often accompanied by a large amount of sometimes confusing detail. This should not blind you to the fact that many figures can be entered very simply from the logic of the trading situation described. For example in the case of Blair you might feel tempted to begin a T-account to compute the closing receivables figure. This kind of working is rarely necessary, since you are told that receivables take two months to pay. Closing receivables will equal total credit sales in the last two months of the period.

Similarly, you may be given a simple statement that a business pays rates at $1,500 a year, followed by a lot of detail to enable you to calculate a prepayment at the beginning and end of the year. If you are preparing a budgeted income statement for the year do not lose sight of the fact that the rates expense can be entered as $1,500 without any calculation at all.

7 Capital expenditure budgets

FAST FORWARD Because of the monetary amounts involved in capital expenditure, the **capital expenditure budget** is one of the principal subsidiary budgets.

7.1 Steps in the preparation of capital expenditure budgets

The steps in the preparation of such a budget are as follows.

Step 1 An **accountant or budget officer should be responsible** for the capital expenditure budget. Their tasks should include communicating between interested parties, providing necessary data to assist in budget preparation, drawing up a timetable to ensure that proper consultation takes place and so on.

Step 2 Sales, production and related budgets cover, in general, a 12-month period. A detailed **capital expenditure budget should be prepared for the budget period but additional budgets should be drawn up for both the medium and long term.** This requires an in-depth consideration of the organisation's requirements for land, buildings, plant, machinery, vehicles, fixtures and fittings and so on for the short, medium and long term.

Step 3 The **budget covering the 12 month period** should be **broken down into monthly** or **quarterly spending**, and details incorporated into the cash budget.

Step 4 Suitable **financing** must be arranged as necessary.

Step 5 The capital expenditure budget should **take account of the principal budget factor**. If available funds are limiting the organisation's activities then they will more than likely limit capital expenditure.

Step 6 As part of the overall budget coordination process, the capital expenditure budget must be **reviewed in relation to the other budgets**. Proposed expansion of production may well require significant fixed asset expenditure which should be reflected in the budget.

Step 7 The capital expenditure budget should be **updated on a regular basis** since both the timing and amount of expenditure can change at short notice.

7.2 Example of a capital expenditure budget

A capital expenditure budget might appear as follows.

XYZ Company: Capital expenditure budget – 20X4

Project	Description/detail of capital investment items	Month	$'000
LV45	Installation of new personal computers and flat screen monitors throughout office and factory	April	100
LV46	Plant replacement of obsolete packing equipment by new automated and electronic machinery	October	500
Budgeted capital expenditure			600

7.3 Depreciation

Any depreciation on budgeted capital expenditure will need to be incorporated into the budgeted income statement, along with depreciation on existing fixed assets. The depreciation on planned disposals of fixed assets also needs to be taken into consideration.

7.3.1 Example: budgeted depreciation.

Suppose, for simplicity, XYZ Company (whose capital expenditure budget is shown above) applies a 10% straight-line depreciation policy to all fixed assets. All fixed assets are under ten years old. Fixed assets had a cost value of $4,000,000 at the beginning of 20X4. Budgeted additions to fixed assets are shown above. The plant being replaced by project LV46 has a cost value of $200,000, and will be disposed of at the very end of September (the new plant becoming operational on 1 October 20X4).

The budgeted depreciation charge for the year is:

	$
Depreciation on fixed assets held at 1 January 20X4 ($4,000,000 × 10%)	400,000
Less: depreciation not charged on disposals (3/12 × 10% × $200,000)	(5,000)
Plus: depreciation on additions	
LV45 (9/12 × 10% × $100,000)	7,500
LV46 (3/12 × 10% × $500,000)	12,500
Budgeted depreciation charge for 20X4	415,000

Chapter Roundup

- Budgeting is a **multi-purpose activity**.

- A budget might be a **forecast**, a **means of allocating resources**, a **yardstick** or a **target.**

- The **budget committee** is the coordinating body in the preparation and administration of budgets.

- The manager responsible for preparing each budget should ideally be the manager responsible for carrying out the budget.

- The **budget manual** is a collection of instructions governing the responsibilities of persons and the procedures, forms and records relating to the preparation and use of budgetary data.

- The first task in the budgetary process is to identify the **principal budget factor**. This is also known as the **key budget factor** or **limiting budget factor**. The principal budget factor is the factor which limits the activities of an organisation.

- **Functional/departmental budgets** include budgets for sales, production, purchases and labour.

- A **cash budget** is a statement in which estimated future cash receipts and payments are tabulated in such a way as to show the forecast cash balance of a business at defined intervals.

- The **usefulness of cash budgets** is that they enable management to make any **forward planning decisions** that may be needed, such as advising their bank of estimated overdraft requirements or strengthening their credit control procedures to ensure that customers pay more quickly.

- The **master budget** provides a consolidation of all the subsidiary budgets and normally consists of a budgeted income statement, budgeted balance sheet and a cash budget.

- Because of the monetary amounts involved in capital expenditure, the **capital expenditure budget** is one of the principal subsidiary budgets.

Quick Quiz

1 Budgets have a number of purposes. Fill in the key words which are missing from the statements below.

   (a) To .... the activities of different departments towards a single plan.

   (b) To .... targets to managers responsible for achieving them.

   (c) To establish a system of .... by comparing budgeted and actual results.

   (d) To compel ....

2 Which of the following is unlikely to be contained with a budget manual?

   A Organisational structures
   B Objectives of the budgetary process
   C Selling overhead budget
   D Administrative details of budget preparation

3   The factor which limits the activities of an organisation is known as:

I   The key budget factor
II   The limiting budget factor
III   The principal budget factor
IV   The main budget factor

A   I, II and IV
B   I and III
C   II and III
D   I, II and III

4   If the principal budget factor is sales demand, in which order would the following budgets be prepared?

Materials usage	Materials purchase	Production	Sales	Cash

1st   [   ]

2nd   [   ]

3rd   [   ]

4th   [   ]

5th   [   ]

5   Match the following cash positions with the appropriate management action.

Short-term surplus   Increase payables

Long-term surplus   Replace/update non-current assets
                            ?
Short-term shortfall   Issue share capital

Long-term shortfall   Increase receivables and inventory

6   Depreciation has an effect on net profit and is therefore included in a cash budget.

True   [   ]

False   [   ]

7   Which of the following are included in the master budget?
I   Budgeted income statement
II   Budgeted balance sheet
III   Budgeted cash flow
IV   Functional budgets

A   I, II and III
B   II and III
C   II, III and IV
D   IV only

Answers to Quick Quiz

1 (a) Coordinate
   (b) Communicate
   (c) Control
   (d) Planning

2 C

3 D

4 1st | Sales |

   2nd | Production |

   3rd | Materials usage |

   4th | Materials purchase |

   5th | Cash |

5 Short term surplus ——→ Increase payables

   Long-term surplus ——→ Replace/update non-current assets

   Short-term shortfall ——→ Issue share capital

   Long-term shortfall ——→ Increase receivables and inventory

6 False. Only cash flow items are included in cash budgets. Depreciation is not a cash flow and so is not included in a cash budget.

7 A

Now try the questions below from the Question Bank

Question numbers	Page
47–51	357

Flexible budgeting

Introduction

You should now be able to **prepare functional budgets, a cash budget and a master budget** and have some idea of the **budgeting process**. This chapter takes the budgeting theme further.

We begin by looking at **flexible budgets**, a vital management planning and control tool. This part of the chapter relies on your understanding of **cost behaviour** covered in Chapter 4.

We'll also take a look at the way in which budgets can be used in a system of reward strategies for managers.

Topic list	Learning outcomes	Syllabus references	Ability required
1 Flexible budgets	E(vi)	E(1)	Analysis
2 Flexible budgets and control	E(v)	E(3), (4), (5), (6)	Application
3 Budgets and management reward	E(vii)	E(6)	Comprehension

1 Flexible budgets

1.1 Fixed budgets versus flexible budgets

FAST FORWARD

- A **fixed budget** is a budget which is set for a single activity level.

- A **flexible budget** is a budget which recognises different cost behaviour patterns and is designed to change as volume of activity changes.

Master budgets are based on planned volumes of production and sales but do not include any provision for the event that actual volumes may differ from the budget. In this sense they may be described as **fixed budgets**.

Key term

A **fixed budget** is a 'budget set prior to the control period and not subsequently changed in response to changes in activity, costs or revenue. It may serve as a benchmark in performance evaluation.' CIMA *Official Terminology*

1.2 Advantages of flexible budgets

A **flexible budget** has two advantages.

(a) At the **planning** stage, it may be helpful to know what the effects would be if the actual outcome differs from the prediction. For example, a company may budget to sell 10,000 units of its product, but may prepare flexible budgets based on sales of, say, 8,000 and 12,000 units. This would enable **contingency plans** to be drawn up if necessary.

(b) At the end of each month or year, actual results may be compared with the relevant activity level in the flexible budget as a **control** procedure.

1.3 Preparation of flexible budgets

Step 1 The first step in the preparation of a flexible budget is the **determination of cost behaviour patterns**, which means **deciding whether costs are fixed, variable or semi-variable**.

- Fixed costs are easy to spot. They remain constant as activity levels change.

- For non-fixed costs, divide each cost figure by the related activity level. If the cost is a variable cost, the cost per unit will remain constant. If the cost is a semi-variable cost, the unit rate will reduce as activity levels increase.

Step 2 The second step in the preparation of a flexible budget is to calculate the **budget cost allowance** for each cost item.

Budget cost allowance = budgeted fixed cost* + (number of units × variable cost per unit)**

* nil for variable cost
** nil for fixed cost

Semi-variable costs therefore need splitting into their fixed and variable components so that the budget cost allowance can be calculated.

Key term

Budget flexing involves 'flexing variable costs from original budgeted levels to the allowances permitted for actual volume achieved while maintaining fixed costs at original budget levels'. CIMA *Official Terminology*

1.3.1 Splitting semi-variable costs

One method for splitting semi-variable costs is the high/low method, which we covered in Chapter 4. Attempt the following question to make sure you remember how to do this.

Question
Cost estimation

The cost of factory power has behaved as follows in past years.

	Units of output produced	Cost of factory power $
20X1	7,900	38,700
20X2	7,700	38,100
20X3	9,800	44,400
20X4	9,100	42,300

Budgeted production for 20X5 is 10,200 units.

Ignoring inflation, the cost of factory power which will be incurred is estimated to be $ ☐ .

Answer

The cost of factory power is estimated to be $ 45,600 .

Workings

	Units	$
20X3 (highest output)	9,800	44,400
20X2 (lowest output)	7,700	38,100
	2,100	6,300

The variable cost per unit is therefore $6,300/2,100 = $3.

The level of fixed cost can be calculated by looking at any output level.

	$
Total cost of factory power in 20X3	44,400
Less variable cost of factory power (9,800 × $3)	29,400
Fixed cost of factory power	15,000

An estimate of costs is 20X5 is as follows.

	$
Fixed cost	15,000
Variable cost of budgeted production (10,200 × $3)	30,600
Total budgeted cost of factory power	45,600

Now you are ready to prepare a flexible budget.

1.4 Example: preparing a flexible budget

(a)   Prepare a budget for 20X6 for the direct labour costs and overhead expenses of a production department flexed at the activity levels of 80%, 90% and 100%, using the information listed below.

(i)   The direct labour hourly rate is expected to be $3.75.

(ii)   100% activity represents 60,000 direct labour hours.

(iii)   Variable costs

Indirect labour	$0.75 per direct labour hour
Consumable supplies	$0.375 per direct labour hour
Canteen and other welfare services	6% of direct and indirect labour costs

(iv)   Semi-variable costs are expected to relate to the direct labour hours in the same manner as for the last five years.

Year	Direct labour hours	Semi-variable costs $
20X1	64,000	20,800
20X2	59,000	19,800
20X3	53,000	18,600
20X4	49,000	17,800
20X5	40,000 (estimate)	16,000 (estimate)

(v)   *Fixed costs*

	$
Depreciation	18,000
Maintenance	10,000
Insurance	4,000
Rates	15,000
Management salaries	25,000

(vi)   Inflation is to be ignored.

(b)   Calculate the budget cost allowance (ie expected expenditure) for 20X6 assuming that 57,000 direct labour hours are worked.

Solution

(a)

	80% level 48,000 hrs $'000	90% level 54,000 hrs $'000	100% level 60,000 hrs $'000
Direct labour	180.00	202.50	225.0
Other variable costs			
Indirect labour	36.00	40.50	45.0
Consumable supplies	18.00	20.25	22.5
Canteen etc	12.96	14.58	16.2
Total variable costs ($5.145 per hour)	246.96	277.83	308.7
Semi-variable costs (W)	17.60	18.80	20.0
Fixed costs			
Depreciation	18.00	18.00	18.0
Maintenance	10.00	10.00	10.0
Insurance	4.00	4.00	4.0
Rates	15.00	15.00	15.0
Management salaries	25.00	25.00	25.0
Budgeted costs	336.56	368.63	400.7

Working

Using the high/low method:

	$
Total cost of 64,000 hours	20,800
Total cost of 40,000 hours	16,000
Variable cost of 24,000 hours	4,800
Variable cost per hour ($4,800/24,000)	$0.20

	$
Total cost of 64,000 hours	20,800
Variable cost of 64,000 hours (× $0.20)	12,800
Fixed costs	8,000

Semi-variable costs are calculated as follows.

			$
60,000 hours	(60,000 × $0.20) + $8,000	=	20,000
54,000 hours	(54,000 × $0.20) + $8,000	=	18,800
48,000 hours	(48,000 × $0.20) + $8,000	=	17,600

(b) The budget cost allowance for 57,000 direct labour hours of work would be as follows.

		$
Variable costs	(57,000 × $5.145)	293,265
Semi-variable costs	($8,000 + (57,000 × $0.20))	19,400
Fixed costs		72,000
		384,665

2 Flexible budgets and control

FAST FORWARD

Control involves **comparing a flexible budget** (based on the actual activity level) with **actual results**. The **differences** between the flexible budget figures and the actual results are **budget variances**.

2.1 Flexible budgets for control

Suppose W Co manufactures a single product, the CL. Budgeted results and actual results for June 20X2 are shown below.

	Budget	Actual results	Variance
Production and sales of the CL (units)	2,000	3,000	
	$	$	$
Sales revenue (a)	20,000	30,000	10,000 (F)
Direct materials	6,000	8,500	2,500 (A)
Direct labour	4,000	4,500	500 (A)
Maintenance	1,000	1,400	400 (A)
Depreciation	2,000	2,200	200 (A)
Rent and rates	1,500	1,600	100 (A)
Other costs	3,600	5,000	1,400 (A)
Total costs (b)	18,100	23,200	5,100
Profit (a) – (b)	1,900	6,800	4,900 (F)

(a)   In this example, the variances are meaningless for purposes of control. Costs were higher than budget because the **volume of output was also higher**; variable costs would be expected to increase above the budgeted costs in the fixed budget. There is no information to show whether control action is needed for any aspect of costs or revenue.

(b)   For control purposes, it is necessary to know the answers to questions such as the following.

- Were actual costs higher than they should have been to produce and sell 3,000 CLs?
- Was actual revenue satisfactory from the sale of 3,000 CLs?

2.1.1 The correct approach to control

Important!

The **correct approach** to control is as follows.

- Identify fixed and variable costs.
- Produce a **flexible budget** based on the **actual activity level**.

In the previous example of W Co, let us suppose that we have the following estimates of cost behaviour.

(a)   Direct materials, direct labour and maintenance costs are variable.

(b)   Rent and rates and depreciation are fixed costs.

(c)   Other costs consist of fixed costs of $1,600 plus a variable cost of $1 per unit made and sold.

The control analysis should therefore be based on a flexible budget as follows.

	Fixed budget (a)	Flexible budget (b)	Actual results (c)	Budget variance (c)-(b)	
Production & sales (units)	2,000	3,000	3,000		
	$	$	$	$	
Sales revenue	20,000	30,000	30,000	0	
Variable costs					
Direct materials	6,000	9,000	8,500	500	(F)
Direct labour	4,000	6,000	4,500	1,500	(F)
Maintenance	1,000	1,500	1,400	100	(F)
Semi-variable costs					
Other costs	3,600	4,600	5,000	400	(A)
Fixed costs					
Depreciation	2,000	2,000	2,200	200	(A)
Rent and rates	1,500	1,500	1,600	100	(A)
Total costs	18,100	24,600	23,200	1,400	(F)
Profit	1,900	5,400	6,800	1,400	(F)

$3,500 (F)　　　　$1,400 (F)
Volume variance　　Expenditure variance

$4,900 (F)
Total variance

Notice that the total variance has not altered. It is still $4,900 (F) as in Section 2.1. The flexible budget comparison merely analyses the total variance into two separate components.

portant!

> Variances are calculated by comparing actual results and the flexible budget, *not* actual results and the original budget.

2.1.2 Interpretation of the control statement

We can analyse the above as follows.

(a) In selling 3,000 units the expected profit should have been, not the fixed budget profit of $1,900, but the flexible budget profit of $5,400. Instead, actual profit was $6,800 ie $1,400 more than we should have expected. This is the $1,400 favourable expenditure variance. The reason for this $1,400 improvement is that, given output and sales of 3,000 units, overall costs were lower than expected (and sales revenue was exactly as expected). For example the direct material cost was $500 lower than expected.

(b) Another reason for the improvement in profit above the fixed budget profit is the **sales volume**. W Co sold 3,000 units of CL instead of 2,000, with the following result.

	$	$
Budgeted sales revenue increased by		10,000
Budgeted variable costs increased by:		
direct materials	3,000	
direct labour	2,000	
maintenance	500	
variable element of other costs	1,000	
Budgeted fixed costs are unchanged		6,500
Budgeted profit increased by		3,500

Budgeted profit was therefore increased by $3,500 because sales volume increased. This is the $3,500 favourable volume variance.

(c)   A full variance analysis statement would be as follows.

	$	$
Fixed budget profit		1,900
Variances		
Sales volume		3,500 (F)
Direct materials cost	500 (F)	
Direct labour cost	1,500 (F)	
Maintenance cost	100 (F)	
Other costs	400 (A)	
Depreciation	200 (A)	
Rent and rates	100 (A)	
Total expenditure variance		1,400 (F)
Actual profit		6,800

Important!

If management believes that any of these variances are large enough to justify it, they will investigate the reasons for them to see whether any corrective action is necessary.

Question   Budget cost allowances

WL Co manufactures and sells a single product, R. Since the R is highly perishable, no inventories are held at any time. WL Co's management uses a flexible budgeting system to control costs. Extracts from the flexible budget are as follows.

Output and sales (units)	4,000	5,500
Budget cost allowances	$	$
Direct material	16,000	22,000
Direct labour	20,000	24,500
Variable production overhead	8,000	11,000
Fixed production overhead	11,000	11,000
Selling and distribution overhead	8,000	9,500
Administration overhead	7,000	7,000
Total expenditure	70,000	85,000

Production and sales of product R amounted to 5,100 units during period 5.

The total budget cost allowances in the flexible budget for period 5 will be:

(a)   Direct material $ ☐

(b)   Direct labour $ ☐

(c)   Variable production overhead $ ☐

(d)   Fixed production overhead $ ☐

(e)   Selling and distribution overhead $ ☐

(f)   Administration overhead $ [   ]

(g)   Production and sales of product R in period 6 amounted to 5,500 units. Budgeted output for the period was 4,000 units. Actual total expenditure was $82,400.

    (i)   The total expenditure variance for period 6 was $ [   ] favourable/adverse (delete as necessary)

    (ii)   The volume variance for period 6 was $ [   ] favourable/adverse (delete as necessary)

Answer

(a)   Direct material $ [20,400]

(b)   Direct labour $ [23,300]

(c)   Variable production overhead $ [10,200]

(d)   Fixed production overhead $ [11,000]

(e)   Selling and distribution overhead $ [9,100]

(f)   Administration overhead $ 7,000

(g)   (i)   The total expenditure variance for period 6 was $ [2,600] favourable/~~adverse~~

    (ii)   The volume variance for period 6 was $ [15,000] ~~favourable~~/adverse

Workings

(a)   Direct material is a variable cost of $16,000/4,000 = $4 per unit
       Budget cost allowance for 5,100 units = 5,100 × $4 = $20,400

(b)   Direct labour is a semi-variable cost which can be analysed using the high-low method.

	Output Units	$
High	5,500	24,500
Low	4,000	20,000
Change	1,500	4,500

Variable cost per unit   = $4,500/1,500 = $3
Substituting in high output, fixed cost   = $24,500 − (5,500 × $3)
                                           = $8,000

Budget cost allowance for 5,100 units:

	$
Variable cost = 5,100 × $3	15,300
Fixed cost	8,000
	23,300

(c)   Variable production overhead per unit = $8,000/4,000 = $2 per unit
       Budget cost allowance for 5,100 units = 5,100 × $2 = $10,200

(d)   Fixed production overhead cost allowance is fixed at $11,000.

(e)   Selling and distribution is a semi-variable cost which can be analysed using the high-low method.

	Output Units	$
High	5,500	9,500
Low	4,000	8,000
Change	1,500	1,500

Variable cost per unit   = $1,500/1,500 = $1

Substituting in high output, fixed cost = $9,500 − (5,500 × $1)

                                            = $4,000

Budget cost allowance for 5,100 units:

	$
Variable cost = 5,100 × $1	5,100
Fixed cost	4,000
	9,100

(f)   Administration overhead cost allowance is fixed at $7,000.

(g)   The budgeted and actual output volumes correspond to the two activity levels provided in the question data. The total budget cost allowance for each activity level can be used as the basis for the variance calculations.

    (i)   Expenditure variance   =   budget cost allowance for 5,500 units − actual expenditure for 5,500 units

                                  = $85,000 − $82,400

                                  = $2,600 favourable

    (ii)   Volume variance = budget cost allowance for original budget of 4,000 units − budget cost allowance for actual volume of 5,500 units

                = $70,000 − $85,000 = $15,000 adverse

3 Budgets and management reward

FAST FORWARD

Budgets can be used in a system of **reward strategies** for managers. They act as targets or benchmarks for managerial performance.

We mentioned at the start of Chapter 10 that one of the reasons for using budgets is to provide a means of evaluating the performance of managers.

Research has shown that if an organisation's **reward system** (promotions, salary increases, bonuses, 'perks') is **connected to a control system**, management **motivation will increase** and management will perceive the **control system** as important, which should **improve its effectiveness**.

For performance evaluation purposes, a system of control using **budgets as targets or benchmarks for managerial performance**, against which actual performance is compared, can be adopted.

This provides a way of evaluating the performance of the manager and good results can be rewarded with a financial bonus or promotion.

The process needs to be carried out so as to **motivate managers**, however, **rather than create resentment and adverse reactions**. The process should not make managers feel under pressure to achieve but should encourage:

- Participation
- Initiative
- Responsibility

It is therefore important that **budget targets** are:

- Under the control of managers (ie they can control the costs and revenues in question)
- Clearly defined
- Attainable (but not too easy to achieve as this will be demotivating)
- Understood and accepted as a target
- Focused on the short, medium and long term

Keeping managers informed of their performance also helps to encourage motivation. Feedback on performance therefore needs to be:

- Frequent
- Up to date
- Accurate
- Relevant (ie relates to items over which the manager has control)

Chapter Roundup

- A **fixed budget** is a budget which is set for a single activity level.

- A **flexible budget** is a budget which recognises different cost behaviour patterns and is designed to change as volume of activity changes.

- **Control** involves **comparing a flexible budget** (based on the actual activity level) with **actual results**. The **differences** between the flexible budget figures and the actual results are **budget variances**.

- Budgets can be used in a system of **reward strategies** for managers. They act as targets or benchmarks for managerial performance.

Quick Quiz

1   *Fill in the blanks with the word 'fixed' or the word 'flexible'.*

   (a)   At the planning stage, a .... budget can show what the effects would be if the actual outcome differs from the prediction.

   (b)   At the end of each period, actual results may be compared with the relevant activity level in the .... budget as a control procedure.

   (c)   Master budgets are .... budgets.

2   Flexible budgets are normally prepared on a marginal costing basis.

   True   ☐

   False   ☐

3   *Fill in the gaps.*

   Budget cost allowance = ... + (........................ × ....)

4   What is the wrong approach to budgetary control?

5   What is the correct approach to budgetary control?

Answers to Quick Quiz

1   (a)   At the planning stage, a **flexible** budget can show what the effects would be if the actual outcome differs from the prediction.

   (b)   At the end of each period, actual results may be compared with the relevant activity level in the **flexible** budget as a control procedure.

   (c)   Master budgets are **fixed** budgets.

2   True

3   Budget cost allowance = budgeted fixed cost + (number of units × variable cost per unit)

4   To compare actual results against a fixed budget.

5   •   To identify fixed and variable costs
   •   To produce a flexible budget using marginal costing techniques

Now try the questions below from the Question Bank

Question numbers	Page
52–56	359

Part E
Costing and accounting systems

Process costing

Introduction

We will look at **costing systems** in this part of the Study Text. These costing systems are used to cost goods or services and which method is used depends on the way in which the goods or services are produced. In Chapter 13 we will look at job, batch and contract costing. In this chapter we will consider **process costing**. Process costing is applied when output consists of a continuous stream of **identical units**. We will begin from basics and look at how to account for the most simple of processes. We will then move on to how to account for any **losses** which might occur, as well as what to do with any **scrapped units** which are sold. Next we will consider how to deal with **closing work in progress** before examining situations involving closing work in progress and losses. We will then go on to have a look at situations involving **opening work in progress** and finally we shall consider how to deal with situations where we have both opening and closing work in progress and losses.

The chapter will conclude with an outline discussion of **joint products** and **by-products**.

Topic list	Learning outcomes	Syllabus references	Ability required
1 The distinguishing features of process costing	D(iii)	D(4)	Analysis
2 The basics of process costing	D(iv)	D(4)	Application
3 Dealing with losses in process	D(iv)	D(4)	Application
4 Accounting for scrap	D(iv)	D(4)	Application
5 Valuing closing work in progress	D(iv)	D(4)	Application
6 Valuing opening work in progress	D(iv)	D(4)	Application
7 Joint products and by-products	D(iii)	D(4)	Application

1 The distinguishing features of process costing

Process costing is a costing method used where it is not possible to identify separate units of production, or jobs, usually because of the continuous nature of the production processes involved.

Process costing is used where there is a continuous flow of identical units and it is common to identify it with **continuous production** such as the following.

- Oil refining
- The manufacture of soap
- Paint manufacture
- Food and drink manufacture

Key terms

Process costing is a 'form of costing applicable to continuous processes where process costs are attributed to the number of units produced. This may involve estimating the number of equivalent units in stock at the start and end of the period under consideration.'

CIMA *Official Terminology*

Don't worry about the term 'equivalent units'. All will become clear as you work through this chapter.

The **features of process costing** which make it different from other methods of costing such as job or batch costing are as follows.

(a) The continuous nature of production in many processes means that there will usually be **closing work in progress which must be valued**. In process costing it is not possible to build up cost records of the cost of each individual unit of output because production in progress is an **indistinguishable homogeneous mass**.

(b) There is often a **loss in process** due to spoilage, wastage, evaporation and so on.

(c) The **output** of one process becomes the **input** to the next until the finished product is made in the final process.

(d) Output from production may be a single product, but there may also be a **by-product** (or by-products) and/or **joint products**.

2 The basics of process costing

2.1 Process accounts

Costs incurred in processes are recorded in what are known as process accounts.

A process account has **two sides**, and on **each side there are two columns** – one for **quantities** (of raw materials, work in progress and finished goods) and one for **costs**.

(a) On the **left hand side** of the process account we record the **inputs** to the process and the **cost of these inputs**. So we might show the quantity of material input to a process during the period and its cost, the cost of labour and the cost of overheads.

(b) On the right hand side of the process account we record what happens to the inputs by the end of the period.

(i)   Some of the input might be converted into **finished goods**, so we show the units of finished goods and the cost of these units.

(ii)   Some of the material input might evaporate or get spilled or damaged, so there would be **losses**. So we record the loss units and the cost of the loss.

(iii)   At the end of a period, some units of input might be in the process of being turned into finished units so would be work in progress (**WIP**). We record the units of WIP and the cost of these units.

The **quantity columns on each side of the account** should total to the **same amount**. Why? Well think about it. If we put 100 kgs of material in to a process (which we record on the left hand side of the account) we should know what has happened to those 100 kgs. Some would be losses maybe, some would be WIP, some would be finished units, but the total should be 100 kgs.

Likewise the **cost of the inputs to the process during a period** (ie the total of the costs recorded on the left hand side of the account) is the **cost of the outputs of the process**. If we have recorded material, labour and overhead costs totalling $1,000 and at the end of the process we have 100 finished units (and no losses or WIP), then that output cost $1,000.

Here's a very simple example of a process account.

PROCESS ACCOUNT

	Units	$		Units	$
Material	1,000	11,000	Closing WIP	200	2,000
Labour		4,000	Finished units	800	16,000
Overhead		3,000			
	1,000	18,000		1,000	18,000

As you can see, the **quantity columns on each side balance** (ie they are the same), **as do the monetary columns**. (Don't worry at this stage about how the costs are split between WIP and finished units.

2.1.1 Debits and credits

You may not have started your Paper C2 studies on financial accounting yet and so won't have come across the terms **debit** and **credit**.

- A **debit** is simply an entry on the **left hand side** of an account
- A **credit** is an entry on the **right hand side** of an account

Don't worry about the terms at this stage. All will become clear as your studies progress.

Before tackling the more complex areas of process costing, we will begin by looking at a very simple process costing example which will illustrate the basic techniques which we will build upon in the remainder of this chapter.

2.2 Example: basics of process costing

Suppose that Purr and Miaow Co make squeaky toys for cats. Production of the toys involves two processes, shaping and colouring. During the year to 31 March 20X3, 1,000,000 units of material worth $500,000 were input to the first process, shaping. Direct labour costs of $200,000 and production overhead costs of $200,000 were also incurred in connection with the shaping process. There were no opening or closing inventories in the shaping department. The process account for shaping for the year ended 31 March 20X3 is as follows.

PROCESS 1 (SHAPING) ACCOUNT

	Units	$		Units	$
Direct materials	1,000,000	500,000	Output to Process 2	1,000,000	900,000
Direct labour		200,000			
Production overheads		200,000			
	1,000,000	900,000		1,000,000	900,000

Assessment focus point

When preparing process accounts, balance off the quantity columns (ie ensure they total to the same amount on both sides) **before** attempting to complete the monetary value columns since they will help you to check that you have missed nothing out. This becomes increasingly important as more complications are introduced into questions.

When using process costing, if a **series of separate processes** is needed to manufacture the finished product, the **output of one process becomes the input to the next** until the final output is made in the final process. In our example, all output from shaping was transferred to the second process, colouring, during the year to 31 March 20X3. An additional 500,000 units of material, costing $300,000, were input to the colouring process. Direct labour costs of $150,000 and production overhead costs of $150,000 were also incurred. There were no opening or closing inventories in the colouring department. The process account for colouring for the year ended 31 March 20X3 is as follows.

PROCESS 2 (COLOURING) ACCOUNT

	Units	$		Units	$
Materials from process 1	1,000,000	900,000	Output to finished		
Added materials		300,000	goods	1,000,000	1,500,000
Direct labour		150,000			
Production overhead		150,000			
	1,000,000	1,500,000		1,000,000	1,500,000

Assessment focus point

Direct labour and production overhead may be treated together in an assessment question as **conversion cost**.

Added materials, labour and overhead in Process 2 are usually **added gradually** throughout the process. Materials from Process 1, in contrast, will often be **introduced in full at the start of the second process**.

2.3 Framework for dealing with process costing

FAST FORWARD

Use our suggested **four-step approach** when dealing with process costing questions.

Step 1	Determine output and losses
Step 2	Calculate cost per unit of output, losses and WIP
Step 3	Calculate total cost of output, losses and WIP
Step 4	Complete accounts

Process costing is centred around **four key steps**. The exact work done at each step will depend on the circumstances of the question, but the approach can always be used. Don't worry about the terms used. We will be looking at their meaning as we work through the chapter.

Step 1   Determine output and losses

- Determine expected output.
- Calculate normal loss and abnormal loss and gain.
- Calculate equivalent units if there is closing work in progress.

Step 2   Calculate cost per unit of output, losses and WIP

Calculate cost per unit or cost per equivalent unit.

Step 3   Calculate total cost of output, losses and WIP

In some examples this will be straightforward. In cases where there is work in progress, a **statement of evaluation** will have to be prepared.

Step 4   Complete accounts

- Complete the process account.
- Write up the other accounts required by the question.

---

essment us point

It always saves time in an assessment if you don't have to think too long about how to approach a question before you begin. This four-step approach can be applied to any process costing question so it would be a good idea to memorise it now. It will be useful as a framework for any workings that you may need to do.

---

3 Dealing with losses in process

FORWARD

Losses may occur in process. If a certain level of loss is expected, this is known as **normal loss**. If losses are greater than expected, the extra loss is **abnormal loss**. If losses are less than expected, the difference is known as **abnormal gain**.

3.1 Losses

During a production process, a loss may occur.

ey terms

Normal loss is 'expected loss, allowed for in the budget, and normally calculated as a percentage of the good output, from a process during a period of time. Normal losses are generally either valued at zero or at their disposal values.'

Abnormal loss is 'any loss in excess of the normal loss allowance'.

Abnormal gain is 'improvement on the accepted or normal loss associated with a production activity'.

CIMA *Official Terminology*

Losses may occur due to wastage, spoilage, evaporation, and so on.

Since normal loss is not given a cost, the cost of producing these units is borne by the 'good' units of output.

Abnormal loss and gain units are valued at the same unit rate as 'good' units. Abnormal events do not therefore affect the cost of good production. Their costs are **analysed separately** in an **abnormal loss or abnormal gain account**.

3.1.1 If you haven't covered bookkeeping yet ...

... you will just need to accept the following facts and learn by rote the correct entries.

(a) In an **abnormal loss account**, the **debit** entry shows the **units (and their value) from the process account**. The **credit** entry shows the **impact on the income statement**.

(b) In an **abnormal gain account**, the **debit** entry shows the **effect on the income statement**, while the **credit** entry shows the **units (and their value) from the process account**.

Once you have covered bookkeeping this will become clear.

3.2 Example: abnormal losses and gains

Suppose that input to a process is 1,000 units at a cost of $4,500. Normal loss is 10% and there are no opening or closing inventories. Determine the accounting entries for the cost of output and the cost of the loss if actual output were as follows.

(a) 860 units (so that actual loss is 140 units)
(b) 920 units (so that actual loss is 80 units)

Solution

Before we demonstrate the use of the 'four-step framework' we will summarise the way that the losses are dealt with.

(a) Normal loss is given no share of cost.

(b) The cost of output is therefore based on the **expected** units of output, which in our example amount to 90% of 1,000 = 900 units.

(c) Abnormal loss is given a cost, which is written off to the income statement via an abnormal loss/gain account.

(d) **Abnormal gain** is treated in the same way, except that being a gain rather than a loss, it appears as a **debit** entry in the process account (as it is a **sort of input**, being additional unexpected units), whereas a **loss** appears as a **credit** entry in this account (as it is a **sort of output**).

(a) **Output is 860 units**

Step 1 Determine output and losses

If actual output is 860 units and the actual loss is 140 units:

	Units
Actual loss	140
Normal loss (10% of 1,000)	100
Abnormal loss	40

Step 2 Calculate cost per unit of output and losses

The cost per unit of output and the cost per unit of abnormal loss are based on expected output.

$$\frac{\text{Costs incurred}}{\text{Expected output}} = \frac{\$4,500}{900\,\text{units}} = \$5 \text{ per unit}$$

Step 3   Calculate total cost of output and losses

Normal loss is not assigned any cost.

	$
Cost of output (860 × $5)	4,300
Normal loss	0
Abnormal loss (40 × $5)	200
	4,500

Step 4   Complete accounts

PROCESS ACCOUNT

	Units	$		Units		$
Cost incurred	1,000	4,500	Normal loss	100		0
			Output (finished			
			goods a/c)	860	(× $5)	4,300
			Abnormal loss	40	(× $5)	200
	1,000	4,500		1,000		4,500

ABNORMAL LOSS ACCOUNT

	Units	$		Units	$
Process a/c	40	200	Income statement	40	200

(b)   **Output is 920 units**

Step 1   Determine output and losses

If actual output is 920 units and the actual loss is 80 units:

	Units
Actual loss	80
Normal loss (10% of 1,000)	100
Abnormal gain	20

Step 2   Calculate cost per unit of output and losses

The cost per unit of output and the cost per unit of abnormal gain are based on **expected** output.

$$\frac{\text{Costs incurred}}{\text{Expected output}} = \frac{\$4,500}{900 \text{ units}} = \$5 \text{ per unit}$$

(Whether there is abnormal loss or gain does not affect the valuation of units of output. The figure of $5 per unit is exactly the same as in the previous paragraph, when there were 40 units of abnormal loss.)

Step 3   Calculate total cost of output and losses

	$
Cost of output (920 × $5)	4,600
Normal loss	0
Abnormal gain (20 × $5)	(100)
	4,500

Step 4   **Complete accounts**

PROCESS ACCOUNT

	Units	$		Units	$
Cost incurred	1,000	4,500	Normal loss	100	0
Abnormal gain a/c	20	(× $5) 100	Output (finished goods a/c)	920	(× $5) 4,600
	1,020	4,600		1,020	4,600

ABNORMAL GAIN

	Units	$		Units	$
Income statement	20	100	Process a/c	20	100

3.3 Example: abnormal losses and gains again

During a four-week period, period 3, costs of input to a process were $29,070. Input was 1,000 units, output was 850 units and normal loss is 10%.

During the next period, period 4, costs of input were again $29,070. Input was again 1,000 units, but output was 950 units.

There were no units of opening or closing inventory.

Required

Prepare the process account and abnormal loss or gain account for each period.

Solution

Step 1   **Determine output and losses**

Period 3

	Units
Actual output	850
Normal loss (10% × 1,000)	100
Abnormal loss	50
Input	1,000

Period 4

	Units
Actual output	950
Normal loss (10% × 1,000)	100
Abnormal gain	(50)
Input	1,000

Step 2   **Calculate cost per unit of output and losses**

For each period the cost per unit is based on expected output.

$$\frac{\text{Cost of input}}{\text{Expected units of output}} = \frac{\$29,070}{900} = \$32.30 \text{ per unit}$$

Step 3   Calculate total cost of output and losses

Period 3	$
Cost of output (850 × $32.30)	27,455
Normal loss	0
Abnormal loss (50 × $32.30)	1,615
	29,070

Period 4	$
Cost of output (950 × $32.30)	30,685
Normal loss	0
Abnormal gain (50 × $32.30)	1,615
	29,070

Step 4   Complete accounts

PROCESS ACCOUNT

	Units	$		Units	$
Period 3					
Cost of input	1,000	29,070	Normal loss	100	0
			Finished goods a/c	850	27,455
			(× $32.30)		
			Abnormal loss a/c	50	1,615
			(× $32.30)		
	1,000	29,070		1,000	29,070
Period 4					
Cost of input	1,000	29,070	Normal loss	100	0
Abnormal gain a/c	50	1,615	Finished goods a/c	950	30,685
(× $32.30)			(× $32.30)		
	1,050	30,685		1,050	30,685

ABNORMAL LOSS OR GAIN ACCOUNT

	$		$
Period 3		**Period 4**	
Abnormal loss in process a/c	1,615	Abnormal gain in process a/c	1,615
Abnormal loss in process a/c	1,615	Abnormal gain in process a/c	1,615

There is a zero balance on this account at the end of period 4.

Question   Cost of output

Charlton Co manufactures a product in a single process operation. Normal loss is 10% of input. Loss occurs at the end of the process. Data for June are as follows.

Opening and closing inventories of work in progress	Nil
Cost of input materials (3,300 units)	$59,100
Direct labour and production overhead	$30,000
Output to finished goods	2,750 units

The full cost of finished output in June was

A $74,250   B $81,000   C $82,500   D $89,100

Answer

The correct answer is C.

Step 1   **Determine output and losses**

	Units
Actual output	2,750
Normal loss (10% × 3,300)	330
Abnormal loss	220
	3,300

Step 2   **Calculate cost per unit of output and losses**

$$\frac{\text{Cost of input}}{\text{Expected units of output}} = \frac{\$89,100}{3,300 - 330} = \$30 \text{ per unit}$$

Step 3   **Calculate total cost of output and losses**

	$
Cost of output (2,750 × $30)	82,500
Normal loss	0
Abnormal loss (220 × $30)	6,600
	89,100

If you were reduced to making a calculated guess, you could have eliminated option D. This is simply the total input cost with no attempt to apportion some of the cost to the abnormal loss.

Option A is incorrect because it results from allocating a full unit cost to the normal loss: remember that normal loss does not carry any of the process cost.

Option B is incorrect because it results from calculating a 10% normal loss based on *output* of 2,750 units (275 units normal loss), rather than on *input* of 3,300 units.

4 Accounting for scrap

ey term

Scrap is 'discarded material having some value'.

CIMA *Official Terminology*

4.1 Basic rules for accounting for scrap

tention!

Again, if you've yet to cover bookkeeping you will just have to learn these debit and credit entries. We suggest you come back to this chapter once you have covered bookkeeping, however, as you'll probably find the whole topic of process costing becomes much clearer.

(a) **Revenue from scrap** is treated, not as an addition to sales revenue, but as a **reduction in costs**.

FORWARD

The **valuation of normal loss is either at scrap value or nil**. It is conventional for the **scrap value of normal loss to be deducted from the cost of materials** before a cost per equivalent unit is calculated.

(b) The scrap value of **normal loss** is therefore used to reduce the material costs of the process.

DEBIT   Scrap account
CREDIT   Process account

with the scrap value of the normal loss.

FORWARD

Abnormal losses and gains never affect the cost of good units of production. The scrap value of abnormal losses is not credited to the process account, and the abnormal loss and gain units **carry the same full cost as a good unit of production**.

(c) The scrap value of **abnormal loss** is used to reduce the cost of abnormal loss.

DEBIT   Scrap account
CREDIT   Abnormal loss account

with the scrap value of abnormal loss, which therefore reduces the write-off of cost to the income statement.

(d) The scrap value of **abnormal gain** arises because the actual units sold as scrap will be less than the scrap value of normal loss. Because there are fewer units of scrap than expected, there will be less revenue from scrap as a direct consequence of the abnormal gain. The abnormal gain account should therefore be debited with the scrap value.

DEBIT   Abnormal gain account
CREDIT   Scrap account

with the scrap value of abnormal gain.

(e) The **scrap account** is completed by recording the **actual cash received** from the sale of scrap.

DEBIT   Cash received
CREDIT   Scrap account

with the cash received from the sale of the actual scrap.

Important!

> The same basic principle therefore applies that only **normal losses** should affect the cost of the good output. The scrap value of **normal loss only** is credited to the process account. The scrap values of abnormal losses and gains are analysed separately in the abnormal loss or gain account.

4.2 Example: scrap and abnormal loss or gain

A factory has two production processes. Normal loss in each process is 10% and scrapped units sell for $0.50 each from process 1 and $3 each from process 2. Relevant information for costing purposes relating to period 5 is as follows

Direct materials added:	Process 1	Process 2
units	2,000	1,250
cost	$8,100	$1,900
Direct labour	$4,000	$10,000
Production overhead	150% of direct labour cost	120% of direct labour cost
Output to process 2/finished goods	1,750 units	2,800 units
Actual production overhead	$17,800	

Required

Prepare the accounts for process 1, process 2, scrap, abnormal loss or gain.

Solution

Step 1 **Determine output and losses**

	Process 1	Process 2
	Units	Units
Output	1,750	2,800
Normal loss (10% of input)	200	300
Abnormal loss	50	-
Abnormal gain	-	(100)
	2,000	3,000*

* 1,750 units from Process 1 + 1,250 units input to process.

Step 2 **Calculate cost per unit of output and losses**

		Process 1		Process 2
		$		$
Cost of input				
- material		8,100		1,900
- from Process 1		-	(1,750 × $10)	17,500
- labour		4,000		10,000
- overhead	(150% × $4,000)	6,000	(120% × $10,000)	12,000
		18,100		41,400
less: scrap value of **normal loss**	(200 × $0.50)	(100)	(300 × $3)	(900)
		18,000		40,500
Expected output				
90% of 2,000		1,800		
90% of 3,000				2,700
Cost per unit				
$18,000 ÷ 1,800		$10		
$40,500 ÷ 2,700				$15

BPP
PROFESSIONAL EDUCATION

Step 3

Calculate total cost of output and losses

	Process 1		Process 2
	$		$
Output (1,750 × $10)	17,500	(2,800 × $15)	42,000
Normal loss (200 × $0.50)*	100	(300 × $3)*	900
Abnormal loss (50 × $10)	500		-
	18,100		42,900
Abnormal gain	-	(100 × $15)	(1,500)
	18,100		41,400

* Remember that normal loss is valued at scrap value only.

Step 4

Complete accounts

PROCESS 1 ACCOUNT

	Units	$		Units	$
Direct material	2,000	8,100	Scrap a/c (normal loss)	200	100
Direct labour		4,000	Process 2 a/c	1,750	17,500
Production			Abnormal loss a/c	50	500
overhead a/c		6,000			
	2,000	18,100		2,000	18,100

PROCESS 2 ACCOUNT

	Units	$		Units	$
Direct materials					
From process 1	1,750	17,500	Scrap a/c (normal loss)	300	900
Added materials	1,250	1,900	Finished goods a/c	2,800	42,000
Direct labour		10,000			
Production o'hd		12,000			
	3,000	41,400			
Abnormal gain	100	1,500			
	3,100	42,900		3,100	42,900

ABNORMAL LOSS ACCOUNT

	$		$
Process 1 (50 units)	500	Scrap a/c: sale of scrap of	
		extra loss (50 units)	25
		Income statement	475
	500		500

ABNORMAL GAIN ACCOUNT

	$		$
Scrap a/c (loss of scrap revenue		Process 2 abnormal gain	1,500
due to abnormal gain,		(100 units)	
100 units × $3)	300		
Income statement	1,200		
	1,500		1,500

SCRAP ACCOUNT

	$		$
Scrap value of normal loss		Cash a/c - cash received	
Process 1 (200 units)	100	Loss in process 1 (250 units)	125
Process 2 (300 units)	900	Loss in process 2 (200 units)	600
Abnormal loss a/c (process 1)	25	Abnormal gain a/c (process 2)	300
	1,025		1,025

Question	Process accounts

Parks Co operates a processing operation involving two stages, the output of process 1 being passed to process 2. The process costs for period 3 were as follows.

Process 1

Material   3,000 kg at $0.25 per kg
Labour $120

Process 2

Material   2,000 kg at $0.40 per kg
Labour $84

General overhead for period 3 amounted to $357 and is absorbed into process costs at a rate of 375% of direct labour costs in process 1 and 496% of direct labour costs in process 2.

The normal output of process 1 is 80% of input and of process 2, 90% of input. Waste matter from process 1 is sold for $0.20 per kg and that from process 2 for $0.30 per kg.

The output for period 3 was as follows.

Process 1   2,300 kgs
Process 2   4,000 kgs

There was no inventory of work in progress at either the beginning or the end of the period and it may be assumed that all available waste matter had been sold at the prices indicated.

Required

Show how the foregoing data would be recorded in process, scrap and abnormal loss/gain accounts by completing the proformas below. (**Hint.** Not all boxes require entries.)

PROCESS 1 ACCOUNT

	kg	$		kg	$
Material			Normal loss to scrap a/c		
Labour			Production transferred to		
General overhead			process 2		
Abnormal gain account			Abnormal loss a/c		

PROCESS 2 ACCOUNT

	kg	$		kg	$
Transferred from process 1	☐	☐	Normal loss to scrap a/c	☐	☐
Material added	☐	☐	Production transferred to		
Labour		☐	finished inventory	☐	☐
General overhead		☐	Abnormal loss	☐	☐
Abnormal gain	☐	☐			
	☐	☐		☐	☐

SCRAP ACCOUNT

	kg	$		kg	$
Normal loss (process 1)	☐	☐	Abnormal gain (process 1)	☐	☐
Normal loss (process 2)	☐	☐	Abnormal gain (process 2)	☐	☐
Abnormal loss (process 1)	☐	☐	Cash	☐	☐
Abnormal loss (process 2)	☐	☐			
	☐	☐		☐	☐

ABNORMAL LOSS AND GAIN ACCOUNT

	kg	$		kg	$
Process 1 (loss)	☐	☐	Scrap value of abnormal		
Process 2 (loss)	☐	☐	loss	☐	☐
Scrap value of abnormal gain	☐	☐	Process 1 (gain)	☐	☐
Income statement		☐	Process 2 (gain)	☐	☐
	☐	☐		☐	☐

Answer

Step 1 — Determine output and losses

	Process 1 kgs		Process 2 kgs
Output	2,300		4,000
Normal loss (20% of 3,000 kgs)	600	(10% of 4,300)	430
Abnormal loss	100		-
Abnormal gain	-		(130)
	3,000		4,300*

* From process 1 (2,300 kgs) + 2,000 kgs added

Step 2   Determine cost per unit of output and losses

		Process 1		Process 2
		$		$
Material (3,000 × $0.25)		750	(2,000 × $0.40)	800
From process 1		-	(2,300 × $0.50)	1,150
Labour		120		84
Overhead (375% × $120)		450	(496% × $84)	417
less: scrap value of **normal** loss				
(600 × $0.20)		(120)	(430 × $0.3)	(129)
		1,200		2,322

Expected output

		Process 1		Process 2
3,000 × 80%		2,400	4,300 × 90%	3,870
Cost per unit ($\dfrac{\$1,320 - \$120}{3,000 - 600}$)		$0.50	($\dfrac{\$2,451 - \$129}{4,300 - 430}$)	$0.60

Step 3   Determine total cost of output and losses

		Process 1		Process 2
		$		$
Output (2,300 × $0.50)		1,150	(4,000 × $0.60)	2,400
Normal loss (scrap)				
(600 × $0.20)		120	(430 × $0.30)	129
Abnormal loss (100 × $0.50)		50		-
		1,320		2,529
Abnormal gain		-	(130 × $0.60)	(78)
		1,320		2,451

Step 4   Complete accounts

PROCESS 1 ACCOUNT

	kg	$		kg	$
Material	3,000	750	Normal loss to scrap a/c		
Labour		120	(20%)	600	120
General overhead		450	Production transferred to		
			process 2	2,300	1,150
			Abnormal loss a/c	100	50
	3,000	1,320		3,000	1,320

PROCESS 2 ACCOUNT

	kg	$		kg	$
Transferred from					
process 1	2,300	1,150	Normal loss to scrap a/c		
Material added	2,000	800	(10%)	430	129
Labour		84	Production transferred to		
General overhead		417	finished inventory	4,000	2,400
	4,300	2,451			
Abnormal gain	130	78			
	4,430	2,529		4,430	2,529

SCRAP ACCOUNT

	kg	$		kg	$
Normal loss (process 1)	600	120	Abnormal gain (process 2)	130	39
Normal loss (process 2)	430	129	Cash	1,000	230
Abnormal loss					
(process 1)	100	20			
	1,130	269		1,130	269

ABNORMAL LOSS AND GAIN ACCOUNT

	kg	$		kg	$
Process 1 (loss)	100	50	Scrap value of		
Scrap value of abnormal			abnormal loss	100	20
gain	130	39	Process 2 (gain)	130	78
Income statement		9			
	230	98		230	98

(*Note.* In this answer, a single account has been prepared for abnormal loss/gain. It is also possible to separate this single account into two separate accounts, one for abnormal gain and one for abnormal loss.)

5 Valuing closing work in progress

T FORWARD

When units are partly completed at the end of a period (ie when there is **closing work in progress**) it is necessary to calculate **the equivalent units of production** in order to determine the cost of a completed unit.

In the examples we have looked at so far we have assumed that opening and closing inventories of work in process have been nil. We must now look at more realistic examples and consider how to allocate the costs incurred in a period between completed output (ie finished units) and partly completed closing inventory.

Some examples will help to illustrate the problem, and the techniques used to share out (apportion) costs between finished output and closing work in progress.

5.1 Example: valuation of closing inventory

Trotter Co is a manufacturer of processed goods. In March 20X3, in one process, there was no opening inventory, but 5,000 units of input were introduced to the process during the month, at the following cost.

	$
Direct materials	16,560
Direct labour	7,360
Production overhead	5,520
	29,440

Of the 5,000 units introduced, 4,000 were completely finished during the month and transferred to the next process. Closing inventory of 1,000 units was only 60% complete with respect to materials and conversion costs.

Solution

(a) The problem in this example is to **divide the costs of production** ($29,440) between the finished output of 4,000 units and the closing inventory of 1,000 units. It is argued, with good reason, that a division of costs in proportion to the number of units of each (4,000:1,000) would not be 'fair' because closing inventory has not been completed, and has not yet 'received' its full amount of materials and conversion costs, but only 60% of the full amount. The 1,000 units of closing inventory, being only 60% complete, are the equivalent of 600 fully worked units.

(b) To apportion costs fairly and proportionately, units of production must be converted into the equivalent of completed units, ie into **equivalent units of production**.

Key term

> **Equivalent units** are 'notional whole units representing incomplete work. Used to apportion costs between work in progress and completed output ...'
> CIMA *Official Terminology*

Step 1   Determine output

For this step in our framework we need to prepare a statement of equivalent units.

STATEMENT OF EQUIVALENT UNITS

	Total units	Completion	Equivalent units
Fully worked units	4,000	100%	4,000
Closing inventory	1,000	60%	600
	5,000		4,600

Step 2   Calculate cost per unit of output, and WIP

For this step in our framework we need to prepare a statement of costs per equivalent unit because equivalent units are the basis for apportioning costs.

STATEMENT OF COSTS PER EQUIVALENT UNIT

$$\frac{\text{Total costs}}{\text{Equivalent units}} = \frac{\$29,440}{4,600}$$

Cost per equivalent unit $6.40

Step 3   Calculate total cost of output and WIP

For this step in our framework a statement of evaluation may now be prepared, to show how the costs should be apportioned between finished output and closing inventory.

STATEMENT OF EVALUATION

Item	Equivalent units	Cost per equivalent unit	Valuation $
Fully worked units	4,000	$6.40	25,600
Closing inventory	600	$6.40	3,840
	4,600		29,440

Step 4   Complete accounts

The process account would be shown as follows.

PROCESS ACCOUNT

	Units	$		Units	$
Direct materials	5,000	16,560	Output to next process	4,000	25,600
Direct labour		7,360	Closing inventory c/f	1,000	3,840
Production o'hd		5,520			
	5,000	29,440		5,000	29,440

5.2 A few hints on preparing accounts

When preparing a process account, it might help to make the entries as follows.

(a)   **Enter the units first**. The units columns are simply memorandum columns, but they help you to make sure that there are no units unaccounted for (for example as loss).

(b)   **Enter the costs of materials, labour and overheads next**. These should be given to you.

(c)   **Enter your valuation of finished output and closing inventory next**. The value of the credit entries should, of course, equal the value of the debit entries.

5.3 Different rates of input

In many industries, materials, labour and overhead may be added at **different rates** during the course of production.

(a)   Output from a previous process (for example the output from process 1 to process 2) may be introduced into the subsequent process all at once, so that closing inventory is 100% complete in respect of these materials.

(b)   Further materials may be **added gradually** during the process, so that closing inventory is only **partially complete** in respect of these added materials.

(c)   Labour and overhead may be 'added' at yet another different rate. When production overhead is absorbed on a labour hour basis, however, we should expect the degree of completion on overhead to be the same as the degree of completion on labour.

When this situation occurs, equivalent units, and a cost per equivalent unit, should be **calculated separately for each type of material, and also for conversion costs**.

5.4 Example: equivalent units and different degrees of completion

Suppose that Shaker Co is a manufacturer of processed goods, and that results in process 2 for April 20X3 were as follows.

Opening inventory	nil
Material input from process 1	4,000 units

Costs of input:	$
material from process 1	6,000
added materials in process 2	1,080
conversion costs	1,720

Output is transferred into the next process, process 3.

Closing work in process amounted to 800 units, complete as to:

process 1 material	100%
added materials	50%
conversion costs	30%

Required

Prepare the account for process 2 for April 20X3.

Solution

Step 1   Determine output and losses

STATEMENT OF EQUIVALENT UNITS (OF PRODUCTION IN THE PERIOD)

					Equivalent units of production			
			Process 1 material		*Added materials*		*Labour and overhead*	
Input	*Output*	*Total*						
Units		Units	Units	%	Units	%	Units	%
4,000	Completed production	3,200	3,200	100	3,200	100	3,200	100
	Closing inventory	800	800	100	400	50	240	30
4,000		4,000	4,000		3,600		3,440	

Step 2   Calculate cost per unit of output, losses and WIP

STATEMENT OF COST (PER EQUIVALENT UNIT)

Input	*Cost*	*Equivalent production in units*	*Cost per unit*
	$		$
Process 1 material	6,000	4,000	1.50
Added materials	1,080	3,600	0.30
Labour and overhead	1,720	3,440	0.50
	8,800		2.30

Step 3   Calculate total cost of output, losses and WIP

STATEMENT OF EVALUATION (OF FINISHED WORK AND CLOSING INVENTORIES)

Production	*Cost element*	*Number of equivalent units*	*Cost per equivalent unit*	*Total*	*Cost*
			$	$	$
Completed production		3,200	2.30		7,360
Closing inventory:	process 1 material	800	1.50	1,200	
	added material	400	0.30	120	
	labour and overhead	240	0.50	120	
					1,440
					8,800

Step 4   Complete accounts

PROCESS ACCOUNT

	Units	$		Units	$
Process 1 material	4,000	6,000	Process 3 a/c	3,200	7,360
Added material		1,080	(finished output)		
Conversion costs		1,720	Closing inventory c/f	800	1,440
	4,000	8,800		4,000	8,800

5.5 Closing work in progress and losses

The previous sections have dealt separately with the following.

(a)   The treatment of loss and scrap.

(b)   The use of equivalent units as a basis for apportioning costs between units of output and units of closing inventory.

We must now look at a situation where both problems occur together. We shall begin with an example where loss has no scrap value.

The rules are as follows.

(a)   Costs should be divided between finished output, closing inventory and abnormal loss/gain using **equivalent units** as a basis of apportionment.

(b)   Units of abnormal loss/gain are often taken to be **one full equivalent unit each**, and are valued on this basis, ie they carry their full 'share' of the process costs.

(c)   **Abnormal loss units are an addition** to the total equivalent units produced but **abnormal gain units are subtracted** in arriving at the total number of equivalent units produced.

(d)   Units of **normal loss are valued at zero equivalent units**, ie they do not carry any of the process costs.

5.6 Example: changes in inventory level and losses

The following data have been collected for a process.

Opening inventory	none	Output to finished goods	2,000 units
Input units	2,800 units	Closing inventory	450 units, 70% complete
Cost of input	$16,695	Total loss	350 units
Normal loss	10%; nil scrap value		

Required

Prepare the process account for the period.

Solution

Step 1 Determine output and losses

STATEMENT OF EQUIVALENT UNITS

	Total units		Equivalent units of work done this period
Completely worked units	2,000	(× 100%)	2,000
Closing inventory	450	(× 70%)	315
Normal loss	280		0
Abnormal loss	70	(× 100%)	70
	2,800		2,385

Step 2 Calculate cost per unit of output, losses and WIP

STATEMENT OF COST PER EQUIVALENT UNIT

$$\frac{\text{Costs incurred}}{\text{Equivalent units of work done}} = \frac{£16,695}{2,385}$$

Cost per equivalent unit $= \$7$

Step 3 Calculate total cost of output, losses and WIP

STATEMENT OF EVALUATION

	Equivalent units	$
Completely worked units	2,000	14,000
Closing inventory	315	2,205
Abnormal loss	70	490
	2,385	16,695

Step 4 Complete accounts

PROCESS ACCOUNT

	Units	$		Units	$
Opening inventory	-	-	Normal loss	280	0
Input costs	2,800	16,695	Finished goods a/c	2,000	14,000
			Abnormal loss a/c	70	490
			Closing inventory c/d	450	2,205
	2,800	16,695		2,800	16,695

5.7 Closing work in progress, loss and scrap

When loss has a **scrap value**, the accounting procedures are the same as those previously described. However, if the equivalent units are a different percentage (of the total units) for materials, labour and overhead, it is a convention that the **scrap value of normal loss** is **deducted from the cost of materials** before a cost per equivalent unit is calculated.

Question

Complete the process account below from the following information.(**Hint.** Not all boxes require entries.)

Opening inventory	Nil
Input units	10,000
Input costs	
Material	$5,150
Labour	$2,700
Normal loss	5% of input
Scrap value of units of loss	$1 per unit
Output to finished goods	8,000 units
Closing inventory	1,000 units
Completion of closing inventory	80% for material
	50% for labour

PROCESS ACCOUNT

	Units	$		Units	$
Material	☐	☐	Completed production	☐	☐
Labour		☐	Closing inventory	☐	☐
Abnormal gain	☐	☐	Normal loss	☐	☐
			Abnormal loss	☐	☐
	☐	☐		☐	☐

Answer

Step 1   Determine output and losses

STATEMENT OF EQUIVALENT UNITS

			Equivalent units		
			Material		Labour
	Total Units	%	Units	%	Units
Completed production	8,000	100	8,000	100	8,000
Closing inventory	1,000	80	800	50	500
Normal loss	500				
Abnormal loss	500	100	500	100	500
	10,000		9,300		9,000

Step 2   Calculate cost per unit of output, losses and WIP

STATEMENT OF COST PER EQUIVALENT UNIT

	Cost $	Cost per Equivalent units	equivalent unit $
Material ($(5,150 – 500))	4,650	9,300	0.50
Labour	2,700	9,000	0.30
	7,350		0.80

Step 3   Calculate total cost of output, losses and WIP

STATEMENT OF EVALUATION

	Equivalent units	Cost per equivalent unit $	Total $	$
Completed production	8,000	0.80		6,400
Closing inventory: material	800	0.50	400	
labour	500	0.30	150	
				550
Abnormal loss	500	0.80		400
				7,350

Step 4   Complete accounts

PROCESS ACCOUNT

	Units	$		Units	$
Material	10,000	5,150	Completed production	8,000	6,400
Labour		2,700	Closing inventory	1,000	550
Abnormal gain	0	0	Normal loss	500	500
			Abnormal loss	500	400
	10,000	7,850		10,000	7,850

6 Valuing opening work in progress

FAST FORWARD

The **weighted average cost method of valuing opening WIP** makes no distinction between units of opening WIP and new units introduced to the process during the current period.

6.1 Weighted average cost method

The weighted average cost method of inventory valuation is a inventory valuation method that calculates a weighted average cost of units produced from both opening inventory and units introduced in the current period. (We studied this method earlier in the Study Text in Chapter 2.)

Important!

With the weighted average cost method no distinction is made between units of opening WIP and new units introduced to the process during the current period. The cost of opening WIP is added to costs incurred during the period, and completed units of opening WIP are each given a value of one full equivalent unit of production.

6.2 Example: weighted average cost method

Magpie Co produces an item which is manufactured in two consecutive processes. Information relating to Process 2 during September 20X3 is as follows.

Opening inventory 800 units

Degree of completion:		$
process 1 materials	100%	4,700
added materials	40%	600
conversion costs	30%	1,000
		6,300

During September 20X3, 3,000 units were transferred from process 1 at a valuation of $18,100. Added materials cost $9,600 and conversion costs were $11,800.

Closing inventory at 30 September 20X3 amounted to 1,000 units which were 100% complete with respect to process 1 materials and 60% complete with respect to added materials. Conversion cost work was 40% complete.

Magpie Co uses a weighted average cost system for the valuation of output and closing inventory.

Required

Prepare the Process 2 account for September 20X3.

Solution

Step 1   Determine output and losses

Opening inventory units count as a full equivalent unit of production when the weighted average cost system is applied. Closing inventory units are assessed in the usual way.

STATEMENT OF EQUIVALENT UNITS

								Equivalent units	
	Total units		Process 1 material		Added material			Conversion costs	
Output to finished goods*	2,800	(100%)	2,800		2,800			2,800	
Closing inventory	1,000	(100%)	1,000	(60%)	600	(40%)		400	
	3,800		3,800		3,400			3,200	

* 3,000 units from Process 1 minus closing inventory of 1,000 units plus opening inventory of 800 units.

Step 2   Calculate cost per unit of output and WIP

The cost of opening inventory is added to costs incurred in September 20X3, and a cost per equivalent unit is then calculated.

STATEMENT OF COSTS PER EQUIVALENT UNIT

	Process 1 material	Added materials	Conversion costs
	$	$	$
Opening inventory	4,700	600	1,000
Added in September 20X3	18,100	9,600	11,800
Total cost	22,800	10,200	12,800
Equivalent units	3,800 units	3,400 units	3,200 units
Cost per equivalent unit	$6	$3	$4

Step 3   Calculate total cost of output and WIP

STATEMENT OF EVALUATION

	Process 1 material $	Added materials $	Conversion costs $	Total cost $
Output to finished goods (2,800 units)	16,800	8,400	11,200	36,400
Closing inventory	6,000	1,800	1,600	9,400
				45,800

Step 4   Complete accounts

PROCESS 2 ACCOUNT

	Units	$		Units	$
Opening inventory b/f	800	6,300	Finished goods a/c	2,800	36,400
Process 1 a/c	3,000	18,100			
Added materials		9,600			
Conversion costs		11,800	Closing inventory c/f	1,000	9,400
	3,800	45,800		3,800	45,800

Assessment focus point	You must be prepared to deal with assessment questions which have opening WIP, closing WIP **and** losses all occurring together in the same process.

6.3 A final question

The following question involves the following process costing situations.

- Normal loss (with and without sale of scrap)
- Abnormal loss
- Abnormal gain
- Opening work in progress
- Closing work in progress

Take time to work through this question carefully and to check your workings against the answer given below. This is an excellent question which should help you to consolidate all of the process costing knowledge that you have acquired while studying this chapter.

 Question   **Watkins Ltd**

W Co has a financial year which ends on 30 April. It operates in a processing industry in which a single product is produced by passing inputs through two sequential processes. A normal loss of 10% of input is expected in each process.

The following account balances have been extracted from its ledger at 31 March 20X0.

	Debit $	Credit $
Process 1 (Materials $4,400; Conversion costs $3,744)	8,144	
Process 2 (Process 1 $4,431; Conversion costs $5,250)	9,681	
Abnormal loss	1,400	
Abnormal gain		300
Overhead control account		250
Sales		585,000
Cost of sales	442,500	
Finished goods inventory	65,000	

W Co uses the weighted average method of accounting for work in process.

During April 20X0 the following transactions occurred.

Process 1	Materials input (kg, $)	4,000 kg	22,000
	Labour cost		$12,000
	Transfer to process 2	2,400 kg	
Process 2	Transfer from process 1	2,400 kg	
	Labour cost		$15,000
	Transfer to finished goods	2,500 kg	
Overhead costs incurred amounted to		$54,000	
Sales to customer were		$52,000	

Overhead costs are absorbed into process costs on the basis of 150% of labour cost.

The losses which arise in process 1 have no scrap value: those arising in process 2 can be sold for $2 per kg.

Details of opening and closing work in process for the month of April 20X0 are as follows.

	Opening	Closing
Process 1	3,000 kg	3,400 kg
Process 2	2,250 kg	2,600 kg

In both processes closing work in process is fully complete as to material cost and 40% complete as to conversion cost.

Inventories of finished goods at 30 April 20X0 were valued at cost of $60,000.

Required

(a) In an account for process 1, the monetary and quantity values for:

(i) transfers to process 2 are ⬚ kgs at $ ⬚

(ii) normal loss are ⬚ kgs at $ ⬚

(iii) abnormal loss are ⬚ kgs at $ ⬚

(iv) abnormal gain are ⬚ kgs at $ ⬚

(v) WIP materials are ⬚ kgs at $ ⬚

(vi) WIP conversion costs are ⬚ kgs at $ ⬚

(b)   In an account for process 2, the monetary and quantity values for:

   (i)   finished goods are [   ] kgs at $ [   ]

   (ii)   normal loss are [   ] kgs at $ [   ]

   (iii) WIP from process 1 are [   ] kgs at $ [   ]

   (iv)   WIP from process 2 are [   ] kgs at $ [   ]

Answer

(a)   **Process 1**

STATEMENT OF EQUIVALENT UNITS

		Equivalent units	
	Total units	Material costs	Conversion costs
Transfers to process 2	2,400	2,400	2,400
Closing WIP	3,400	(100%) 3,400	(40%) 1,360
Normal loss (10% × 4,000)	400	0	0
Abnormal loss	800	800	800
	7,000	6,600	4,560

STATEMENT OF COSTS PER EQUIVALENT UNIT

$$\frac{\text{Costs incurred}}{\text{Equivalent units}} = \text{Cost per equivalent unit}$$

$$\therefore \text{Materials cost per equivalent unit} = \frac{\$4,400 + \$22,000}{6,600}$$

$$= \frac{\$26,400}{6,600} = \$4$$

$$\therefore \text{Conversion costs per equivalent unit} = \frac{\$3,744 + \$12,000 + \$18,000}{4,560}$$

$$= \frac{\$33,744}{4,560} = \$7.40$$

STATEMENT OF EVALUATION

	Materials	Conversion costs	Total
	$	$	$
Transfers to process 2	9,600	17,760	27,360
Abnormal loss	3,200	5,920	9,120
Closing WIP	13,600	10,064	23,664
	26,400	33,744	60,144

PROCESS 1 ACCOUNT

	Kg	$		Kg	$
WIP materials	3,000	4,400	Process 2	2,400	27,360
WIP conversion costs	-	3,744	Normal loss	400	-
Materials	4,000	22,000	Abnormal loss	800	9,120
Labour	-	12,000	WIP materials	3,400	13,600
Overhead	-	18,000	WIP conversion costs	-	10,064
	7,000	60,144		7,000	60,144

The monetary and quantity values for:

(i) **transfer to process 2 are** $\boxed{2,400}$ **kgs at $** $\boxed{27,360}$

(ii) **normal loss are** $\boxed{400}$ **kgs at $** $\boxed{0}$

(iii) **abnormal loss are** $\boxed{800}$ **kgs at $** $\boxed{9,120}$

(iv) **abnormal gain are** $\boxed{0}$ **kgs at $** $\boxed{0}$

(v) **WIP materials are** $\boxed{3,400}$ **kgs at $** $\boxed{13,600}$

(vi) **WIP conversion costs are** $\boxed{0}$ **kgs at $** $\boxed{10,064}$

(b) **Process 2**

STATEMENT OF EQUIVALENT UNITS

	Total units	Process 1	Conversion costs
Finished goods	2,500	2,500	2,500
Normal loss	240	0	0
Abnormal gain	(690)	(690)	(690)
Closing WIP	2,600*	2,600	1,040 **
	4,650	4,410	2,850

* Total input units   = opening WIP + input = 2,250 + 2,400 = 4,650
    Total output units   = finished goods + closing WIP + normal loss – abnormal gain
                      = 2,500 + 2,600 + 240 – 690
                      = 4,650

** 2,600 × 40%   = 1,040

STATEMENT OF COSTS PER EQUIVALENT UNIT

Process 1 $= \dfrac{\$4,431 + \$27,360 - 480}{4,410} = \$7.10$

Conversion costs $= \dfrac{\$5,250 + \$15,000 + \$22,500}{2,850} = \$15.00$

STATEMENT OF EVALUATION

	Process 1 $	Conversion costs $	Total $
Finished goods	17,750	37,500	55,250
Abnormal gain	4,899	10,350	15,249
Closing WIP	18,460	15,600	34,060
	41,109	63,450	104,559

PROCESS 2 ACCOUNT

	Kg	$		Kg	$
WIP Process 1	2,250	4,431	Finished goods	2,500	55,250
WIP conversion costs	-	5,250	Normal loss	240	480
Process 1	2,400	27,360	WIP Process 1	2,600	18,460
Labour	-	15,000	WIP conversion costs	-	15,600
Overhead	-	22,500			
Abnormal gain	690	15,249			
	5,340	89,790		5,340	89,790

The monetary and quantity values for:

(i)   **finished goods are** | 2,500 | **kgs at $** | 55,250 |

(ii)   **normal loss are** | 240 | **kgs at $** | 480 |

(iii)   **WIP from process 1 are** | 2,600 | **kgs at $** | 18,460 |

(iv)   **WIP from process 2 are** | 0 | **kgs at $** | 15,600 |

7 Joint products and by-products

7.1 Joint products

> **Joint products** are two or more products separated in a process each of which has a **significant value** compared to the other.

Key term

> **Joint products** are 'two or more products produced by the same process and separated in processing, each having a sufficiently high saleable value to merit recognition as a main product'.   CIMA *Official terminology*

Joint products:

- Are produced in the **same process**
- Are **indistinguishable** from each other until the **separation point**
- Have a **substantial sales value** (after further processing, if necessary)
- **May require further processing** after the separation point

For example in the oil refining industry the following joint products all arise from the same process.

- Diesel fuel
- Petrol
- Paraffin
- Lubricants

7.2 By-products

> A **by-product** is an **incidental product** from a process which has an **insignificant value** compared to the main product(s).

ey term

> A **by-product** is 'output of some value produced incidentally while manufacturing the main product'.
>
> CIMA *Official terminology*

A by-product is a product which is similarly produced at the same time and from the same common process as the 'main product' or joint products. The distinguishing feature of a by-product is its **relatively low sales value** in comparison to the main product. In the timber industry, for example, by-products include sawdust, small offcuts and bark.

7.3 Distinguishing joint products from by-products

The answer lies in management attitudes to their products, which in turn is reflected in the cost accounting system.

(a)   A **joint product** is regarded as an important saleable item, and so it should be **separately costed**. The profitability of each joint product should be assessed in the cost accounts.

(b)   A **by-product** is not important as a saleable item, and whatever revenue it earns is a 'bonus' for the organisation. It is not worth costing by-products separately, because of their relative insignificance. It is therefore equally irrelevant to consider a by-product's profitability. The only question is how to account for the 'bonus' net revenue that a by-product earns.

7.4 Accounting for joint and by-products

The point at which joint and by-products become separately identifiable is known as the **split-off point** or **separation point**. Costs incurred up to this point are called **common costs** or **joint costs**.

Common or joint costs need to be allocated (apportioned) in some manner to each of the joint products. In the following sketched example, there are two different split-off points.

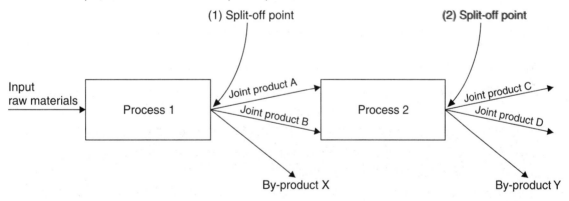

7.5 Apportioning common costs

Reasons for apportioning common costs to individual joint products are as follows.

(a)   To put a value to closing inventories of each joint product.

(b)   To record the costs and therefore the profit from each joint product. This is of limited value however, because the costs and therefore profit from one joint product are influenced by the share of costs assigned to the other joint products. Management decisions would be based on the apparent relative profitability of the products which has arisen due to the arbitrary apportionment of the joint costs.

(c)   Perhaps to assist in pricing decisions.

Here are some examples of the common costs problem.

(a) How to spread the common costs of oil refining between the joint products made (petrol, naphtha, kerosene and so on).

(b) How to spread the common costs of running the telephone network between telephone calls in peak rate times and cheap rate times, or between local calls and long-distance calls.

7.5.1 Methods of apportioning common costs

The main methods that might be used to establish a basis for apportioning or allocating common costs to each product are as follows.

- Physical measurement (eg weight of output)

- Relative sales value apportionment method 1; sales value at split-off point

- Relative sales value apportionment method 2; sales value of end product less further processing costs after split-off point, ie the net realisable value of each product at the split-off point.

7.6 Accounting for by-products

Despite the fact that the by-product has a **small value relative to that of the main product**, it does have some commercial value and its accounting treatment usually consists of one of the following.

(a) **Income** (minus any post-separation further processing or selling costs) from the sale of the by-product **may be added to sales of the main product**, thereby increasing sales revenue for the period.

(b) The sales of the by-product may be treated as a **separate, incidental source of income** against which are set only post-separation costs (if any) of the by-product. The revenue would be recorded in the income statement as **'other income'**.

(c) The **sales income of the by-product may be deducted from the cost of production** or cost of sales of the main product.

(d) The **net realisable value of the by-product may be deducted from the cost of production of the main product.** The net realisable value is the final saleable value of the by-product minus any post-separation costs.

The choice of method will be influenced by the circumstances of production and ease of calculation, as much as by conceptual correctness. The most common method is method (d). Notice that this method is the same as the accounting treatment of a **normal loss which is sold for scrap**.

Question

Split-off point

Mark the split-off point on the diagram above.

PROFESSIONAL EDUCATION

Answer

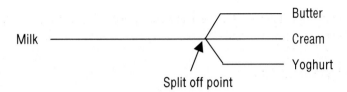

Chapter Roundup

- **Process costing** is a costing method used where it is not possible to identify separate units of production, or jobs, usually because of the continuous nature of the production processes involved.

- A process account has **two sides**, and on **each side there are two columns** – one for **quantities** (of raw materials, work in progress and finished goods) and one for **costs**.

- Use our suggested **four-step approach** when dealing with process costing questions.

  Step 1   Determine output and losses

  Step 2   Calculate cost per unit of output, losses and WIP

  Step 3   Calculate total cost of output, losses and WIP

  Step 4   Complete accounts

- **Losses** may occur in process. If a certain level of loss is expected, this is known as **normal loss**. If losses are greater than expected, the extra loss is **abnormal loss**. If losses are less than expected, the difference is known as **abnormal gain**.

- The **valuation of normal loss is either at scrap value or nil**. It is conventional for the **scrap value of normal loss to be deducted from the cost of materials** before a cost per equivalent unit is calculated.

- Abnormal losses and gains never affect the cost of good units of production. The scrap value of abnormal losses is not credited to the process account, and the abnormal loss and gain units **carry the same full cost as a good unit of production**.

- When units are partly completed at the end of a period (ie when there is **closing work in progress**) it is necessary to calculate the **equivalent units of production** in order to determine the cost of a completed unit.

- The **weighted average cost** method of valuing opening WIP makes no distinction between units of opening WIP and new units introduced to the process during the current period.

- **Joint products** are two or more products separated in a process, each of which has a **significant value** compared to the other.

- A **by-product** is an **incidental product** from a process which has an **insignificant value** compared to the main product(s).

Quick Quiz

1   *Choose the correct words from those highlighted.*

Process costing is often identified with **construction of large buildings/paint manufacture/services provided in a supermarket**.

2   Process costing is centred around four key steps. What are they?

Step 1   ....

Step 2   ....

Step 3   ....

Step 4   ....

3   Abnormal gains result when actual loss is less than normal or expected loss.

True   ☐

False   ☐

4   *Match the types of loss with the correct method of valuation.*

Normal loss (no scrap value)　　　　　　　　　　Same value as good output (positive cost)

Abnormal loss　　　　　　　　　**?**　　No value

Abnormal gain　　　　　　　　　　　　　　Same value as good output (negative cost)

5   How is revenue from scrap treated?

A   As an addition to sales revenue
B   As a reduction in costs of processing
C   As a bonus to employees
D   Any of the above

6   When there is closing WIP at the end of a process, the first step in the four-step approach to process costing questions is to draw up a statement of evaluation.

True   ☐

False   ☐

7   *Choose the correct words from those highlighted.*

The weighted average cost method of inventory valuation **makes no distinction/makes a distinction** between units of opening WIP and new units introduced to the process during the current period.

8   *Match the type of product with the correct sales value.*

Joint product　　　　　　　　　　　Sales value is relatively significant

　　　　　　　　　　?

By-product　　　　　　　　　　　Sales value is not relatively significant

Answers to Quick Quiz

1   Process costing is often identified with **paint manufacture**.

2   **Step 1**   Determine output and losses

   Step 2   Calculate cost per unit of output, losses and WIP

   Step 3   Calculate total cost of output, losses and WIP

   Step 4   Complete accounts

3   True

4   Normal loss (no scrap value) ⟶ Same value as good output (positive cost)

   Abnormal loss ⟶ No value

   Abnormal gain ⟶ Same value as good output (negative cost)

5   B

6   False. The first step is to calculate the equivalent units of production by drawing up a statement of equivalent units.

7   The weighted average cost method of inventory valuation **makes no distinction** between units of opening WIP and new units introduced to the process during the current period.

8   Joint product ⟶ Sales value is relatively significant

   By-product ⟶ Sales value is not relatively significant

Now try the questions below from the Question Bank

Question numbers	Page
57–70	360

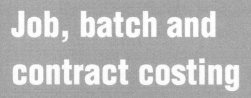

Job, batch and contract costing

Introduction

A **costing method** is designed to suit the way goods are processed or manufactured or the way services are provided. Each organisation's costing method will therefore have unique features but costing methods of firms in the same line of business will more than likely have common aspects. We've already looked at process costing, which is used when production is a continuous flow of identical units.

In this chapter we will be looking at **specific order costing** methods, specific order costing being the 'basic cost accounting method applicable if work consists of separately identifiable batches, contracts or jobs' (CIMA *Official Terminology*).

This chapter begins by covering **job costing** and then moves on to **batch costing**, the procedure for which is similar to job costing.

The third costing method considered in this chapter is **contract costing**. Contract costing is similar to job costing but the job is of such importance that a formal contract is made between the supplier and the customer. We will see how to record contract costs, how to account for any profits and losses arising on contracts at the end of an accounting period and we will look briefly at how contract balances are disclosed in financial accounts.

Topic list	Learning outcomes	Syllabus references	Ability required
1 Job costing	D(iii)	D(4)	Analysis
2 Job costing example	D(iv)	D(4)	Application
3 Job costing for internal services	D(iii)	D(4)	Analysis
4 Batch costing	D(iii), (iv)	D(4)	Analysis, Application
5 Contracts and contract costing	D(iii)	D(4)	Analysis
6 Contract costs	D(iv)	D(4)	Application
7 Progress payments and retentions	D(iv)	D(4)	Application
8 Profits on contracts	D(iv)	D(4)	Application
9 Losses on incomplete contracts	D(iv)	D(4)	Application
10 Disclosure of long-term contracts in financial accounts	D(iv)	D(4)	Application

1 Job costing

Job costing is the costing method used where work is undertaken to customers' special requirements and each order is of comparatively short duration.

The work relating to a job is usually carried out within a factory or workshop and moves through processes and operations as a **continuously identifiable unit**.

Key terms

A **job** is a 'customer order or task of relatively short duration'.

Job costing is a 'form of specific order costing where costs are attributed to individual jobs'.

CIMA Official Terminology

1.1 Procedure for the performance of jobs

The normal procedure which is adopted in jobbing concerns involves the following.

(a) The prospective customer approaches the supplier and indicates the requirements of the job.

(b) A responsible official sees the prospective customer and agrees with him the precise details of the items to be supplied, for example the quantity, quality, size and colour of the goods, the date of delivery and any special requirements.

(c) The estimating department of the organisation then prepares an estimate for the job. This will include the cost of the materials to be used, the wages expected to be paid, the appropriate amount for factory, administration, selling and distribution overhead, the cost where appropriate of additional equipment needed specially for the job, and finally the supplier's **profit margin**. The total of these items will represent the quoted **selling price**.

(d) At the appropriate time, the job will be 'loaded' on to the factory floor. This means that as soon as all materials, labour and equipment are available and subject to the scheduling of other orders, the job will be started. In an efficient organisation, the start of the job will be timed to ensure that while it will be ready for the customer by the promised date of delivery it will not be loaded too early, otherwise storage space will have to be found for the product until the date it is required by (and was promised to) the customer.

1.2 Recording job costs

A separate record must be maintained to show the details of individual jobs. In **manual** systems, these are known as **job cost cards** or **job cost sheets**. In **computerised** systems, job costs will be collected in **job accounts**.

1.2.1 Job accounts

Job accounts are very much like the process accounts we encountered in Chapter 12. Inputs to a job are recorded on the left-hand side of the account, outputs on the right-hand side.

1.2.2 Collecting job costs

Key points on the process of collecting job costs are as follows.

(a) Some labour costs, such as overtime premium, might be charged either directly to a job or else as an overhead cost, depending on the circumstances in which the costs have arisen.

(b) The relevant costs of materials issued, direct labour performed and direct expenses incurred are charged to a job account in the work in progress ledger, the work in progress ledger recording the cost of all WIP. You will cover ledger accounts in detail in Chapter 14.

(c) The job account is allocated with the job's share of the factory overhead, based on the absorption rate(s) in operation. If the job is incomplete at the end of an accounting period, it is valued at factory cost in the closing balance sheet (where a system of absorption costing is in operation).

(d) On completion of the job, the job account is charged with the appropriate administration, selling and distribution overhead, after which the total cost of the job can be ascertained. The job is transferred to finished goods.

(e) The difference between the agreed selling price and the total actual cost will be the supplier's profit (or loss).

(f) When delivery is made to the customer, the costs become a cost of sale.

Question
Job costing

Twist and Tern Co is a company that carries out jobbing work. One of the jobs carried out in February was job 1357, to which the following information relates.

Direct material Y: 400 kilos were issued from stores at a cost of $5 per kilo.

Direct material Z: 800 kilos were issued from stores at a cost of $6 per kilo.

60 kilos were returned.

Department P: 320 labour hours were worked, of which 100 hours were done in overtime.

Department Q: 200 labour hours were worked, of which 100 hours were done in overtime.

Overtime work is not normal in Department P, where basic pay is $8 per hour plus an overtime premium of $2 per hour. Overtime work was done in Department Q in February because of a request by the customer of another job to complete his job quickly. Basic pay in Department Q is $10 per hour and overtime premium is $3 per hour.

Overhead is absorbed at the rate of $3 per direct labour hour in both departments.

(a) The direct materials cost of job 1357 is $ [   ].

(b) The direct labour cost of job 1357 is $ [   ].

(c) The full production cost of job 1357 is $ [   ].

Answer

(a) **The direct materials cost is $ 6,440**

Workings

	$
Direct material Y (400 kilos × $5)	2,000
Direct material Z (800 − 60 kilos × $6)	4,440
Total direct material cost	6,440

(b) **The direct labour cost is $ 4,560**

Workings

	$
Department P (320 hours × $8)	2,560
Department Q (200 hours × $10)	2,000
Total direct labour cost	4,560

In Department P, overtime premium will be charged to overhead. In Department Q, overtime premium will be charged to the job of the customer who asked for overtime to be worked.

(c) **The full production cost is $ 12,560**

Workings

	$
Direct material cost	6,440
Direct labour cost	4,560
Production overhead (520 hours × $3)	1,560
	12,560

1.3 Job costing and computerisation

Job costing cards exist in **manual** systems, but it is increasingly likely that in large organisations the job costing system will be **computerised**, using accounting software specifically designed to deal with job costing requirements. A computerised job accounting system is likely to contain the following features.

(a) Every job will be given a job code number, which will determine how the data relating to the job is stored.

(b) A separate set of codes will be given for the type of costs that any job is likely to incur. Thus, 'direct wages', say, will have the same code whichever job they are allocated to.

(c) In a sophisticated system, costs can be analysed both by job (for example all costs related to Job 456), but also by type (for example direct wages incurred on all jobs). It is thus easy to perform variance analysis and to make comparisons between jobs.

(d) A job costing system might have facilities built into it which incorporate other factors relating to the performance of the job. In complex jobs, sophisticated planning techniques might be employed to ensure that the job is performed in the minimum time possible. Time management features therefore may be incorporated into job costing software.

1.4 Cost plus pricing

FORWARD The usual method of fixing prices within a jobbing concern is **cost plus pricing**.

As you know from Chapter 4, cost plus pricing is where a desired profit margin is added to total costs to arrive at the selling price.

The **disadvantages** of cost plus pricing are as follows.

(a) There are no incentives to **control costs** as a profit is guaranteed.

(b) There is no motive to tackle **inefficiencies** or **waste**.

(c) It does not take into account any significant differences in actual and estimated volumes of activity. Since the overhead absorption rate is based upon estimated volumes, there may be **under-/over-absorbed overheads** not taken into account.

(d) Because overheads are apportioned in an arbitrary way, this may lead to **under and over pricing**.

portant! | The cost plus system is often adopted where one-off jobs are carried out to customers' specifications.

essment | Assessment questions may require you to accumulate costs to arrive at a job cost, and then to determine a **job price** by
us point | adding a profit of, say, 30 per cent **on sales**. To do this, you need to jot down the following crucial formula.

	%
Sales price	100
Profit	30
Cost	70

Once the job costs have been accumulated, the profit margin can be added as (cost × 30/70). A common error would be to simply add 30 per cent to cost, so it is vital that you read any assessment question carefully.

Question

Selling prices

The total cost of job 259 is $4,200.

(a) When profit is calculated as 25 per cent of sales, the correct selling price for the job is $ _____

(b) When profit is calculated as 25 per cent of cost, the correct selling price for the job is $ _____

Answer

If you have difficulty working out the correct amount, simply jot down the cost and selling price structures as percentages in each case.

(a) **The correct selling price is $ 5,600 .**

Workings

Profit is calculated as a percentage of sales, so selling price must be written as 100%.

	%
Cost	75
Profit	25
Selling price	100

Selling price = $4,200 × 100/75 = $5,600

(b)   **The correct selling price is $ 5,250 .**

Workings

Profit is calculated as a percentage of cost, so cost must be written as 100%.

	%
Cost	100
Profit	25
Selling price	125

Selling price = $4,200 × 125/100 = $5,250

2 Job costing example

An example may help to illustrate the principles of job costing.

FM Co is a jobbing company. On 1 June 20X2, there was one uncompleted job in the factory. The job card for this work is summarised as follows.

Job card, job no 6832

Costs to date	$
Direct materials	630
Direct labour (120 hours)	840
Factory overhead ($2 per direct labour hour)	240
Factory cost to date	1,710

During June, three new jobs were started in the factory, and costs of production were as follows.

Direct materials	$
Issued to: Job 6832	2,390
Job 6833	1,680
Job 6834	3,950
Job 6835	4,420
Damaged inventory written off from stores	2,300

Material transfers	$
Job 6834 to Job 6833	250
Job 6832 to 6834	620

Materials returned to store	$
From Job 6832	870
From Job 6835	170

Direct labour hours recorded	
Job 6832	430 hrs
Job 6833	650 hrs
Job 6834	280 hrs
Job 6835	410 hrs

The cost of labour hours during June 20X2 was $8 per hour, and production overhead is absorbed at the rate of $2 per direct labour hour. Production overheads incurred during the month amounted to $3,800. Completed jobs were delivered to customers as soon as they were completed, and the invoiced amounts were as follows.

Job 6832	$8,500
Job 6834	$9,000
Job 6835	$9,500

Administration and marketing overheads are added to the cost of sales at the rate of 20% of factory cost. Actual costs incurred during June 20X2 amounted to $4,418.

Required

(a)   Prepare the job accounts for each individual job during June 20X2. (Remember inputs to the job go on the left-hand side of the account, outputs on the right-hand side.)

(b)   Prepare the summarised job cost cards for each job, and calculate the profit on each completed job.

Solution

(a)   **Job accounts**

JOB 6832

	$		$
Balance b/f	1,710	Job 6834 a/c	620
Materials	2,390	(materials transfer)	
Labour	3,440	To stores (materials returned)	870
Production overhead	860	Cost of sales (balance)	6,910
	8,400		8,400

JOB 6833

	$		$
Materials	1,680	Balance c/f	8,430
Labour	5,200		
Production overhead	1,300		
Job 6834 a/c (materials transfer)	250		
	8,430		8,430

JOB 6834

	$		$
Materials	3,950	Job 6833 a/c (materials transfer)	250
Labour	2,240		
Production overhead	560	Cost of sales (balance)	7,120
Job 6832 a/c (materials transfer)	620		
	7,370		7,370

JOB 6835

	$		$
Materials	4,420	To stores (materials returned)	170
Labour	3,280		
Production overhead	820	Cost of sales (balance)	8,350
	8,520		8,520

(b)   **Job cards, summarised**

	Job 6832	Job 6833	Job 6834	Job 6835
	$	$	$	$
Materials	1,530*	1,930	4,320 **	4,250
Labour	4,280	5,200	2,240	3,280
Production overhead	1,100	1,300	560	820
Factory cost	6,910	(c/f) 8,430	7,120	8,350
Admin & marketing o'hd (20%)	1,382		1,424	1,670
Cost of sale	8,292		8,544	10,020
Invoice value	8,500		9,000	9,500
Profit/(loss) on job	208		456	(520)

* $(630 + 2,390 − 620 − 870)   ** $(3,950 + 620 − 250)

We will return to this example in the next chapter and see how the costing of individual jobs fits in with the recording of total costs in a system of what are known as control accounts. Don't worry about this now, though. Just make sure at this stage that you can follow the principle of 'inputs to the job on the left hand side, outputs on the right hand side'.

Question   Selling price of jobs

A furniture-making business manufactures quality furniture to customers' orders. It has three production departments (A, B and C) which have overhead absorption rates (per direct labour hour) of $12.86, $12.40 and $14.03 respectively.

Two pieces of furniture are to be manufactured for customers. Direct costs are as follows.

	Job XYZ	Job MNO
Direct material	$154	$108
Direct labour	20 hours dept A	16 hours dept A
	12 hours dept B	10 hours dept B
	10 hours dept C	14 hours dept C

Labour rates are as follows: $7.60(A); $7.00 (B); $6.80 (C)

The firm quotes prices to customers that reflect a required profit of 25% on selling price.

(a)   (i)   The total cost of job XYZ is $ ⬚ .

(ii)   The selling price of job XYZ is $ ⬚ .

(b)   (i)   The total cost of job MNO is $ ⬚ .

(ii)   The selling price of job MNO is $ ⬚ .

Answer

(a)   (i)   **The total cost of job XYZ is $** 1,004.30

(ii)   **The selling price of job XYZ is $** 1,339.07

(b)   (i)   **The total cost of job MNO is $** 920.98

(ii)   **The selling price of job MNO is $** 1,227.97

Workings

			Job XYZ		Job MNO
			$		$
Direct material			154.00		108.00
Direct labour:	dept A	(20 × 7.60)	152.00	(16 × 7.60)	121.60
	dept B	(12 × 7.00)	84.00	(10 × 7.00)	70.00
	dept C	(10 × 6.80)	68.00	(14 × 6.80)	95.20
Total direct cost			458.00		394.80
Overhead:	dept A	(20 × 12.86)	257.20	(16 × 12.86)	205.76
	dept B	(12 × 12.40)	148.80	(10 × 12.40)	124.00
	dept C	(10 × 14.03)	140.30	(14 × 14.03)	196.42
Total cost			1,004.30		920.98
Profit (note)			334.77		306.99
Quoted selling price			1,339.07		1,227.97

Note. If profit is 25% on selling price, this is the same as $33^{1}/_{3}$% (25/75) on cost:

	%
Selling price	100
Cost	75
Profit	25

Question

Closing work in progress

A firm uses job costing and recovers overheads on direct labour.

Three jobs were worked on during a period, the details of which are as follows.

	Job 1	Job 2	Job 3
	$	$	$
Opening work in progress	8,500	0	46,000
Material in period	17,150	29,025	0
Labour for period	12,500	23,000	4,500

The overheads for the period were exactly as budgeted, $140,000.

Jobs 1 and 2 were the only incomplete jobs.

What was the value of closing work in progress?

A $81,900   B $90,175   C $140,675   D $214,425

Answer

The correct answer is D.

Total labour cost = $12,500 + $23,000 + $4,500 = $40,000

Overhead absorption rate = $\dfrac{£140,000}{£40,000} \times 100\% = 350\%$ of direct labour cost

Closing work in progress valuation

		Job 1		Job 2	Total
		$		$	$
Costs given in question		38,150		52,025	90,175
Overhead absorbed	(12,500 × 350%)	43,750	(23,000 × 350%)	80,500	124,250
					214,425

We can eliminate **option B** because $90,175 is simply the total of the costs allocated to Jobs 1 and 2, with no absorption of overheads. **Option A** is an even lower cost figure, therefore it can also be eliminated.

Option C is wrong because it is a simple total of all allocated costs, including Job 3 which is not incomplete.

3 Job costing for internal services

An **internal job costing** system can be used for costing the work of service departments.

Job costing systems may be used to **control the costs** of **internal service departments**, such as the maintenance department. A job costing system enables the cost of a specific job to be charged to a user department. Therefore instead of apportioning the total costs of service departments, each job done is charged to the individual user department.

3.1 Advantages of internal job costing systems

An **internal job costing system** for service departments will have the following advantages.

(a) **Realistic apportionment**. The identification of expenses with jobs and the subsequent charging of these to the department(s) responsible means that costs are borne by those who incurred them.

(b) **Increased responsibility and awareness**. User departments will be aware that they are charged for the specific services used and may be more careful to use the facility more efficiently. They will also appreciate the true cost of the facilities that they are using and can take decisions accordingly.

(c) **Control of service department costs**. The service department may be restricted to charging a standard cost to user departments for specific jobs carried out. It will then be possible to measure the efficiency or inefficiency of the service department by recording the difference between the standard charges and the actual expenditure.

(d) **Budget information**. This information will ease the budgeting process, as the purpose and cost of service department expenditure can be separately identified.

4 Batch costing

Batch costing is similar to job costing in that each batch of similar articles is separately identifiable. The **cost per unit** manufactured in a batch is the total batch cost divided by the number of units in the batch.

Batch costing is a 'form of specific order costing where costs are attributed to batches of product (unit costs can be calculated by dividing by the number of products in the batch)'.   CIMA *Official Terminology*

4.1 Example: batch costing

A company manufactures widgets to order and has the following budgeted overheads for the year, based on normal activity levels.

Department	Budgeted overheads $	Budgeted activity
Welding	6,000	1,500 labour hours
Assembly	10,000	1,000 labour hours

Selling and administrative overheads are 20% of factory cost. An order for 250 widgets type X128, made as Batch 5997, incurred the following costs.

Materials $12,000

Labour   100 hours welding shop at $10/hour; 200 hours assembly shop at $8/hour

$500 was paid for the hire of special X-ray equipment for testing the welds.

Required

Calculate the cost per unit for Batch 5997.

Solution

The first step is to calculate the overhead absorption rate for the production departments.

Welding $= \dfrac{\$6,000}{1,500} = \$4$ per labour hour   Assembly $= \dfrac{\$10,000}{1,000} = \$10$ per labour hour

		Total cost – Batch no 5997	
		$	$
Direct material			12,000
Direct expense			500
Direct labour	100 × $10.00 =	1,000	
	200 × $8.00 =	1,600	
			2,600
Prime cost			15,100
Overheads	100 × $4 =	400	
	200 × $10 =	2,000	
			2,400
Factory cost			17,500
Selling and administrative cost (20% of factory cost)			3,500
Total cost			21,000

Cost per unit $= \dfrac{\$21,000}{250} = \$84.00$

✏️   **25% profit on selling price**

A printing firm is proposing offering a leaflet advertising service to local traders.

The following costs have been estimated for a batch of 10,000 leaflets.

Setting up machine	6 hours at $10 per hour
Artwork	$20 per batch
Paper	$1.80 per 100 sheets
Other printing materials	$15
Direct labour cost	4 hours at $6 per hour

Fixed overheads allocated to this side of the business are $1,000 per annum incurred at an even rate throughout the year. Overheads are recovered on the basis of orders received, which are expected to be two per week for 50 weeks in the year.

The management requires 25% profit on selling price.

(a)   The selling price, to the nearest cent, per thousand leaflets, for quantities of:

    (i)   5,000 leaflets is $ ▢

    (ii)   10,000 leaflets is $ ▢

(b)   During the latest week, the firm sold two batches of 10,000 leaflets and one batch of 5,000 leaflets. All costs and selling prices were as estimated.

    The profit for the week was $ ▢

🟦 **Answer**

(a)   (i)   **The selling price is $**   **53.20**

       (ii)   **The selling price is $**   **41.20**

    Workings

    Expected orders per annum = 2 orders × 50 weeks = 100 orders

$$\therefore \text{Fixed overhead per order} = \frac{\$1,000}{100} = \$10$$

    Calculation of price per 1,000 leaflets

Batch size: (leaflets)	5,000	10,000
	$	$
Setting up machine	60.00	60.00
Artwork	20.00	20.00
Paper	90.00	180.00
Other printing materials	7.50	15.00
Direct labour cost	12.00	24.00
Fixed overhead	10.00	10.00
Total cost	199.50	309.00
Profit	66.50	103.00
Selling price	266.00	412.00
Price per 1,000 leaflets	53.20	41.20

    The profit is 25% on selling price ie cost (75) + profit (25) = selling price (100), and thus profit = 1/3 cost

(b) **The profit for the week was $** 282.50

Workings

		$	$
Batch profit	$66.50 × 1		66.50
	$103.00 × 2		206.00
			272.50
Plus over-absorbed overhead:			
Overhead absorbed 3 batches × $10		30.00	
Overhead incurred $1,000/50 weeks		20.00	
			10.00
Profit for the week			282.50

5 Contracts and contract costing

- A **contract** is a cost unit or cost centre which is charged with the direct costs of production and an apportionment of head office overheads.

- **Contract costing** is a form of job costing which applies where the job is on a large scale and for a long duration. The majority of costs relating to a contract are direct costs.

In industries such as building and construction work, civil engineering and shipbuilding, job costing is not usually appropriate. **Contract costing** is.

Key terms

Contract costing is a 'form of specific order costing where costs are attributed to contracts'. CIMA *Official Terminology*

5.1 Features of contract costing

- A **formal contract** is made between customer and supplier.
- Work is undertaken to **customers' special requirements.**
- The work is for a **relatively long duration.**
- The work is frequently **constructional in nature.**
- The method of costing is **similar to job costing.**
- The work is frequently **based on site.**
- It is not unusual for a site to have its own cashier and time-keeper.

5.2 Potential problems in contract costing

(a) **Identifying direct costs**: because of the large size of the job, many cost items which are usually thought of as production overhead are charged as direct costs of the contract (for example supervision, hire of plant, depreciation and so on).

(b) **Low indirect costs**: because many costs normally classed as overheads are charged as direct costs of a contract, the absorption rate for overheads should only apply a share of the cost of those cost items which are not already direct costs.

(c)   **Difficulties of cost control**: because of the size of some contracts and some sites, there are often cost control problems (material usage and losses, pilferage, labour supervision, damage to and loss of plant and tools and so on).

(d)   **Dividing the profit between different accounting periods**: when a contract covers two or more accounting periods, how should the profit (or loss) on the contract be divided between the periods?

6 Contract costs

6.1 Contract accounts

FAST FORWARD

Contract costs are collected in **contract accounts**.

Guess what contract accounts are similar to? Yes, that's right, the process accounts and job accounts we have covered already. Inputs are recorded on the left hand side, outputs on the right.

6.2 Direct materials

The direct materials used on a contract may be obtained in two ways.

6.2.1 Materials obtained from the company's central stores

(a)   A material requisition note must be sent to the store keeper from the contract site. The requisition note provides a record of the cost of the materials issued to the contract.

Contract managers prefer to have too much material, rather than run out. This means that they will often requisition more material than actually needed and the surplus material will need to be returned to stores. As with job costing, the **material returned** is classified as an output and **recorded on the right hand side of the account**.

(b)   **Materials on site** which relate to an **incomplete contract** should be **carried forward** as 'closing inventory of materials on site'.

6.2.2 Materials obtained from the company's suppliers (direct)

The entire invoice cost will be charged directly to the contract.

6.3 Direct labour

It is usual for direct labour on a contract site to be **paid on an hourly basis**. Employees who work on several contracts at the same time will have to record the time spent on each contract on time sheets. Each contract will then be charged with the cost of these recorded hours.

6.4 The cost of supervision and subcontractors

The **cost of supervision**, which is usually a production overhead in unit costing, job costing and so on, will be a **direct cost** of a contract.

On large contracts, much work may be done by **subcontractors**. The invoices of subcontractors will be treated as a **direct expense** to the contract.

6.5 The cost of plant

A feature of most contract work is the amount of plant used. Plant used on a contract may be **owned** by the company, or **hired** from a plant hire firm.

(a)   If the plant is **hired**, the cost will be a **direct expense** of the contract.
(b)   If the plant is **owned**, a **variety of accounting methods** may be employed.

6.5.1 Method one: charging depreciation

The contract may be charged depreciation on the plant, on a straight line or reducing balance basis. For example if a company has some plant which cost $10,000 and is depreciated at 10% per annum straight line (to a residual value of nil) and a contract makes use of the plant for six months, a depreciation charge of $500 would be made against the contract. The disadvantage of this method of costing for plant is that the contract site manager is not made directly responsible and accountable for the actual plant in his charge. The contract manager must be responsible for receipt of the plant, returning the plant after it has been used and proper care of the plant while it is being used.

6.5.2 Method two: charging the contract with current book value

A **more common method** of costing for plant is to **charge the contract with the change in book value of the plant during the period**.

For example, suppose contract number 123 obtained some plant and loose tools from central store on 1 January 20X2. The book value of the plant was $100,000 and the book value of the loose tools was $8,000. On 1 October 20X2, some plant was removed from the site: this plant had a written down value on 1 October of $20,000. At 31 December 20X2, the plant remaining on site had a written down value of $60,000 and the loose tools had a written down value of $5,000.

CONTRACT 123 ACCOUNT

	$		$
1 January 20X2		*1 October 20X2*	
Plant issued to site	100,000	Plant transferred	20,000
Loose tools issued to site	8,000	*31 December 20X2*	
		Plant value c/f	60,000
		Loose tools value c/f	5,000
		Depreciation (bal fig)	23,000
	108,000		108,000

The difference between the values on the debit and the credit sides of the account ($20,000 for plant and $3,000 for loose tools) is the depreciation cost of the equipment for the year.

6.5.3 Method three: using a plant account

A third method of accounting for plant costs is to **open a plant account, which is charged with the depreciation costs and the running costs** (repairs, fuel and so on) **of the equipment**. A notional hire charge is then made to contracts using the plant. For example suppose that a company owns some equipment which is depreciated at the rate of $100 per month. Running costs in May 20X3 are $300. The plant is used on 20 days in the month, 12 days on Contract X and 8 days on Contract Y. The accounting entries would be as follows.

PLANT ACCOUNT

	$		$
Depreciation	100	Contract X (hire for 12 days)	240
Running costs (wages a/c, stores a/c)	300	Contract Y (hire for 8 days)	160
	400		400

CONTRACT X

	$		$
Plant account (notional hire)	240		

CONTRACT Y

	$		$
Plant account (notional hire)	160		

6.6 Overhead costs

Overhead costs are **added periodically** (for example at the end of an accounting period) and are **based on predetermined overhead absorption rates for the period**. You may come across examples where a share of head office general costs is absorbed as an overhead cost to the contract, but this should not happen if the contract is unfinished at the end of the period, because only production overheads should be included in the value of any closing work in progress.

6.7 Recording contract costs

If we ignore, for the moment, profits on a part-finished contract (we'll come to this in a minute), a typical contract account might appear as shown below. Check the items in the account carefully, and notice how the cost (or value) of the work done emerges as work in progress. On an unfinished contract, where no profits are taken mid-way through the contract, this cost of work in progress is carried forward as a closing inventory balance. Here's an example.

CONTRACT 794

	$		$
Materials requisition from stores	15,247	Materials returned to stores or	
Materials and equipment purchased	36,300	transferred to other sites	2,100
Maintenance and operating costs		Proceeds from sale of materials	
of plant and vehicles	14,444	on site and jobbing work for	
Hire charges for plant and		other customers	600
vehicles not owned	6,500	Book value of plant transferred	4,800
Tools and consumables	8,570	Materials on site c/d	7,194
Book value of plant on site b/d	14,300	Book value of plant on site c/d	6,640
Direct wages	23,890		21,334
Supervisors' and engineers' salaries			
(proportion relating to time spent		Cost of work done c/d	
on the contract)	13,000	(balancing item)	139,917
Other site expenses	12,000		
Overheads (apportioned perhaps on			
the basis of direct labour hours)	17,000		
	161,251		161,251
Materials on site b/d	7,194		
Book value of plant on site b/d	6,640		
Cost of work done b/d	139,917		

7 Progress payments and retentions

A customer is likely to be required under the terms of the contract to make **progress payments** which are calculated as the **value of work done** and certified by the architect or engineer minus a **retention** minus the payments made to date.

7.1 Progress payment due

	The value of work done and certified by the architect or engineer
minus	**a retention (commonly 10%)**
minus	**the payments made to date**
equals	**payment due.**

Thus, if an architect's certificate assesses the value of work done on a contract to be $125,000 and if the retention is 10%, and if $92,000 has already been paid in progress payments the current payment = $125,000 – $12,500 – $92,000 = $20,500

7.2 Retention monies

Retention monies are released either when the contract is completed and accepted by the customer or within an agreed period after this date.

8 Profits on contracts

You may have noticed that the progress payments do not necessarily give rise to profit immediately because of **retentions**. So how are **profits calculated on contracts**?

8.1 Example: profits on contracts completed in one accounting period

If a contract is started and completed in the same accounting period, the calculation of the profit is straightforward, sales minus the cost of the contract. Suppose that a contract, No. 6548, has the following costs.

	$
Direct materials (less returns)	40,000
Direct labour	35,000
Direct expenses	8,000
Plant costs	6,000
Overhead	11,000
	100,000

The work began on 1 February 20X3 and was completed on 15 November 20X3 in the contractor's same accounting year.

The contract price was $120,000 and on 20 November the inspecting engineer issued the final certificate of work done. At that date the customer had already paid $90,000 and the remaining $30,000 was still outstanding at the end of the contractor's accounting period. The contract account would appear as follows.

CONTRACT 6548 ACCOUNT

	$		$
Materials less returns	40,000	Cost of sales (Income	100,000
Labour	35,000	statement)	
Expenses	8,000		
Plant cost	6,000		
Overhead	11,000		
	100,000		100,000

The profit on the contract will be treated in the income statement as follows.

	$
Revenue	120,000
Cost of sales	(100,000)
	20,000

8.2 Taking profits on incomplete contracts

The long duration of a contract usually means that an **estimate** must be made of the profit earned on each **incomplete contract** at the end of the accounting period. This avoids excessive fluctuations in reported profits.

A more difficult problem emerges when a contract is **incomplete** at the end of an accounting period. The contractor may have spent considerable sums of money on the work, and received substantial progress payments, and even if the work is not finished, the contractor will want to claim some profit on the work done so far.

Suppose that a company starts four new contracts in its accounting year to 31 December 20X1, but at the end of the year, none of them has been completed. All of the contracts are eventually completed in the first few months of 20X2 and they make profits of $40,000, $50,000, $60,000 and $70,000 respectively, $220,000 in total. If profits are not taken until the contracts are finished, the company would make no profits at all in 20X1, when most of the work was done, and $220,000 in 20X2. Such violent fluctuations in profitability would be confusing not only to the company's management, but also to shareholders and the investing public at large.

The problem arises because **contracts are for long-term work**, and it is a well-established practice that some profits should be taken in an accounting period, even if the contract is incomplete.

8.2.1 Example: profits on incomplete contracts

Suppose that contract 246 is started on 1 July 20X2. Costs to 31 December 20X2, when the company's accounting year ends, are derived from the following information.

	$
Direct materials issued from store	18,000
Materials returned to store	400
Direct labour	15,500
Plant issued, at book value 1 July 20X2	32,000
Written-down value of plant 31 December 20X2	24,000
Materials on site, 31 December 20X2	1,600
Overhead costs	2,000

As at 31 December, certificates had been issued for work valued at $50,000 and the contractee had made progress payments of $45,000. The company has calculated that more work has been done since the last certificates were issued, and that the cost of work done but not yet certified is $8,000.

Solution

The contract account would be prepared as follows.

CONTRACT 246 ACCOUNT

	$	$		$
Materials	18,000		Value of plant c/d	24,000
Less returns	400		Materials on site c/d	1,600
		17,600	Cost of work done not	
Labour		15,500	certified c/d	8,000
Plant issued at book value		32,000	Cost of sales (income statement)	33,500
Overheads		2,000		
		67,100		67,100

Points to note

(a) **The work done, but not yet certified, must be valued at cost,** and not at the value of the unissued certificates. It would be imprudent to suppose that the work has been done to the complete satisfaction of the architect or engineer, who may not issue certificates until further work is done.

(b) It would appear that $50,000 should be recognised as revenue and $33,500 as cost of sales leaving $16,500 as net profit. However it is often considered imprudent to claim this full amount of profit, and it is commonly argued that the profit taken should be a more conservative figure (in our example, less than $16,500, so that amounts taken to revenue and cost of sales relating to the contract should be less than $50,000 and $33,500 respectively).

(c) We have ignored retentions here.

8.3 Estimating the size of the profit

There are several different ways of calculating contract profits, but the overriding consideration must be the application of the prudence concept. **If a loss is expected on a contract, the total expected loss should be taken into account as soon as it is recognised, even if the contract is not complete.**

The method of calculating profit on an incomplete contract may vary and you should follow the instructions carefully in any question on contract costing.

The **concept of prudence** should be applied when estimating the size of the profit on an incomplete contract and the guidelines in the following paragraphs should be noted.

8.4 Guidelines for estimating profits

(a) **If the contract is in its early stages, no profit should be taken**. Profit should only be taken when the outcome of the contract can be assessed with reasonable accuracy.

(b) **For a contract on which substantial costs have been incurred, but which is not yet near completion** (that is, it is in the region of 30% to 85% complete) a formula which has often been used in the past is as follows.

> **Profit taken = $^2/_3$ (or $^3/_4$) of the notional profit**

where notional profit = (the value of work certified to date) − (the cost of the work certified).

In the example above, the notional profit for contract 246 is $16,500 ($(50,000 - 33,500)) and the profit taken for the period using the above formula would be calculated as follows.

$$^2/_3 \text{ of } \$16,500 = \$11,000 \text{ (or } ^3/_4 \text{ of } \$16,500 = \$12,375)$$

(c) **Where the contractee withholds a retention**, or **where progress payments are not made as soon as work certificates are issued**, it would be more prudent to reduce the profit taken by the proportion of retentions to the value of work certified.

> **Profit taken = $^2/_3$ (or $^3/_4$) × notional profit × $\dfrac{\text{cash received on account}}{\text{value of work certified}}$**

In our example of contract 246, this would be:

$$^2/_3 \times \$16,500 \times \frac{\$45,000}{\$50,000} = \$9,900$$

(d) **If the contract is nearing completion, the size of the eventual profit should be foreseeable with reasonable certainty and there is no need to be excessively prudent.** The profit taken may be calculated by one of three methods.

(i) **Work certified to date minus the cost of work certified**. In our example, this would be the full $16,500.

(ii) > **Profit taken = $\dfrac{\text{cost of work done}}{\text{estimated total cost of contract}}$ × estimated total profit**

In our example, if the estimated total cost of the contract 246 is $64,000 and the estimated total profit on the contract is $18,000, the profit taken would be:

$$\frac{\$(33,500 + 8,000)}{\$64,000} \times \$18,000 = \$11,672$$

(iii) > **Profit taken = $\dfrac{\text{value of work certified}}{\text{contract price}}$ × estimated total profit**

This is perhaps the most-favoured of the three methods. In our example of contract 246, if the final contract price is $82,000 and the estimated total profit is $18,000 the profit taken would be:

$$\frac{\$50,000}{\$82,000} \times \$18,000 = \$10,976$$

Some companies may feel that it is prudent to reduce the profit attributed to the current accounting period still further, to allow for retentions of cash by the contractee. In our example, the profit taken would now be:

$$\frac{\$50,000}{\$82,000} \times \$18,000 \times \frac{\$45,000}{\$50,000} = \$9,878$$

This formula simplifies to:

$$\frac{\text{cash received to date}}{\text{contract price}} \times \text{estimated total profit from the contract}$$

(e) **A loss on the contract may be foreseen**. The method of dealing with losses is covered in the next section.

Important!

It should be apparent from these different formulae that the profit taken on an incomplete contract will depend on two things.

- The degree of completion
- The choice of formula

Question

Profits on contracts

LS Company is a construction company. Data relating to one of its contracts, XYZ, for the year to 31 December 20X2, are as follows.

	$'000
Value of work certified to 31 December 20X1	500
Cost of work certified to 31 December 20X1	360
Plant on site b/f at 1 January 20X2	30
Materials on site b/f at 1 January 20X2	10
Cost of contract to 1 January 20X2 b/f	370
Materials issued from store	190
Sub-contractors' costs	200
Wages and salaries	200
Overheads absorbed by contract in 20X2	100
Plant on site c/f at 31 December 20X2	15
Materials on site c/f at 31 December 20X2	5
Value of work certified to 31 December 20X2	1,200
Cost of work certified to 31 December 20X2	950

No profit has been taken on the contract prior to 20X2. There are no retentions.

(a) The total cumulative cost of contract XYZ to the end of December 20X2 is $ [____] .

(b) Revenue on the contract is taken as the value of work certified. The gross profit for the contract for the year to 31 December 20X2 is $ [____] .

Answer

(a) **The cost is $ 1,080,000 .**

Workings

CONTRACT ACCOUNT

	$'000		$'000
Cost of contract b/f	370	Plant on site c/f	15
Plant on site b/f	30	Materials on site c/f	5
Materials on site b/f	10	Cost of contract c/f (balance)	1,080
Materials from stores	190		
Sub-contractors' costs	200		
Wages and salaries	200		
Overheads	100		
	1,100		1,100

(b) **The profit is $ 250,000 .**

Workings

No profit had been taken on the contract prior to 20X2, and so profit is quite simply calculated as follows.

	$'000
Value of work certified to 31.12.X2	1,200
Cost of work certified to 31.12.X2	950
Gross profit to 31.12.X2	250

9 Losses on incomplete contracts

FAST FORWARD

Any **loss** on a contract should be deducted from the amounts for long-term contracts included under inventories in the balance sheet. If the resulting balance is a credit, it should be disclosed separately under accounts payable or allowance for liabilities and charges.

At the end of an accounting period, it may be that instead of finding that the contract is profitable, a loss is expected. When this occurs, the **total expected loss should be taken into account as soon as it is recognised, even though the contract is not yet complete.** The contract account should be debited with the **anticipated future loss** (final cost of contract – full contract price – (cost of work at present – value of work certified at present)) and the income statement debited with the total expected loss (final cost of contract – full contract price).

The same accounting procedure would be followed on completed contracts, as well as incomplete contracts, but it is essential that the full amount of the loss on the total contract, if foreseeable, should be charged against company profits at the earliest opportunity, even if a contract is incomplete. This means that in the next accounting period, the contract should break even, making neither a profit nor a loss, because the full loss has already been charged to the income statement.

9.1 Example: loss on contract

Contract 257 was begun on 22 March 20X3. By 31 December 20X3, the end of the contractor's accounting year, costs incurred were as follows.

	$
Materials issued	24,000
Materials on site, 31 December	2,000
Labour	36,000
Plant issued to site 22 March	40,000
Written-down value of plant, 31 December	28,000
Overheads	6,000

The contract is expected to end in February 20X4 and at 31 December 20X3, the cost accountant estimated that the final cost of the contract would be $95,000. The full contract price is $90,000. Work certified at 31 December was valued at $72,000. The contractee has made progress payments up to 31 December of $63,000.

Required

Prepare the contract account.

Solution

CONTRACT 257 ACCOUNT

	$		$
Materials issued	24,000	Materials on site c/f	2,000
Labour	36,000	Plant at written-down value, c/f	28,000
Plant issued, written-down value	40,000	Cost of work done c/d (balancing	
Overheads	6,000	figure)	76,000
	106,000		106,000
Cost of work done, b/d	76,000	Cost of sales (P&L)	77,000
Anticipated future loss*	1,000		
	77,000		77,000

* The total estimated loss on the contract is $5,000 ($90,000 – $95,000). Of this amount $4,000 has been lost in the current period ($76,000 – $72,000) and so $1,000 is anticipated as arising in the future: the company will invoice $18,000 ($90,000 – $72,000) and will incur costs of $19,000 ($95,000 – $76,000). This is taken as a loss in the current period.

The loss is posted $72,000 to revenue and $77,000 to cost of sales ($5,000 net).

Question   **Contract account**

Jibby Co's year end is 30 April. At 30 April 20X4 costs of $43,750 have been incurred on contract N53. The value of work certified at the period end is $38,615. The contract price is $57,500 but it is anticipated that the final costs at 30 September 20X4, when the contract is expected to end, will be $63,111.

(a)   The anticipated future loss on the contract is $ _____.

(b)   The revenue figure for the period to 30 April 20X4 is $ _____.

(c)   The cost of sales figure for the period to 30 April 20X4 is $ _____.

Answer

(a)   The anticipated future loss on the contract is $ 476 .

(b)   The revenue figure for the period to 30 April 20X4 is $ 36,815 .

(c)   The cost of sales figure for the period to 30 April 20X4 is $ 44,226 .

Workings

CONTRACT N53

	$		$
Cost of work done b/d	43,750	Cost of sales	44,226
Anticipated future loss*	476		
	44,226		44,226

*$[(63,111 − 57,500) − (43,750 − 38,615)] = $476

10 Disclosure of long-term contracts in financial accounts

FAST FORWARD

SSAP 9 defines how inventories and work in progress should be valued in the financial accounts, and makes particular reference to long-term contract work in progress and profits. Although there is no requirement that cost accounting procedures should be the same as financial accounting procedures and standards, it is generally thought that **conformity between the financial and cost accounts is desirable in contract costing**.

10.1 SSAP 9 requirements – income statement

(a)   The income statement will contain revenue and related costs deemed to accrue to the contract over the period, so that the income statement reflects the net profit on the contract taken in the period.

(b)   The profit taken needs to reflect the proportion of the work carried out at the accounting date, and to take account of any known inequalities of profitability at the various stages of a contract.

(c)   Where the outcome of a contract cannot be reasonably assessed before its completion, no profits should be taken on the incomplete contract.

(d)   The amount of profit taken to the income statement for an incomplete contract should be judged with prudence.

(e)   If it is expected that there will be a loss on the contract as a whole, provision needs to be made for the whole of the loss as soon as it is recognised (in accordance with the prudence concept). The amount of the loss should be deducted from the amounts for long-term contracts included under inventories, and where a credit balance results, it should be disclosed separately under accounts payable or allowances for liabilities and charges.

10.2 SSAP 9 disclosures – balance sheet

Balances relating to long-term contracts are split into two elements.

(a) Work done on long-term contracts not yet recognised in the income statement is disclosed under 'inventories' as 'long-term contract balances'.

(b) The difference between

(i)	amounts recognised as revenue	X
(ii)	progress payments received	(X)
		X

will be recognised in accounts receivable as 'amounts recoverable on long-term contracts' if (i) is greater than (ii), or will be offset against the balances in (a) above if (ii) is greater than (i).

Question
          Income statement and balance sheet

During its financial year ended 30 June 20X7 Beavers Co, an engineering company, has worked on several contracts. Information relating to one of them is given below.

Contract X201

Date commenced	1 July 20X6
Estimated completion date	30 Sept 20X7
Contract price	$240,000
Proportion of work certified as satisfactorily completed (and invoiced) up to June 20X7	$180,000
Amount received from contractee	$150,000
Costs up to 30 June 20X7	
Wages	$91,000
Materials sent to site	$36,000
Other contract costs	$18,000
Proportion of head office costs	$6,000
Plant and equipment transferred to the site (at book value on 1 July 20X6)	$9,000

The plant and equipment is expected to have a book value of about $1,000 when the contract is completed.

Inventory of materials at site on 30 June 20X7	$3,000
Expected additional costs to complete the contract	
Wages	$10,000
Materials (including inventory at 30 June 20X7)	$12,000
Other (including head office costs)	$8,000

Company policy is to recognise profit on contracts as follows.

$$\text{Profit to be recognised} = \frac{\text{value of work certified}}{\text{total contract value}} \times \text{estimated total contract profit}$$

(a)   The contract account has been partially completed as at 30 June 20X7 as follows.

CONTRACT ACCOUNT X201

	$		$
Wages	91,000	Inventory c/d	3,000
Materials	36,000	Plant c/d	A
Other costs	18,000	Costs incurred to date	
Head office costs	6,000		
Plant and equipment transferred	9,000		
	160,000		160,000

The value to be entered in the account as A is $ ☐

(b)   The profit to be recognised on the contract to date is $ ☐

(c)   The amounts to be shown on the company balance sheet as at 30 June 20X7 in respect of contract X201 are:

(i)   Inventories: long-term contract balances $ ☐

(ii)   Receivables: amounts recoverable on long-term contracts $ ☐

Answer

(a)   **The value to be entered in the account as A is $ 2,600 .**

Working

Total expected loss of value of plant = $8,000

Proportion to be allocated to contract to date = 12 months/15 months × $8,000 = $6,400.

∴ Value of plant c/d = $9,000 − $6,400 = $2,600

(b)   **The profit to be recognised on the contract to date is $ 40,500 .**

Working

	$	$	$
Contract price			240,000
Actual costs to date			
Wages	91,000		
Materials	33,000		
Other costs	18,000		
HO costs	6,000		
Plant	6,400		
		154,400	
Expected future costs			
Wages	10,000		
Materials	12,000		
Other costs	8,000		
Plant	1,600		
		31,600	
			186,000
Estimated total profit			54,000

Proportion recognised in the current year:

$$\frac{£180,000}{£240,000} \times \$54,000 = \$40,500$$

(c) (i) **Inventories: long-term contract balances \$** 14,900 see (W1)

     (ii) **Receivables: amounts recoverable on long-term contracts \$** 30,000 see (W2)

Workings

1   Profit recognised = \$40,500

    Value of work certified = \$180,000

    ∴ Amount allocated to cost of sales = \$180,000 − \$40,500
                             = \$139,500

	$
Costs incurred to date	154,400
Less allocated to cost of sales	139,500
Inventories: long-term contract balances	14,900

2 Amounts recognised as revenue	180,000
Less progress payments received	150,000
Receivables: amounts recoverable on long-term contracts	30,000

Chapter Roundup

- **Job costing** is the costing method used where work is undertaken to customers' special requirements and each order is of comparatively short duration.

- The usual method of fixing prices within a jobbing concern is **cost plus pricing**.

- An **internal job costing system** can be used for costing the work of service departments.

- **Batch costing** is similar to job costing in that each batch of similar articles is separately identifiable. The **cost per unit** manufactured in a batch is the total batch cost divided by the number of units in the batch.

- A **contract** is a cost unit or cost centre which is charged with the direct costs of production and an apportionment of head office overheads.

- **Contract costing** is a form of job costing which applies where the job is on a large scale and for a long duration. The majority of costs relating to a contract are direct costs.

- Contract costs are collected in **contract accounts**.

- A customer is likely to be required under the terms of the contract to make **progress payments** which are calculated as the **value of work done** and certified by the architect or engineer minus a **retention** minus the payments made to date.

- The long duration of a contract usually means that an **estimate** must be made of the profit earned on each **incomplete contract** at the end of the accounting period. This avoids excessive fluctuations in reported profits.

- There are several different ways of calculating contract profits, but the overriding consideration must be the application of the prudence concept. **If a loss is expected on a contract, the total expected loss should be taken into account as soon as it is recognised, even if the contract is not complete.**

- Any **loss** on a contract should be deducted from the amounts for long-term contracts included under inventories in the balance sheet. If the resulting balance is a credit, it should be disclosed separately under accounts payable or allowances for liabilities and charges.

- **SSAP 9** defines how inventories and work in progress should be valued in the financial accounts, and makes particular reference to long-term contract work in progress and profits. Although there is no requirement that cost accounting procedures should be the same as financial accounting procedures and standards, it is generally thought that **conformity between the financial and cost accounts is desirable in contract costing.**

Quick Quiz

1   Which of the following are not characteristics of job costing?

    I   Customer driven production
    II   Complete production possible within a single accounting period
    III   Homogeneous products

A   I and II only
B   I and III only
C   II and III only
D   III only

2   The cost of a job is $100,000

    (a)   If profit is 25% of the job cost, the price of the job = $ ☐

    (b)   If there is a 25% margin, the price of the job = $ ☐

3   List six features of contract costing

    • ....
    • ....
    • ....
    • ....
    • ....
    • ....

4   What are the three methods of calculating profit on a contract which is nearing completion?

    (a)   ....   minus   ....

    (b) $\dfrac{........................}{........................}$ ×   ....

    (c) $\dfrac{........................}{........................}$ ×   ....

5   How would you account for a loss on an incomplete contract?

6   The following information is available for contract AF3.

Contract price	$15 million
Cost of work to date	$5,040,000
Estimated costs to completion	$3,960,000

The amount of profit to be recognised on the contract is

A $0   B $3,360,000   C $6,000,000   D $8,400,000

Answers to Quick Quiz

1   D

2   (a) $100,000 + (25% × $100,000) = $100,000 + $25,000 = $125,000

     (b)   Profit is 25 per cent of the selling price, therefore selling price should be written as 100%:

	%
Selling price	100
Profit	25
Cost	75

∴ Price = $100,000 × 100/75 = $133,333.

3   •   A formal contract is made between customer and supplier
     •   Work is undertaken to customers' special requirements
     •   The work is for a relatively long duration
     •   The work is frequently constructional in nature
     •   The method of costing is similar to job costing
     •   The work is frequently based on site

4   (a)   Work certified to date – cost of work certified

     (b) $\dfrac{\text{Cost of work done}}{\text{Estimated total cost of contract}} \times$ estimated total profit on contract

     (c) $\dfrac{\text{Value of work certified}}{\text{Contract price}} \times$ estimated total profit on contract

5   If a loss is expected on an incomplete contract, the total expected loss should be taken into account as soon as it is recognised, even though the contract is not yet complete.

6   B   Total cost to completion = $5,040,000 + $3,960,000 = $9,000,000

     Percentage of total cost incurred to date = $5,040,000/$9,000,000 = 56%

     Therefore it is acceptable to recognise a profit. This eliminates option A.

     Profit to be recognised = $\dfrac{\text{Cost of work done}}{\text{Estimated total cost of contract}} \times$ estimated total profit

     $= \dfrac{£5,040,000}{£9,000,000} \times \$(15,000,000 - 9,000,000)$

     $= \$3,360,000$

Now try the questions below from the Question Bank

Question numbers	Page
71–78	363

Cost bookkeeping

Introduction

In Part A of this Study Text you saw how to determine the major elements of the cost of a unit of product - **material**, **labour**, **overhead** - and how to build up these elements into a total cost. In Chapters 12 and 13 you saw how costs are recorded depending on the costing method adopted by an organisation. But what you don't know how to do is account for costs within a cost accounting system. This chapter will teach you. It will teach you **cost bookkeeping**.

The overall bookkeeping routine will vary from organisation to organisation but either an **integrated** or an **interlocking** system will be used. For the purposes of this Paper C1 syllabus you **only need to know about integrated systems**, however.

In the last part of this chapter we will look at how a standard costing system is used in conjunction with an integrated system of cost bookkeeping.

Topic list	Learning outcomes	Syllabus references	Ability required
1 Accounting for costs	D(i)	D(2)	Comprehension
2 Integrated systems	D(i), (ii)	D(1), (2)	Comprehension, Application
3 Standard cost bookkeeping	D(ii)	D(3)	Application

1 Accounting for costs

FAST FORWARD

Cost bookkeeping is based on the principles of **double entry**, the **golden rule** of which is that for **every entry made in one account, there must be a corresponding balancing entry in another account**.

1.1 Cost accounting systems

There are **no statutory requirements** to keep detailed cost records and so some small firms only keep traditional financial accounts and prepare cost information in an ad-hoc fashion. This approach is, however, unsatisfactory for all but the smallest organisations: most firms therefore maintain some form of cost accounting system.

Cost accounting systems range from simple analysis systems to computer based accounting systems. Often systems are tailored to the users' requirements and therefore incorporate unique features. All systems will incorporate a number of common aspects and all records will be maintained using the **principles of double entry**.

1.2 Principles of double entry bookkeeping

The principles of double entry bookkeeping are not described in this chapter, but if you have not yet begun your studies of basic financial accounting, you may not be familiar with the concept of 'debits and credits'. Nevertheless you may still be able to follow the explanations below, provided that you remember the 'golden rule' of double entry bookkeeping, that for every entry made in one account, there must be a corresponding balancing entry in another account.

2 Integrated systems

FAST FORWARD

Integrated systems combine both financial and cost accounts in one system of ledger accounts.

Key term

Integrated accounts are a 'set of accounting records that integrates both financial and cost accounts using a common input of data for all accounting purposes'.
CIMA *Official Terminology*

2.1 The principal accounts in a system of integrated accounts

- (a) **The resources accounts**

  - Materials control account or stores control account
  - Wages (and salaries) control account
  - Production overhead control account
  - Administration overhead control account
  - Selling and distribution overhead control account

- (b) **Accounts which record the cost of production items from the start of production work through to cost of sales**

  - Work in progress control account
  - Finished goods control account
  - Cost of sales control account

- (c) Sales account

- (d) Income statement

2.2 Accounting entries in an integrated system

ORWARD

The basic entries in an interpreted system are as follows:

- **Expenditure** on materials, wages and overheads

    - DR   Resources account
    - CR   Cash or accounts payable

- **Work in progress**

    - DR   WIP (for overhead, this is **overhead absorbed**)
    - CR   Resources account (for overhead, this is **overhead absorbed**)

- **Finished goods**

    - DR   Finished goods
    - CR   WIP

- **Cost of sales**

    - DR   Cost of sales
    - CR   Finished goods

The accounting entries in an integrated system can be confusing and it is important to keep in mind some general principles.

2.2.1 Materials, wages and overheads expenditure

When **expenditure** is incurred on materials, wages or overheads, the actual amounts paid or payable are debited to the appropriate **resources accounts**. The credit entries are made in the cash or accounts payable accounts.

2.2.2 Work in progress

When production begins, **resources are allocated to work in progress**. This is recorded by crediting the resources accounts and debiting the work in progress account. In the case of production overheads, the amount credited to the overhead account and debited to work in progress should be the amount of overhead absorbed. If this differs from the amount of overhead incurred, there will be a difference on the overhead control account; this should be written off to an under-/over-absorbed overhead account. (One other point to remember is that when **indirect** materials and labour are allocated to production, the entries are to credit the materials and wages accounts and debit **production overhead account**.)

2.2.3 Finished goods

As **finished goods** are produced, work in progress is reduced. This is recorded by debiting the finished goods control account and crediting the work in progress control account.

2.2.4 Cost of sales

At the end of the period, the cost of goods sold is transferred from the finished goods account to the cost of sales account, and from there to the income statement.

2.2.5 Non-production overheads

The balances on the administration overhead control account and the selling and distribution overhead control account are usually transferred direct to the income statement at the period end.

2.2.6 Sales

Sales are debited to the receivables control account and credited to the sales account.

2.2.7 Profits

Profit is established by transferring to the income statement the balances on the sales account, cost of sales account and under-/over-absorbed overhead account.

2.3 Accounting entries in full costing and marginal costing systems

Cost bookkeeping can appear quite daunting to begin with. You may find it useful to study the two diagrams on the following pages, which illustrate the (simplified) operation of integrated systems using absorption costing and marginal costing. Follow the entries through the various control accounts and note the differences between the two diagrams. Yo will then be ready to work through an example.

Cost accounting using absorption costing

Diagram: Cost accounting using absorption costing

STORES

£		£
X		X
X		

Credit purchases
Cash purchases

WAGES

£		£
X		X
X		

Cash wages

Indirect wages

WIP

£		£
X		X
X		
X		

Direct materials
Direct wages
Ohds absorbed

FG

£		£
X		X

FG transferred

OHDs

£		£
X		X
X	X	X
X		
X		
X		

Indirect materials
Credit expenses
Cash expenses
Depreciation
Selling and distribution overheads
Balance on a/c - under- or over- absorbed overheads

COST P/L

£		£
X		X
		X
		X

COS
Sales
Balance on a/c - profit or loss for period

SALES

£		£
X		X

Sales

Cost accounting using marginal costing

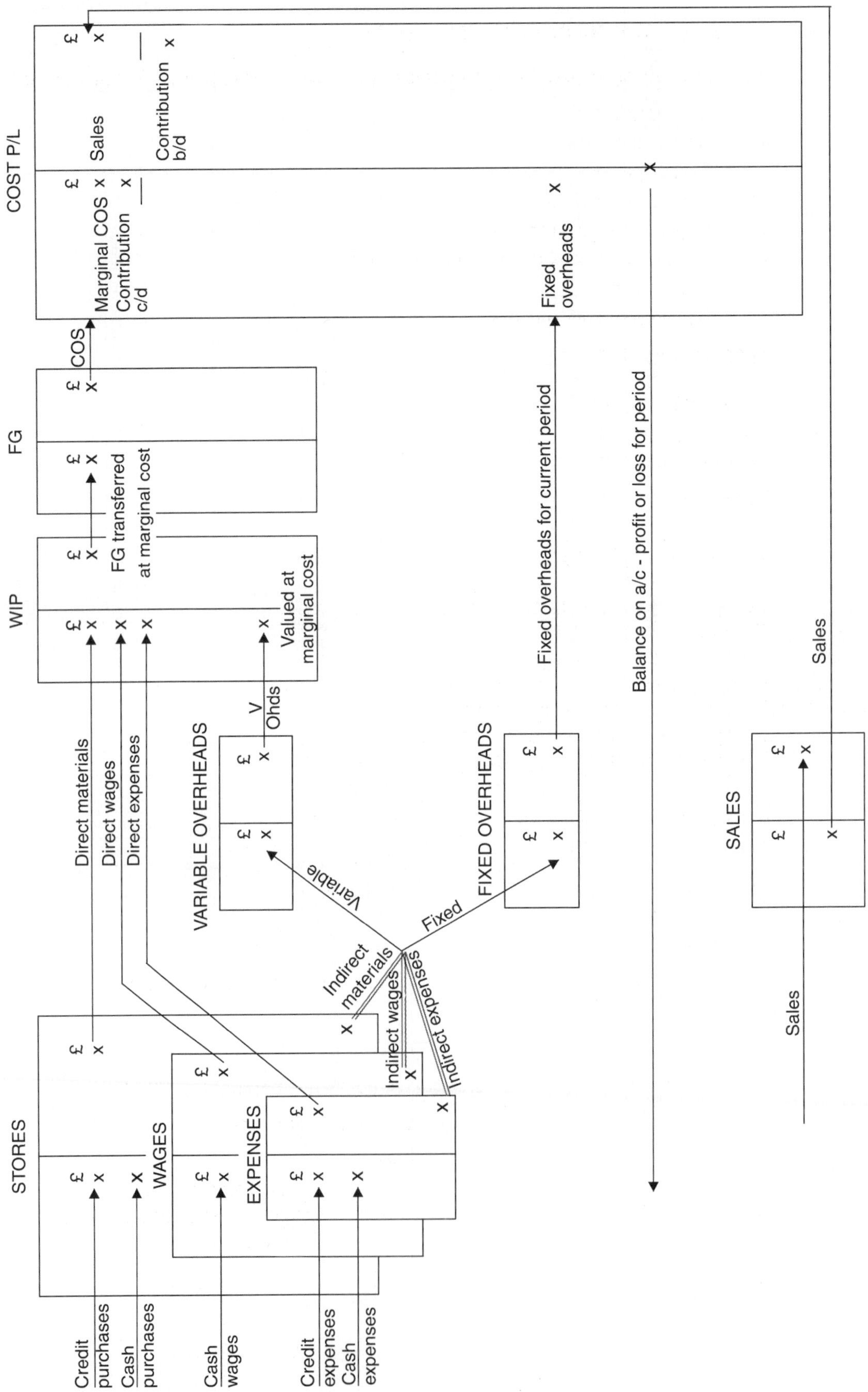

2.4 Example: integrated accounts

Using the information given below for October, you are required to prepare the following accounts.

- Raw materials control
- Work in progress control
- Finished goods control
- Production overhead control
- Wages and salaries control
- Selling and administration overhead control
- Cost of sales
- Trading and profit and loss

Balances as at 1 October

	$'000
Raw materials control	10
Work in progress control	15
Finished goods control	18

Transactions for October

	$'000
Materials received from suppliers on credit	50
Materials issued to production	42
Materials issued to production service departments	5
Direct wages incurred	30
Production indirect wages incurred	13
Selling and administration salaries incurred	12
Production expenses paid as incurred	8
Selling and administration expenses paid as incurred	9
Allowance for depreciation: production equipment	3
selling and administration equipment	2
Wages and salaries paid: direct wages	28
production indirect wages	13
selling and administration salaries	12
Production completed and transferred to finished goods store	90
Production cost of goods sold	97
Sales on credit	145

Production overhead is absorbed at the rate of 80 per cent of direct wages incurred.

Solution

The figures in brackets refer to the explanations which follow after the ledger accounts.

RAW MATERIALS CONTROL

	$'000		$'000
Balance b/d	10	Work in progress (1)	42
Accounts payable	50	Production overhead control (1)	5
		Balance c/d	13
	60		60
Balance b/d	13		

WORK IN PROGRESS CONTROL

	$'000		$'000
Balance b/d	15	Finished goods control (4)	90
Raw materials control (1)	42	Balance c/d (4)	21
Wages and salaries control (2)	30		
Production overhead control (3)	24		
	111		111
Balance b/d	21		

FINISHED GOODS CONTROL

	$'000		$'000
Balance b/d	18	Cost of sales (5)	97
Work in progress control (4)	90	Balance c/d (5)	11
	108		108
Balance b/d	11		

PRODUCTION OVERHEAD CONTROL

	$'000		$'000
Raw materials control (1)	5	Work in progress control (3)	24
Wages and salaries control (2)	13	Under absorption to income	
Bank (6)	8	statement (8)	5
Allowance for depreciation (6)	3		
	29		29

WAGES AND SALARIES CONTROL

	$'000		$'000
Bank (7)	53	Work in progress control (2)	30
Balance c/d (7)	2	Production overhead control (2)	13
		Selling and admin o/h control (2)	12
	55		55
		Balance b/d	2

SELLING AND ADMINISTRATION OVERHEAD CONTROL

	$'000		$'000
Bank (6)	9	Income statement	23
Wages and salaries control (2)	12		
Allowance for depreciation (6)	2		
	23		23

COST OF SALES

	$'000		$'000
Finished goods control (5)	97	Income statement	97

TRADING AND INCOME STATEMENT

	$'000		$'000
Cost of sales (5)	97	Sales – receivables	145
Gross profit c/d	48		
	145		145
Under-absorbed overhead (8)	5	Gross profit b/d	48
Selling and admin o/h	23		
Net profit for October	20		
	48		48

Notes

1   The materials issued to production are charged as **direct materials** to work in progress. The materials issued to production service departments are **indirect materials**. The cost of indirect materials is 'collected' in the production overhead control account, pending its later absorption, along with all the other production overheads, into the value of work in progress.

2   The wages and salaries **incurred** are debited to the relevant control accounts:

- direct wages to work in progress
- indirect wages to production overhead control
- selling and administration salaries to selling and administration overhead control

The credit entry for wages **incurred** is made in the wages and salaries control account.

3   Once the direct material and direct wages have been debited to work in progress, the next step is to **absorb production overheads**, using the predetermined overhead absorption rate. The work in progress account is charged with 80 per cent of wages incurred: $30,000 \times 80\% = \$24,000$.

4   Now that all of the elements of production cost have been charged to work in progress, the **production cost of goods completed** can be transferred to the finished goods control account. The balance on the work in progress account presents the inventory at the end of October.

5   The **production cost of goods sold** is transferred from the finished goods account to the cost of sales account. The balance on the finished goods account represents the inventory at the end of October.

6   The production expenses incurred and the depreciation on production machinery are debited in the production overhead control account. Thus they are 'collected' with the other production overheads, for later **absorption into work in progress**.

7   The total amount of wages **paid** ($28,000 + $13,000 + $12,000) is debited to the wages and salaries control account. The balance remaining on the account is the difference between the wages paid and the wages incurred. This represents a $2,000 accrual for wages, which is carried down into next month's accounts.

8   The balance remaining on the production overhead control account is the difference between the production overhead incurred, and the amount absorbed into work in progress. On this occasion the overhead is **underabsorbed** and is transferred as a debit in the income statement.

2.5 Job costing and cost bookkeeping

Do you remember at the end of the job costing example in the last chapter we said we'd be encountering it again? Well now we are!

2.5.1 Example: job costing and cost bookkeeping

This example will show you how to integrate your job costing and cost bookkeeping knowledge, and you'll see how to incorporate job accounts into an integrated ledger system.

We reproduce below the job accounts from Chapter 13, this time with some additional information about the accounts to which the corresponding double entry is made (in brackets).

JOB 6832

	$		$
Balance b/f	1,710	Job 6834 a/c	620
Materials (stores a/c)	2,390	(materials transfer)	
Labour (wages a/c)	3,440	Stores a/c (materials returned)	870
Production overhead (o'hd a/c)	860	Cost of sales a/c (balance)	6,910
	8,400		8,400

JOB 6833

	$		$
Materials (stores a/c)	1,680	Balance c/f	8,430
Labour (wages a/c)	5,200		
Production overhead (o'hd a/c)	1,300		
Job 6834 a/c (materials transfer)	250		
	8,430		8,430

JOB 6834

	$		$
Materials (stores a/c)	3,950	Job 6833 a/c (materials transfer)	250
Labour (wages a/c)	2,240		
Production overhead (o'hd a/c)	560	Cost of sales a/c (balance)	7,120
Job 6832 a/c (materials transfer)	620		
	7,370		7,370

JOB 6835

	$		$
Materials (stores a/c)	4,420	Stores a/c (materials returned)	170
Labour (wages a/c)	3,280		
Production overhead (o'hd a/c)	820	Cost of sales a/c (balance)	8,350
	8,520		8,520

Required

Show how the costs recorded in the job accounts above would be shown in the company's cost control accounts.

Solution

STORES CONTROL (incomplete)

	$		$
WIP a/c (returns)	1,040	WIP a/c	
		(2,390 + 1,680 + 3,950 + 4,420)	12,440
		Income statement:	
		inventory written off	2,300

WORK IN PROGRESS CONTROL

	$		$
Balance b/f	1,710	Stores control a/c (returns)	1,040
Stores control a/c	12,440	Cost of sales a/c	
Wages control a/c	*14,160	(6,910 + 7,120 + 8,350)	22,380
Production o'hd control a/c	**3,540	Balance c/f (Job No 6833)	8,430
	31,850		31,850

* 1,770 hours at $8 per hour
** 1,770 hours at $2 per hour

COST OF SALES CONTROL

	$		$
WIP control a/c	22,380	Income statement	26,856
Admin & marketing o'hd a/c			
(1,382 + 1,424 + 1,670)	4,476		
	26,856		26,856

SALES

	$		$
Income statement	27,000	Receivables	27,000
		(8,500 + 9,000 + 9,500)	
	27,000		27,000

PRODUCTION OVERHEAD CONTROL

	$		$
Overhead incurred – payables	3,800	WIP a/c	3,540
		Under-absorbed o'hd a/c	260
	3,800		3,800

UNDER-/OVER-ABSORBED OVERHEADS

	$		$
Production o'hd control a/c	260	Admin & marketing o'hd a/c	58
		Income statement	202
	260		260

ADMIN & MARKETING OVERHEAD CONTROL

	$		$
Overhead incurred – payables	4,418	Cost of sales a/c	4,476
Over absorbed o'hd a/c	58		
	4,476		4,476

INCOME STATEMENT

	$		$
Cost of sales a/c	26,856	Sales a/c	27,000
Stores a/c (inventory written off)	2,300	Loss	2,358
Under-absorbed overhead a/c	202		
	29,358		29,358

The loss of $2,358 is the sum of the profits/losses on each completed job $(208 + 456 − 520) = $144, minus the total of under-absorbed overhead ($202) and the inventory write-off ($2,300).

2.6 Contract costing and cost bookkeeping

In Chapter 13 you saw how to draw up contract accounts. Having looked at integrated systems you're now in a position to consider the other ledger accounts that are affected by the recording of contract costs and revenues.

Look back at Example 8.1 in the previous chapter. Here's how we account for the contract revenue (the price is $120,000) and for amount of $30,000 outstanding from the customer (contractee or debtor).

WORK CERTIFIED ACCOUNT

	$		$
Revenue (income statement)	120,000	Contractee account	120,000
	120,000		120,000

CONTRACTEE (CUSTOMER) ACCOUNT

	$		$
Work certified a/c - value of work certified	120,000	Cash	90,000
		Balance c/f (account receivable in balance sheet)	30,000
	120,000		120,000

Question   Cost bookkeeping and contract costing

Look back at Example 8.2.1 of Chapter 13. Complete the following work certified and contractee accounts.

WORK CERTIFIED ACCOUNT

	$		$
Revenue	☐	Contractee account	☐
	☐		☐

CONTRACTEE ACCOUNT

	$		$
Work certified account	☐	Cash	☐
		Balance c/f	☐
	☐		☐

Answer

WORK CERTIFIED ACCOUNT

	$			$
Revenue	50,000	Contractee account		50,000
	50,000			50,000

CONTRACTEE ACCOUNT

	$		$
Work certified account	50,000	Cash (progress payment)	45,000
		Balance c/f	5,000
	50,000		50,000

2.7 Bookkeeping entries for wages

Accounting for wages often causes difficulties for students, so let's look at another example. This example goes a bit further than the data in the last example, because it shows you how to deal with deductions for income tax, national insurance and so on.

2.7.1 Example: the wages control account

The following details were extracted from a weekly payroll for 750 employees at a factory.

	Direct workers	Indirect workers	Total
Analysis of gross pay:	$	$	$
Ordinary time	36,000	22,000	58,000
Overtime: basic wage	8,700	5,430	14,130
premium	4,350	2,715	7,065
Shift allowance	3,465	1,830	5,295
Sick pay	950	500	1,450
Idle time	3,200	-	3,200
	56,665	32,475	89,140
Net wages paid to employees	$45,605	$24,220	$69,825

Required

Prepare the wages control account for the week.

Solution

(a)   The **wages control account** acts as a sort of 'collecting place' for net wages paid and deductions made from gross pay. The gross pay is then analysed between direct and indirect wages.

(b)   The first step is to determine which wage costs are direct and which are indirect. The direct wages will be debited to the work in progress account and the indirect wages will be debited to the production overhead account.

(c)   There are in fact only two items of direct wages cost in this example - the ordinary time ($36,000) and the basic overtime wage ($8,700) paid to direct workers. All other payments (including the overtime premium) are indirect wages.

(d)   The net wages paid are debited to the control account, and the balance then represents the deductions which have been made for income tax, national insurance, and so on.

WAGES CONTROL ACCOUNT

	$		$
Bank: net wages paid	69,825	Work in progress – direct labour	44,700
Deductions control accounts*		Production overhead control:	
($89,140 – $69,825)	19,315	Indirect labour	27,430
		Overtime premium	7,065
		Shift allowance	5,295
		Sick pay	1,450
		Idle time	3,200
	89,140		89,140

* In practice there would be a separate deductions control account for each type of deduction made (such as PAYE, National Insurance).

Question

Raw materials inventory control account

The following information relates to E Co for March.

Opening balance of raw materials	$12,000
Raw materials purchased on credit	$80,000
Raw materials issued: to production	$73,000
to production maintenance	$8,000
Raw materials returned to supplier	$2,000

The balance c/d at the end of March on the raw materials inventory control account is $ ⌷ .

Answer

The balance c/d is $ 9,000 .

Workings

RAW MATERIALS INVENTORY CONTROL

	$		$
Balance b/d	12,000	Work in progress	73,000
Accounts payable	80,000	Production overhead control	8,000
		Accounts payable	2,000
		Balance c/d	9,000
	92,000		92,000
Balance b/d	9,000		

2.8 Manufacturing accounts

ORWARD

> The **ledger accounts related to production** can be consolidated into a **manufacturing account**.

Suppose an organisation has the following ledger accounts for control period 2.

RAW MATERIALS CONTROL

	$'000		$'000
Balance b/d	50	WIP	250
Purchases	275	Balance c/d	75
	325		325

WIP CONTROL

	$'000		$'000
Balances b/d	40	Finished goods control	810
Raw materials control	250		
Wages and salaries control	380		
Production overhead control	200	Balance c/d	60
	870		870

The **manufacturing** account is as follows.

MANUFACTURING ACCOUNT

	$'000		$'000
Raw materials (opening stock)	50	Raw materials consumed	250
Purchases	275	Raw materials (closing stock)	75
	325		325
WIP (opening stock)	40	WIP (closing stock)	60
Raw materials consumed	250	Manufacturing (or factory or production)	
Wages and salaries	380	cost of goods produced	810
Production overheads	200		
	870		870

2.9 The advantage and disadvantage of integrated systems

(a)   The **advantage** of integrated systems over systems which have separate systems for cost and financial accounting is the **saving in administrative effort**. Only one set of accounts needs to be maintained instead of two and the possible confusion arising from having two sets of accounts with different figures (such as for inventory values and profits) does not exist.

(b)   The **disadvantage** of integrated accounts is that one set of accounts is expected to fulfil two different purposes.

- Stewardship of the business, and external reporting
- Provision of internal management information

(c)   At times, these different purposes may conflict; for example, the valuation of inventories in an integrated system will conform to the requirements of SSAP 9, whereas for management information purposes it might be preferable to value closing inventories at, say, marginal cost or replacement cost.

(d)   In practice, however, computers have overcome these disadvantages and most modern cost accounting systems are integrated systems, incorporating coding systems which allow basic data to be analysed and presented in different ways for different purposes.

Question
Production overhead control account

The following information relates to Jamboree Co.

Production overheads incurred	$50,000
Labour hours worked	5,000
Production overhead absorption rate	$11 per labour hour

Delete the incorrect words and fill in the missing figure in the statement below.

The production overhead is **under/over** absorbed by $ [   ]. This amount is a **debit/credit** to the production overhead control account.

Answer

The production overhead is **over** absorbed by $ 5,000 . This amount is a **debit** to the production overhead control account.

Workings

PRODUCTION OVERHEAD CONTROL ACCOUNT

	$		$
Cash/payables	50,000	Work in progress control	
Over-absorbed overhead to profit		(5,000 hr × $11)	55,000
and loss	5,000		
	55,000		55,000

Question
Accounting entries

At the end of a period, in an integrated cost and financial accounting system, the accounting entries for $18,000 overheads under-absorbed would be

A	Debit work-in-progress control account	Credit overhead control account
B	Debit income statement	Credit work-in-progress control account
C	Debit income statement	Credit overhead control account
D	Debit overhead control account	Credit income statement

Answer

The correct answer is C.

Eliminate the incorrect options first. The only overhead charge made to work in progress (WIP) is the overhead absorbed into production based on the predetermined rate. Under or over absorption does not affect WIP. This eliminates A and B. Under-absorbed overhead means that overhead charges have been too low therefore there must be a further debit to income statement. This eliminates D, and the correct answer is C.

Question

Look back at Example 4.2 of Chapter 12.

Delete the incorrect words and fill in the missing figure in the statement below.

In the production overhead account for that example, there would be **under/over** absorption of overhead of $☐,
which would be a **debit/credit** in the account.

Answer

In the production overhead account for that example, there would be **over** absorption of overhead of $ 200 which
would be a **debit** in the account.

Workings

PRODUCTION OVERHEAD ACCOUNT

	$		$
Overhead incurred	17,800	Process 1 a/c	6,000
Over-absorbed overhead a/c		Process 2 a/c	12,000
(or P & L a/c)	200		
	18,000		18,000

3 Standard cost bookkeeping

When an organisation runs a standard costing system, the variances need to be included in the ledger accounts. This is
known as standard cost bookkeeping. Don't panic, it's not as complicated as it sounds.

3.1 Basic principles

There are some possible variations in accounting method between one organisation's system and others, especially in
the method of recording overhead variances, but the following are the basic principles.

3.1.1 Where the variances are recorded

In a **standard cost bookkeeping system**, the variances are recorded as follows:

(a)   The **material price variance** is recorded in the **stores control account**.

(b)   The **labour rate variance** is recorded in the **wages control account**.

(c)   The following variances are recorded in the **work in progress account**.

- Material usage variance
- Idle time variance
- Labour efficiency variance
- Variable overhead efficiency variance

(d)   The **production overhead expenditure variance** will be recorded in the **production overhead control account**.

(e)   The **production overhead volume variance** may be recorded in the **fixed production overhead account**. (*Note*. Alternatively, you may find the volume variance recorded in the **work in progress account**.)

(f)   **Sales variances do not appear in the books of account.** Sales are recorded in the sales account at actual invoiced value.

(g)   The balance of variances in the variance accounts at the end of a period may be **written off to the income statement.**

3.1.2 When the variances are recorded

The general principle in standard cost bookkeeping is that cost variances should be recorded as **early as possible**. They are recorded in the relevant account **in which they arise** and the appropriate double entry is taken to a variance account.

(a)   **Material price variances** are apparent when materials are purchased, and they are therefore recorded in the **stores account**. If a price variance is adverse, we should credit the stores account and debit a variance account with the amount of the variance.

(b)   **Material usage variances** do not occur until output is actually produced in the factory, and they are therefore recorded in the **work in progress account**. If a usage variance is favourable, we should debit the work in progress account and credit a variance account with the value of the variance.

3.1.3 Adverse and favourable variances

Adverse variances are **debited** to the relevant variance account; **favourable** variances are **credited** in the relevant variance account.

The actual process is best demonstrated with an example. Work carefully through the one which follows, ensuring that you look at how the various variances are recorded.

3.2 Example: cost bookkeeping and variances

Zed Co operates an integrated accounting system and a standard marginal costing system and prepares its final accounts monthly. You are provided with the following information.

Balances as at 1 October

	$'000
Plant and machinery, at cost	600
Inventory – raw materials	520
Wages payable	40
Inventory – finished goods	132

Data for the month of October

Materials purchased on credit	400,000 kgs at $4.90 per kg
Issued to production	328,000 kgs
Direct wages incurred	225,000 hours at $4.20 per hour
Direct wages paid	$920,000
Variable overhead incurred	$1,385,000
Sales	$4,875,000
Production and sales	39,000 units

Additional data

Inventories of raw materials and finished goods are maintained at standard cost.

Standard data

Direct material price	$5.00 per kg
Direct material usage	8 kgs per unit
Direct wages	$4.00 per hour
Direct labour	6 hours per unit
Variable overhead	6 labour hours per unit at $6 per hour
Budgeted output	10,000 units per week

Required

(a) Calculate the appropriate cost variances for October.

(b) Show the following ledger accounts for October.

    (i)   Stores ledger control account
    (ii)   Direct wages control account
    (iii)   Variable overhead control account
    (iv)   Work in progress control account
    (v)   Finished goods control account
    (vi)   Cost of sales control account
    (vii)   Sales account
    (viii) Variances account
    (ix)   Income statement

Solution

(a)   We will begin by determining the standard unit cost and calculating the variances.

Standard marginal cost per unit	$
Direct materials (8 kgs × $5)	40
Direct labour (6 hrs × $4)	24
Variable production overhead (6 hrs × $6)	36
	100

Direct material price variance	$'000
400,000 kgs should cost (× $5)	2,000
but did cost (400,000 × $4.90)	1,960
	40 (F)

Direct material usage variance	
39,000 units should use (× 8)	312,000 kgs
but did use	328,000 kgs
Variance in kg	16,000 kgs (A)
× standard price per kg	× $5
	$80,000 (A)

Direct labour rate variance	$'000
225,000 hours should cost (× $4)	900
but did cost (225,000 × $4.20)	945
	45 (A)

Direct labour efficiency variance	
39,000 units should take (× 6 hrs)	234,000 hrs
but did take	225,000 hrs
Variance in hours	9,000 hrs (F)
× standard rate per hour	× $4
	$36,000 (F)

Variable overhead expenditure variance	$
225,000 hours should cost (× $6)	1,350,000
but did cost	1,385,000
	35,000 (A)

Variable overhead efficiency variance	
Labour efficiency variance in hours	9,000 hrs (F)
× standard rate per hour	× $6
	$54,000 (F)

(b)   (i)   STORES LEDGER CONTROL ACCOUNT

	$'000		$'000
Balance b/f	520	Work in progress	
Payables		(328,000 × $5)	1,640
(400,000 × $4.90)	1,960	Balance c/d	880
Material price variance	40		
	2,520		2,520
Balance b/d	880		

Notes

(1)   Materials are issued from store at standard price.

(2)   The material price variance is recorded in this account. It is a favourable variance, therefore it is recorded as a credit in the variance account.

(ii)   DIRECT WAGES CONTROL ACCOUNT

	$'000		$'000
Bank	920	Balance b/f	40
Balance c/d	65	Work in progress	
		(225,000 hrs × $4)	900
		Labour rate variance	45
	985		985
		Balance b/d	65

Notes

(1)   Labour hours are charged to work in progress at the standard rate per hour.

(2)   The labour rate variance is recorded in this account. It is an adverse variance, therefore it is recorded as a debit in the variance account.

VARIABLE OVERHEAD CONTROL ACCOUNT

	$'000		$'000
Payables	1,385	Variable overhead expenditure variance	35
		Work in progress	
		(225,000 × $6)	1,350
	1,385		1,385

Notes

(1)   Variable overhead is charged to work in progress at the standard rate per hour.

(2)   The variable overhead expenditure variance is recorded in this account. It is an adverse variance and so is a debit in the variance account.

(iv)

WORK IN PROGRESS CONTROL ACCOUNT

	$'000		$'000
Stores ledger control	1,640	Finished goods	
Direct wages control	900	(39,000 × $100)	3,900
Variable overhead control	1,350	*Direct material usage*	
Direct labour		*variance*	80
efficiency variance	36		
Variable overhead efficiency	54		
	3,980		3,980

Notes

(1)   Output is transferred to the finished goods account at standard marginal production cost.

(2)   The efficiency variances appear in this account.

(v)

FINISHED GOODS CONTROL ACCOUNT

	$'000		$'000
Balance b/f	132	Cost of sales (39,000 × $100)	3,900
Work in progress	3,900	Balance c/d	132
	4,032		4,032
Balance b/d	132		

(vi)

COST OF SALES CONTROL ACCOUNT

	$'000		$'000
Finished goods	3,900	Income statement	3,900

(vii)

SALES ACCOUNT

	$'000		$'000
Income statement	4,875	Bank/receivables	4,875

(viii)

VARIANCES ACCOUNT

	$'000		$'000
Wages (labour rate)	45	Stores (material price)	40
WIP (o/hd expenditure)	35	WIP (labour efficiency)	36
WIP (material usage)	80	WIP (o/hd efficiency)	54
		Income statement	30
	160		160

Assessment focus point

The variances are recorded in a variances account as part of the double entry system. The balance on the account at the end of the period is written off to the income statement. Sometimes a separate account is used for each variance, but the double entry principles would be the same. An adverse variance is debited in the relevant variance account; a favourable variance is credited in the variance account.

(ix)

INCOME STATEMENT

	$'000		$'000
Cost of sales	3,900	Sales	4,875
Variances	30		
Gross profit for month	945		
	4,875		4,875

3.3 Example: journal entries

Suppose that 4 kgs of material A are required to make one unit of product TS, each kilogram costing $10. It takes direct labour 5 hours to make one unit of product TS. The labour force is paid $4.50 per hour.

During the period the following results were recorded.

Material A: 8,200 kgs purchased on credit *	$95,000
Material A: kgs issued to production*	8,200 kgs
Units of product TS produced*	1,600
Direct labour hours worked*	10,000
Cost of direct labour*	$32,000

Required

(a)   Calculate the following variances for the period.

    (i)   Material price variance
    (ii)   Material usage variance
    (iii)   Labour rate variance
    (iv)   Labour efficiency variance

(b)   Prepare journal entries for the transactions marked * above, together with the variances calculated in (a).

    Note

    You should make the following assumptions.

    (i)   An integrated accounting system is maintained.
    (ii)   There are no opening or closing inventories of work in progress.

Solution

(a)

			$
(i)	8,200 kgs should cost (× $10)		82,000
	but did cost		95,000
	Material price variance		13,000 (A)
(ii)	1,600 units of TS should use (× 4 kgs)		6,400 kgs
	but did use		8,200 kgs
	Usage variance in kgs		1,800 kgs (A)
	× standard price per kg		× $10
	Material usage variance		$18,000 (A)
(iii)			$
	10,000 hours should cost (× $4.50)		45,000
	but did cost		32,000
	Labour rate variance		13,000 (F)
(iv)	1,600 units of TS should take (× 5 hrs)		8,000 hrs
	but did take		10,000 hrs
	Efficiency variance in hrs		2,000 hrs (A)
	× standard rate per hour		× $4.50
	Labour efficiency variance		$9,000 (A)

(b) (i)

	$	$
Stores ledger control account (8,200 kgs × $10)	82,000	
Material price variance	13,000	
Payables		95,000

The purchase of materials on credit

(ii)

	$	$
Work in progress control account	82,000	
Stores ledger control account		82,000

The issue of material A to production

(iii)

Material usage variance	18,000	
Work in progress control account		18,000

The recording of the material A usage variance

(iv)

Work in progress control account (10,000 hrs × $4.50)	45,000	
Direct labour control account		32,000
Direct labour rate variance		13,000

The charging of labour to work in progress

(v)

Direct labour efficiency variance	9,000	
Work in progress control account		9,000

The recording of the labour efficiency variance

(vi)

Finished goods control account (1,600 × $62.50 (W))	100,000	
Work in progress control account		100,000

The transfer of finished goods from work in progress

Working

Standard cost of product TS

	$
Material A (4 kgs × $10)	40.00
Direct labour (5 hrs × $4.50)	22.50
	62.50

Question   **Journal entries**

A company uses raw material J in production. The standard price for material J is $3 per metre. During the month 6,000 metres were purchased for $18,600, of which 5,000 metres were issued to production.

Required

Show the journal entries to record the above transactions in integrated accounts in the following separate circumstances.

(a) When raw material inventory is valued at standard cost, that is the direct materials price variance is extracted on receipt.

(b) When raw materials inventory is valued at actual cost, that is the direct materials price variance is extracted as the materials are used.

BPP
PROFESSIONAL EDUCATION

Answer

(a)

		$	$
	Raw material inventory (6,000 × $3)	18,000	
	Direct material price variance	600	
	Payables		18,600
	Purchase on credit of 6,000 metres of material J		
	Work in progress (5,000 × $3)	15,000	
	Raw material inventory		15,000
	Issue to production of 5,000 metres of J		

		$	$
(b)	Raw material inventory	18,600	
	Payables		18,600
	Purchase on credit of 6,000 metres of material J		
	Work in progress	15,000	
	Direct material price variance (5,000 × $(3.10 – 3.00))	500	
	Raw material inventory		15,500
	Issue to production of 5,000 metres of material J		

Note that in both cases the material is charged to work in progress at standard price. In (b) the price variance is extracted only on the material which has been used up, the inventory being valued at actual cost.

Question
Integrated accounting issues

A firm uses standard costing and an integrated accounting system. The double entry for an adverse material usage variance is

A	DR stores control account	CR work-in-progress control account
B	DR material usage variance account	CR stores control account
C	DR work-in-progress control account	CR material usage variance account
D	DR material usage variance account	CR work-in-progress control account

Answer

The correct answer is D.

The usage variance arises during production therefore the correct account to be credited is work-in-progress. Option D is correct.

An adverse variance is debited to the relevant variance account. Therefore we can eliminate the incorrect options A and C.

Option B has the correct debit entry for the adverse variance but the credit entry is incorrect.

Chapter Roundup

- **Cost bookkeeping** is based on the principles of **double entry**, the **golden rule** of which is that for **every entry made in one account, there must be a corresponding balancing entry in another account**.

- **Integrated systems** combine both financial and cost accounts in one system of ledger accounts.

- The basic entries in an interpreted system are as follows:

Expenditure on materials, wages and overheads

- – DR Resources account
- – CR Cash or accounts payable

Work in progress

- – DR WIP (for overhead, this is overhead absorbed)
- – CR Resources accounts (for overhead, this is **overhead absorbed**)

Finished goods

- – DR Finished goods
- – CR WIP

Cost of sales

- – DR Cost of sales
- – CR Finished goods

- The **ledger accounts** related to production can be consolidated into a **manufacturing account**.

- In a **standard cost bookkeeping system**, the variances are recorded as follows:

   - – The **material price variance** is recorded in the **stores control account**.

   - – The **labour rate variance** is recorded in the **wages control account**.

   - – The following variances are recorded in the **work in progress account**.

      Material usage variance
      Idle time variance
      Labour efficiency variance
      Variable overhead efficiency variance

   - – The **production overhead expenditure variance** will be recorded in the **production overhead control account**.

   - – The **production overhead volume variance** may be recorded in **the fixed production overhead account**. (Note. Alternatively, you may find the volume variance recorded in the **work in progress account**.)

   - – **Sales variances do not appear in the books of account**. Sales are recorded in the sales account at actual invoiced value.

   - – The balance of variances in the variance accounts at the end of a period may be **written off to the income statement**.

- The general principle in standard cost bookkeeping is that cost variances should be recorded as **early as possible**. They are recorded in the relevant account **in which they arise** and the appropriate double entry is taken to a variance account.

- **Adverse** variances are **debited** to the relevant variance account; **favourable** variances are **credited** in the relevant variance account.

Quick Quiz

1   What is the double entry for the following in an integrated accounts system?

(a)   Production overhead absorbed in the cost of production
(b)   Completed work transferred from the production process to inventory

2   GF Co bought $100,000 worth of materials and issued $75,000 to production. Which of the following entries represents the correct bookkeeping treatment? (Select three options.)

I	Dr	Raw materials	$75,000
II	Dr	Raw materials	$100,000
III	Dr	Work-in-progress	$75,000
IV	Cr	Raw materials	$75,000
V	Cr	Raw materials	$100,000
VI	Dr	Work-in-progress	$75,000
VII	Dr	Work-in-progress	$100,000

3   The wages control account for X Co for October looks like this.

WAGES CONTROL ACCOUNT

	$'000		$'000
Bank	110	Work in progress	101
		Production overhead	7
		Balance c/d	2
	110		110

Indicate whether the following statements are true or false.

		True	False
I	Total wages incurred during October was $110,000	☐	☐
II	Indirect wages incurred during October was $7,000	☐	☐
III	Wages accrued at the end of October were $2,000	☐	☐

4   The material usage variance is recorded in the raw materials control account.

True   ☐

False   ☐

5   What is the double entry for recording sales variances in cost accounts?

Answers to Quick Quiz

1   (a)   Dr   Work in progress control account
         Cr   Production overhead account

    (b)   Dr   Finished goods control account
         Cr   Work in progress control account

2   II
    IV
    VI

    Costs incurred are debited to the materials account, and those issued as direct materials to production are credited to the materials account and subsequently debited to the work-in-progress account.

3   I   False. Total wages *paid* was $100,000.
    II   True. Indirect wages of $7,000 were charged to production overhead.
    III   False. Wages were prepaid at the end of October

4   False. Material usage variances are recorded in the WIP account.

5   Sales variances do not appear in the books of account.
    Sales are recorded in the sales account at actual invoiced value.

Now try the questions below from the Question Bank

Question numbers	Page
79–86	365

Service costing

Introduction

So far in this Study Text we have looked at different types of cost and different cost accounting systems and the inference has been that we have been discussing a **manufacturing** organisation. Most of the cost accounting principles we have looked at so far can also be applied to **service organisations**, however.

In this chapter we will therefore look at the costing method used by service organisations which we will call **service costing**. As you study this chapter, you will see how the knowledge you have built up can be applied easily to service organisations.

In the final section of this chapter, and indeed of this Study Text, we'll think about managerial reports, and the type of information managers of a range of organisations require.

Topic list	Learning outcomes	Syllabus references	Ability required
1 Service costing	D(x)	D(6)	Analysis
2 Management reports	D(viii), (ix), (x)	D(6)	Comprehension, Application, Analysis

1 Service costing

Service organisations do not make or sell tangible goods.

1.1 What are service organisations?

Profit-seeking service organisations include accountancy firms, law firms, management consultants, transport companies, banks, insurance companies and hotels. **Almost all not-for-profit organisations** - hospitals, schools, libraries and so on – are also service organisations. Service organisations also include **charities** and the **public sector**.

1.2 Service costing versus other costing methods

(a)   With many services, the **cost of direct materials consumed will be relatively small** compared to the labour, direct expenses and overheads cost. In product costing the direct materials are often a greater proportion of the total cost.

(b)   Because of the difficulty of identifying costs with specific cost units in service costing, the **indirect costs tend to represent a higher proportion** of total cost compared with product costing.

(c)   The **output** of most service organisations is often **intangible** and hence difficult to define. It is therefore **difficult to establish a measurable cost unit**.

(d)   The service industry includes such a **wide range of organisations** which provide such different services and have such **different cost structures** that **costing will vary** considerably from one service to another.

(e)   There is often a **high fixed cost of maintaining an organisation's total capacity**, which may be **very under utilised at certain times**. Consider the demand for railway and bus services, for example. Demand at midday is likely to be much lower than demand during the rush hours. The costing system must therefore be comprehensive enough to show the effects of this type of demand on the costs of operation. This often involves the analysis of costs into fixed and variable components, and the use of marginal costing techniques and breakeven analysis. **'Cut-price' prices** can then be offered, which might produce a low but still positive contribution to the organisation's high operational fixed costs.

You should bear in mind, however, that service organisations often have **large-scale operations** (think about power stations, large city hospitals) that require **sophisticated cost control techniques to manage the very high level of costs involved**. One such technique is control using flexible budgets, which we looked at in Chapter 11, and which can apply equally to service organisations as to manufacturing ones.

1.3 Characteristics of services

Specific characteristics of services

- Intangibility
- Simultaneity
- Perishability
- Heterogeneity

Consider the service of providing a haircut.

(a) A haircut is **intangible** in itself, and the performance of the service comprises many other intangible factors, like the music in the salon, the personality of the hairdresser, the quality of the coffee.

(b) The production and consumption of a haircut are **simultaneous,** and therefore it cannot be inspected for quality in advance, nor can it be returned if it is not what was required.

(c) Haircuts are **perishable,** that is, they cannot be stored. You cannot buy them in bulk, and the hairdresser cannot do them in advance and keep them stocked away in case of heavy demand. The incidence of work in progress in service organisations is less frequent than in other types of organisation.

(d) A haircut is **heterogeneous** and so the exact service received will vary each time: not only will two hairdressers cut hair differently, but a hairdresser will not consistently deliver the same standard of haircut.

1.4 Cost units and service costing

FORWARD

One main problem with service costing is being able to define a **realistic cost unit** that represents a suitable measure of the service provided. If the service is a function of two activity variables, a **composite cost unit** may be more appropriate.

A particular problem with service costing is the difficulty in defining a realistic cost unit that represents a suitable measure of the service provided. Frequently, a **composite cost unit** may be deemed more appropriate if the service is a function of two activity variables. Hotels, for example, may use the **'occupied bed-night'** as an appropriate unit for cost ascertainment and control. You may remember that we discussed such cost units in Chapter 1.

essment us point

An objective test question in a previous syllabus assessment asked candidates to identify characteristics of service costing from a number of different characteristics listed. The two relevant characteristics in the particular list provided were:

- High levels of indirect cost as a proportion of total cost
- Use of composite cost units

A similar question may come up in your computer-based assessment: be prepared!

1.4.1 Typical cost units used by companies operating in a service industry

Service	Cost unit
Road, rail and air transport services	Passenger-kilometre, tonne-kilometre
Hotels	Occupied bed-night
Education	Full-time student
Hospitals	Patient-day
Catering establishments	Meal served

Each organisation will need to ascertain the cost unit most appropriate to its activities.

sessment cus point

Make sure that you are familiar with suitable composite cost units for common forms of service operation such as transport.

1.4.2 Cost per unit

Average cost per unit of service = $\dfrac{\text{Total costs incurred in the period}}{\text{Number of service units supplied in the period}}$

1.4.3 The use of unit cost measures in not-for-profit organisations

The success of not-for-profit organisations cannot be judged in terms of profitability, nor against competition.

Not-for-profit organisations include **private sector** organisations such as charities and churches and **much of the public sector** (the National Health Service, the police, schools and so on).

Commercial organisations generally have profit or market competition as the objectives which guide the process of managing resources economically, efficiently and effectively. However, **not-for-profit organisations cannot** by definition **be judged by profitability nor do they generally have to be successful against competition**, so other methods of assessing performance have to be used.

Most **financial measures** of performance for not-for-profits therefore tend to be **cost based**. Costs are collected relative to some measure of output and a **unit cost** calculated as described above.

Unit cost measures in not-for-profit organisations have three main **uses**.

(a) **As a measure of relative efficiency**

   Efficiency means **getting out as much as possible for what goes in**.

   Most not-for-profit organisations do not face competition but this does not mean that all not-for-profit organisations are unique. Bodies like local governments, health services and so on can **compare** their performance **against each other. Unit cost measurements** like 'cost per patient day' or 'cost of borrowing one library book' can be established to allow organisations to assess whether they are doing better or worse than their counterparts.

   Bear in mind, however, that the comparisons are only valid if, say, the hospitals cater for broadly the same type of patients, the same illnesses, are similarly equipped and so on. **Cost comparisons are only valid if like is being compared with like**.

(b) **As a measure of efficiency over time**

   Unit costs of the same organisation can be compared from period to period. This will help to highlight whether efficiency is increasing or decreasing over time.

(c) **As an aid to cost control**

   If unit costs are produced on a regular basis and compared with other similar organisations, this will help to control costs and should engender a more cost-conscious attitude.

1.4.4 Example: cost units in not-for-profit organisations

Suppose that at a cost of $40,000 and 4,000 hours (**inputs**) in an average year, two policemen travel 8,000 miles and are instrumental in 200 arrests (**outputs**). A large number of **possibly meaningful measures** can be derived from these few figures.

		$40,000	4,000 hours	8,000 miles	200 arrests
Cost	$40,000		$40,000/4,000 = $10 per hour	$40,000/8,000 = $5 per mile	$40,000/200 = $200 per arrest
Time	4,000 hrs	4,000/$40,000 = 6 minutes patrolling per $1 spent		4,000/8,000 = ½ hour to patrol 1 mile	4,000/200 = 20 hours per arrest
Miles	8,000	8,000/$40,000 = 0.2 of a mile per $1	8,000/4,000 = 2 miles patrolled per hour		8,000/200 = 40 miles per arrest
Arrests	200	200/$40,000 = 1 arrest per $200	200/4,000 = 1 arrest every 20 hours	200/8,000 = 1 arrest every 40 miles	

These measures do not necessarily identify cause and effect or personal responsibility and accountability. Actual performance needs to be **compared** to the following.

- **Standards**, if there are any
- Similar external activities
- Similar internal activities

- **Targets**
- Over time – ie as trends

1.4.5 Limitations of using unit costs

(a) **Quality of performance is ignored**. Cost per patient day tells us nothing about the quality of the care provided, whether the patients are cured and so on.

(b) **The input mix will vary**. For example, the average cost per patient in a intensive care ward is likely to be higher than the average cost per patient in a post-operative recovery ward.

(c) **Inputs rather than objectives are measured**. Inputs might be the number of eye operations carried out in a hospital but cost per eye operation does not give any indication of the objective of the eye department in a hospital, which might be something along the lines of improving the quality of life of people with eye problems.

(d) **Regional differences are not taken into consideration**. For example, the cost of refuse collection in rural areas will probably be higher than in towns and cities because of the distance to be travelled.

The following examples will illustrate the principles involved in service costing and the further considerations to bear in mind when costing services.

1.5 Example: costing an educational establishment

A university offers a range of degree courses. The university organisation structure consists of three faculties each with a number of teaching departments. In addition, there is a university administrative/management function and a central services function.

(a)   The following cost information is available for the year ended 30 June 20X3.

(i)   **Occupancy costs**

Total $1,500,000

Such costs are apportioned on the basis of area used which is as follows.

	Square metres
Faculties	7,500
Teaching departments	20,000
Administration/management	7,000
Central services	3,000

(ii)   **Administrative/management costs**

Direct costs: $1,775,000
Indirect costs: an apportionment of occupancy costs

Direct and indirect costs are charged to degree courses on a percentage basis.

(iii)   **Faculty costs**

Direct costs: $700,000
Indirect costs: an apportionment of occupancy costs and central service costs

Direct and indirect costs are charged to teaching departments.

(iv)   **Teaching departments**

Direct costs: $5,525,000
Indirect costs: an apportionment of occupancy costs and central service costs plus all faculty costs

Direct and indirect costs are charged to degree courses on a percentage basis.

(v)   **Central services**

Direct costs: $1,000,000
Indirect costs: an apportionment of occupancy costs

(b)   Direct and indirect costs of central services have, in previous years, been charged to users on a percentage basis. A study has now been completed which has estimated what user areas would have paid external suppliers for the same services on an individual basis. For the year ended 30 June 20X3, the apportionment of the central services cost is to be recalculated in a manner which recognises the cost savings achieved by using the central services facilities instead of using external service companies. This is to be done by apportioning the overall savings to user areas in proportion to their share of the estimated external costs.

The estimated external costs of service provision are as follows.

	$'000
Faculties	240
Teaching departments	800
Degree courses:	
Business studies	32
Mechanical engineering	48
Catering studies	32
All other degrees	448
	1,600

(c) Additional data relating to the degree courses is as follows.

	Degree course		
	Business studies	Mechanical engineering	Catering studies
Number of graduates	80	50	120
Apportioned costs (as % of totals)			
Teaching departments	3.0%	2.5%	7%
Administration/management	2.5%	5.0%	4%

Central services are to be apportioned as detailed in (b) above.

The total number of undergraduates from the university in the year to 30 June 20X3 was 2,500.

Required

(a) Calculate the average cost per undergraduate for the year ended 30 June 20X3.

(b) Calculate the average cost per undergraduate for each of the degrees in business studies, mechanical engineering and catering studies, showing all relevant cost analysis.

Solution

(a) The average cost per undergraduate is as follows.

	Total costs for university
	$'000
Occupancy	1,500
Admin/management	1,775
Faculty	700
Teaching departments	5,525
Central services	1,000
	10,500
Number of undergraduates	2,500
Average cost per undergraduate for year ended 30 June 20X3	$4,200

(b)   Average cost per undergraduate for each course is as follows.

	Business studies $	Mechanical engineering $	Catering studies $
Teaching department costs			
(W1 and using % in question)	241,590	201,325	563,710
Admin/management costs			
(W1 and using % in question)	51,375	102,750	82,200
Central services (W2)	22,400	33,600	22,400
	315,365	337,675	668,310
Number of undergraduates	80	50	120
Average cost per undergraduate for year			
ended 30 June 20X3	$3,942	$6,754	$5,569

Workings

1   Cost allocation and apportionment

Cost item	Basis of apportionment	Teaching departments $'000	Admin/ management $'000	Central services $'000	Faculties $'000
Direct costs	allocation	5,525	1,775	1,000	700
Occupancy costs	area used	800	280	120	300
Central services reapportioned	(W2)	560	-	(1,120)	168
Faculty costs reallocated	allocation	1,168	-	-	(1,168)
		8,053	2,055		

2   Apportioning savings to user areas on the basis given in the question gives the same result as apportioning internal costs in proportion to the external costs.

	External costs $'000	Apportionment of internal central service costs $'000
Faculties	240	168.0
Teaching	800	560.0
Degree courses:		
Business studies	32	22.4
Mechanical engineering	48	33.6
Catering studies	32	22.4
All other degrees	448	313.6
	1,600	1,120.0

 Question

Service cost units

Briefly describe cost units that are appropriate to a transport business.

Answer

The cost unit is the basic measure of control in an organisation, used to monitor cost and activity levels. The cost unit selected must be measurable and appropriate for the type of cost and activity. Possible cost units which could be suggested are as follows.

Cost per kilometre

- Variable cost per kilometre

- Fixed cost per kilometre – however this is not particularly useful for control purposes because it will tend to vary with the kilometres run.

- Total cost of each vehicle per kilometre – this suffers from the same problem as above

- Maintenance cost of each vehicle per kilometre

Cost per tonne-kilometre

This can be more useful than a cost per kilometre for control purposes, because it combines the distance travelled and the load carried, both of which affect cost.

Cost per operating hour

Once again, many costs can be related to this cost unit, including the following.

- Total cost of each vehicle per operating hour

- Variable costs per operating hour

- Fixed costs per operating hour – this suffers from the same problems as the fixed cost per kilometre in terms of its usefulness for control purposes.

Question

Cost per tonne – killometre

Carry Co operates a small fleet of delivery vehicles. Expected costs are as follows.

Loading	1 hour per tonne loaded
Loading costs:	
Labour (casual)	$2 per hour
Equipment depreciation	$80 per week
Supervision	$80 per week
Drivers' wages (fixed)	$100 per man per week
Petrol	10c per kilometre
Repairs	5c per kilometre
Depreciation	$80 per week per vehicle
Supervision	$120 per week
Other general expenses (fixed)	$200 per week

There are two drivers and two vehicles in the fleet.

During a slack week, only six journeys were made.

Journey	Tonnes carried (one way)	One-way distance of journey Kilometres
1	5	100
2	8	20
3	2	60
4	4	50
5	6	200
6	5	300

The expected average full cost per tonne-kilometre for the week is $ _____ .

Answer

The expected average full cost per tonne-kilometre for the week is $ | 0.304 |

Workings

Variable costs

Journey	1	2	3	4	5	6
	$	$	$	$	$	$
Loading labour	10	16	4	8	12	10
Petrol (both ways)	20	4	12	10	40	60
Repairs (both ways)	10	2	6	5	20	30
	40	22	22	23	72	100

Total costs

	$
Variable costs (total for journeys 1 to 6)	279
Loading equipment depreciation	80
Loading supervision	80
Drivers' wages	200
Vehicles depreciation	160
Drivers' supervision	120
Other costs	200
	1,119

Journey	Tonnes	One-way distance Kilometres	Tonne-kilometres
1	5	100	500
2	8	20	160
3	2	60	120
4	4	50	200
5	6	200	1,200
6	5	300	1,500
			3,680

Cost per tonne-kilometre $\dfrac{\$1,119}{3,680} = \$0.304$

Note that the large element of fixed costs may distort this measure but that a variable cost per tonne-kilometre of $279/3,680 = \$0.076$ may be useful for budgetary control.

Hourly rates

Mr G and Mrs H have recently formed a consultancy business, and have sought your advice concerning costs and fees. Both wish to receive a salary of $20,000 in the first year of trading. They have purchased two cars at a cost of $13,000 each and expect to use them for three years. At the end of this time each of the cars has an expected resale value of $4,000. Straight-line depreciation is to be applied.

Mr G and Mrs H expect to work for eight hours per day, five days per week for 45 weeks per year. They refer to this as *available time.* 25% of the available time is expected to be used for dealing with administrative matters related to their own business, and in the first year it is expected that there will be idle time which will average 22.5% of the available time. The remainder of the available time is expected to be chargeable to clients.

Mr G and Mrs H agreed that their fee structure should comprise the following.

- An hourly rate for productive client work
- An hourly rate for travelling to/from clients
- A rate per mile travelled to/from clients

They expect that the travelling time will equal 25% of their chargeable time, and will amount to a total of 18,000 miles. They have agreed that this time should be charged at one-third of their normal hourly rate.

Apart from the costs referred to above, Mr G and Mrs H have estimated their other costs for the first twelve months as follows.

	$
Electricity	1,200
Fuel for vehicles	1,800
Insurance – professional liability and office	600
insurance – vehicles	800
Mobile telephones	1,200
Office rent and rates	8,400
Office telephone/facsimile	1,800
Postage and stationery	500
Secretarial costs	8,400
Servicing and repairs of vehicles	1,200
Vehicle road tax	280

The consultancy business should break even after paying the required salaries.

If costs are classified as either professional services costs or vehicle costs, then, on the basis of the above data and costs,

(a)   the hourly rate for productive client work is $ ☐

(b)   the hourly rate for travelling to/from clients is $ ☐

(c)   the rate per mile travelled to/from clients is $ ☐

Answer

(a) **The rate is $** | 39.43 |

(b) **The rate is $** | 13.14 |

(c) **The rate is $** | 0.56 |

Workings

Cost analysis

	Professional services costs	*Vehicle costs*
	$	$
Electricity	1,200	
Fuel for vehicles		1,800
Insurance: professional liability and office	600	
vehicles		800
Mobile telephones (note 1)	1,200	
Office rent and rates	8,400	
Office telephone/fax	1,800	
Postage and stationery	500	
Secretarial costs	8,400	
Servicing and repairs of vehicles		1,200
Vehicle road tax		280
Vehicle depreciation (note 2)		6,000
Salaries	40,000	
	62,100	10,080

Notes

1   It is assumed that mobile telephones are used in providing professional services and that their use is not consequent on travelling.

2   Annual depreciation = $\dfrac{\$13,000 - \$4,000}{3} \times 2 \text{ cars} = \$6,000$

Analysis of available time

Total hours per annum	$(8 \times 5 \times 45) \times 2$ people =	3,600 available hours
Less: administration	25.0%	
idle time	22.5%	
	$47.5\% \times 3,600 =$	(1,710) hours
		1,890 hours
Travelling time (25%)		427.5 hours
Productive time (75%)		1,417.5 hours

Rates

Travelling time is to be charged at one third of the normal hourly rate.

'Weighted' chargeable time	=	1,417.5 + (472.5/3)
	=	1,575 hours
∴ Rate per productive hour	=	$62,100/1,575
(a) Hourly rate for productive client work	=	$39.43
(b) Hourly rate for travelling (÷ 3)	=	$13.14
(c) Rate per mile travelled	=	$10,080/18,000
	=	$0.56

1.6 Job costing and services

Remember that job costing applies where work is undertaken to customers' special requirements. An organisation may therefore be working in the service sector but may supply one-off services which meet particular customers' special requirements; in such a situation job costing may be more appropriate than service costing. For example, a consultancy business, although part of the service sector, could use job costing.

2 Management reports

FORWARD

Management reports based on cost accounting information should be formatted to aid management to cost products and services, and to plan, control and make decisions.

We finish this Study Text by referring you back to the very first sections of the very first chapter.

Cost accounting provides **information** for management to enable them to **cost products or services**, and to **plan**, **control** and **make decisions**.

The **format of cost accounting reports** is entirely at **management discretion**. Each organisation can devise its own management accounting system and format of reports.

So, whatever the type of organisation, be it production or service, commercial or not-for-profit, private sector or public sector, the **cost accounting management reports should be formatted in the most appropriate way so as to provide information to management to enable them to cost products/services, plan, control and make decision**.

As you have worked through this part of the Study Text in particular you should have noticed the sort of information management of organisations in job, batch, process and service industries need.

2.1 Information for management

For example, suppose a private hospital has three main revenue earning departments – maternity, surgical and orthopaedic. These departments are supported by many other departments, some of which also earn revenue by charging for services undertaken for external customers.

The radiology department is one of these departments. In addition to undertaking x-ray work for the above three hospital departments, it charges for external work involved in carrying out x-rays on patients who have been referred to it by doctors in general practice. After this work has been done, patients may continue their treatment within the hospital.

Let's have a think about the **type of information** which ought to be provided within the hospital for **operational control** and for **making proper charges for services**.

2.1.1 Information for operational control

(a) **Responsibility centres**

For effective operational control each department within the hospital should be a **separate cost** or **profit centre** with a manager responsible for the performance of each centre.

Those centres which have a measurable output, such as the maternity, surgical, orthopaedic and radiolog departments, can be designated as profit centres since it is possible to determine their **revenue** and therefore their **profit**. Other departments would operate as cost centres, responsible for the **control of their own costs**.

(b) **Coding systems**

The information system should contain an efficient coding system to ensure that all costs and revenues are charged and credited to the **correct responsibility centre**.

(c) **Control reports**

The costs and revenues collected for each centre should be reported to the manager of the centre on a **regular basis**, at least **monthly**.

The reports should show separately **controllable** and **uncontrollable** items. For example the costs directly incurred by the department, which are under the control of the **responsibility centre** manager, should be separated from the **uncontrollable costs**. The latter would include items such as central administration charges. Although there is an argument for excluding these charges altogether, it can be useful to show them on the **control reports** so that managers are aware of the cost of providing them with administrative support services.

(d) **Establishing a basis for comparison**

The most effective way of achieving **operational control** is to **compare** each department's **costs**, and **revenues** if appropriate, with some form of yardstick.

The best basis of comparison is a **budget**, which should be divided into **time periods** according to the frequency with which **control reports** will be prepared.

Variances can then be calculated and analysed. A system of **exception reporting** should be adopted so that the busy manager's attention is drawn to those areas where management action is most urgently needed.

(e) **Determining appropriate cost units**

For those departments with measurable activity a suitable **cost unit** or a series of cost units should be established. This is particularly applicable where **output** can be **standardised**, or where **activities** can be **analysed** into a series of standard tasks such as taking an x-ray.

The cost units can be used to **control costs** by establishing a **standard cost** and providing mangers with information which compares actual unit cost with standard and which identifies any **variances**.

(f) **Flexible budgets**

Control information can be improved if it is based on a system of **flexible budgets**. This is particularly relevant if **activity levels fluctuate** and a significant proportion of costs is **variable**.

Once a cost unit has been established the budget cost allowance for the period can be determined based on the actual activity achieved. This will enable a more **realistic budget comparison** for more **effective operational control**.

(g) **Ad hoc reports and future projections**

As well as routine reports, the hospital information system should be capable of providing **ad hoc advice** for managers on the cost and revenue affects of **proposed activities**. For example it should be possible to project future costs for the purpose of tendering for work.

2.1.2 Information for charging for services

A well designed information system will provide the basis for making **proper charges** for services.

Once a suitable cost unit has been established the system should be capable of accurately measuring the **units of activity** so that the correct charge is made for services provided.

For tendering and quotation purposes it will be necessary to be able to **project costs** in order to determine a **reasonable price** to be charged. This will require an understanding of the **cost behaviour pattern** for each department.

The **standard cost** used for **operational control** could provide the basis for charging for services. An activity based analysis may provide a better understanding of the cost of services provided. For example the process of taking an x-ray could be broken down into a series of activities with a separate **cost driver** for each (the cost per patient transported to x-ray, and the cost per film processed for example).

Once a realistic standard cost has been established, management can decide on the required margin to be added to achieve a price for the service provided.

2.2 Figures for management

Here are some figures that might be highlighted in some (or many) management reports.

(a) **Gross revenue** is income (at invoice values) received for goods and services over some given period of time. It is used as an indicator of the level of demand for the organisation's product or services.

(b) **Value-added** is **sales less cost of bought-in materials and services**, and represents the wealth or value created by an organisation's operations. It is affected only by costs incurred internally, such as labour, and is therefore useful as a target.

(c) **Contribution** is the difference between sales revenue and variable costs of sale. It is used in decision making as fixed costs are not relevant to many business decisions.

(d) **Gross margin** is the ratio of gross profit to sales revenue and is used to look into the relationship between production/purchasing costs and sales revenues and to analyse the pure trading activities of an organisation. It can be increased by raising prices and/or by negotiating lower prices with suppliers. It is calculated as ((sales – cost of sales)/sales for the period) × 100%.

(e) **Marketing expense** may be compared to revenue on a period by period basis to see whether the expenditure has produced the desired increase in sales and in which areas.

(f) **General and administrative expenses** need to be carefully controlled in order to keep net profit margins at an acceptable level. They may be targeted as an area for cost reduction if the organisation is trying to improve its profitability.

Chapter Roundup

- **Service organisations** do not make or sell tangible goods.

- **Specific characteristics of services**

  - Intangibility
  - Simultaneity
  - Perishability
  - Heterogeneity

- One main problem with service costing is being able to define a **realistic cost unit** that represents a suitable measure of the service provided. If the service is a function of two activity variables, a **composite cost unit** may be more appropriate

- Average cost per unit of service $= \dfrac{\text{Total costs incurred in the period}}{\text{Number of service units supplied in the period}}$

- **The success of not-for-profit organisations** cannot be judged in terms of profitability, nor against competition.

- **Management reports** based on cost accounting information should be formatted to aid management to cost products and services, and to plan, control and make decisions.

Quick Quiz

1   With many services the cost of direct materials will be relatively high.

    True   ☐

    False   ☐

2   Match up the following services with their typical cost units

Service		Cost unit
Hotels		Patient-day
Education	?	Meal served
Hospitals		Full-time student
Catering organisations		Occupied bed-night

3   What are the specific characteristics of services.

    I   Intangibility
    II   Heterogeneity
    III   Perishability
    IV   Consistency
    V   Regularity
    VI   Simultaneity

    A   I, III, V and VI
    B   II, III, IV and V
    C   I, II, III and VI
    D   II, IV, V and VI

4   Average cost per unit of service = $\dfrac{\text{..........................}}{\text{..........................}}$

5   Value added is:

    A   Sales less cost of materials and services
    B   Sales less labour cost
    C   Sales less internally generated costs
    D   Sales less cost of bought-in materials and services

Answers to Quick Quiz

1   False. Labour, direct expenses and overheads will be a greater proportion of total cost.

2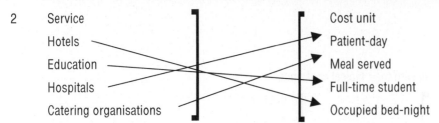

3   C

4   Average cost per unit of service = $\dfrac{\text{Total costs incurred in the period}}{\text{Number of service units supplied in the period}}$

5   D

Now try the questions below from the Question Bank

Question numbers	Page
87–92	368

Question Bank

1   Which of the following are part of the prime cost for a manufacturing company?

A   Maintenance cost of a machine used in production
B   Salary cost of a supervisor overseeing direct employees
C   Cost of a canteen used by production employees
D   Royalties payable to the designer of the basic product

2   Employee A is a carpenter and normally works 36 hours per week, which is treated as direct labour. The standard rate of pay is $7.00 per hour. A premium of 50% of his basic hourly rate is paid for all overtime hours worked. During the last week of October, Employee A worked for 42 hours. The overtime hours worked were for the following reasons:

Machine breakdown: 4 hours
To complete a special job at the request of a customer: 2 hours

How much of Employee A's earnings for the last week of October would have been treated as direct wages?

A $315.00
B $252.00
C $273.00
D $294.00

3   **Fill in the blanks** in the statements below, using the words in the box.

 •   Costs can be divided into the following three categories (1)................; (2).............. ; (3) ....

 •   There are a number of different ways in which costs can be classified.

     –   (4)............ and (5)............ (or overhead) costs

     –   (6).............................costs (production costs, distribution and selling costs, administration costs and financing costs)

     –   Fixed and (7)............ costs

 •   A (8)............. is a unit of product which has costs attached to it. A (9) .... is a type of responsibility centre where managers are responsible for expenses only.

 •   A (10)............. cost tends to vary with the level of activity. A (11) .... cost is unaffected by changes in the level of activity.

• Cost centre	• Direct	• Fixed	• Cost unit
• Variable	• Variable	• Indirect	• Other costs
• Material	• Functional	• Labour	

4   Direct costs are:

A   costs which can neither be identified with a cost centre nor identified with a single cost unit
B   costs which can be identified with a single cost unit
C   costs incurred as a direct result of a particular decision
D   costs incurred which can be attributed to a particular accounting period

5   A system of accounting that segregates revenue and costs into areas of personal responsibility in order to monitor and assess the performance of each part of the organisation is known as:

    A   Control accounting
    B   Responsibility accounting
    C   Controllable accounting
    D   Centre accounting

6   800 units of component L valued at a price of $4.20 each were in inventory on 1 May.

The following receipts and issues were recorded during May.

9 May	Received	2,500 units at $4.50 per unit
21 May	Received	1,800 units at $4.80 per unit
24 May	Issued	4,500 units

Using the LIFO method of inventory valuation, the total value of the components issued on 24 May was:

    A $18,900
    B $20,370
    C $20,730
    D $21,600

Questions 7 and 8 are based on the following data.

Date		Units	Unit Price $	Value $
1 Jan	Balance b/f	100	5.00	500.00
3 Mar	Issue	40		
4 June	Receipt	50	5.50	275.00
6 June	Receipt	50	6.00	300.00
9 Sept	Issue	70		

7   If the first-in, first-out method of pricing had been used the value of the issue on 9 September would have been:

    A $350
    B $355
    C $395
    D $420

8   If the last-in, first-out method of pricing had been used the value of the issue on 9 September would have been:

    A $350
    B $395
    C $410
    D $420

Questions 9 and 10 are based on the following data.

At the beginning of week 3 there were 200 units of Product G held in the stores. Eighty of these units had been purchased for $8.00 each in week 2 and 120 had been purchased for $9.00 each in week 1.

On day 3 of week 3 a further 60 units were received into stores at a purchase cost of $10.00 each.

The only issue of Product G occurred on day 4 of week 3, when 75 units were issued to production.

9   Using the LIFO valuation method, what was the total cost of the units issued on day 4?

    A $500.05
    B $580.75
    C $720.00
    D $980.00

10   The total cost of the units issued on day 4 using AVCO valuation method is, to the nearest $, $ [_____].

11   Factory overheads can be absorbed by which of the following methods?

    1   Direct labour hours
    2   Machine hours
    3   As a % of prime cost
    4    $x per unit

    A   1, 2, 3 or 4
    B   1 and 2 only
    C   1, 2 or 3 only
    D   2, 3 or 4 only

12   Which of the following would be the most appropriate basis for apportioning machinery insurance costs to cost centres within a factory?

    A   The number of machines in each cost centre
    B   The floor area occupied by the machinery in each cost centre
    C   The value of the machinery in each cost centre
    D   The operating hours of the machinery in each cost centre

13   Department L production overheads are absorbed using a direct labour hour rate. Budgeted production overheads for the department were $480,000 and the actual labour hours were 100,000. Actual production overheads amounted to $516,000.

Based on the above data, and assuming that the production overheads were over absorbed by $24,000, what was the overhead absorption rate per labour hour?

    A $4.80
    B $4.92
    C $5.16
    D $5.40

14   AC Co absorbs production overhead in the assembly department on the basis of direct labour hours. Budgeted direct labour hours for the period were 200,000. The production overhead absorption rate for the period was $2 per direct labour hour.

Actual results for the period were as follows.

Direct labour hours worked	220,000
Production overheads incurred	$480,000

Which one of the following statements is correct?

    A   Production overheads were $40,000 over absorbed
    B   Production overheads were $40,000 under absorbed
    C   Production overheads were $80,000 under absorbed
    D   No under or over absorption occurred

15   The budgeted production overheads and other budget data of Eiffel Co are as follows.

	Production dept X
Budget	
Overhead cost	$36,000
Direct materials cost	$32,000
Direct labour cost	$40,000
Machine hours	10,000
Direct labour hours	18,000

What would be the absorption rate for Department X using the various bases of apportionment?

(a)   % of direct material cost =

(b)   % of direct labour cost =

(c)   % of total direct cost =

(d)   Rate per machine hour =

(e)   Rate per direct labour hour =

16   Cost and selling price details for product Q are as follows.

	$ per unit
Direct material	4.20
Direct labour	3.00
Variable overhead	1.00
Fixed overhead	2.80
	11.00
Profit	4.00
Selling price	15.00

Budgeted production for month	10,000 units
Actual production for month	12,000 units
Actual sales for month	11,200 units
Actual fixed overhead cost incurred during month	$31,000

(a)   Based on the above data, the marginal costing profit for the month is

   A $44,800
   B $45,160
   C $50,600
   D $76,160

(b)   Based on the above data, the absorption costing profit for the month is

   A $42,200
   B $44,800
   C $45,160
   D $47,400

17   B Company makes a product which has a variable production cost of $21 per unit and a sales price of $39 per unit. At the beginning of 20X5, there was no opening inventory and sales during the year were 50,000 units. Fixed costs (production, administration, sales and distribution) totalled $328,000. Production was 70,000 units.

(a)   The contribution per unit is $ [   ].

(b)   The profit per unit is $ [   ].

18   A Co requires a 25% return on sales. The full cost of product R is $27.

The selling price of product R should be $ [   ].

19   R Co expects to sell 10,000 units of product Y in the coming year. The organisation makes an annual investment of $1,700,000 in production of product R and requires a return of 22% on its investment. The full cost of product Y is $15.

The required selling price of product Y is $ [   ].

20   (a)   Product S's unit cost is $5. A selling price is based on a margin of 25%. The selling price is $ [   ] to the nearest cent.

(b)   Product H sells for $175. The mark-up is 12%. The unit cost of product H is $ [   ] to the nearest cent.

21   DP Co is preparing its estimate of distribution costs for the next period. Based on previous experience, a linear relationship has been identified between sales volume and distribution costs. The following information has been collected concerning distribution costs.

Sales volume	Distribution cost
Units	$
22,000	58,600
34,000	73,000

What would be the estimated distribution costs for a sales volume of 28,000 units?

A $32,200
B $33,600
C $65,800
D $74,582

22   A delivery driver for a courier company is paid a salary of $1,000 per month, plus an extra 12 cents per delivery made. This labour cost is best described as:

A   a variable cost
B   a step cost
C   a fixed cost
D   a semi-variable cost

23   The following is a graph of cost against level of activity

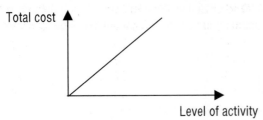

Total cost

Level of activity

To which one of the following costs does the graph correspond?

A   Sales commission payable per unit up to a maximum amount of commission

B   Electricity bills made up of a standing charge and a variable charge

C   Bonus payments to employees, paid per unit when production reaches a certain level

D   Machine rental costs, where a fixed amount is payable up to a certain level of output, and thereafter an additional rate per unit is payable

24   Identify which type of cost is being described in (a)-(d) below.

VARIABLE COST	FIXED COST	STEPPED FIXED COST	SEMI-VARIABLE COST

(a)   This type of cost stays the same, no matter how many products you produce

(b)   This type of cost increases as you produce more products. The sum of these costs are also known as the marginal cost of a product

(c)   This type of cost is fixed but only within certain levels of activity

(d)   This type of cost contains both fixed and variable elements

25   Total cost

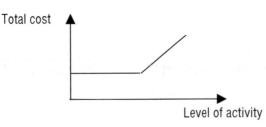

Level of activity

Which of the following costs is depicted by this graph?

A   Labour costs where employees are paid a guaranteed wage. When output exceeds an agreed level a bonus is paid for each additional unit produced.

B   Labour costs where employees are paid a guaranteed wage plus a bonus per unit for all units produced.

C   Gas costs which comprise a standing charge each period and an additional charge for each unit of gas consumed.

D   Rental of a car which comprises a fixed charge per month plus an additional charge for mileage.

26 J Co manufactures three products, details of which are as follows.

	Product K $ per unit	Product L $ per unit	Product M $ per unit
Selling price	105	133	133
Direct materials ($3/litre)	15	6	21
Direct labour ($8/hour)	24	32	24
Variable overhead	9	12	9
Fixed overhead	23	50	42

In a period when direct labour is restricted in supply, the most and least profitable use of labour are:

	Most profitable	Least profitable
A	K	M
B	L	K
C	M	K
D	M	L

27 V Co manufactures three products which have the following selling prices and costs per unit.

	V1 $	V2 $	V3 $
Selling price	30.00	36.00	34.00
Costs per unit			
Direct materials	8.00	10.00	20.00
Direct labour	4.00	8.00	3.60
Overhead			
Variable	2.00	4.00	1.80
Fixed	9.00	6.00	2.70
	23.00	28.00	28.10
Profit per unit	7.00	8.00	5.90

All three products use the same type of labour.

In a period in which labour is in short supply, the rank order of production is:

V1 ....

V2 ....

V3 ....

28 Product N generates a contribution to sales ratio of 20%. Annual fixed costs are $80,000.

The breakeven point, in terms of units sold per annum,

A is 96,000
B is 400,000
C is 480,000
D cannot be calculated without more information

29

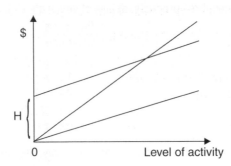

(a)   H on the graph indicates the value of

     A   contribution
     B   fixed cost
     C   sales value
     D   variable cost

(b)   This graph is known as a

     A   contribution breakeven chart
     B   conventional breakeven chart
     C   profit-volume chart
     D   semi-variable cost chart

30   S Co manufactures a single product, V. Data for the product are as follows.

	$ per unit
Selling price	40
Direct material cost	8
Direct labour cost	6
Variable production overhead cost	4
Variable selling overhead cost	2
Fixed overhead cost	10
Profit per unit	10

The profit/volume ratio for product V is [   ]

31   Fast Fandango Co manufactures a single product, the FF, which sells for $10. At 75% capacity, which is the normal level of activity for the factory, sales are $600,000 per period.

The cost of these sales are as follows.

Direct cost per unit	$3
Production overhead	$156,000 (including variable costs of $30,000)
Sales costs	$ 80,000
Distribution costs	$ 60,000 (including variable costs of $15,000)
Administration overhead	$ 40,000 (including variable costs of $9,000)

The sales costs are fixed with the exception of sales commission which is 5% of sales value.

(a)   The contribution per unit of product FF is $ [   ]

(b)   The fixed cost per period is $ [   ]

(c)   The breakeven volume of sales per period is [   ] units

32 A factory manufactures three components A, B and C.

During week 26, the following data were recorded.

Labour grade	Number of employees	Rate per hour $	Individual hours worked
I	6	12.00	40
II	18	9.60	42
III	4	8.40	40
IV	1	4.80	44

Output and standard times during the same week were as follows.

Component	Output	Standard minutes (each)
A	444	30
B	900	54
C	480	66

The normal working week is 38 hours. Overtime is paid at a premium of 50% of the normal hourly rate.

A group incentive scheme is in operation. The time saved is expressed as a percentage of hours worked and is shared between the group as a proportion of the hours worked by each grade.

The bonus rate paid is 75% of the normal hourly rate.

(a) The overtime premium payable to each grade of labour is:

Grade I $ ☐

Grade II $ ☐

Grade III $ ☐

Grade IV $ ☐

(b) The number of standard hours produced is ☐

(c) The amount of bonus payable in total to all employees is $ ☐

33 Standard costing provides which of the following? Tick all that apply.

(a) Targets and measures of performance   ☐

(b) Information for budgeting   ☐

(c) Simplification of inventory control systems   ☐

(d) Actual future costs   ☐

34 CC Co manufactures a carbonated drink, which is sold in 1 litre bottles. During the bottling process there is a 20% loss of liquid input due to spillage and evaporation. The standard usage of liquid per bottle is

A   0.80 litres
B   1.00 litres
C   1.20 litres
D   1.25 litres

35 PM Co is in the process of setting standard unit costs for next period. Period J uses two types of material, P and S. 7 kg of material P and 3 kg of material S are needed, at a standard price of $4 per kg and $9 per kg respectively.

Direct labour will cost $7 per hour and each unit of J requires 5 hours of labour.

Production overheads are to be recovered at the rate of $6 per direct labour hour, and general overhead is to be absorbed at a rate of ten per cent of production cost.

The standard prime cost for one unit of product J will be:

A $55
B $90
C $120
D $132

36 Calculate the standard cost of producing 100 wheels for a toy car using the information given below. Fill in the shaded box.

	Bending	Cutting	Assembly
Standard labour rates of pay per hour $	4	6	5
Standard labour rates per 100 wheels (hours)	0.8	0.5	1.2

STANDARD COST CARD			
Toy car wheels	Part number 5917B - 100 wheels		Date:
	Quantity	Rate/price	Total $
Direct materials			
Tyres	100	10c each	
Steel strip	50	$10.40 per 100	
Wire	1000	2c each	
Direct labour	hours	$	
Bending			
Cutting			
Assembly			
STANDARD COST			

37   SG Co has extracted the following details from the standard cost card of one of its products.

Direct labour 3.5 hours @ $9.20 per hour

During period 4, SG Co produced 1,600 units of product and incurred direct labour cost of $55,100 for 5,800 hours.

The direct labour rate and efficiency variances for period 4 were

	Rate	Efficiency
	$	$
A	1,740 adverse	1,840 adverse
B	1,740 adverse	1,900 adverse
C	1,740 adverse	1,840 favourable
D	1,740 favourable	1,840 favourable

38   Which of the following would help to explain a favourable direct material price variance?

		Would help to explain variance	Would not help to explain variance
(a)	The standard price per unit of direct material was unrealistically high		
(b)	Output quantity was greater than budgeted and it was possible to obtain bulk purchase discounts		
(c)	The material purchased was of a higher quality than standard		

39   SL Co has budgeted to make and sell 4,200 units of product S during the period.

The standard variable overhead cost per unit is $4.

During the period covered by the budget, the actual results were as follows.

Production and sales   5,000 units
Variable overhead incurred $17,500

The variable overhead total variance for the period was

A $2,500 favourable
B $700 favourable
C $2,500 adverse
D $700 adverse

Questions 40 and 41 are based on the following data.

Standard costing is used to control the material costs of product Alpha. No material inventories are held.

The following data are available for product Alpha during May.

	Budget	Actual
Production units	6,000	6,300
Material usage	48,000 kg	51,150 kg
Material cost	$576,000	$562,650

40   The material usage variance for May is:

A $750 (A)
B $6,000 (A)
C $9,000 (A)
D $28,800 (F)

41   The material price variance for May is:

A $8,900 (F)
B $51,150 (F)
C $62,000 (F)
D $64,100 (F)

42   Standard and budgeted data for the latest period for a company's single product are as follows:

Budgeted sales volume	19,680 units
Actual sales volume	18,780 units
Standard selling price per unit	$27.10
Standard variable cost per unit	$21.70
Actual sales revenue	$529,596

The sales price variance for the period is:

A $3,732 (A)
B $20,658 (A)
C $20,658 (F)
D $24,390 (A)

43   P Co has the following data relating to its budgeted sales for October 20X7:

Budgeted sales	$100,000
Budgeted selling price per unit	$8.00
Budgeted contribution per unit	$2.50

During October 20X7, actual sales were 11,000 units for a sales revenue of $99,000.

P Co uses a marginal costing system.

The sales variances for October 20X7 were:

	Price	Volume
	$	$
A	11,000 (F)	3,750 (A)
B	11,000 (F)	6,000 (A)
C	12,500 (F)	12,000 (A)
D	12,500 (A)	12,000 (A)

44   J Co uses a standard costing system and has the following data relating to one of its products.

	$	$
Selling price		9.00
Variable cost	4.00	
Fixed costs	3.00	
		7.00
Profit per unit		2.00

Its budgeted sales for October 20X5 were 800 units, but the actual sales were 850 units. The revenue earned from these sales was $7,480.

If a profit reconciliation statement were to be drawn up using marginal costing principles, the sales variances would be

	Price	Volume
A	$160 (A)	$100 (F)
B	$160 (A)	$250 (F)
C	$170 (A)	$240 (F)
D	$170 (A)	$250 (F)

45 J Co operates a standard cost accounting system. The following information has been extracted from its standard cost card and budgets.

Budgeted sales volume	5,000 units
Standard sales price	$10.00 per unit
Standard variable cost	$5.60 per unit
Standard total cost	$7.50 per unit

If it used a standard marginal cost accounting system and its actual sales were 4,500 units at a selling price of $12.00, its sales volume variance would be

A $1,250 adverse
B $2,200 adverse
C $2,250 adverse
D $3,200 adverse

46 Which of the following would help to explain a favourable sales volume variance?

(i) Increased competitor activity led to a reduction in the number of units sold.

(ii) Customers were given discounts at a higher level than standard in order to encourage increased sales.

(iii) The unit cost of production was lower than standard and selling prices were maintained at the standard level, so that a higher contribution was achieved per unit sold.

(iv) Higher quality material supplies led to improvements in the quality of the final output, which customers found attractive.

A (i), (ii) and (iv) only
B (ii), (iii) and (iv) only
C (ii) and (iv) only
D (ii) only

47 PG Co makes a single product and is preparing its material usage budget for next year. Each unit of product requires 2 kg of material, and 5,000 units of product are to be produced next year.

Opening inventory of material is budgeted to be 800 kg and PG Co budgets to increase material inventory at the end of next year by 20%.

The material usage budget for next year is

A 8,000 kg
B 9,840 kg
C 10,000 kg
D 10,160 kg

48   In a situation where there are no production resource limitations, which of the following must be available for the material usage budget to be completed? Tick all that apply.

     (a)   Production volume from the production budget   ☐

     (b)   Budgeted change in materials inventory   ☐

     (c)   Standard material usage per unit   ☐

49   The following details have been extracted from the accounts receivable records of PR Co.

Invoices paid in the month after sale	80%
Invoices paid in the second month after sale	10%
Invoices paid in the third month after sale	5%
Bad debts (irrecoverable debts)	5%

Invoices are issued on the last day of each month, and customers paying in the month after sale are entitled to deduct a 1% settlement discount.

Credit sales values for January to April are budgeted as follows.

January	February	March	April
$35,000	$40,000	$60,000	$45,000

The amount budgeted to be received from credit sales in April is

A $43,640
B $53,270
C $53,750
D $55,020

50   If a company has no production resource limitations, in which order would the following budgets be prepared?

	Order
Material usage budget	
Sales budget	
Material purchase budget	
Finished goods inventory budget	
Production budget	
Material inventory budget	

51   When preparing a production budget, the quantity to be produced equals

A   sales quantity + opening inventory + closing inventory
B   sales quantity − opening inventory + closing inventory
C   sales quantity − opening inventory − closing inventory
D   sales quantity + opening inventory − closing inventory

52 The following extract is taken from the distribution cost budget of DC Co:

Volume delivered (units)   8,000   14,000
Distribution cost $7,200 $10,500

The budgeted cost allowance for distribution cost for a delivery volume of 12,000 units is

A $6,600
B $9,000
C $9,400
D $10,800

53 Which of the following best describes a flexible budget?

A   A budget which is designed to be easily updated to reflect recent changes in unit costs or selling prices

B   A budget which can be flexed when actual costs are known, to provide a realistic forecast for the forthcoming period

C   A budget which, by recognising different cost behaviour patterns, is designed to change as the volume of activity changes

D   A budget which is prepared on a spreadsheet, with the flexibility to add new costs items to prepare new forecasts as circumstances change during the year

54

		True	False
(a)	Budgetary control procedures are useful only to maintain control over an organisation's expenditure		
(b)	A prerequisite of flexible budgeting is a knowledge of cost behaviour patterns		
(c)	Fixed budgets are not useful for control purposes		

55 A flexible budget is

A   a budget comprising variable production costs only
B   a budget which is updated with actual costs and revenues as they occur during the budget period
C   a budget which shows the costs and revenues at different levels of activity
D   a budget which is prepared using a computer spreadsheet model

56 The following extract is taken from the production cost budget of W Co:

Production units   2,000   3,000
Production cost $17,760 $20,640

The budget cost allowance for an activity level of 4,000 units is

A $11,520
B $23,520
C $27,520
D $35,520

57 PC Co makes a product in two processes. The following data is available for the latest period, for process 1.

Opening work in progress of 200 units was valued as follows.

Material	$2,400
Labour	$1,200
Overhead	$400

No losses occur in the process.

Units added and costs incurred during the period:

Material	$6,000 (500 units)
Labour	$3,350
Overhead	$1,490

Closing work in progress of 100 units had reached the following degrees of completion:

Material	100%
Labour	50%
Overhead	30%

PC Co uses the weighted average method of inventory valuation.

(a) How many equivalent units are used when calculating the cost per unit in relation to overhead?

    A   500
    B   600
    C   630
    D   700

(b) The value of the units transferred to process 2 was

    A $7,200
    B $13,200
    C $14,840
    D $15,400

58 A company needs to produce 340 litres of Chemical X. There is a normal loss of 10% of the material input into the process. During a given month the company did produce 340 litres of good production, although there was an abnormal loss of 5% of the material input into the process.

How many litres of material were input into the process during the month?

    A   357 litres
    B   374 litres
    C   391 litres
    D   400 litres

59   20,000 litres of liquid were put into a process at the beginning of the month at a cost of $4,400. The output of finished product was 17,000 litres. The normal level of waste in this process is 20% and the waste which is identified at the end of the process can be sold at $0.50 per litre. Use this information to complete the process account below.

PROCESS ACCOUNT

	Litres	$		Litres	$
Materials			Normal waste		
Abnormal gains	_____	_____	Finished goods	_____	_____
	=====	=====		=====	=====

60   Bonto Co produces a simple product in two processes, process R and process X. The following information relates to process X for period 4.

Work in progress at start of period - nil.
Material transferred from process R during the period - 2,500 kgs valued at $7,145.
Wages paid - 234½ hours at $4 per hour.
Other direct costs allocated - $463.

Normal waste during processing - 5% of process R input. This has a scrap value of 16c per kg.

At the end of period 4 there were 2,100 kgs transferred to finished inventory, and 150 kgs remained in work in progress.

The work in progress is 100% complete so far as materials are concerned, but only 80% of labour costs and 60% of other direct costs have been incurred.

(a)   During the period there was an abnormal [   ] of [   ] kg

(b)   The cost per equivalent unit of each cost element during the period was:

Materials $ [   ]

Labour $ [   ]

Other direct costs $ [   ]

61   What is an equivalent unit?

A   A unit of output which is identical to all others manufactured in the same process
B   Notional whole units used to represent uncompleted work
C   A unit of product in relation to which costs are ascertained
D   The amount of work achievable, at standard efficiency levels, in an hour

The following information relates to questions 62 and 63.

Patacake Co produces a certain food item in a manufacturing process. On 1 November, there was no opening stock of work in process. During November, 500 units of material were input to the process, with a cost of $9,000. Direct labour costs in November were $3,840. Production overhead is absorbed at the rate of 200% of direct labour costs. Closing stock on 30 November consisted of 100 units which were 100% complete as to materials and 80% complete as to labour and overhead. There was no loss in process.

62   The full production cost of completed units during November was

    A $10,400
    B $16,416
    C $16,800
    D $20,520

63   The value of the closing work in progress on 30 November is

    A $2,440
    B $3,720
    C $4,200
    D $20,520

64   In process costing, a joint product is

    A   A product which is later divided into many parts

    B   A product which is produced simultaneously with other products and is of similar value to at least one of the other products

    C   A product which is produced simultaneously with other products but which is of a greater value than any of the other products

    D   A product produced jointly with another organisation

65   What is a by-product?

    A   A product produced at the same time as other products which has no value

    B   A product produced at the same time as other products which requires further processing to put it in a saleable state

    C   A product produced at the same time as other products which has a relatively low volume compared with the other products

    D   A product produced at the same time as other products which has a relatively low value compared with the other products

66   In process costing, if an abnormal loss arises, the process account is generally

    A   debited with the scrap value of the abnormal loss units
    B   debited with the full production cost of the abnormal loss units
    C   credited with the scrap value of the abnormal loss units
    D   credited with the full production cost of the abnormal loss units

67   A food manufacturing process has a normal wastage of 10% of input. In a period, 3,000 kgs of material were input and there was an abnormal loss of 75 kg. No stocks are held at the beginning or end of the process.

    The quantity of good production achieved was ☐ kg.

68   A company makes a product, which passes through a single process.

    Details of the process for the last period are as follows.

Materials	5,000 kg at 50c per kg
Labour	$700
Production overheads	200% of labour

Normal losses are 10% of input in the process, and without further processing any losses can be sold as scrap for 20c per kg.

The output for the period was 4,200 kg from the process.

There was no work in progress at the beginning or end of the period.

The value credited to the process account for the scrap value of the normal loss for the period will be $ ⬚

69   A company makes a product, which passes through a single process.

Details of the process for the last period are as follows.

Materials	5,000 kg at 50c per kg
Labour	$700
Production overheads	200% of labour

Normal losses are 10% of input in the process, and without further processing any losses can be sold as scrap for 20c per kg.

The output for the period was 4,200 kg from the process.

There was no work in progress at the beginning or end of the period.

The value of the abnormal loss for the period is $ ⬚

70   A product is manufactured as a result of two processes, 1 and 2. Details of process 2 for the latest period were as follows.

Opening work in progress	Nil
Materials transferred from process 1	10,000 kg valued at $40,800
Labour and overhead costs	$8,424
Output transferred to finished goods	8,000 kg
Closing work in progress	900 kg

Normal loss is 10% of input and losses have a scrap value of $0.30 per kg.

Closing work in progress is 100% complete for material, and 75% complete for both labour and overheads.

The value of the closing work in progress for the period was $ ⬚

71   A construction company has the following data concerning one of its contracts.

	$
Contract price	1,800,000
Estimated total cost to complete contract	1,200,000
Value of work certified to date	1,170,000

No difficulties are foreseen on the contract.

The profit to be recognised on the contract to date is $ ⬚

72 Contract number 724 commenced on 1 May and plant with a book value of $600,000 was delivered to the site from central stores. On 1 October further plant was delivered, with a book value of $48,000.

Company policy is to depreciate plant at a rate of 25% of the book value each year.

The book value of the plant on site as at 31 December is

A $103,000
B $486,000
C $545,000
D $648,000

73 PA Co operates a job costing system. The company's standard net profit margin is 20 per cent of sales.

The estimated costs for job 173 are as follows.

Direct materials	5 metres @ $20 per metre
Direct labour	14 hours @ $8 per hour

Variable production overheads are recovered at the rate of $3 per direct labour hour.

Fixed production overheads for the year are budgeted to be $200,000 and are to be recovered on the basis of the total of 40,000 direct labour hours for the year.

Other overheads, in relation to selling, distribution and administration, are recovered at the rate of $80 per job.

The price to be quoted for job 173 is, to the nearest $

A $404
B $424
C $485
D $505

74 Which of the following is a feature of job costing?

A   Production is carried out in accordance with the wishes of the customer
B   Associated with continuous production of large volumes of low-cost items
C   Establishes the cost of services rendered
D   Costs are charged over the units produced in the period

75 A firm uses job costing and recovers overheads as a percentage of direct labour cost.

Three jobs were worked on during a period, the details of which are as follows.

	Job 1	Job 2	Job 3
	$	$	$
Opening work in progress	8,500	0	46,000
Material in period	17,150	29,025	0
Labour for period	12,500	23,000	4,500

The overheads for the period were exactly as budgeted, $140,000.

Job 3 was completed during the period and consisted of 2,400 identical circuit boards. The firm adds 50% to total production costs to arrive at a selling price.

What is the selling price of a circuit board?

A   It cannot be calculated without more information
B $31.56
C $41.41
D $55.21

76   P Co manufactures ring binders which are embossed with the customer's own logo. A customer has ordered a batch of 300 binders. The following data illustrate the cost for a typical batch of 100 binders.

	$
Direct materials	30
Direct wages	10
Machine set up	3
Design and artwork	15
	58

Direct employees are paid on a piecework basis.

P Co absorbs production overhead at a rate of 20 per cent of direct wages cost. Five per cent is added to the total production cost of each batch to allow for selling, distribution and administration overhead.

P Co requires a profit margin of 25 per cent of sales value.

The selling price for a batch of 300 binders (to the nearest cent) will be

A $189.00
B $193.20
C $201.60
D $252.00

77   JC Co operates a job costing system. The company's standard net profit margin is 20 per cent of sales value.

The estimated costs for job B124 are as follows.

Direct materials   3 kg @ $5 per kg

Direct labour   4 hours @ $9 per hour

Production overheads are budgeted to be $240,000 for the period, to be recovered on the basis of a total of 30,000 labour hours.

Other overheads, related to selling, distribution and administration, are budgeted to be $150,000 for the period. They are to be recovered on the basis of the total budgeted production cost of $750,000 for the period.

The price to be quoted for job B124 is $ ☐

78   In which of the following situation(s) will job costing normally be used?

☐   Production is continuous

☐   Production of the product can be completed in a single accounting period

☐   Production relates to a single special order

79   In a standard cost bookkeeping system, when the actual wage rate paid per hour is higher than the standard wage rate per hour, the accounting entries to record this are

	Debit	Credit
A	Labour rate variance account	Wages control account
B	Labour rate variance account	Work in progress control account
C	Wages control account	Labour rate variance account
D	Work in progress control account	Labour rate variance account

80   Which of the following statements is correct?

A   An adverse direct material cost variance will always be a combination of an adverse material price varianc
      and an adverse material usage variance

B   An adverse direct material cost variance will always be a combination of an adverse material price varianc
      and a favourable material usage variance

C   An adverse direct material cost variance can be a combination of a favourable material price variance and
      favourable material usage variance

D   An adverse direct material cost variance can be a combination of a favourable material price variance and
      an adverse material usage variance

81   PB Co maintains a standard cost bookkeeping system. The work in progress account for the latest period is as
      follows.

WORK IN PROGRESS CONTROL ACCOUNT

	$'000		$'000
Stores account	724	Finished goods control	3,004
Wages control	1,210	Material usage variance	180
Production overhead control	1,050		
Labour efficiency variance	200		
	3,184		3,184

Which of the following statements is/are consistent with the entries in the work in progress account?

		Consistent with the account entries	Not consistent with the account entries
(a)	The material used in production was more than the standard allowed for the number of units produced	☐	☐
(b)	All of the material issued to production was completely processed during the period	☐	☐
(c)	The number of labour hours worked was greater than the standard allowed for the number of units produced	☐	☐

82 Libra Co uses standard costing and an integrated accounting system. The double entry for a favourable labour efficiency variance is (delete as appropriate):

DR

| DIRECT LABOUR EFFICIENCY VARIANCE ACCOUNT |
| WORK IN PROGRESS CONTROL ACCOUNT |
| DIRECT LABOUR CONTROL ACCOUNT |
| DIRECT LABOUR RATE VARIANCE ACCOUNT |

CR

| DIRECT LABOUR EFFICIENCY VARIANCE ACCOUNT |
| WORK IN PROGRESS CONTROL ACCOUNT |
| DIRECT LABOUR CONTROL ACCOUNT |
| DIRECT LABOUR RATE VARIANCE ACCOUNT |

83 A firm operates an integrated cost and financial accounting system. The accounting entries for direct wages incurred would be:

	Debit	*Credit*
A	Wages control account	Work in progress account
B	Wages control account	Bank account
C	Work in progress account	Wages control account
D	Bank account	Wages control account

84 In the same integrated system, the firm's entries for production overhead absorbed would be:

	Debit	*Credit*
A	Finished goods inventory account	Overhead control account
B	Income statement	Overhead control account
C	Work in progress control account	Overhead control account
D	Overhead control account	Work in progress control account

85 LE Co operates an integrated accounting system. The raw materials control account at 31 May is as follows.

RAW MATERIALS CONTROL

	$		$
Balance b/f	18,000	?	71,000
Bank	76,000	Production overhead control	6,000
		Balance c/f	17,000
	94,000		94,000

The $71,000 credit entry is the value of the transfer to the

A   cost of sales account
B   account payable control account
C   finished goods control account
D   work in progress control account

86 In cost bookkeeping, when material costs are debited to the materials account, the corresponding credit entry is to which of the following accounts?

Cash

Suppliers

Work-in-progress

87 Which of the following would be appropriate cost units for a passenger coach company?

	Appropriate	Not appropriate
(a) Vehicle cost per passenger-kilometre		
(b) Fuel cost for each vehicle per kilometre		
(c) Fixed cost per kilometre		

88 The following information is available for the Whiteley Hotel for the latest thirty day period.

Number of rooms available per night   40
Percentage occupancy achieved   65%
Room servicing cost incurred $3,900

The room servicing cost per occupied room-night last period, to the nearest penny, was:

A $3.25
B $5.00
C $97.50
D $150.00

89 Consider the following features and identify whether they relate to job costing, contract costing, service costing or none of these costing methods.

J =   Job costing
C =   Contract costing
S =   Service costing
N =   None of these costing methods

(i)   Production is carried out in accordance with the wishes of the customer

(ii)   Work is usually of a relatively long duration

(iii)   Work is usually undertaken on the contractor's premises

(iv)   Costs are averaged over the units produced in the period

(v)   It establishes the costs of services rendered

90 The following information relates to two hospitals for the year ended 31 December 20X5.

	St Matthew's	St Mark's
Number of in-patients	15,400	710
Average stay per in-patient	10 days	156 days
Total number of out-patient attendances	130,000	3,500
Number of available beds	510	320
Average number of beds occupied	402	307

Cost analysis	In-patients $	Out-patients $	In-patients $	Out-patients $
Patient care services				
Direct treatment services and supplies (eg nursing staff)	6,213,900	1,076,400	1,793,204	70,490
Medical supporting services:				
Diagnostic (eg pathology)	480,480	312,000	22,152	20,650
Other services (eg occupational therapy)	237,160	288,600	77,532	27,790
General services				
Patient related (eg catering)	634,480	15,600	399,843	7,700
General (eg administration)	2,196,760	947,700	1,412,900	56,700

Note. In-patients are those who receive treatment while remaining in hospital. Out-patients visit hospital during the day to receive treatment.

(a)   The cost per in-patient day at each hospital is (to the nearest penny):

    (i)   St Matthew's $ ⬚

    (ii)   St Mark's $ ⬚

(b)   The cost per out-patient attendance at each hospital is (to the nearest penny):

    (i)   St Matthew's $ ⬚

    (ii)   St Mark's $ ⬚

(c)   The bed occupation percentage at each hospital is (to one decimal place):

    (i)   St Matthew's   % ⬚

    (ii)   St Mark's   % ⬚

The following information relates to questions 91 and 92.

Happy Returns Co operates a haulage business with three vehicles. During week 26 it is expected that all three vehicles will be used at a total cost of $10,390; 3,950 kilometres will be travelled (including return journeys when empty) as shown in the following table.

Journey	Tonnes carried (one way)	Kilometres (one way)
1	34	180
2	28	265
3	40	390
4	32	115
5	26	220
6	40	480
7	29	90
8	26	100
9	25	135
	280	1,975

91 The total of tonne-kilometres in week 26 =

92 The average cost per tonne-kilometre for week 26 = $ _____ per tonne-kilometre (to the nearest penny).

Answer Bank

1   D   Royalty costs can be traced directly to cost units and are therefore direct expenses and a part of prime cost.

Options A, B and C are all **indirect costs** which cannot be traced directly to cost units. They would be classified as **production overheads** and are not a part of prime cost.

2   C   The overtime premium paid at the specific request of a customer would be treated as a direct cost because it can be traced to a specific cost unit.

The four hours of machine breakdown time is idle time. It cannot be traced to a specific cost unit therefore it is an indirect cost.

The direct wages cost is as follows.

	$
Basic pay for active hours: 38 hours × $7.00	266.00
Overtime premium re: customer request 2 hours × $3.50	7.00
	273.00

Option A is incorrect because it is the employee's total wages for the week, both direct and indirect.

Option B is the basic pay for a 36 hour week, making no allowance for the overtime worked at the customer's request.

If you selected **option D** you calculated the basic pay for all of the hours worked, but you made no allowance for either the idle time or the overtime premium.

3   (1)   Material
       (2)   Labour
       (3)   Other costs
       (4)   Direct
       (5)   Indirect
       (6)   Functional
       (7)   Variable
       (8)   Cost unit
       (9)   Cost centre
      (10)   Variable
      (11)   Fixed

4   B   You need to learn this definition.

5   B   Responsibility accounting requires costs to be classified as controllable or uncontrollable.

6   C   The LIFO method uses the price of the latest batches first:

		$
1,800	× $4.80	8,640
2,500	× $4.50	11,250
200	× $4.20	840
4,500		20,730

Option A is incorrect because it values all issues at the opening inventory price of $4.20.

Option B is the value of the issues using the FIFO method. If you selected **option D** you valued all the issues at the latest price of $4.80. However, only 1,800 units were received at this price. The remaining units must be valued at the price of the next latest batch received, until that batch is used up, and so on.

7   B   Using FIFO, the issue on 9 September would consist of the remaining 60 units from the opening balance (40 units were issued on 3 March) plus 10 units from the batch received on 4 June.

	$
60 units × $5	300
10 units × $5.50	55
	355

If you selected **option A** you used the opening inventory rate of $5 for all the units issued: you didn't notice that 40 of these units had already been issued on 3 March.

If you selected **option C** you ignored the opening inventory and based your calculations only on the receipts during the year.

Option D is incorrect because it values all the issues at the latest price paid, $6 per unit.

8   C   Using LIFO, the issue on 9 September would consist of the 50 units received on 6 June, plus 20 of the units received on 4 June.

	$
50 units × $6	300
20 units × $5.50	110
	410

Option A is incorrect because it is based on the opening inventory rate of $5 per unit – this is certainly not the latest batch received.

Option B if a FIFO calculation based on the receipts on 4 and 6 June.

Option D is incorrect because it values all the issues at the latest price paid, $6 per unit. However there were only 50 units in this batch. The price for the remaining 20 units issued is the $5.50 per unit paid for the next latest batch received.

9   C

		$
60	units received on day 3 of week 3 @ $10.00	600.00
15	units received in week 2 @ $8.00	120.00
75		720.00

10   Cost in $ | 669 |

Value of units held on day 4:

			$
Wk 1	80	× $8 =	640
Wk 2	120	× $9 =	1,080
Wk 3	60	× $10 =	600
	260		2,320

∴ Issues are priced at $2,320/260 = $8.92
∴ Total cost is $8.92 × 75 = $669

11   A   All of the overhead absorption methods are suitable, depending on the circumstances.

Method 1, direct labour hours, is suitable in a labour-intensive environment. **Method 2**, machine hours, is suitable in a machine-intensive environment. **Method 3**, a percentage of prime cost, can be used if it is difficult to obtain the necessary information to use a time-based method. **Method 4**, a rate per unit, is suitable if all cost units are identical.

12   C   The insurance cost is likely to be linked to the cost of replacing the machines, therefore the most appropriate basis for apportionment is the value of machinery.

Options A, **B and D** would all be possible apportionment bases in the absence of better information, but option C is preferable.

13   D

	$
Actual overheads	516,000
Over absorbed overheads	24,000
Overheads absorbed by 100,000 hours	540,000

∴ Overhead absorption rate = $540,000/100,000 = $5.40 per labour hour

Option A is incorrect because it is based on the budgeted overhead and the actual labour hours.

If you selected **option B** you deducted the over absorbed overheads by mistake, at the beginning of the calculation. If overhead is over absorbed, then the overhead absorbed must be higher than the actual overhead incurred.

Option C is incorrect because it is the actual overhead per direct labour hour.

14   B

	$
Overhead absorbed 220,000 hours × $2	440,000
Overhead incurred	480,000
Overhead under absorbed	40,000

Option A is the correct monetary amount, but the overhead incurred is more than the overhead absorbed, therefore there is an under absorption. **Option C** is the difference between the original budgeted overhead and the actual overhead incurred. This takes no account of the amount of overhead absorbed based on the activity achieved.

Option D is incorrect because there is a difference between the overhead incurred and the overhead absorbed.

15   (a)   % of direct material cost = | 112.5% |

(b)   % of direct labour cost = | 90% |

(c)   % of total direct cost = | 50% |

(d)   Rate per machine hour = | $3.60 |

(e)   Rate per direct labour hour = | $2 |

Workings

(a)   % of direct materials cost $\dfrac{\$36,000}{\$32,000} \times 100\% = 112.5\%$

(b)   % of direct labour cost $\dfrac{\$36,000}{\$40,000} \times 100\% = 90\%$

(c)   % of total direct cost $\dfrac{\$36,000}{\$72,000} \times 100\% = 50\%$

(d)   Rate per machine hour $\dfrac{\$36,000}{10,000\,\text{hrs}}$ = $3.60 per machine hour

(e)   Rate per direct labour hour $\dfrac{\$36,000}{18,000\,\text{hrs}}$ = $2 per direct labour hour

16   (a)   B

Contribution per unit	=	$15 – $(4.20 + 3.00 + 1.00)
	=	$6.80
Contribution for month	=	$6.80 × 11,200 units
	=	$76,160
Less fixed costs incurred	=	$31,000
Marginal costing profit		$45,160

Option A bases the profit on the actual sales volume at $4 per unit profit. This utilises a unit rate for fixed overhead which is not valid under marginal costing.

If you selected option C you used the correct method but you based your calculations on the units produced rather than the units sold.

If you selected option D you calculated the correct contribution but you forgot to deduct the fixed overhead.

(b)   D

	$
Sales 11,200 units × $15	168,000
Absorption costs for 11,200 units (× $11)	123,200
	44,800
Over absorbed fixed overhead for month (see working)	2,600
Absorption costing profit	47,400

Working	$
Overhead absorbed into production (12,000 units × $2.80)	33,600
Overhead incurred	31,000
Overhead over absorbed	2,600

If you selected **option A** you calculated all the figures correctly but you subtracted the over absorbed overhead instead of adding it to profit.

Option B makes no allowance for the over absorbed overhead, and **option C** is the marginal costing profit.

17   (a)   The contribution per unit is $900,000/50,000 = $ | 18 |

(b)   The profit per unit is $572,000/50,000 = $ | 11.44 |

	$'000	$'000
Sales (at $39 per unit)		1,950
Opening inventory	–	
Variable production cost ($21 × 70,000)	1,470	
Less closing inventory ($21 × 20,000)	420	
Variable cost of sales		1,050
Contribution		900
Less fixed costs		328
Profit		572

18   The selling price is $ $\boxed{36}$

Selling price = $27/0.75 = $36

19   The selling price is $ $\boxed{52.40}$

Required return = 0.22 × $1.7m = $374,000

Expected cost = 10,000 × $15 = $150,000

Expected revenue   = $(374,000 + 150,000)
                      = $524,000

∴ Selling price = $524,000/10,000 = $52.40

20   (a)   The selling price is $ $\boxed{6.67}$

Selling price = $5/0.75 = $6.67

(b)   The cost is $ $\boxed{156.25}$

Cost = $175/1.12 = $156.25

21   C   Using the high-low method.

	Units	$
High sales	34,000	73,000
Low sales	22,000	58,600
Variable cost of	12,000	14,400

Variable cost per unit $14,400/12,000 = $1.20

Fixed cost   = $73,000 − (34,000 × $1.20)
              = $32,200

Estimated distribution costs for a sales volume of 28,000 units:

	$
Fixed cost	32,200
Variable cost (28,000 × $1.20)	33,600
	65,800

Options A and B are the fixed cost and variable cost respectively, rather than the total cost. If you selected **option D** you simply calculated an average unit cost rate without allowing for the constant nature of the fixed costs.

22   D   The driver's wages are part fixed ($1,000 per month) and part variable (12 cents per delivery). Therefore the wages are a semi-variable cost.

If you chose options A or C you were considering only part of the cost.

Option B, a step cost, is a cost which remains constant up to a certain level and then increases to a higher, constant level of fixed cost.

23　C　The depicted cost is zero up to a certain level of output, then it increases at a constant rate per unit of output. The description of bonus payments fits this pattern.

Graphs for the other options would look like this.

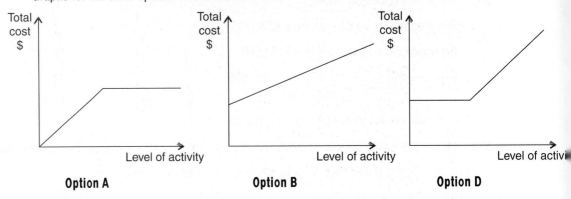

Option A　　　　**Option B**　　　　**Option D**

24　(a)

FIXED COST
(b) VARIABLE COST
(c) STEPPED FIXED COST
(d) SEMI-VARIABLE COST

25　A　Costs B, C and D would be depicted as follows.

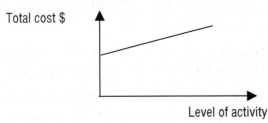

26　C

	Product K	Product L	Product M
Contribution per unit	$57	$83	$79
Labour hours per unit	3	4	3
Contribution per labour hour	$19	$20.75	$26.33
Ranking	3	2	1

Therefore M is the most profitable and K is the least profitable.

If you selected **option A** you reversed the ranking. **Option B** ranks the products according to the contribution per unit, but this takes no account of the **limiting factor**. If you selected **option D** you ranked the products according to their profit per unit, but this takes no account of the **limiting factor** and is **distorted by the fixed costs**.

27 V1 = 1st
    V2 = 3rd
    V3 = 2nd

	V1	V2	V3
	$	$	$
Selling price per unit	30	36	34.00
Variable costs per unit	14	22	25.40
Contribution per unit	16	14	8.60
Labour cost per unit	$4	$8	$3.60
Contribution per $ of labour cost	$4	$1.75	$2.39
Rank order of production	1	3	2

28 D The breakeven point cannot be calculated in terms of units because we do not know the unit selling price.

Option C gives the breakeven point in terms of sales value:

$$\frac{\$80,000}{0.2} = \$400,000$$

To convert this to a number of units we would need to divide by the selling price per unit.

29 (a) B The distance H is the total cost at zero activity, ie the fixed cost. **Option A**, contribution, is the distance between the sales line and the variable cost line, which are the two lines that pass through the origin. Sales value (**option C**) is represented by the steepest of the two lines passing through the origin. Variable cost (**option D**) is represented by the less steep of the two lines passing through the origin.

(b) A The chart shows the variable cost line and the contribution can be read directly as the distance between this and the sales value line. Therefore this is a contribution breakeven chart.

A conventional breakeven chart (**option B**) shows the fixed cost line instead of the variable cost line. A profit volume chart (**option C**) plots a single line to indicate the profit at any level of activity. **Option D** is not a generally recognised description of a chart used for breakeven analysis.

30 The profit/volume ratio for product V is 50 %

The profit/volume ratio (P/V ratio) is another term used to describe the contribution/sales ratio (C/S ratio)

$$\text{P/V ratio} = \frac{\text{Contribution per unit}}{\text{Selling price per unit}}$$

$$= \frac{\$(40-8-6-4-2)}{\$40} \times 100\% = 50\%$$

31   (a)   The contribution per unit of product FF is $5.60.

Workings

Sales are 60,000 units at the normal level of activity. Variable costs at 60,000 units of production/sales a▪
as follows.

	$	$ per unit
Production overhead	30,000	0.50
Sales costs (5% of $600,000)	30,000	0.50
Distribution costs	15,000	0.25
Administration overhead	9,000	0.15
	84,000	1.40
Direct costs	180,000	3.00
Total variable costs	264,000	4.40
Sales revenue	600,000	10.00
Contribution	336,000	5.60

(b)   The fixed cost per period is $252,000.

Fixed costs	$
Production overhead	126,000
Sales costs	50,000
Distribution costs	45,000
Administration overhead	31,000
	252,000

(c)   The breakeven volume of sales per period is 45,000 units.

Workings

$$\text{Breakeven point} = \frac{\text{fixed costs}}{\text{contribution per unit}}$$

$$= \frac{\$252,000}{\$5.60}$$

$$= 45,000 \text{ units}$$

32   (a)   Grade I $72.00
           Grade II $345.60
           Grade III $33.60
           Grade IV $14.40

Workings

Grade	Overtime premium (50% of basic rate) $/hour (a)	Overtime hours payable (b)		Overtime premium $ ((a) × (b))
I	6.00	2 hrs × 6 =	12	72.00
II	4.80	4 hrs × 18 =	72	345.60
III	4.20	2 hrs × 4 =	8	33.60
IV	2.40	6 hrs × 1 =	6	14.40

(b) The number of standard hours produced is 1,560.

Workings

Component		Standard hours
A	$444 \times \dfrac{30}{60}$ hours	222
B	$900 \times \dfrac{54}{60}$ hours	810
C	$480 \times \dfrac{66}{60}$ hours	528
		1,560

(c) The amount of bonus payable in total to all employees is $2,630.88.

Workings

Actual time taken

Grade		Hours
I	6×40 hrs	240
II	18×42 hrs	756
III	4×40 hrs	160
IV	1×44 hrs	44
		1,200

∴ Time saved = (1,560 – 1,200) hrs = 360 hrs

Time saved as a percentage of hours worked = $\dfrac{360}{1,200} \times 100\% = 30\%$

Calculation of bonus payable

Grade	Bonus hours		75% basic rate $	Bonus payable $
I	$240 \times 30\%$	= 72.0	× 9.00	648.00
II	$756 \times 30\%$	= 226.8	× 7.20	1,632.96
III	$160 \times 30\%$	= 48.0	× 6.30	302.40
IV	$44 \times 30\%$	= 13.2	× 3.60	47.52
				2,630.88

33 (a) Targets and measures of performance   ✓

(b) Information for budgeting   ✓

(c) Simplification of inventory control systems   ✓

(d) Actual future costs

Standard costing provides targets for achievement, and yardsticks against which actual performance can be monitored (**item (a)**). It also provides the unit cost information for evaluating the volume figures contained in a budget (**item (b)**). Inventory control systems are simplified with standard costing. Once the variances have been eliminated, all inventory units are evaluated at standard price (**item (c)**).

Item (d) is incorrect because standard costs are an estimate of what will happen in the future, and a unit cost target that the organisation is aiming to achieve.

34   D   Required liquid input = 1 litre $\times \dfrac{100}{80}$ = 1.25 litres

If you selected **option A** you **deducted** 20 per cent from the required output, instead of **adding extra** to allow for losses, whereas **option B** makes **no allowance** for losses.

Option C simply adds an extra 20 per cent to the completed output, but the wastage is 20 per cent of the liquid input, not 20 per cent of output.

35   B

		$ per unit	$ per unit
Material P	7 kg × $4	28	
Material S	3 kg × $9	27	
			55
Direct labour 5hr × $7			35
Standard prime cost of product J			90

Option A is the **standard material cost** and **option C** is the **standard total production cost**, including overheads which are not part of prime cost.

Option D includes the absorption of **general overhead**; always **read the question carefully**!

36

STANDARD COST CARD			
Toy car wheels	Part number 5917B - 100 wheels		Date:
	Quantity	Rate/price	Total $
Direct materials			
Tyres	100	10c each	10.00
Steel strip	50	$10.40 per 100	5.20
Wire	1000	2c each	20.00
			35.20
Direct labour	hours	$	
Bending	4	0.8	3.20
Cutting	6	0.5	3.00
Assembly	5	1.2	6.00
			12.20
STANDARD COST			47.40

37   A

	$
5,800 hours should have cost (× $9.20)	53,360
but did cost	55,100
Labour rate variance	1,740 (A)
1,600 units should take (× 3.5 hours)	5,600 hrs
but did take	5,800 hrs
Variance in hours	200 hrs (A)
× standard rate per hour	× $9.20
Labour efficiency variance	$1,840 (A)

If you selected option B you valued the efficiency variance in hours at the actual rate per hour instead of the standard rate per hour.

If you selected option C or option D you calculated the money values of the variances correctly but misinterpreted their direction.

38

		Would help to explain variance	Would not help to explain variance
(a)	The standard price per unit of direct material was unrealistically high	✓	
(b)	Output quantity was greater than budgeted and it was possible to obtain bulk purchase discounts	✓	
(c)	The material purchased was of a higher quality than standard		✓

Statement (a) is consistent with a favourable material price variance. If the standard is high then actual prices are likely to be below the standard.

Statement (b) is consistent with a favourable material price variance. Bulk purchase discounts would not have been allowed at the same level in the standard, because purchases were greater than expected.

Statement (c) is not consistent with a favourable material price variance. Higher quality material is likely to cost more than standard, resulting in an adverse material price variance.

39   A   **Variable overhead total variance**

	$
Budgeted 5,000 units should cost (× $4)	20,000
But did cost	17,500
Variable overhead total variance	2,500 (F)

The variance is favourable because the actual expenditure was less than the amount budgeted.

If you selected an incorrect option you misinterpreted the direction of the variance or calculated one element of it only.

40   C   Standard price per kg of material = $576,000/48,000 = $12

Standard material usage per unit = 48,000 kg/6,000 = 8 kg per unit

6,300 units should have used (× 8 kg)	50,400	kg
but did use	51,150	kg
Usage variance in kg	750	kg (A)
× standard price per kg	× $12	
Material usage variance	$9,000	(A)

41   B

	$	
51,150 kg of material should have cost (× $12 (from question 40))	613,800	
but did cost	562,650	
Material price variance	51,150	(F)

42   C

	$	
18,780 units should sell for (× $27.10)	508,938	
but did sell for	529,596	
Sales price variance	20,658	(F)

43   A

	$	
11,000 units should have sold for (× $8)	88,000	
but did sell for	99,000	
Selling price variance	11,000	(F)
Budgeted sales volume ($100,000 ÷ $8)	12,500	units
Actual sales volume	11,000	units
Sales volume variance in units	1,500	units (A)
× standard contribution per unit	× $2.50	
Sales volume contribution variance	$3,750	(A)

44   D

Actual sales	850	units
Budgeted sales	800	units
Variance in units	50	units (F)
× standard contribution per unit ($(9 − 4))	× $5	
Sales volume contribution variance	$250	(F)

	$	
Revenue for 850 units should have been (× $9)	7,650	
but was	7,480	
Selling price variance	170	(A)

45   B   Since J Co uses a standard marginal costing system, the sales volume variance will be valued at the standard contribution of $4.40 per unit ($10.00 − $5.60).

Budgeted sales volume	5,000	units
Actual sales volume	4,500	units
Sales volume variance in units	500	units (A)
× standard contribution per unit	× $4.40	
Sales volume contribution variance in $	$2,200	(A)

46   C   **Situation (i)** would result in an adverse sales volume variance because volumes were reduced.

Situation (ii) would result in a favourable sales volume variance, evaluated at the standard contribution achievable on the extra sales volume above standard.

A higher contribution per unit (**situation (iii)**) would not affect the sales volume variance because the variance is evaluated at standard contribution per unit.

Situation (iv) would lead to an increased sales volume and hence a favourable sales volume variance.

47   C   Material usage budget = 5,000 units produced × 2 kg per unit

                            = 10,000 kg

Option D is the material purchases budget. If you selected this you need to read the question more carefully. If you selected **option B** you adjusted incorrectly for the inventory change in attempting to calculate the purchases budget, but the material usage budget was required. If you selected **option A** you seem to have taken 20 per cent of the usage budget as the correct answer: the change in material inventory will have no effect at all on the usage budget for the year.

48   (a)   Production volume from the production budget

     (b)   Budgeted change in materials inventory

     (c)   Standard material usage per unit

Since there are no production resource limitations, the production budget would be prepared before the material usage budget (a). The standard material usage per unit (c) would then indicate the total material usage required to produce the budgeted production volume.

It would not be necessary to know the budgeted change in materials inventory (b) since this would affect the material purchases, rather than the material usage.

49   B

		Received in April
		$
March sales	$60,000 × 80% × 99%*	47,520
February sales	$40,000 × 10%	4,000
January sales	$35,000 × 5%	1,750
		53,270

*This reduction allows for the 1% settlement discount.

If you selected **option A** you misinterpreted 'month **after** sale' to be the month the sale was made. The invoices are issued on the last day of each month, therefore cash receipts in respect of each month's sales will begin in the following month.

Option C makes no allowance for the settlement discount and **option D** includes the receipt of bad debts; those amounts will never be received cash.

50

	Order
Material usage budget	4
Sales budget	1
Material purchase budget	6
Finished goods inventory budget	2
Production budget	3
Material inventory budget	5

51   B   Sales = opening inventory + production – closing inventory

∴ Production = sales – opening inventory + closing inventory

52   C

	Units	$
High activity	14,000	10,500
Low activity	8,000	7,200
Increase	6,000	3,300

Variable cost per unit = $3,300/6,000 = $0.55

Fixed cost, substituting in high activity = $10,500 – (14,000 × 0.55)
= $2,800

Budget cost allowance to distribute 12,000 units:

	$
Variable cost (12,000 × $0.55)	6,600
Fixed cost	2,800
	9,400

If you selected **option A** you did not include an allowance for fixed cost, and if you selected **option B** or **D** you calculated the answer on a pro rata basis from the data given. This does not take account of the fixed element of the distribution cost.

53   C   A flexible budget identifies fixed costs separately from variable costs. The allowance for variable costs can be flexed to derive a realistic target in the light of the actual activity level achieved.

54

		True	False
(a)	Budgetary control procedures are useful only to maintain control over an organisation's expenditure		✓
(b)	A prerequisite of flexible budgeting is a knowledge of cost behaviour patterns	✓	
(c)	Fixed budgets are not useful for control purposes		✓

Comments

(a) Budgetary control procedures can also be useful to maintain control over an organisation's revenue.

(b) A knowledge of cost behaviour patterns is necessary so that the variable cost allowance can be flexed in line with changes in activity.

(c) Fixed budgets may be useful for control purposes when:

    (i) Variable costs are negligible or non-existent

    (ii) Activity levels are not subject to change

55   C   Learn this definition.

56   B

			Change
Production units	2,000	3,000	+1,000
Production cost	$17,760	$20,640	$2,880

Variable cost per unit $= \dfrac{\$2,880}{1,000} = \$2.88$; Fixed costs $= \$17,760 - (2,000 \times \$2.88) = \$12,000$

Therefore, budget cost allowance for activity level of 4,000 units $= \$12,000 + (4,000 \times \$2.88) = \$23,520$

57   (a)   C   STATEMENT OF EQUIVALENT UNITS

	Total Units		Materials		Equivalent units Labour		Overheads
Output to process 2*	600		600		600		600
Closing WIP	100	(100%)	100	(50%)	50	(30%)	30
	700		700		650		630

*500 units input + opening WIP 200 units – closing WIP 100 units.

Option A is incorrect because it is the number of units input to the process, taking no account of opening and closing work in progress. **Option B** is the completed output, taking no account of the work done on the closing inventory.

Option D is the total number of units worked on during the period, but they are not all complete in respect of overhead cost.

(b)   B   STATEMENT OF COSTS PER EQUIVALENT UNIT

	Materials $	Labour $	Overheads $	Total
Opening inventory	2,400	1,200	400	
Added during period	6,000	3,350	1,490	
Total cost	8,400	4,550	1,890	
Equivalent units	700	650	630	
Cost per equivalent unit	$12	$7	$3	$22

Value of units transferred to process 2 = 600 units $\times$ $22 = $13,200

Option A is incorrect because it represents only the material cost of the units transferred. **Option C** is all of the costs incurred in the process during the period, but some of these costs must be allocated to the closing work in progress. **Option D** is the value of 700 completed units: but only 600 units were transferred to the next process.

58   D   The total loss was 15% of the material input. The 340 litres of good output therefore represents 85% of the total material input.

Therefore, material input = $\dfrac{340}{0.85}$ = 400 litres

Options A and B are incorrect because they represent a further five per cent and ten per cent respectively added to the units of good production.

If you selected **option C** you simply added 15 per cent to the 340 litres of good production. However, the losses are stated as a percentage of input, not as a percentage of output.

59

PROCESS ACCOUNT

	Litres	$		Litres	$
Materials	20,000	4,400	Normal waste		
			(4,000 × $0.50)	4,000	2,000
			Finished goods	17,000	2,550
Abnormal gain	1,000	150			
	21,000	4,550		21,000	4,550

Workings

Normal loss = 20% × 20,000 litres = 4,000 litres

Expected output = 20,000 − 4,000 = 16,000 litres

$$\text{Cost per unit} = \frac{\text{Process costs - scrap proceeds of normal loss}}{\text{Expected output}}$$

$$= \frac{\$4,400 - (4,000 \times \$0.50)}{16,000 \,\text{litres}}$$

$$= \frac{\$4,400 - \$2,000}{16,000 \,\text{litres}}$$

$$= \frac{\$2,400}{16,000 \,\text{litres}}$$

$$= \$0.15$$

60   (a)   During the period there was an abnormal loss of 125 kg.

Workings

Loss in process	2,500 kg − (2,100 + 150)kg	= 250 kg
Normal loss	5% × 2,500 kg	= 125 kg
∴ Abnormal loss		= 125 kg

(b)

Materials	$3.00
Labour	$0.40
Other direct costs	$0.20

Workings

STATEMENT OF EQUIVALENT UNITS OF PRODUCTION

Equivalent units

	Total Units	Materials Units	%	Labour Units	%	Other direct costs Units	%
Normal loss	125	0		0		0	
Abnormal loss	125	125	100	125	100	125	100
Finished inventory	2,100	2,100	100	2,100	100	2,100	100
Work in progress	150	150	100	120	80	90	60
	2,500	2,375		2,345		2,315	
Costs		*$7,125		$938		$463	
Cost per equivalent unit	$3.60	$3.00		$0.40		$0.20	

* $7,145 less scrap value of normal loss $20 = $7,125.

61 B This is the correct definition of an equivalent unit.

62 C *Step 1.* Determine output

Equivalent units

Input Units	Output	Total Units	Materials Units	%	Labour and overhead Units	%
	Finished units (balance)	400	400	100	400	100
500	Closing stock	100	100	100	80	80
500		500	500		480	

Step 2. Calculate the cost per equivalent unit

Input	Cost $	Equivalent production in units	Cost per unit $
Materials	9,000	500	18
Labour and overhead	11,520	480	24
			42

Step 3. Calculate total cost of output

Cost of completed units = $42 × 400 units = $16,800

If you selected option A you omitted the absorption of overhead at the rate of 200 per cent of direct labour costs. If you selected option B you did not allow for the fact that the work in progress was incomplete. Option D is the total process cost for the period, some of which must be allocated to the work in progress.

63 B Using the data from answer 62 above, extend **step 3** to calculate the value of the work in progress.

	Cost element	Number of equivalent units	Cost per equivalent unit $	Total $
Work in progress:	Materials	100	18	1,800
	Labour and overhead	80	24	1,920
				3,720

If you selected option A you omitted the absorption of overhead into the process costs. If you selected option C you did not allow for the fact that the work in progress was incomplete. Option D is the total process cost for the period, some of which must be allocated to the completed output.

64   **B**   Joint products are two or more products produced by the same process and separated in processing, each having a sufficiently high saleable value to merit recognition as a main product.

A joint product may be subject to further processing, as implied in option A, but this is not the case for all joint products.

65   **D**   A by-product is output of some value produced in manufacturing something else (the main product).

Option A is incorrect because a by-product has some value.

Option B is incorrect because this description could also apply to a joint product.

Option C is incorrect because the value of the product described could be relatively high, even though the output volume is relatively low.

66   **D**   The abnormal loss units are valued at their **full production cost** and **credited** to the process account, so that their occurrence does not affect the cost of good production. Therefore the correct answer is D.

Options A and C are incorrect because the scrap value of the abnormal loss is debited to the **scrap account** and credited to the **abnormal loss account**, it has no impact on the process account.

67   The quantity of good production achieved was $\boxed{2,625}$ kg.

Good production   = input − normal loss − abnormal loss
                            = 3,000 − (10% × 3,000) − 75
                            = 3,000 − 300 − 75
                            = 2,635 kg

68   The value credited to the process account for the scrap value of the normal loss for the period will be $\$\boxed{100}$

Normal loss   = 10% × input
                = 10% × 5,000 kg
                = 500 kg

When scrap has a value, normal loss is valued at the value of the scrap ie 20p per kg.

Normal loss   = $0.20 × 500 kg
                = $100

69   The value of the abnormal loss for the period is $\$\boxed{300}$

	kg
Input	5,000
Normal loss (10% × 5,000 kg)	(500)
Abnormal loss	(300)
Output	4,200

Cost per kg $= \dfrac{\text{Input costs} - \text{scrap value of normal loss}}{\text{Expected output}}$

$$= \frac{\$4,600^* - \$100}{5,000 - 500}$$

$$= \frac{\$4,500}{4,500} = \$1.00$$

Value of abnormal loss = 300 × $1.00 = $300

	$
*Materials (5,000 kg × 0.5)	2,500
Labour	700
Production overhead	1,400
	4,600

70 The value of the closing work in progress for the period was $ 4,698

STATEMENT OF EQUIVALENT UNITS

	Total units	Materials units		Labour and overhead units	
Completed output	8,000	(100%)	8,000	(100%)	8,000
Normal loss	1,000	(0%)	-	(0%)	-
Abnormal loss	100	(100%)	100	(100%)	100
Closing WIP	900	(100%)	900	(75%)	675
	10,000		9,000		8,775

STATEMENT OF COST PER EQUIVALENT UNIT

	Materials	Labour and overhead
Total costs	*$40,500	$8,424
Equivalent units	9,000	8,775
Cost per equivalent unit	$4.50	$0.96

* $40,800 less scrap value normal loss $300 = $40,500

Value of work in progress:

	$
Materials 900 equivalent units × $4.50	4,050
Labour and overhead 675 equivalent units × $0.96	648
	4,698

71 The profit to be recognised on the contract is $390,000

Workings

Approximate degree of completion = $1,170,000/$1,800,000 = 65%

Since the contract is 65% complete and no difficulties are foreseen, it is reasonable to recognise a profit.

Profit to be recognised   = 65% × final contract profit
                           = 65% × $(1,800,000 − 1,200,000)
                           = $390,000

72 C

	$
Book value of plant delivered to site	648,000
Depreciation on plant delivered:	
1 May $600,000 × 25% × 8/12	(100,000)
1 October $48,000 × 25% × 3/12	(3,000)
Book value of plant on site as at 31 December	545,000

Option A is the figure for depreciation to be charged to contract 724. If you selected **option B** you charged a full year's depreciation rather than allowing for the fact that the two items of plant were delivered on 1 May and 1 October respectively. If you selected **option D** you made no allowance for depreciation at all.

73   D

	$
Direct materials (5 × $20)	100
Direct labour (14 × $8)	112
Variable overhead (14 × $3)	42
Fixed overhead (14 × $5*)	70
Other overhead	80
Total cost of job 173	404
Profit margin (× 20/80)	101
Selling price	505

*Fixed production overhead absorption rate = $\dfrac{\$200,000}{40,000}$ = $5 per direct labour hour

Option A is the total cost, but a profit margin should be added to this to determine the selling price. If you selected **option B** you added only $5 for fixed production overhead: but this is the hourly rate, which must be multiplied by the number of direct labour hours. If you selected **option C** you calculated 20 per cent of cost to determine the profit: but the data states that profit is calculated as 20 per cent of the sales value.

74   A   Job costing is a costing method applied where work is **undertaken to customers' special requirements.** Option B describes process costing, C describes service costing and D describes absorption costing.

75   C   Workings

Total labour cost incurred during period   = $(12,500 + 23,000 + 4,500)
                                             = $40,000

∴ Overhead absorption rate = ($140,000/$40,000) × 100%
                            = 350% of labour cost

	$
Opening WIP	46,000
Labour for period	4,500
Overhead absorbed ($4,500 × 350%)	15,750
Total production cost	66,250
50% mark up	33,125
Sales value of job 3	99,375
Selling price per circuit board = $99,375 ÷ 2,400	$41.41

Option B is the selling price without the inclusion of any overhead absorbed. If you selected option D you calculated a 50 per cent margin based on the selling price, instead of a 50% mark up on cost.

76   C   Since wages are paid on a piecework basis they are a variable cost which will increase in line with the number of binders. The machine set-up cost and design costs are fixed costs for each batch which will not be affected by the number of binders in the batch.

For a batch of 300 binders:

	$
Direct materials (30 × 3)	90.00
Direct wages (10 × 3)	30.00
Machine set up	3.00
Design and artwork	15.00
Production overhead (30 × 20%)	6.00
Total production cost	144.00
Selling, distribution and administration overhead (+ 5%)	7.20
Total cost	151.20
Profit (25% margin = $33^1/_3$% of cost)	50.40
Selling price for a batch of 300	201.60

If you selected option A you calculated the cost correctly, but added a profit mark up of 25% of cost, instead of a margin of 25% of selling price.

If you selected option B you failed to absorb the appropriate amount of fixed overhead. If you selected option D you treated all of the costs as variable costs.

77   The price to be quoted for job B124 is $ 124.50

Production overhead absorption rate = $240,000/30,000 = $8 per labour hour

Other overhead absorption rate = ($150,000/$750,000) × 100% = 20% of total production cost

Job B124	$
Direct materials (3 kgs × $5)	15.00
Direct labour (4 hours × $9)	36.00
Production overhead (4 hours × $8)	32.00
Total production cost	83.00
Other overhead (20% × $83)	16.60
Total cost	99.60
Profit margin: 20% of sales (× $^{20}/_{80}$)	24.90
Price to be quoted	124.50

78   ✓   Production of the product can be completed in a single accounting period

      ✓   Production relates to a single special order

Job costing is appropriate where each cost unit is **separately identifiable** and is of relatively **short duration**.

79   A   The labour rate variance is recorded in the wages control account. Since the actual rate paid was higher than the standard rate, the labour rate variance is adverse. Therefore the variance will be debited in the labour rate variance account.

Options B and **D** are incorrect because it is the labour efficiency variance that is recorded in the work in progress account, not the labour rate variance.

If you selected **option C** you identified the correct accounts, but you reversed the debit and credit.

80   D   Direct material cost variance = material price variance + material usage variance

The adverse material usage variance could be larger than the favourable material price variance. The total of the two variances would therefore represent a net result of an adverse total direct material cost variance.

The situation in **option A** would sometimes arise, but not always, because of the possibility of the situation described in **option D**.

Option B could sometimes be correct, depending on the magnitude of each of the variances. However it will not always be correct as stated in the wording.

Option C is incorrect because the sum of the two favourable variances would always be a larger favourable variance.

81

		Consistent with the account entries	Not consistent with the account entries
(a)	The material used in production was more than the standard allowed for the number of units produced	✓	
(b)	All of the material issued to production was completely processed during the period	✓	
(c)	The number of labour hours worked was greater than the standard allowed for the number of units produced		✓

Statement (a) is correct because the resulting adverse usage variance is a debit in the variance account.

Statement (b) is correct because there is no opening or closing balance on the work in progress account.

Statement (c) is incorrect because the labour efficiency variance will be transferred as a credit in the variance account. Therefore it is a favourable variance and the number of labour hours worked was actually lower than the standard allowed.

82   DR | WORK IN PROGRESS CONTROL ACCOUNT |

        CR | DIRECT LABOUR EFFICIENCY VARIANCE ACCOUNT |

83   C   The **direct costs of production**, of which direct wages are a part, are **debited to the work in progress account**. The credit entry is made in the **wages control account**, where the wages cost has been 'collected', as it is paid or accrued, prior to **its analysis** between direct and indirect wages.

If you selected option A you identified the correct accounts but your **entries were reversed**.

Option B represents the entries for direct wages paid, and option D is the (incorrect) reversal of these entries.

84   C   Overhead is absorbed into the cost of production for the period by debiting the work in progress account with the appropriate amount of overhead based on the predetermined overhead absorption rate. The credit entry is made in the overhead control account, where the overhead has been 'collected' in the debit side, as it is paid or accrued.

If you selected **option D** you identified the correct accounts but your **entries were reversed**.

Option A is incorrect because the cost of production must first be 'collected' in the **work in progress account** before the final transfer of the cost of completed production to the finished goods account.

Option B represents the entries, usually made at the end of a period, to account for any production overhead under absorbed.

85   D   There are two possible transfers from the raw materials control account:

- the cost of direct materials is transferred to the work in progress account
- the cost of indirect materials is transferred to the production overhead control account

The transfer of the cost of indirect materials to the production overhead control account is already shown as $6,000. Therefore the $71,000 must represent the issue of direct materials to work in progress.

86   Cash   ✓

       Payables   ✓

       Work-in-progress

Note. When materials are purchased, they are either paid for in cash (credit cash account) or purchased on credit (credit/supplier account)

87

		Appropriate	Not appropriate
(a)	Vehicle cost per passenger-kilometre	✓	
(b)	Fuel cost for each vehicle per kilometre	✓	
(c)	Fixed cost per kilometre		✓

The vehicle cost per passenger-kilometre (a) is appropriate for cost control purposes because it **combines** the distance travelled and the number of passengers carried, **both of which affect cost**.

The fuel cost for each vehicle per kilometre (b) can be useful for control purposes because it **focuses on a particular aspect** of the cost of operating each vehicle.

The fixed cost per kilometre (c) is not particularly useful for control purposes because it **varies with the number of kilometres travelled**.

88   B   Number of occupied room-nights   = 40 rooms × 30 nights × 65%
$$= 780$$

Room servicing cost per occupied room-night $= \dfrac{\$3,900}{780} = \$5$

Option A is the cost per available room-night. This makes no allowance for the 65% occupancy achieved. If you selected **option C** you simply divided $3,900 by 40 rooms. This does not account for the number of nights in the period, nor the percentage occupancy achieved. If you selected **option D** you calculated the cost per occupied room, rather than the cost per occupied room-night.

89

(i)	Production is carried out in accordance with the wishes of the customer	J
(ii)	Work is usually of a relatively long duration	C
(iii)	Work is usually undertaken on the contractor's premises	N
(iv)	Costs are averaged over the units produced in the period	S
(v)	It establishes the costs of services rendered	S

90 (a) (i) St Matthew's $63.40
        (ii) St Mark's $33.46

Workings

Number of in-patient days = number of in-patients × average stay

St Matthew's = 15,400 × 10 days   = 154,000
St Mark's   = 710 × 156 days   = 110,760

St Matthew's cost per in-patient day = total cost ÷ 154,000
                                      = $9,762,780 ÷ 154,000
                                      = $63.40

St Mark's cost per in-patient day   = $3,705,631 ÷ 110,760
                                      = $33.46

(b) (i) St Matthew's $20.31 (Total cost $2,640,300 ÷ 130,000)
    (ii) St Mark's $52.38 (Total cost $183,330 ÷ 3,500)

(c) (i) St Matthew's 78.8%
    (ii) St Mark's   95.9%

Workings

St Matthew's = $\frac{402}{510}$ × 100% = 78.8%

St Mark's   = $\frac{307}{320}$ × 100% = 95.9%

91   66,325

Working

Calculation of tonne-km

Journey	Tonnes	Km	Tonne-km
1	34	180	6,120
2	28	265	7,420
3	40	390	15,600
4	32	115	3,680
5	26	220	5,720
6	40	480	19,200
7	29	90	2,610
8	26	100	2,600
9	25	135	3,375
	280	1,975	66,325

92 $ 0.16   per tonne-kilometre (to the nearest penny).

Working

Average cost per tonne-kilometre = $\frac{\text{Total cost}}{\text{Total tonne - kilometres}}$

= $\frac{\$10,390}{66,325}$

= $0.16 per tonne-kilometre (to the nearest penny)

Index

Note. **Key terms** and their page references are given in **bold**

ABC, 66
Abnormal gain, 235
Abnormal loss, 235
Absorbed overhead, 61
Absorption, 52
Absorption base, 53
Absorption costing, 44
Absorption rate, 52
Activity based costing (ABC), 66, **67**
Administration costs, 16
Administration overhead, 13
Allocation, 44
Apportion, 45
Apportionment bases, 45
Attainable standards, 150
AVCO, 35
Average cost, 35

Bases of apportionment, 45
Basic standards, 150
Batch costing, 277
Blanket absorption rates, 59
Bonus schemes, 156
Breakeven analysis, 114
Breakeven arithmetic, 117
Breakeven chart, 122
Breakeven point, 80, **114**
Budget, 197
Budget committee, 197
Budget cost allowance, 218
Budget flexing, 218
Budget manual, 199
Budget period, 198
Budget preparation, 197, 199
Budget purposes, 196
Budget variances, 222
Budgeted balance sheet, 210
Budgeted income statement, 210
Budgeting, 196
Budgets and management reward, 226
By-product, 260, 261

C/S ratio, 115
Capital expenditure budgets, 212
Cash budget, 205

Classification by nature, 10
Classification by purpose, 11
Classification by responsibility, 11
Code, 20
Committed fixed costs, 19
Common costs, 261
Composite codes, 21
Composite cost units, 8, 327
Concept of cost, 9
Contract, 279
Contract accounts, 280
Contract costing, 279
Contract costing and cost bookkeeping, 308
Contribution, 78, 114, 339
Contribution breakeven chart, 125
Contribution/sales (C/S) ratio, 115
Control, 222
Controllable cost, 19
Cost, 10
Cost accountant, 4
Cost accounting, 4
Cost accounting systems, 5, 298
Cost behaviour, 100, 110
Cost behaviour patterns, 100
Cost bookkeeping, 297
Cost bookkeeping and variances, 315
Cost centres, 7, 345
Cost classification, 10, 17
Cost codes, 20
Cost drivers, 68
Cost elements, 11
Cost measurement, 9
Cost object, 7
Cost per unit for services, 328
Cost plus pricing, 271
Cost pools, 68
Cost unit, 7, 345
Cost units and service costing, 327
Cost-volume-profit (CVP) analysis, 114
Credits, 233
Cumulative weighted average pricing, 35
Current standards, 150
CVP analysis, 114

Debits, 233
Departmental absorption rates, 59

Departmental budget, 200
Departments, 6
Depreciation, 213
Differential piecework schemes, 155
Direct cost, 11
Direct expenses, 12, 13
Direct labour cost, 13
Direct labour efficiency variance, 167
Direct labour idle time variance, 169
Direct labour rate variance, 167
Direct labour total variance, 164, 167
Direct labour variances, 167
Direct material, 12
Direct material price variance, 164
Direct material usage variance, 164
Direct material variances, 164
Direct materials cost, 13
Direct method, 49
Direct wages, 12
Discretionary fixed costs, 19
Distribution overhead, 14
Double entry bookkeeping, 298
Dual responsibility, 19

Economic cost, 9
Economic value, 9
Equivalent units, 248
Expenses, 345

FIFO, 31
FIFO (first in, first out), 31
Financial accounting, 5
Financial accounts, 5
Finished goods inventory budget, 200
First in, first out, 31
Fixed budget, 218
Fixed cost, 18, 100
Flexible budget, 218
Flexible budgeting, 217
Forecast, 197
Full cost plus pricing, 87
Functional budgets, 201
Functional costs, 16
Functions, 6

General and administrative expenses, 339
Gross margin, 339
Gross revenue, 339

Group bonus scheme, 157

Heterogeneity, 326
High day-rate system, 156
High/low method, 107
Historical costs versus standard costs, 147

Ideal standards, 149
Idle time variance, 169
Incentive schemes, 156
Incentive schemes involving shares, 157
Indirect cost, 13
Individual bonus scheme, 156
Information for management, 337
Intangibility, 326
Integrated accounts, 298
Integrated systems, 298
Inter-relationships between variances, 190
Inventory valuation, 30
Inventory valuation and profitability, 38
Inventory valuation using absorption costing and
    marginal costing, 81

Job, 268
Job accounts, 268
Job costing, 268
Job costing and computerisation, 270
Job costing and cost bookkeeping, 305
Job costing and services, 337
Job costing for internal services, 276
Joint costs, 261
Joint products, 260

Key budget factor, 199
Key factor, 132

Labour, 345
Labour budget, 200
Last in, first out, 34
LIFO, 34
LIFO (last in, first out), 34
Limiting budget factor, 199
Limiting factor, 132
Limiting factor analysis, 132
Line of best fit, 109
Line of best fit method, 109
Losses on incomplete contracts, 288

Machine usage budget, 200
Management accounting, 4
Management accounts, 5
Management by exception, **147**
Management reports, 337
Manufacturing accounts, 311
Manufacturing cost, 16
Margin of safety, **116**
Marginal cost, **78**
Marginal cost plus pricing, 91
Marginal costing, 78, **79**
Margins, 92
Marketing expense, 339
Mark-ups, 92
Master budget, 210, 218
Materials, 29, 345
Materials inventory budget, 200
Materials usage budget, 200
Mixed cost, 104
Motivation and budgets, 196

Non-controllable costs, 19
Non-linear variable costs, 103
Normal loss, **235**
Not-for-profit organisations, 328

Objective classification, 11, 21
Operating statements, 179
Over-absorbed overhead, **61**
Over absorption of overhead, 61
Overhead, **13**
Overhead absorption, 52
Overhead absorption rate, **52**
Overhead allocation, 44
Overhead apportionment, 45
Overhead costs, 43

P/V graph, 126
P/V ratio, 115
Performance standards, 149
Period cost, **16**
Perishability, 326
Piecework schemes, 154
Pricing decisions, 87
Prime cost, **12**
Principal budget factor, 199, **200**
Process accounts, 232

Process costing, **232**
Process costing and losses, 235
Process costing and opening work in progress, 254
Product cost, **16**
Production budget, 200
Production overhead, 13
Profit sharing scheme, 157
Profit/volume (P/V) graph, 126
Profit/volume ratio, 115
Profits on contracts, 283
Progress payments, 283
Prudence, 285

Raw materials purchases budget, 200
Re-apportion, **49**
Relevant range, **105**
Remuneration methods, 153
Repeated distribution method, 49
Resource allocation, 197
Responsibility accounting, **18**, 196
Responsibility centre, **18**
Retention monies, 283
Return on investment, 90
Return on sales, 90
Reward strategies, 226

Sales budget, 200
Sales price variance, **178**
Sales variances, 178
Sales volume contribution variance, **178**
Scattergraph method, 109
Scrap, **241**
Selling overhead, 14
Semi-fixed costs, 104
Semi-variable cost, **18**, **104**
Service cost centre cost apportionment, 49
Service costing, 325
Service industry costing, 326
Service organisations, 326
Simultaneity, 326
Single factory overhead absorption rates, 60
SSAP 9 disclosures – balance sheet, 291
SSAP 9 requirements – income statement, 290
Standard cost, **144**
Standard cost bookkeeping, 313
Standard costing, 144, **146**
Standard hour, 153
Standard operation sheet, 149

Standard product specification, 149
Standard time allowances, 154
Step cost, 102
Straight piece rate scheme, 154
Subjective classification, 10, 21

Target profit, 118
Target return on investment, 90
Target return on sales, 90
Time-based systems, 153

Uncontrollable cost, 19
Under-absorbed overhead, 61
Under absorption of overhead, 61
Unit cost measures, 328

Value-added, 339
Variable cost, 18, 101

Variable costing, 79
Variable overhead total variance, 172
Variable overhead variances, 172
Variable production overhead efficiency variance, 172, 173
Variable production overhead expenditure variance, 172, 173
Variable production overhead total variance, 172
Variable production total overhead variances, 172
Variance, 164
Variance analysis, 164
Variances – reasons for, 173

Wages control account, 309
Weighted average cost method, 254
Weighted average price, 35

BPP)))
PROFESSIONAL EDUCATION

Review Form & Free Prize Draw – Paper C1 Fundamentals of Management Accounting (7/06)

All original review forms from the entire BPP range, completed with genuine comments, will be entered into one of two draws on 31 January 2007 and 31 July 2007. The names on the first four forms picked out on each occasion will be sent a cheque for £50.

Name: _____   **Address:** _____

_____

_____

How have you used this Study Text?
(Tick one box only)

☐ Home study (book only)

☐ On a course: college _____

☐ With 'correspondence' package

☐ Other _____

Why did you decide to purchase this Study Text? *(Tick one box only)*

☐ Have used BPP Texts in the past

☐ Recommendation by friend/colleague

☐ Recommendation by a lecturer at college

☐ Saw information on BPP website

☐ Saw advertising

☐ Other _____

Which BPP products have you used?

Text ☑   Success CD ☐   Learn Online ☐

Kit ☐   i-Learn ☐   Home Study Package ☐

Passcard ☐   i-Pass ☐   Home Study PLUS ☐

MCQ cards ☐

During the past six months do you recall seeing/receiving any of the following?
(Tick as many boxes as are relevant)

☐ Our advertisement in *Financial Management*

☐ Our advertisement in *Pass*

☐ Our advertisement in *PQ*

☐ Our brochure with a letter through the post

☐ Our website www.bpp.com

Which (if any) aspects of our advertising do you find useful?
(Tick as many boxes as are relevant)

☐ Prices and publication dates of new editions

☐ Information on Text content

☐ Facility to order books off-the-page

☐ None of the above

Your ratings, comments and suggestions would be appreciated on the following areas.

	Very useful	Useful	Not useful
Introductory section (Key study steps, personal study)	☐	☐	☐
Chapter introductions	☐	☐	☐
Key terms	☐	☐	☐
Quality of explanations	☐	☐	☐
Assessment focus points	☐	☐	☐
Questions and answers in each chapter	☐	☐	☐
Fast forwards and chapter roundups	☐	☐	☐
Quick quizzes	☐	☐	☐
Question Bank	☐	☐	☐
Answer Bank	☐	☐	☐
Index	☐	☐	☐
Icons	☐	☐	☐

Overall opinion of this Study Text	Excellent ☐	Good ☐	Adequate ☐	Poor ☐

Do you intend to continue using BPP products?   Yes ☐   No ☐

On the reverse of this page are noted particular areas of the text about which we would welcome your feedback.

The BPP author of this edition can be e-mailed at: helendarch@bpp.com

Please return this form to: Janice Ross, CIMA Certificate Publishing Manager, BPP Professional Education, FREEPOST, London, W12 8BR

Review Form & Free Prize Draw (continued)

TELL US WHAT YOU THINK

Please note any further comments and suggestions/errors below

Free Prize Draw Rules

1   Closing date for 31 January 2007 draw is 31 December 2006. Closing date for 31 July 2007 draw is 30 June 2007.

2   Restricted to entries with UK and Eire addresses only. BPP employees, their families and business associates are excluded.

3   No purchase necessary. Entry forms are available upon request from BPP Professional Education. No more than one entry per title, per person. Draw restricted to persons aged 16 and over.

4   Winners will be notified by post and receive their cheques not later than 6 weeks after the relevant draw date.

5   The decision of the promoter in all matters is final and binding. No correspondence will be entered into.